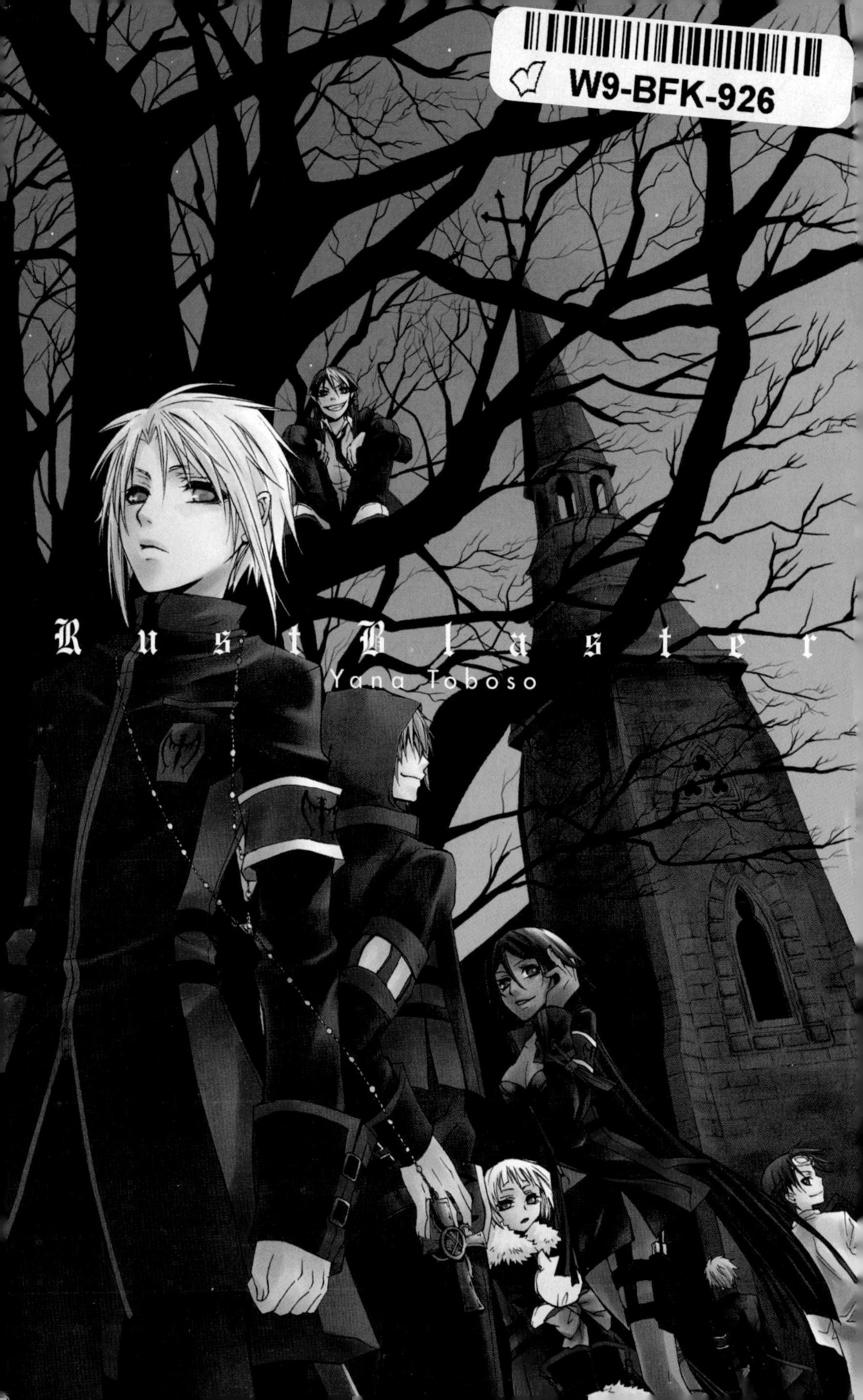
Rust Blaster
Yana Toboso

RustBlaster

Contents

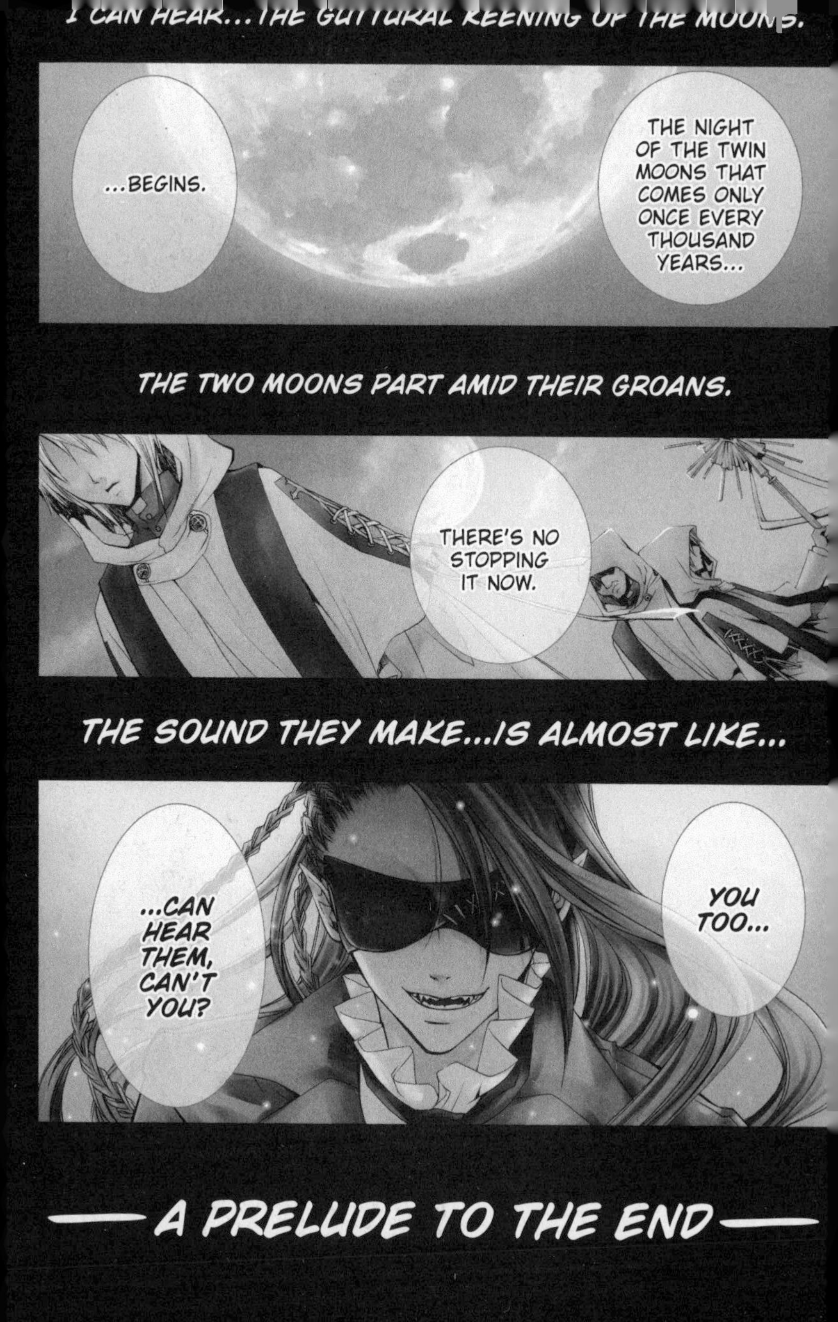
I CAN HEAR...THE GUTTURAL KEENING OF THE MOONS.
THE NIGHT OF THE TWIN MOONS THAT COMES ONLY ONCE EVERY THOUSAND YEARS...
...BEGINS.
THE TWO MOONS PART AMID THEIR GROANS.
THERE'S NO STOPPING IT NOW.
THE SOUND THEY MAKE...IS ALMOST LIKE...
YOU TOO...
...CAN HEAR THEM, CAN'T YOU?
—A PRELUDE TO THE END—

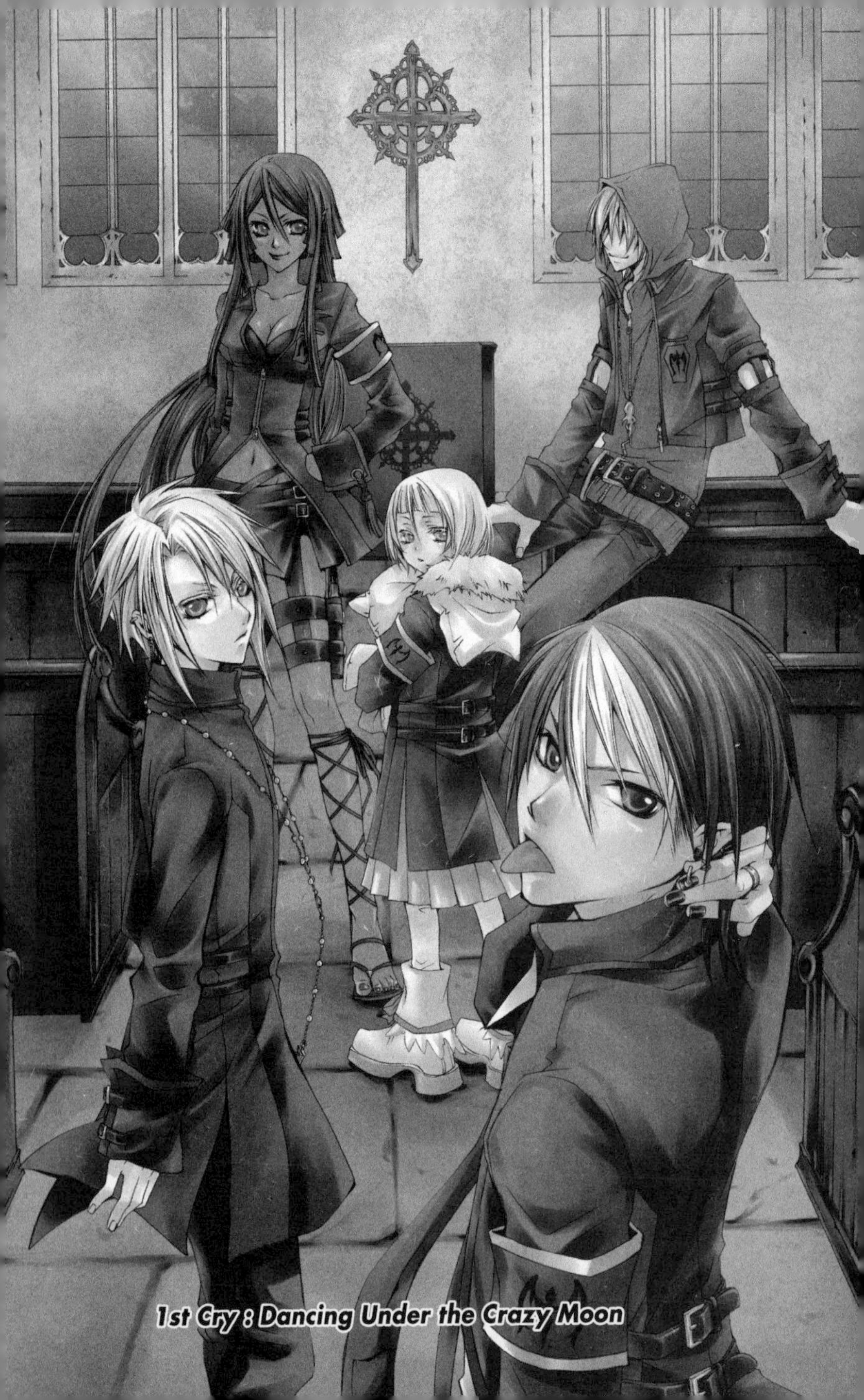
1st Cry : Dancing Under the Crazy Moon

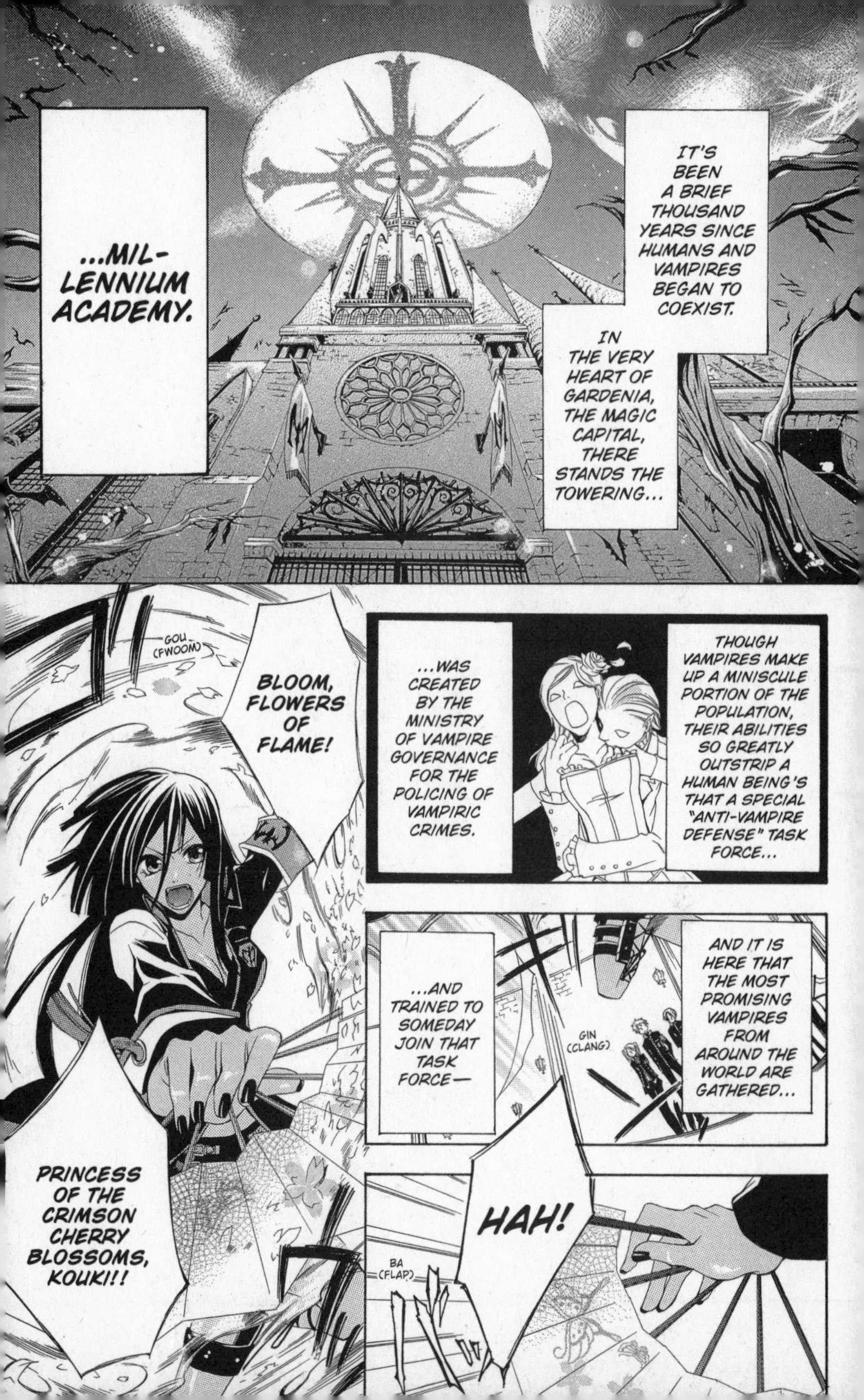
IT'S BEEN A BRIEF THOUSAND YEARS SINCE HUMANS AND VAMPIRES BEGAN TO COEXIST.
IN THE VERY HEART OF GARDENIA, THE MAGIC CAPITAL, THERE STANDS THE TOWERING...
...MIL-LENNIUM ACADEMY.
THOUGH VAMPIRES MAKE UP A MINISCULE PORTION OF THE POPULATION, THEIR ABILITIES SO GREATLY OUTSTRIP A HUMAN BEING'S THAT A SPECIAL "ANTI-VAMPIRE DEFENSE" TASK FORCE...
...WAS CREATED BY THE MINISTRY OF VAMPIRE GOVERNANCE FOR THE POLICING OF VAMPIRIC CRIMES.
AND IT IS HERE THAT THE MOST PROMISING VAMPIRES FROM AROUND THE WORLD ARE GATHERED...
GIN (CLANG)
...AND TRAINED TO SOMEDAY JOIN THAT TASK FORCE—
HAH!
BA (FLAP)
GOU (FWOOM)
BLOOM, FLOWERS OF FLAME!
PRINCESS OF THE CRIMSON CHERRY BLOSSOMS, KOUKI!!

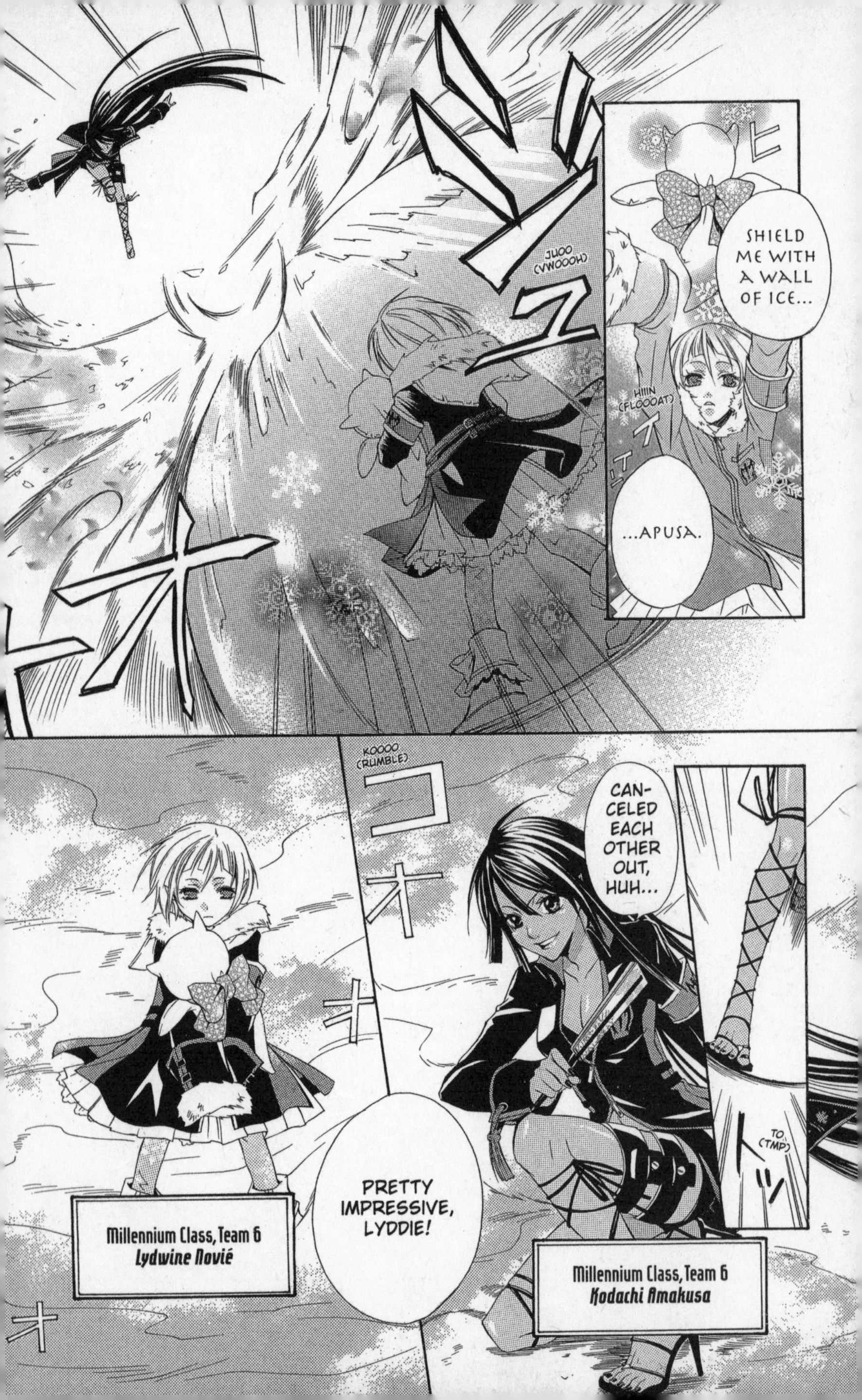
SHIELD ME WITH A WALL OF ICE...
HIIN (FLOOOAT)
...APUSA.
JUOO (VWOOOH)
TO (TMP)
KOOOO (RUMBLE)
CAN-CELED EACH OTHER OUT, HUH...
PRETTY IMPRESSIVE, LYDDIE!
Millennium Class, Team 6
Kodachi Amakusa
Millennium Class, Team 6
Lydwine Novié

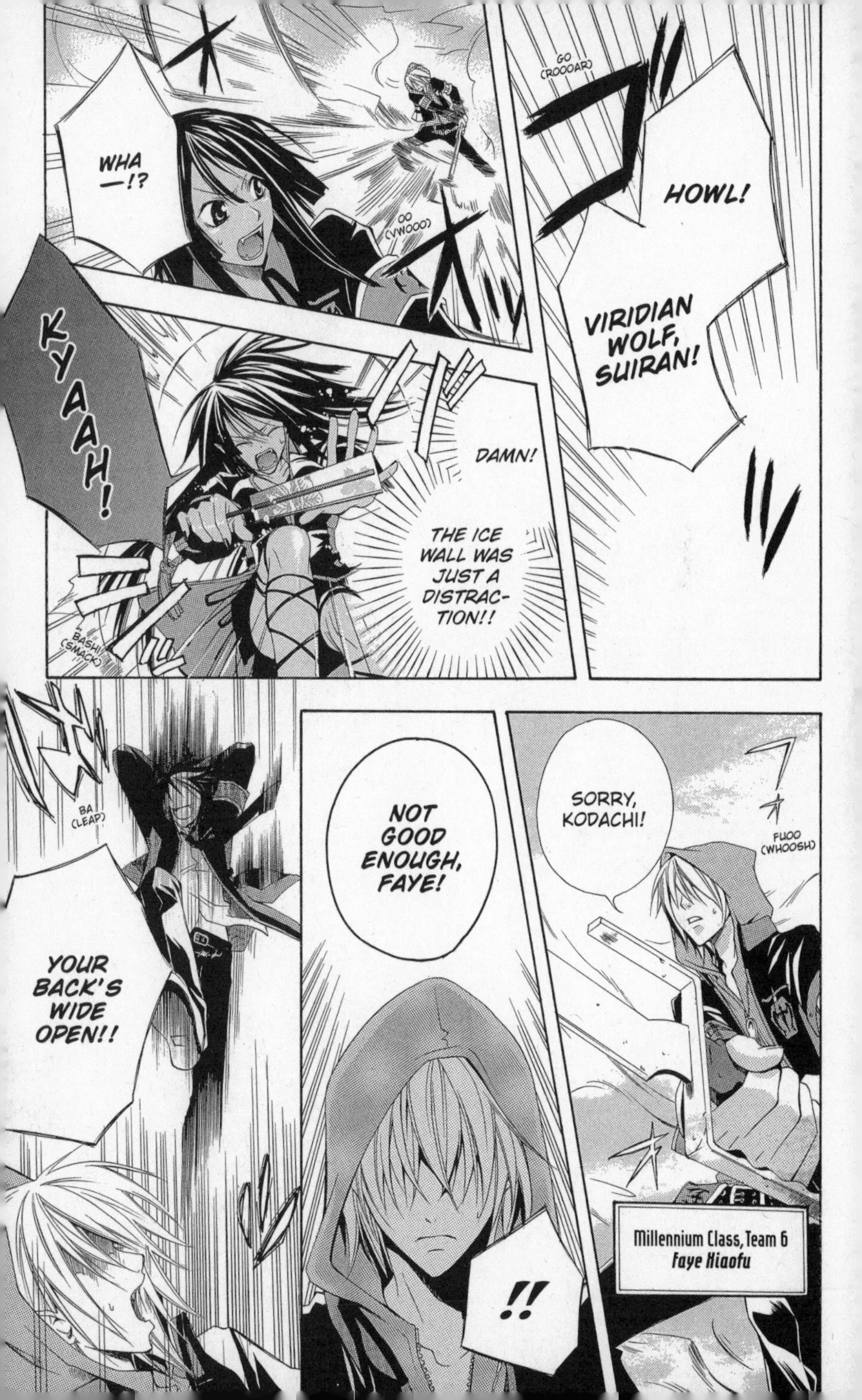
GO
(ROOOAR)
HOWL!
VIRIDIAN WOLF, SUIRAN!
WHA—!?
OO
(VWOOO)
DAMN!
THE ICE WALL WAS JUST A DISTRAC-TION!!
KYAAAH!
BASHI
(SMACK)
FUOO
(WHOOSH)
SORRY, KODACHI!
Millennium Class, Team 6
Faye Xiaofu
NOT GOOD ENOUGH, FAYE!
!!
BA
(LEAP)
YOUR BACK'S WIDE OPEN!!

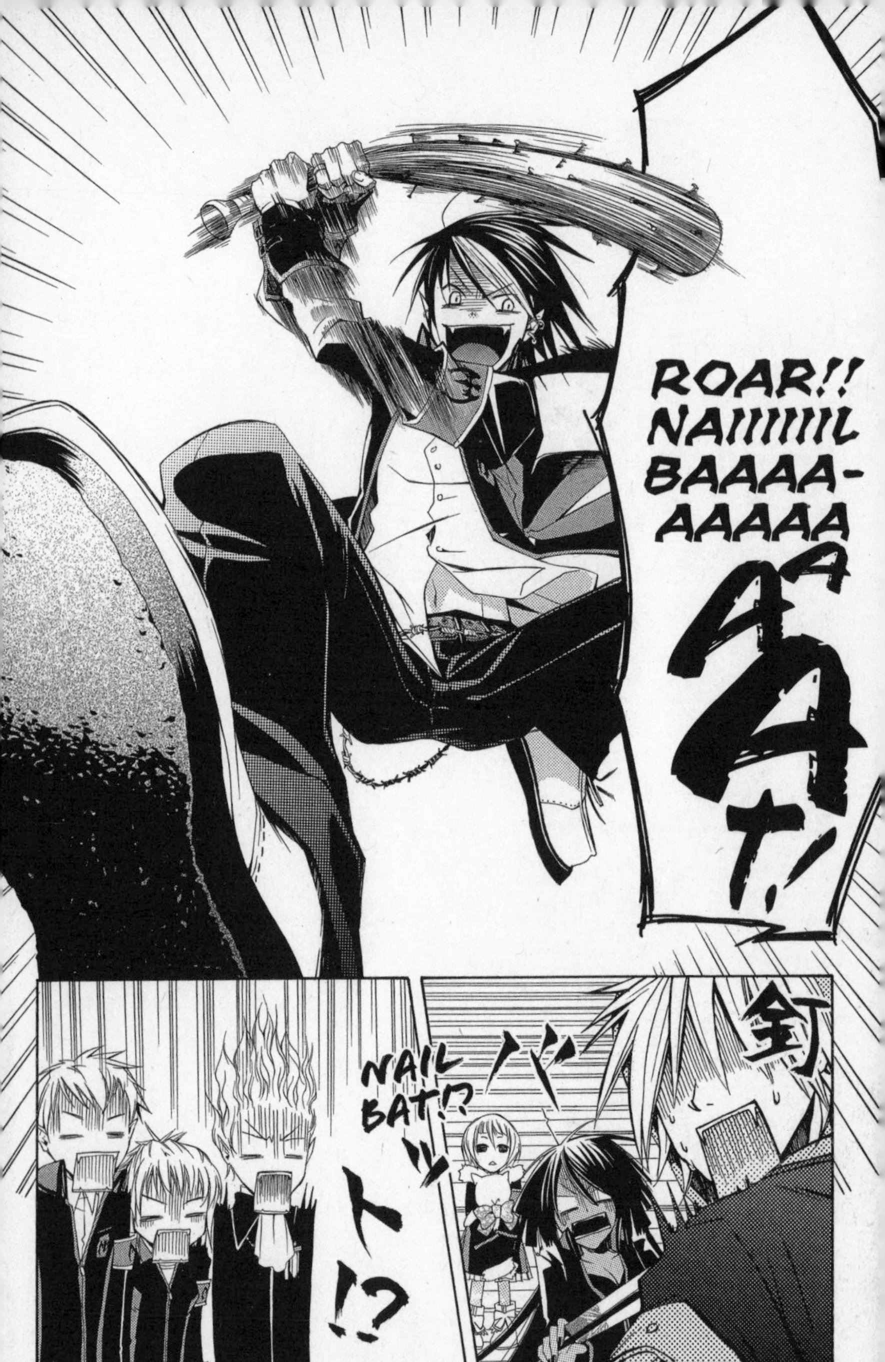
ROAR!!
NAIIIIIL
BAAAA-
AAAAA
釘
NAIL BAT!?

↑ TEACHER

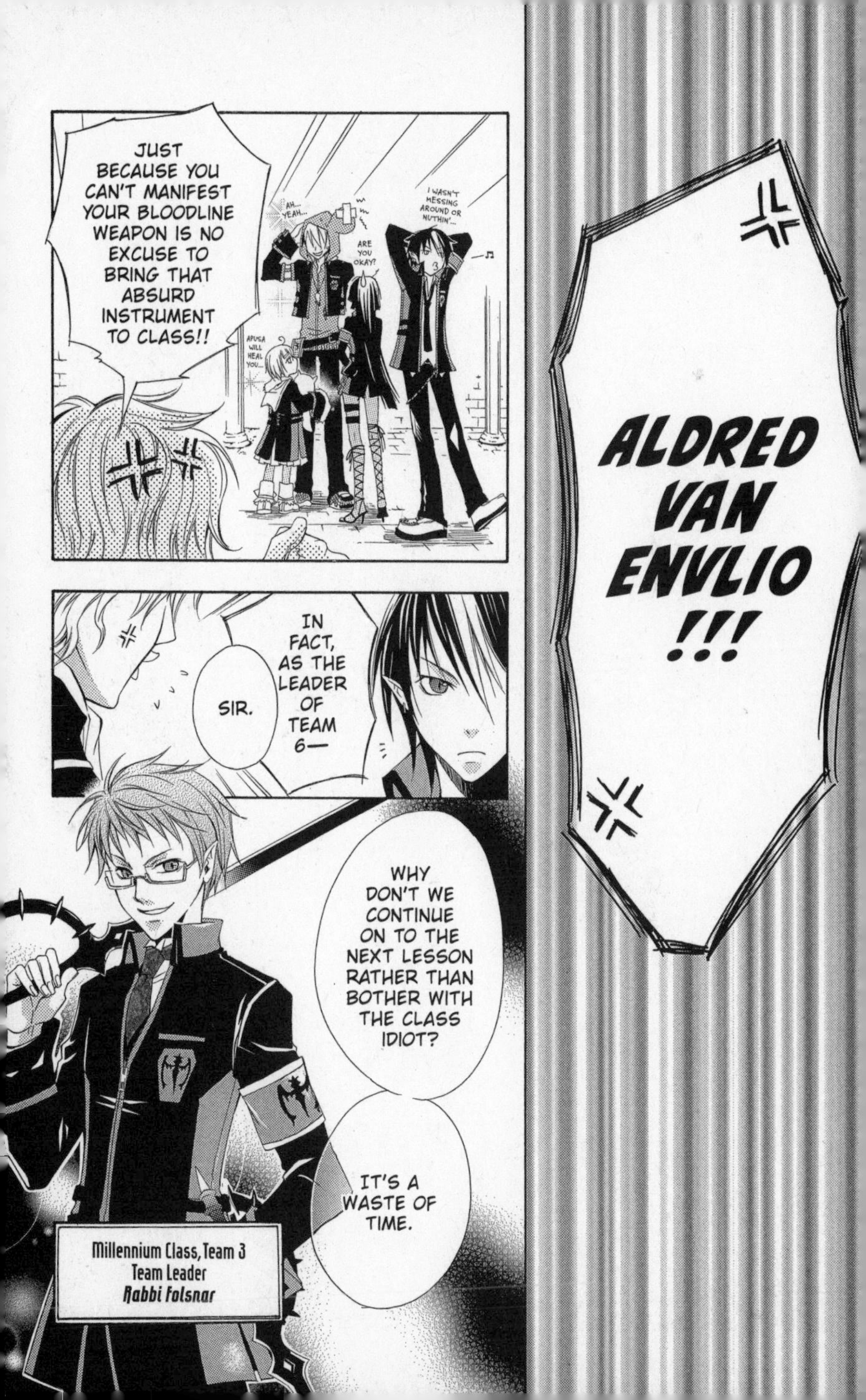
ALDRED VAN ENVLIO!!!
JUST BECAUSE YOU CAN'T MANIFEST YOUR BLOODLINE WEAPON IS NO EXCUSE TO BRING THAT ABSURD INSTRUMENT TO CLASS!!
I WASN'T MESSING AROUND OR NUTHIN'...
AH... YEAH...
ARE YOU OKAY?
APUSA WILL HEAL YOU...
IN FACT, AS THE LEADER OF TEAM 6—
SIR.
WHY DON'T WE CONTINUE ON TO THE NEXT LESSON RATHER THAN BOTHER WITH THE CLASS IDIOT?
IT'S A WASTE OF TIME.
Millennium Class, Team 3
Team Leader
Rabbi Folsnar

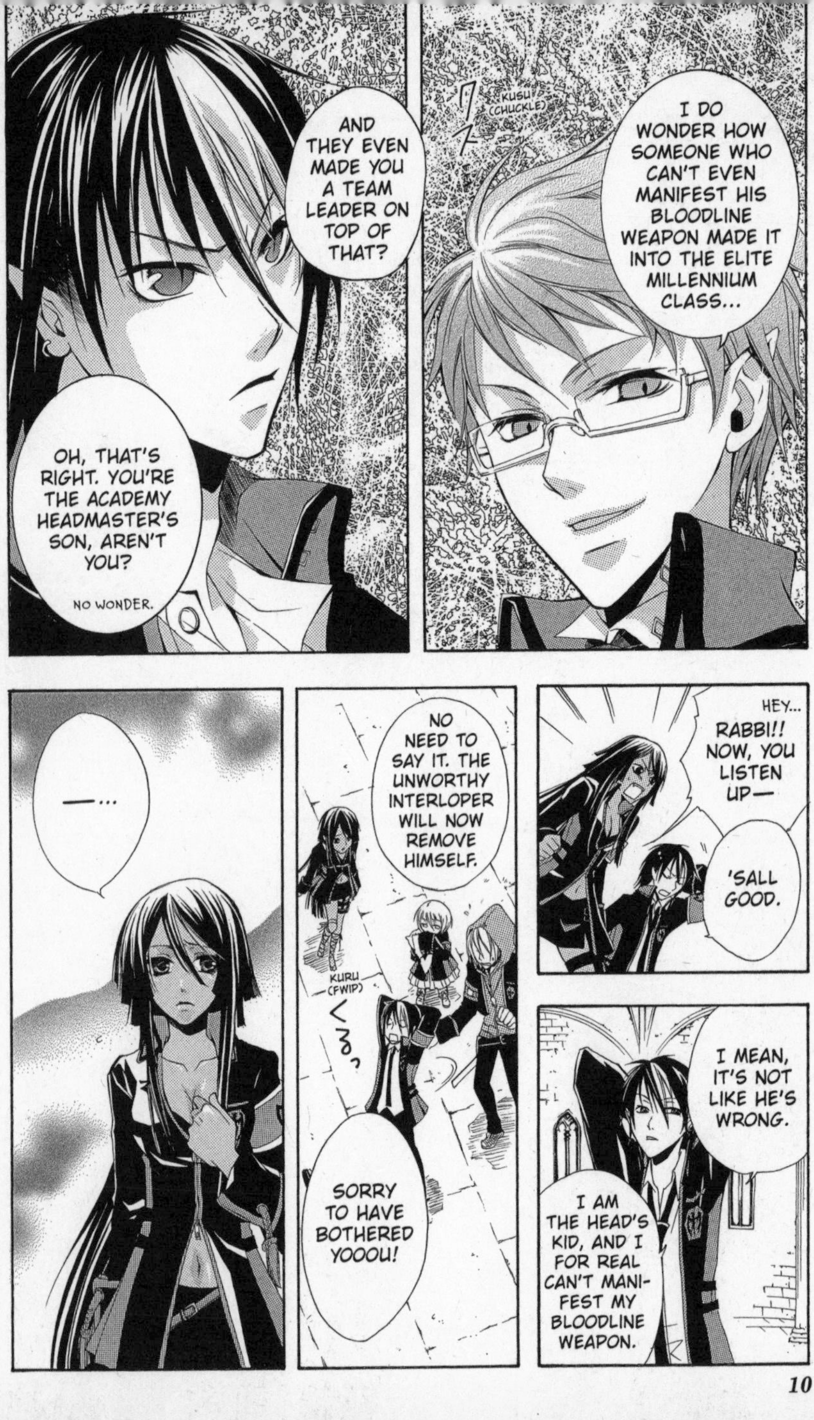
KUSU (CHUCKLE)
I DO WONDER HOW SOMEONE WHO CAN'T EVEN MANIFEST HIS BLOODLINE WEAPON MADE IT INTO THE ELITE MILLENNIUM CLASS...
AND THEY EVEN MADE YOU A TEAM LEADER ON TOP OF THAT?
OH, THAT'S RIGHT. YOU'RE THE ACADEMY HEADMASTER'S SON, AREN'T YOU?
NO WONDER.
HEY... RABBI!! NOW, YOU LISTEN UP—
'SALL GOOD.
I MEAN, IT'S NOT LIKE HE'S WRONG.
I AM THE HEAD'S KID, AND I FOR REAL CAN'T MANI-FEST MY BLOODLINE WEAPON.
NO NEED TO SAY IT. THE UNWORTHY INTERLOPER WILL NOW REMOVE HIMSELF.
KURU (FWIP)
SORRY TO HAVE BOTHERED YOOOU!
—...

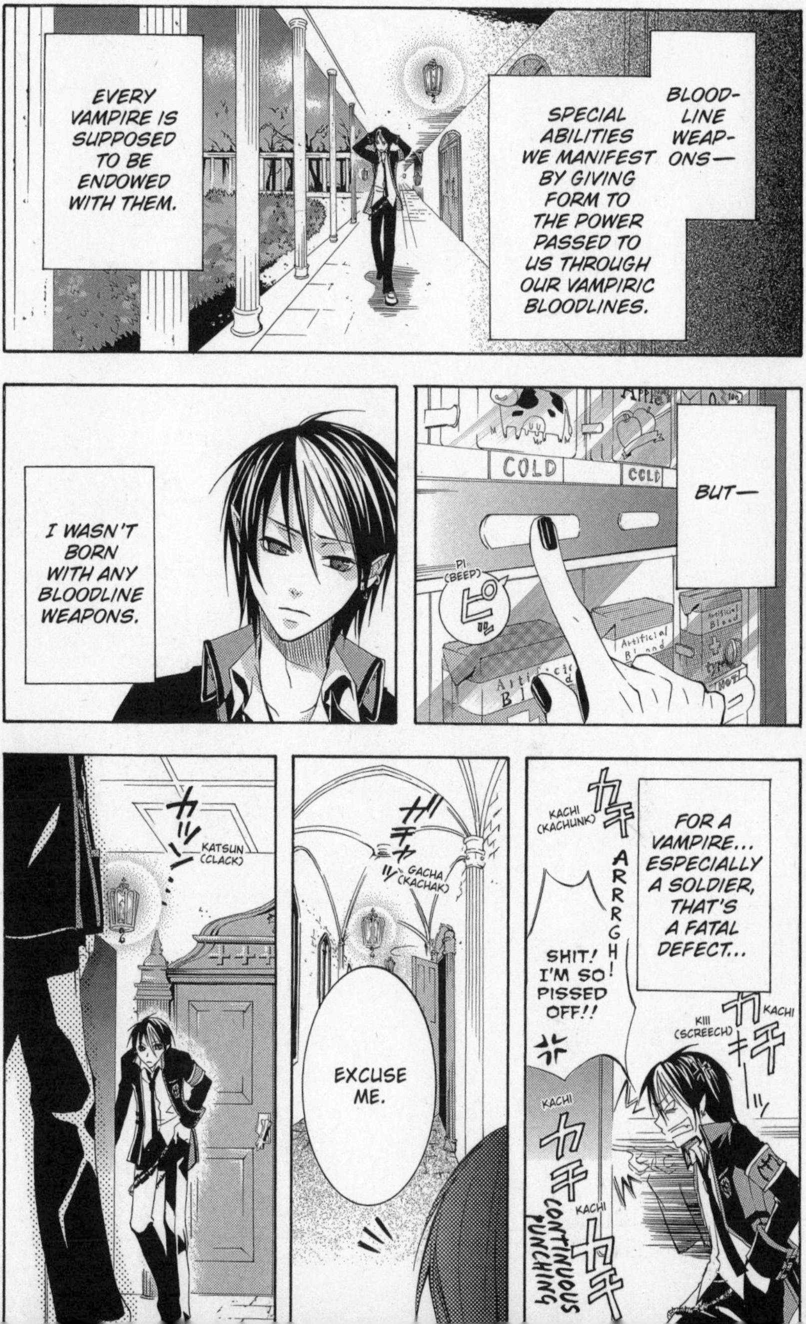
BLOOD-LINE WEAP-ONS—
SPECIAL ABILITIES WE MANIFEST BY GIVING FORM TO THE POWER PASSED TO US THROUGH OUR VAMPIRIC BLOODLINES.
EVERY VAMPIRE IS SUPPOSED TO BE ENDOWED WITH THEM.
BUT—
COLD
COLD
PI (BEEP)
I WASN'T BORN WITH ANY BLOODLINE WEAPONS.
FOR A VAMPIRE... ESPECIALLY A SOLDIER, THAT'S A FATAL DEFECT...
KACHI (KACHUNK)
ARRRGH!
SHIT! I'M SO PISSED OFF!!
KACHI
KIII (SCREECH)
KACHI
KACHI
CONTINUOUS PUNCHING
GACHA (KACHAK)
EXCUSE ME.
KATSUN (CLACK)

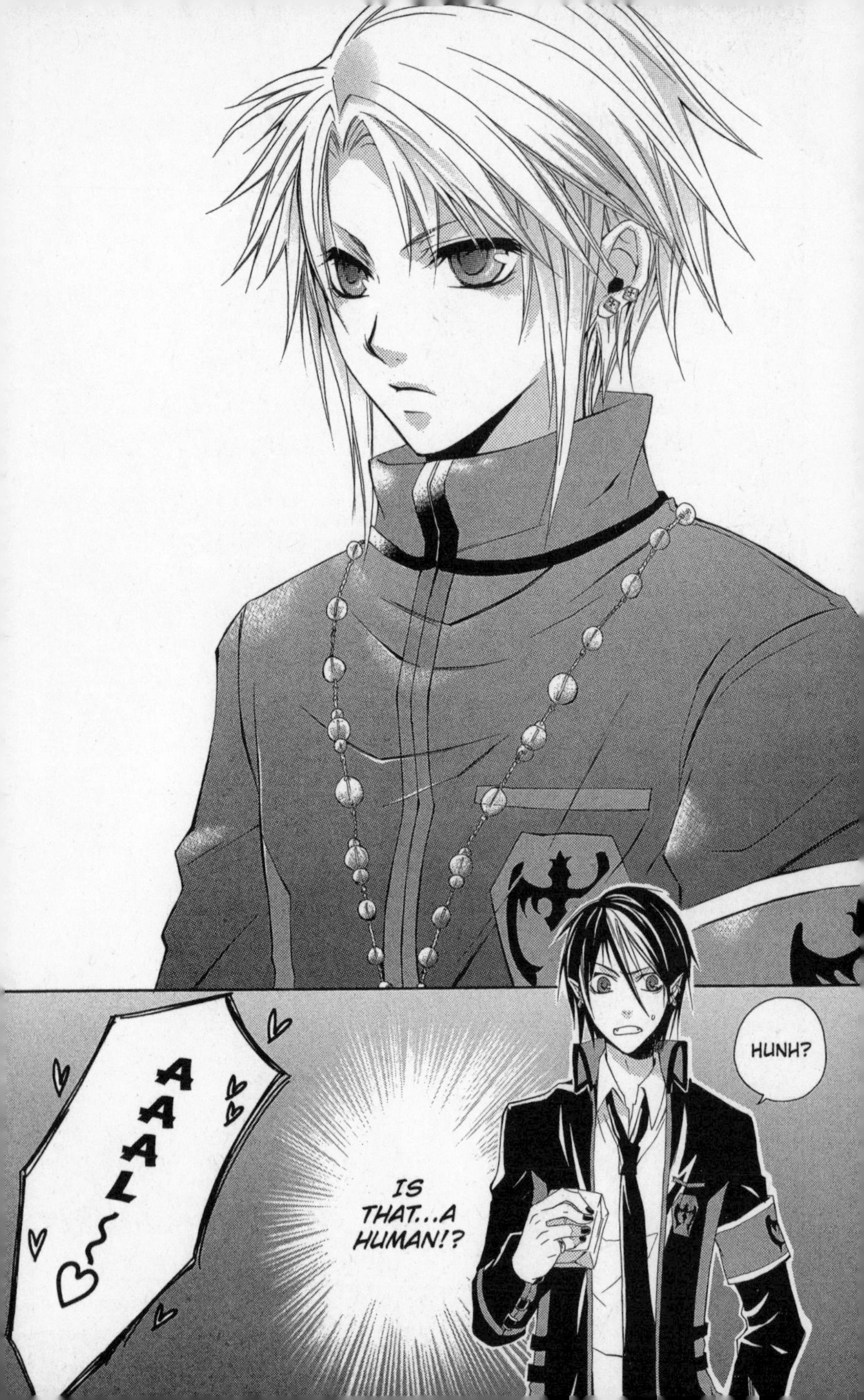
HUNH?
AAAL~
IS THAT...A HUMAN!?

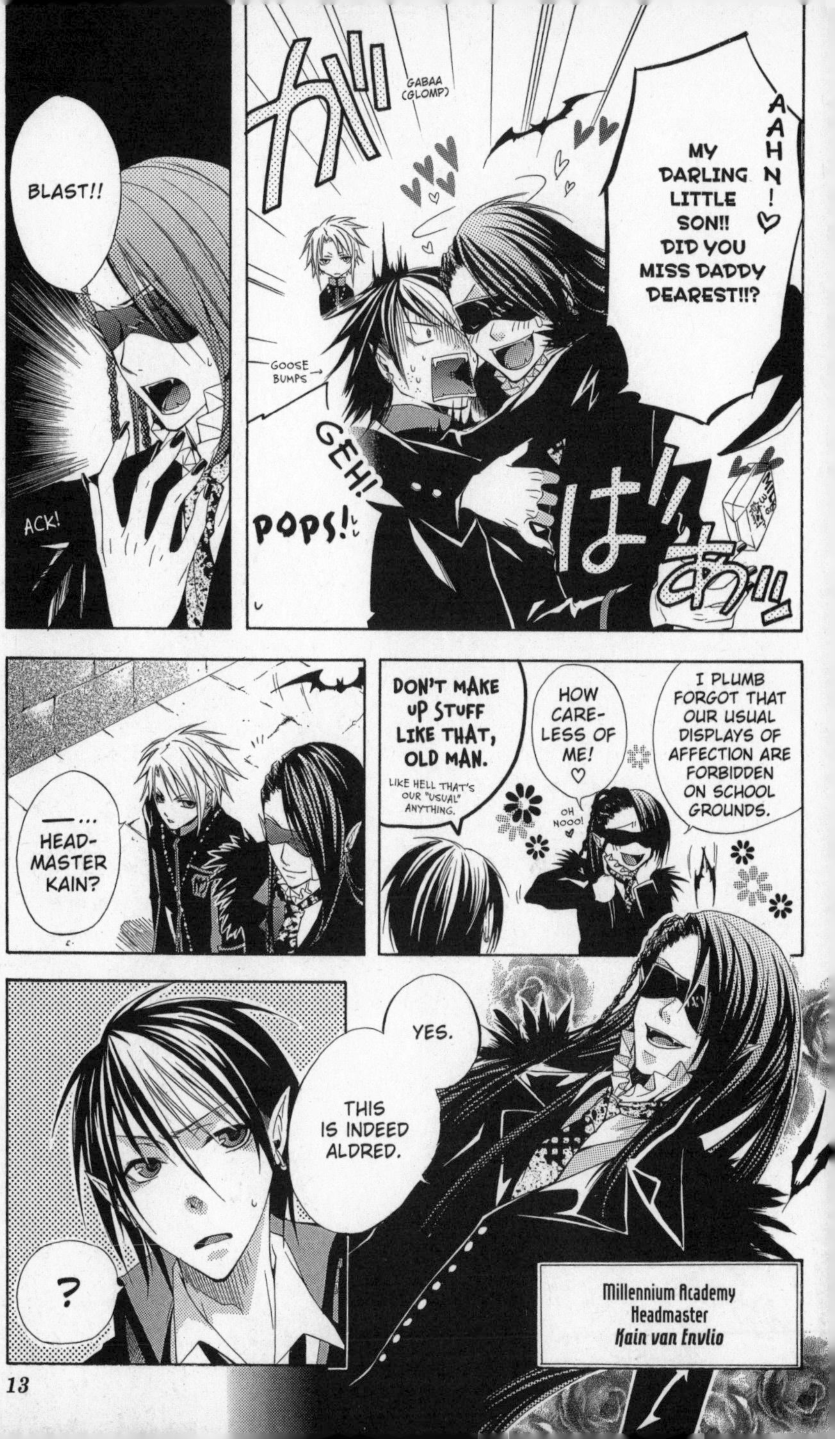

GABAA (GLOMP)
AAHN! ♡
MY DARLING LITTLE SON!! DID YOU MISS DADDY DEAREST!!?
GOOSE BUMPS
GEH!
POPS!
BLAST!!
ACK!
I PLUMB FORGOT THAT OUR USUAL DISPLAYS OF AFFECTION ARE FORBIDDEN ON SCHOOL GROUNDS.
HOW CARELESS OF ME! ♡
OH NOOO!
DON'T MAKE UP STUFF LIKE THAT, OLD MAN.
LIKE HELL THAT'S OUR "USUAL" ANYTHING.
—... HEADMASTER KAIN?
YES.
THIS IS INDEED ALDRED.
?
Millennium Academy Headmaster Kain van Envlio

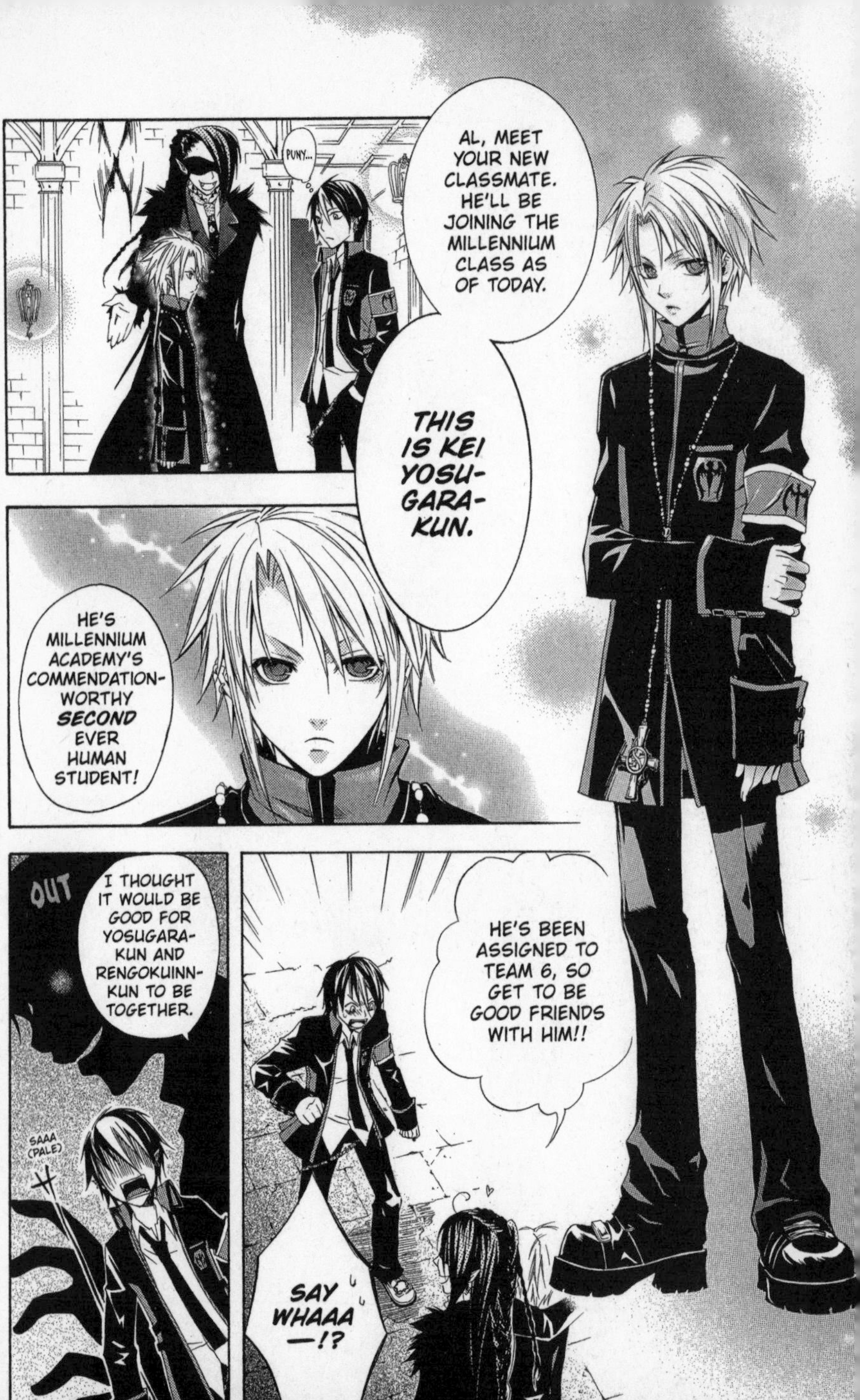
AL, MEET YOUR NEW CLASSMATE. HE'LL BE JOINING THE MILLENNIUM CLASS AS OF TODAY.
THIS IS KEI YOSU-GARA-KUN.
PUNY...
HE'S MILLENNIUM ACADEMY'S COMMENDATION-WORTHY SECOND EVER HUMAN STUDENT!
HE'S BEEN ASSIGNED TO TEAM 6, SO GET TO BE GOOD FRIENDS WITH HIM!!
SAY WHAAA —!?
I THOUGHT IT WOULD BE GOOD FOR YOSUGARA-KUN AND RENGOKUINN-KUN TO BE TOGETHER.
OUT
SAAA (PALE)

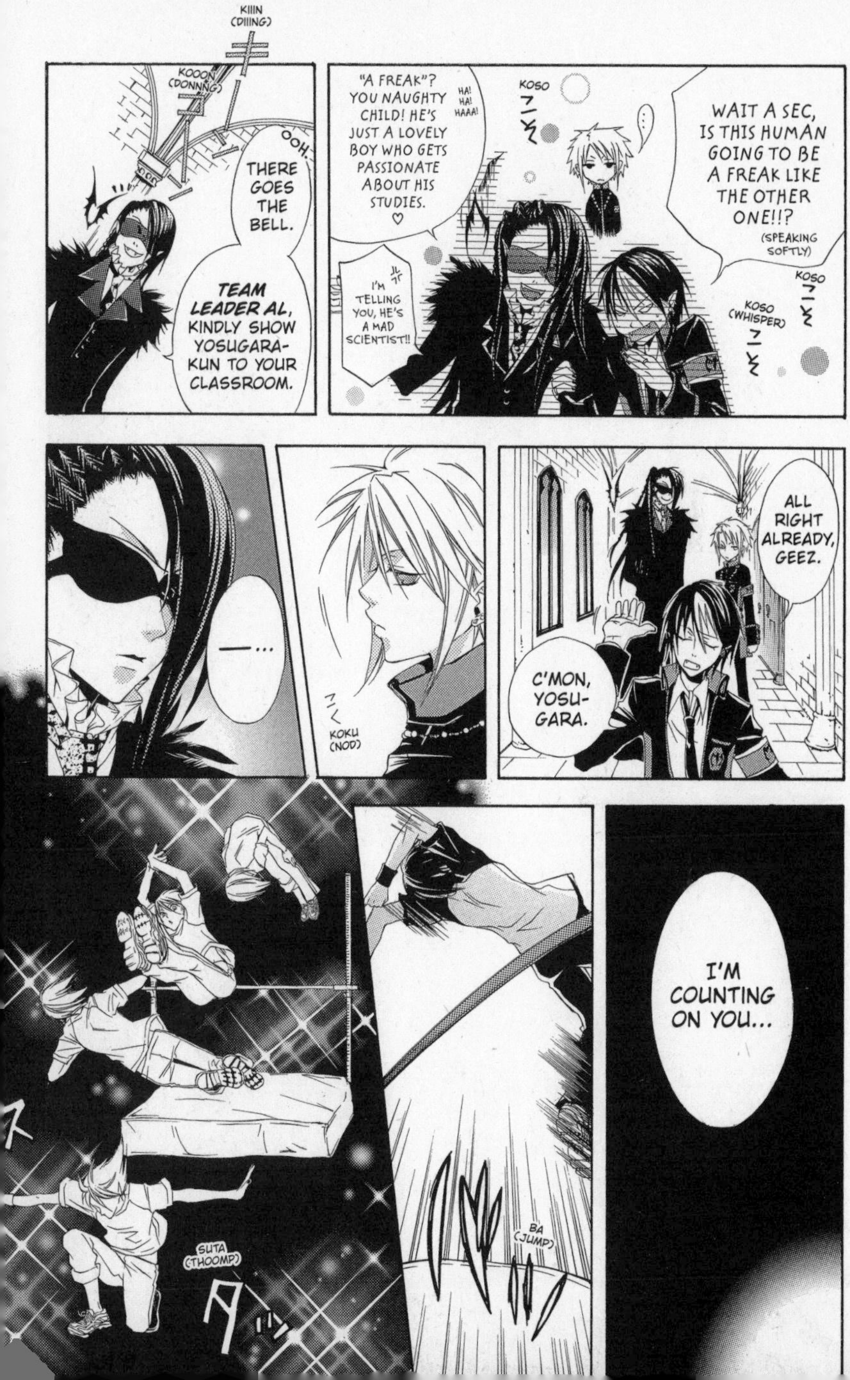
KOSO
WAIT A SEC, IS THIS HUMAN GOING TO BE A FREAK LIKE THE OTHER ONE!!?
(SPEAKING SOFTLY)
KOSO
KOSO (WHISPER)
...
"A FREAK"? YOU NAUGHTY CHILD! HE'S JUST A LOVELY BOY WHO GETS PASSIONATE ABOUT HIS STUDIES. ♡
HA! HA! HAAA!
I'M TELLING YOU, HE'S A MAD SCIENTIST!!
KIIIN (DIIING)
KOOON (DONNNG)
OOH.
THERE GOES THE BELL.
TEAM LEADER AL, KINDLY SHOW YOSUGARA-KUN TO YOUR CLASSROOM.
ALL RIGHT ALREADY, GEEZ.
C'MON, YOSU-GARA.
KOKU (NOD)
—...
I'M COUNTING ON YOU...
BA (JUMP)
SUTA (THOOMP)

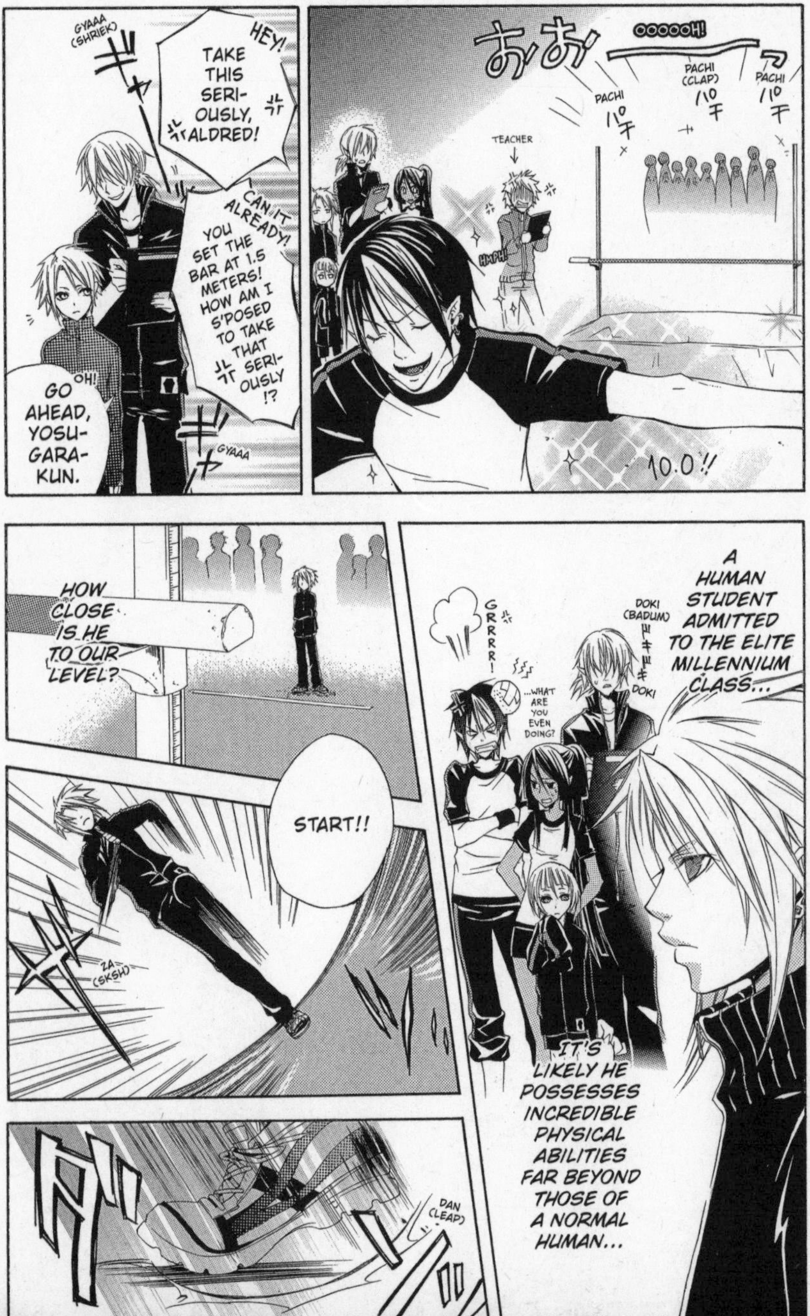
おお—ッ
OOOOOH!
PACHI
PACHI (CLAP)
PACHI
TEACHER
HMPH!
10.0!!
HEY!
TAKE THIS SERI-OUSLY, ALDRED!
GYAAA (SHRIEK)
CAN IT ALREADY! YOU SET THE BAR AT 1.5 METERS! HOW AM I S'POSED TO TAKE THAT SERI-OUSLY!?
GYAAA
OH!
GO AHEAD, YOSU-GARA-KUN.
A HUMAN STUDENT ADMITTED TO THE ELITE MILLENNIUM CLASS...
DOKI (BADUM)
DOKI
GRRRR!
...WHAT ARE YOU EVEN DOING?
IT'S LIKELY HE POSSESSES INCREDIBLE PHYSICAL ABILITIES FAR BEYOND THOSE OF A NORMAL HUMAN...
HOW CLOSE IS HE TO OUR LEVEL?
START!!
ZA (SKSH)
DAN (LEAP)

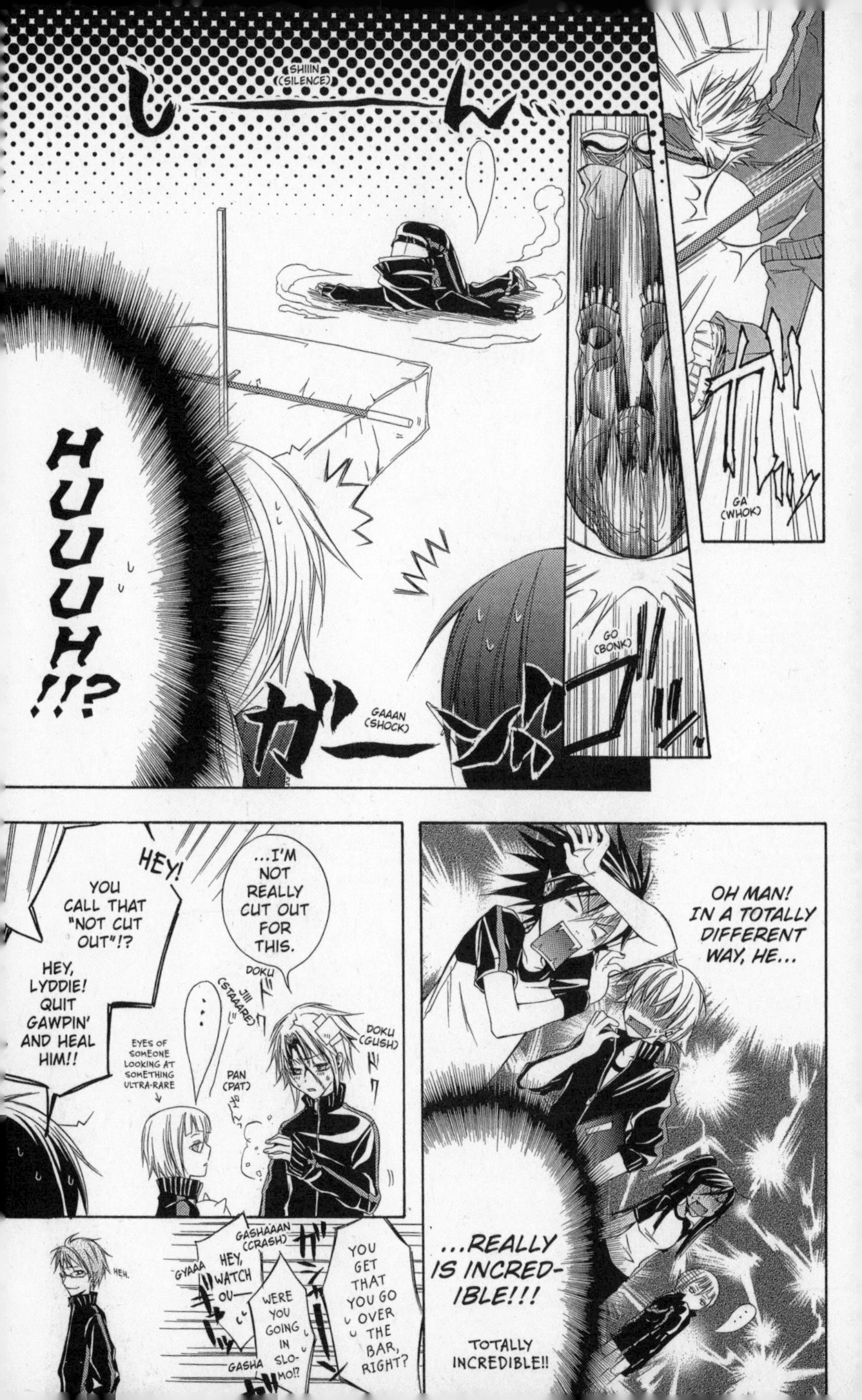
GA (WHOK)
GO (BONK)
SHIIIN (SILENCE)
...
HUUUH!!?
GAAAN (SHOCK)
OH MAN! IN A TOTALLY DIFFERENT WAY, HE...
...REALLY IS INCREDIBLE!!!
TOTALLY INCREDIBLE!!
...
...I'M NOT REALLY CUT OUT FOR THIS.
HEY! YOU CALL THAT "NOT CUT OUT"!?
HEY, LYDDIE! QUIT GAWPIN' AND HEAL HIM!!
DOKU (GUSH)
DOKU
JIIII (STAAARE)
...
PAN (PAT)
EYES OF SOMEONE LOOKING AT SOMETHING ULTRA-RARE
YOU GET THAT YOU GO OVER THE BAR, RIGHT?
GASHAAAN (CRASH)
WERE YOU GOING IN SLO-MO!?
HEY, WATCH OU—
GYAAA
GASHA
HEH.

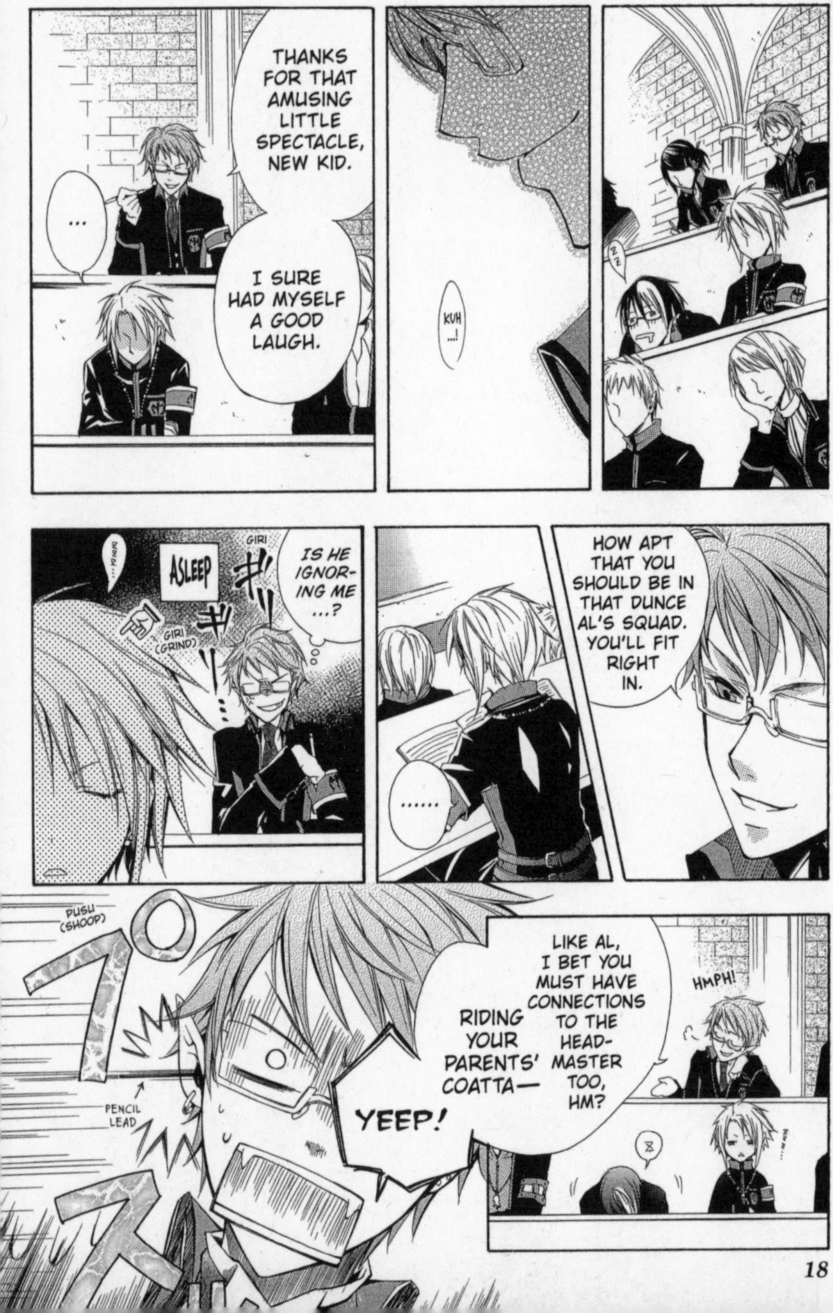
Z Z
KUH ...!
THANKS FOR THAT AMUSING LITTLE SPECTACLE, NEW KID.
I SURE HAD MYSELF A GOOD LAUGH.
...
HOW APT THAT YOU SHOULD BE IN THAT DUNCE AL'S SQUAD. YOU'LL FIT RIGHT IN.
......
IS HE IGNORING ME ...?
GIRI
GIRI (GRIND)
ASLEEP
HMPH!
LIKE AL, I BET YOU MUST HAVE CONNECTIONS TO THE HEADMASTER TOO, HM?
RIDING YOUR PARENTS' COATTA—
YEEP!
PUSU (SHOOP)
PENCIL LEAD

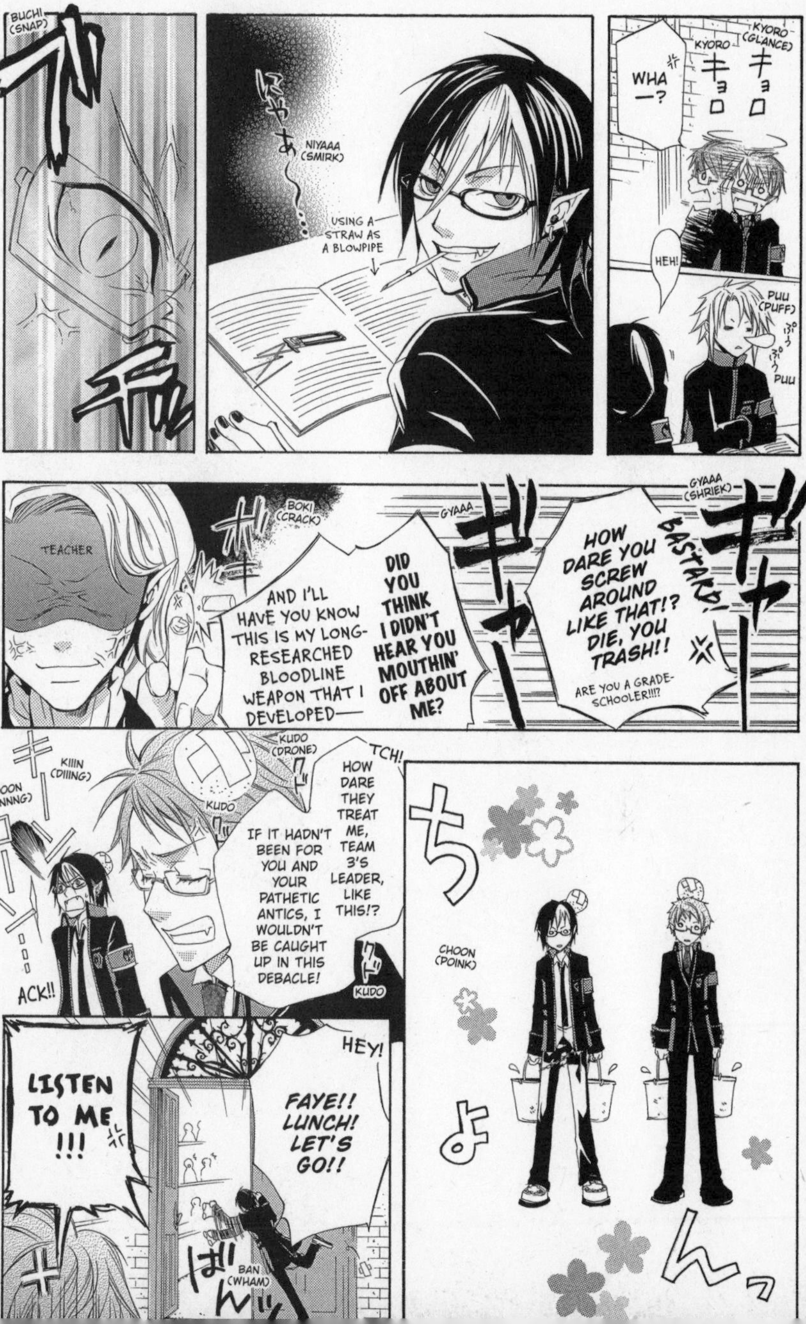
KYORO
KYORO (GLANCE)
WHA—?
HEH!
PUU (PUFF)
PUU
NIYAAA (SMIRK)
USING A STRAW AS A BLOWPIPE
BUCHI (SNAP)
GYAAA (SHRIEK)
HOW DARE YOU SCREW AROUND LIKE THAT!? DIE, YOU TRASH!!
BASTARD!
ARE YOU A GRADE-SCHOOLER!!!?
GYAAA
DID YOU THINK I DIDN'T HEAR YOU MOUTHIN' OFF ABOUT ME?
AND I'LL HAVE YOU KNOW THIS IS MY LONG-RESEARCHED BLOODLINE WEAPON THAT I DEVELOPED—
BOKI (CRACK)
TEACHER
CHOON (POINK)
TCH!
HOW DARE THEY TREAT ME, TEAM 3'S LEADER, LIKE THIS!?
KUDO (DRONE)
KUDO
IF IT HADN'T BEEN FOR YOU AND YOUR PATHETIC ANTICS, I WOULDN'T BE CAUGHT UP IN THIS DEBACLE!
KUDO
KIIIN (DIIING)
KOOON (DONNNG)
ACK!!
HEY!
FAYE!! LUNCH! LET'S GO!!
BAN (WHAM)
LISTEN TO ME!!!

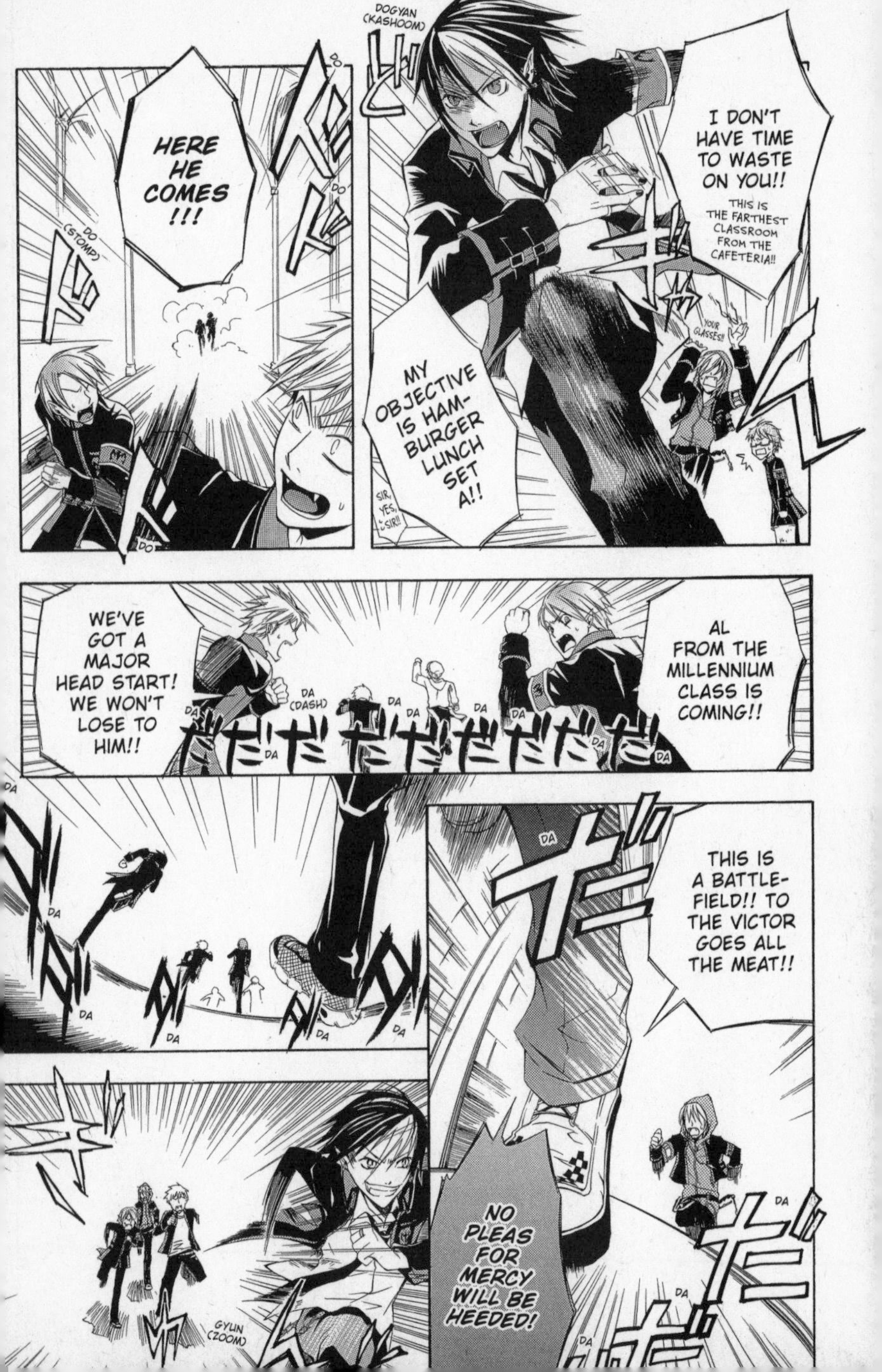
DOGYAN (KASHOOM)
I DON'T HAVE TIME TO WASTE ON YOU!!
THIS IS THE FARTHEST CLASSROOM FROM THE CAFETERIA!!
YOUR GLASSES!!
MY OBJECTIVE IS HAM-BURGER LUNCH SET A!!
SIR, YES, SIR!!
DO
HERE HE COMES!!!
DO
DO (STOMP)
DO
AL FROM THE MILLENNIUM CLASS IS COMING!!
WE'VE GOT A MAJOR HEAD START! WE WON'T LOSE TO HIM!!
DA (DASH)
DA
DA
THIS IS A BATTLE-FIELD!! TO THE VICTOR GOES ALL THE MEAT!!
DA
DA
NO PLEAS FOR MERCY WILL BE HEEDED!
GYUN (ZOOM)
DA

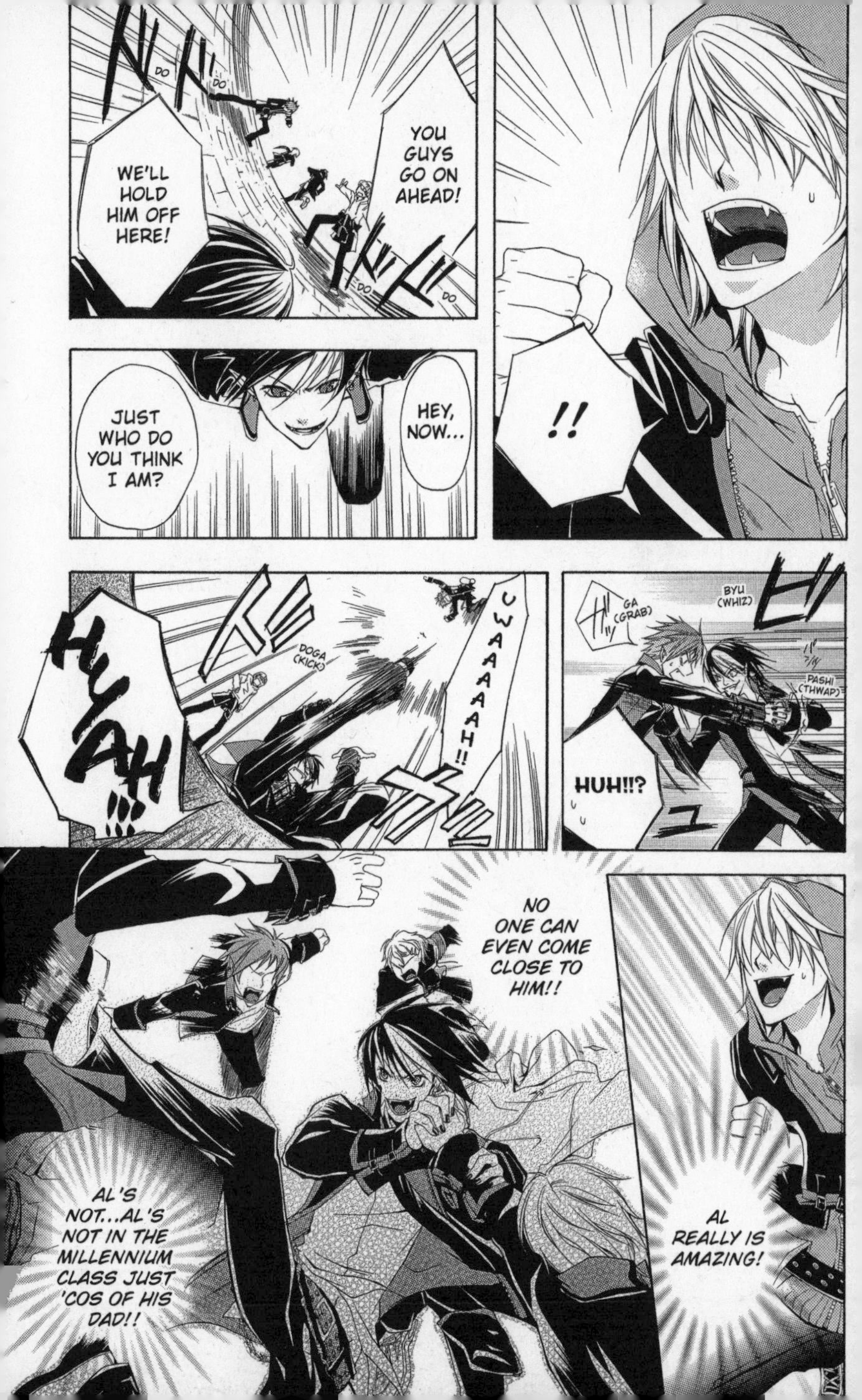
!!
YOU GUYS GO ON AHEAD!
WE'LL HOLD HIM OFF HERE!
DO DO
DO DO
HEY, NOW...
JUST WHO DO YOU THINK I AM?
BYU (WHIZ)
GA (GRAB)
PASHI (THWAP)
HUH!!?
UWAAAAAAAH!!
DOGA (KICK)
HIYAH!!!
AL REALLY IS AMAZING!
NO ONE CAN EVEN COME CLOSE TO HIM!!
AL'S NOT...AL'S NOT IN THE MILLENNIUM CLASS JUST 'COS OF HIS DAD!!

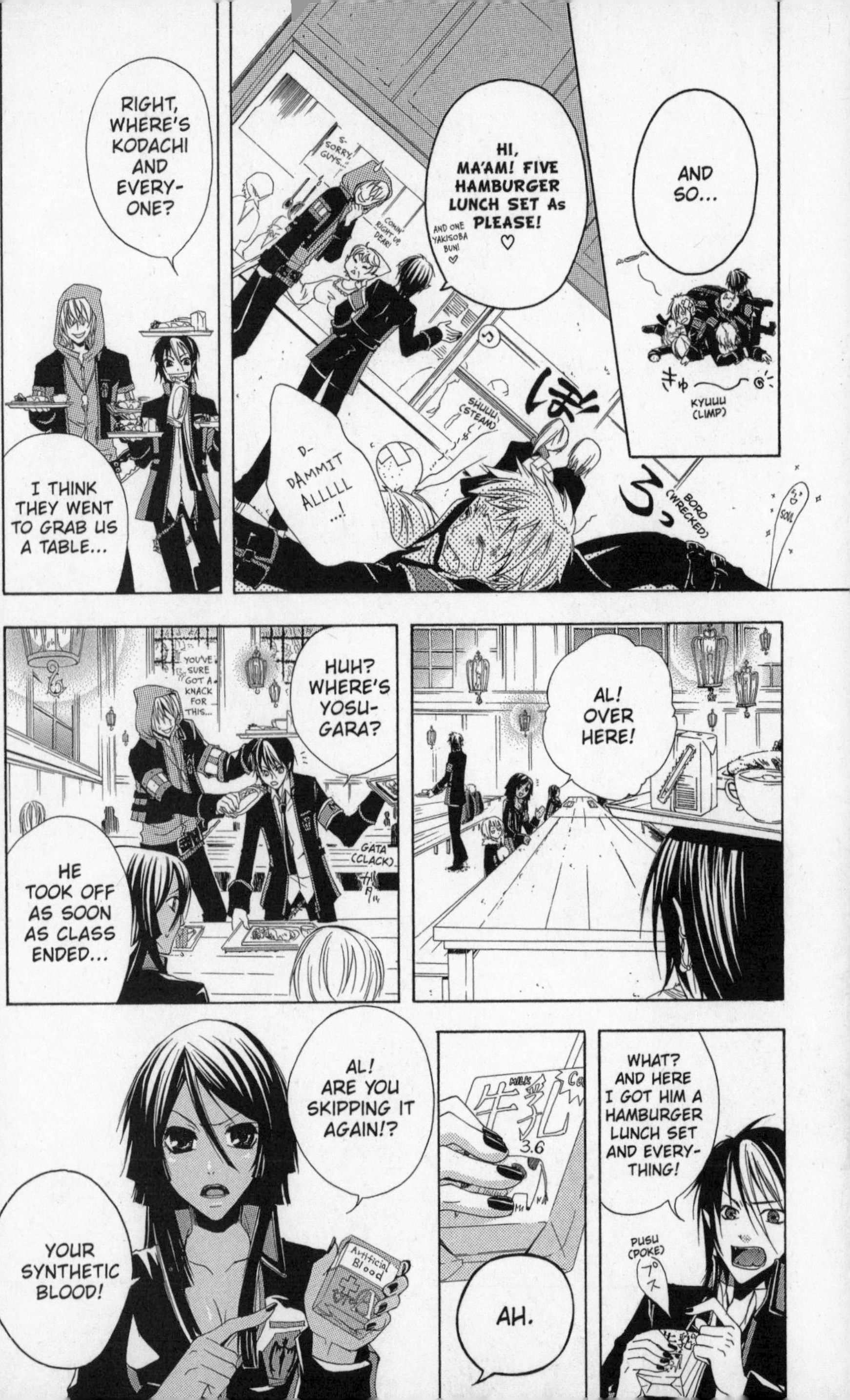
AND SO...
KYUUU (LIMP)
BORO (WRECKED)
SOUL
HI, MA'AM! FIVE HAMBURGER LUNCH SET As PLEASE! ♡
AND ONE YAKISOBA BUN! ♡
COMIN' RIGHT UP, DEAR!
S-SORRY, GUYS...
SHUUU (STEAM)
D-DAMMIT ALLLLL...!
RIGHT, WHERE'S KODACHI AND EVERY-ONE?
I THINK THEY WENT TO GRAB US A TABLE...
AL! OVER HERE!
HUH? WHERE'S YOSU-GARA?
YOU'VE SURE GOT A KNACK FOR THIS...
GATA (CLACK)
HE TOOK OFF AS SOON AS CLASS ENDED...
WHAT? AND HERE I GOT HIM A HAMBURGER LUNCH SET AND EVERY-THING!
PUSU (POKE)
牛乳
MILK
3.6
AH.
AL! ARE YOU SKIPPING IT AGAIN!?
YOUR SYNTHETIC BLOOD!
Artificial Blood

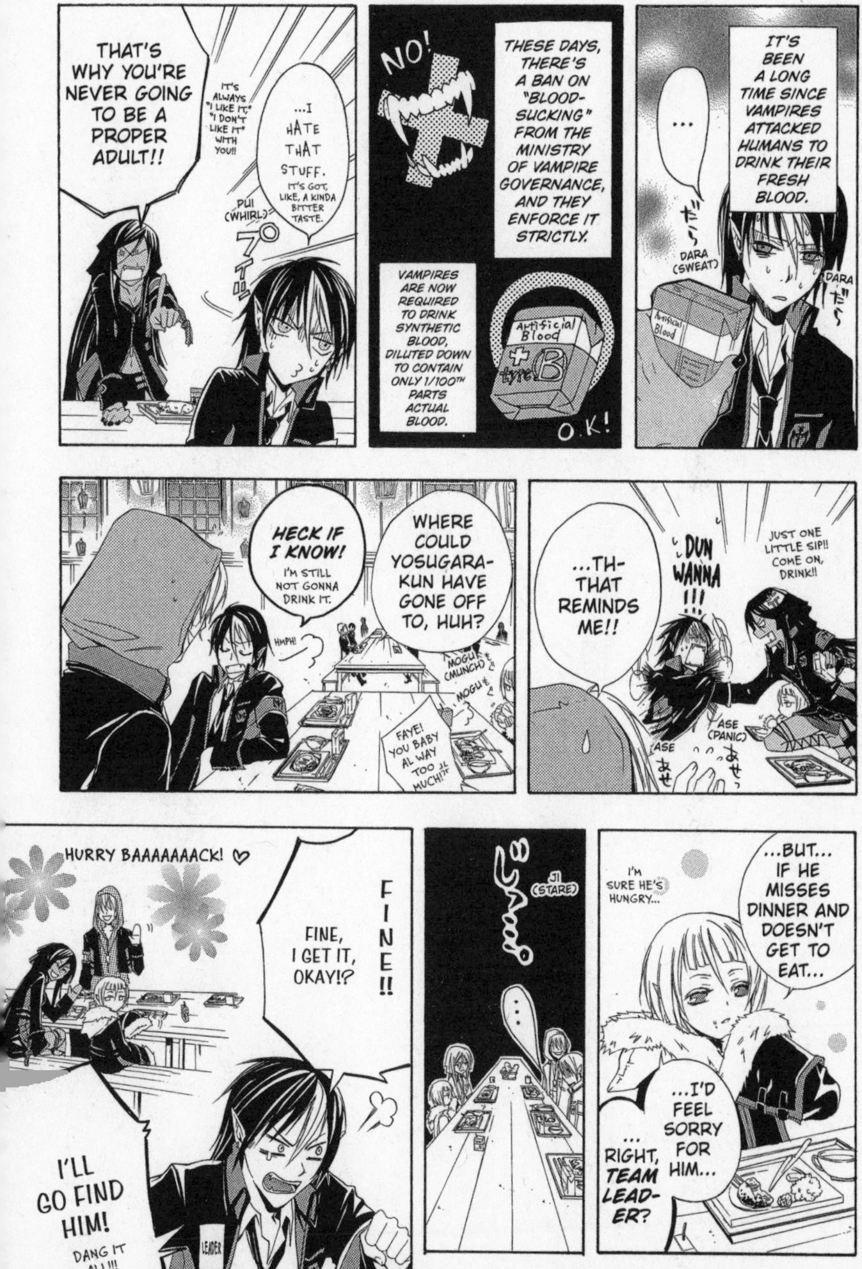
IT'S BEEN A LONG TIME SINCE VAMPIRES ATTACKED HUMANS TO DRINK THEIR FRESH BLOOD.
...
DARA (SWEAT)
DARA
Artificial Blood
THESE DAYS, THERE'S A BAN ON "BLOOD-SUCKING" FROM THE MINISTRY OF VAMPIRE GOVERNANCE, AND THEY ENFORCE IT STRICTLY.
NO!
VAMPIRES ARE NOW REQUIRED TO DRINK SYNTHETIC BLOOD, DILUTED DOWN TO CONTAIN ONLY 1/100TH PARTS ACTUAL BLOOD.
Artificial Blood
type B
O.K!
...I HATE THAT STUFF.
IT'S GOT, LIKE, A KINDA BITTER TASTE.
IT'S ALWAYS "I LIKE IT," "I DON'T LIKE IT" WITH YOU!!
THAT'S WHY YOU'RE NEVER GOING TO BE A PROPER ADULT!!
PUI (WHIRL)
JUST ONE LITTLE SIP!! COME ON, DRINK!!
DUN WANNA!!!
...TH-THAT REMINDS ME!!
ASE (PANIC)
ASE
WHERE COULD YOSUGARA-KUN HAVE GONE OFF TO, HUH?
MOGU (MUNCH)
MOGU
FAYE! YOU BABY AL WAY TOO MUCH!
HECK IF I KNOW!
I'M STILL NOT GONNA DRINK IT.
HMPH!
...BUT... IF HE MISSES DINNER AND DOESN'T GET TO EAT...
I'M SURE HE'S HUNGRY...
...I'D FEEL SORRY FOR HIM...
...RIGHT, TEAM LEADER?
JI (STARE)
...
FINE!!
FINE, I GET IT, OKAY!?
HURRY BAAAAAAACK! ♡
I'LL GO FIND HIM!
DANG IT ALL!!!
LEADER

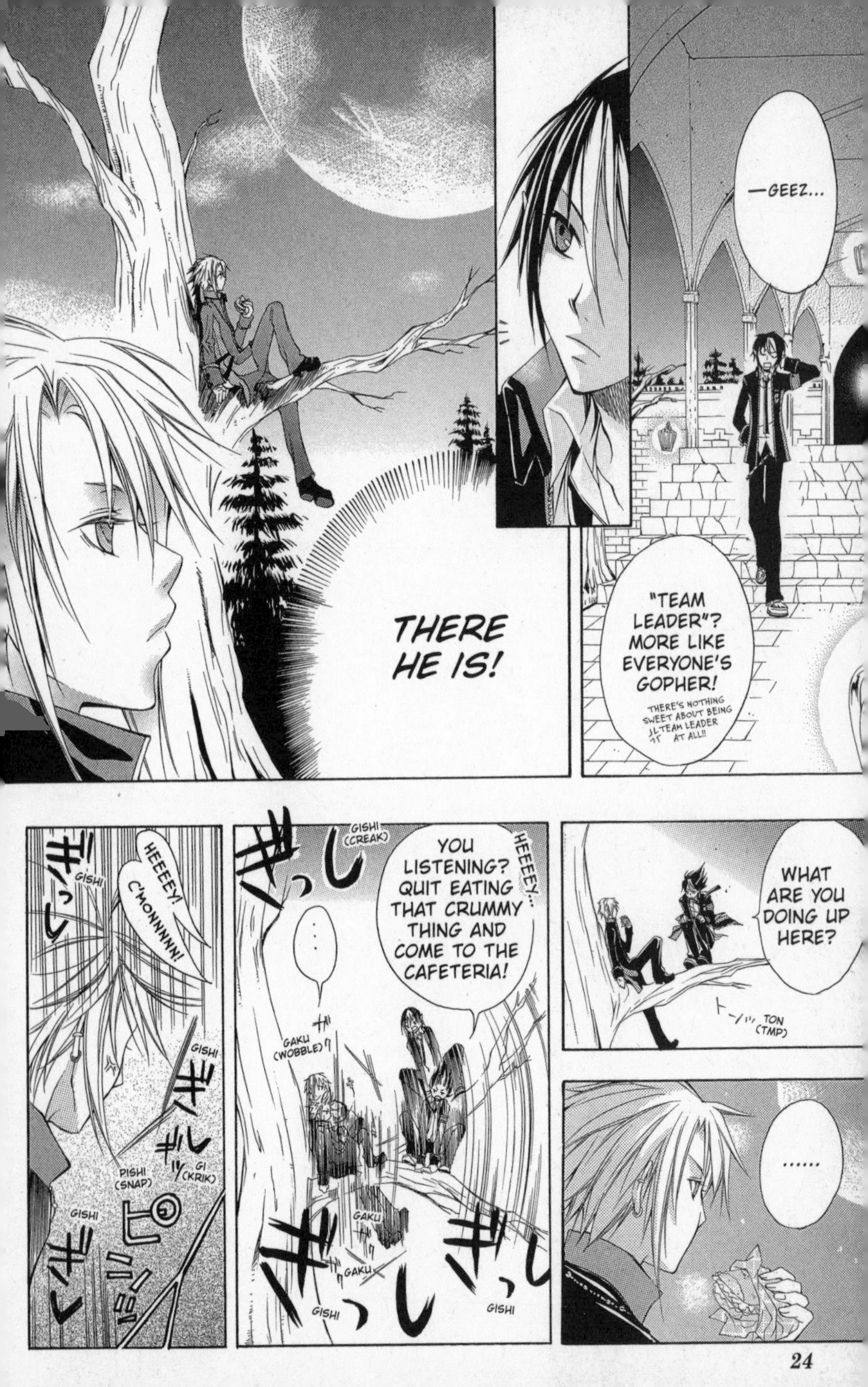

—GEEZ...
"TEAM LEADER"? MORE LIKE EVERYONE'S GOPHER!
THERE'S NOTHING SWEET ABOUT BEING TEAM LEADER AT ALL!!
THERE HE IS!
WHAT ARE YOU DOING UP HERE?
TON (TMP)
......
HEEEEY...
YOU LISTENING? QUIT EATING THAT CRUMMY THING AND COME TO THE CAFETERIA!
GISHI (CREAK)
...
GAKU (WOBBLE)
GAKU
GAKU
GISHI
GISHI
HEEEEY! C'MONNNNN!
GISHI
GISHI
PISHI (SNAP)
GI (KRIK)
GISHI

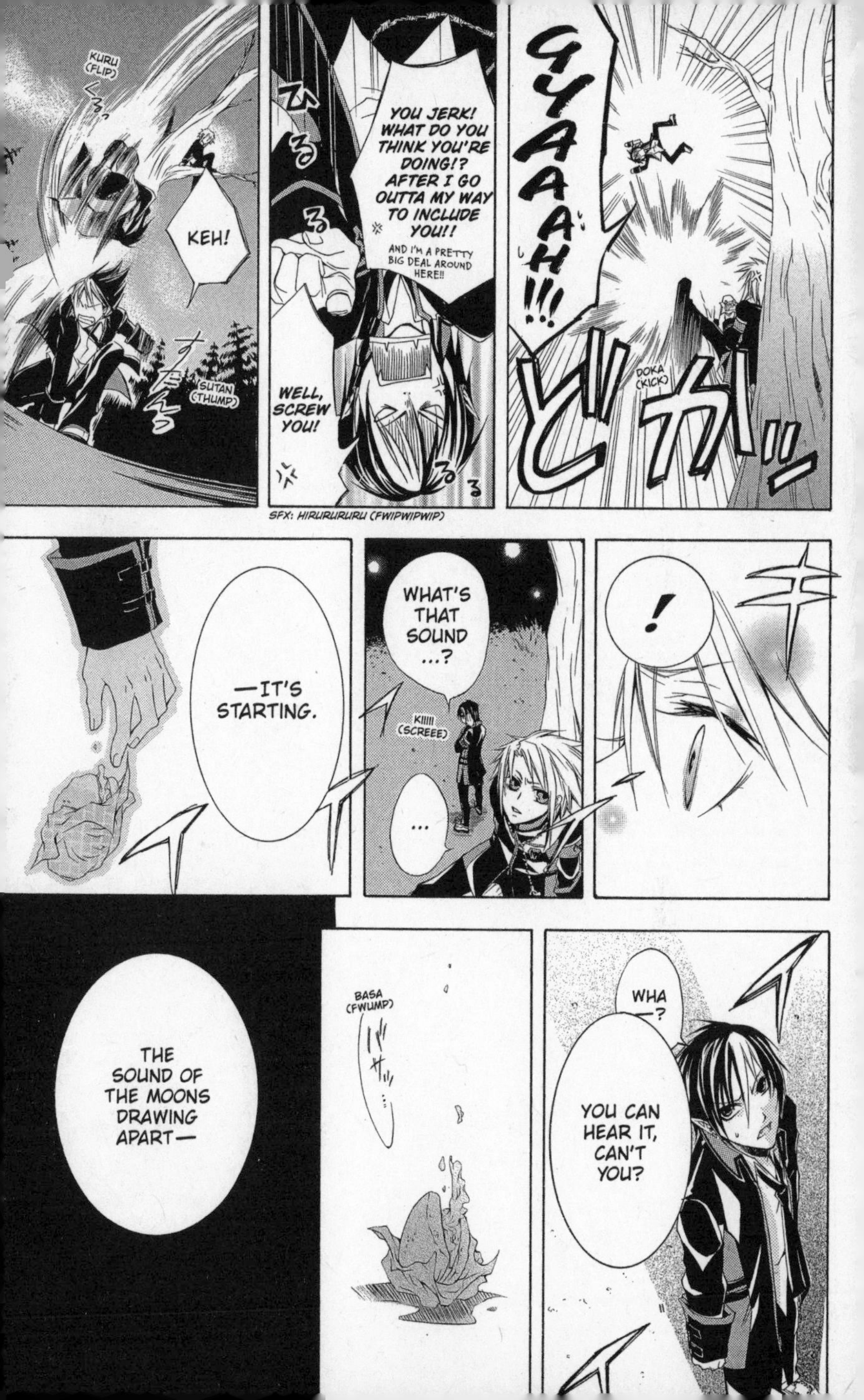
GYAAAAH!!!
DOKA (KICK)
YOU JERK! WHAT DO YOU THINK YOU'RE DOING!? AFTER I GO OUTTA MY WAY TO INCLUDE YOU!!
AND I'M A PRETTY BIG DEAL AROUND HERE!!
WELL, SCREW YOU!
SFX: HIRURURURU (FWIPWIPWIP)
KURU (FLIP)
KEH!
SUTAN (THUMP)
!
WHAT'S THAT SOUND ...?
KIIII (SCREEE)
...
—IT'S STARTING.
WHA—?
YOU CAN HEAR IT, CAN'T YOU?
BASA (FWUMP)
THE SOUND OF THE MOONS DRAWING APART—

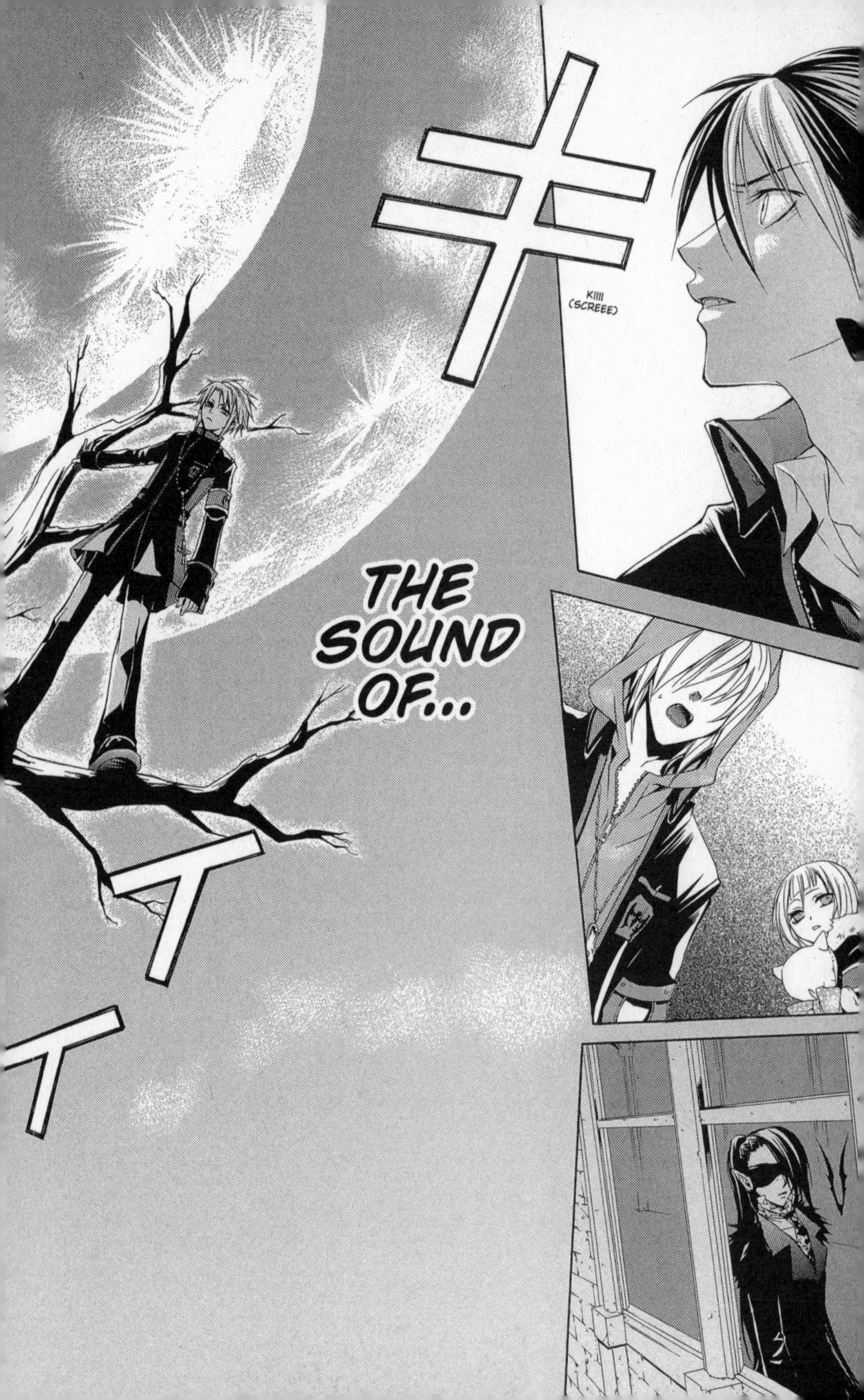
KIIII
(SCREEE)
THE SOUND OF...

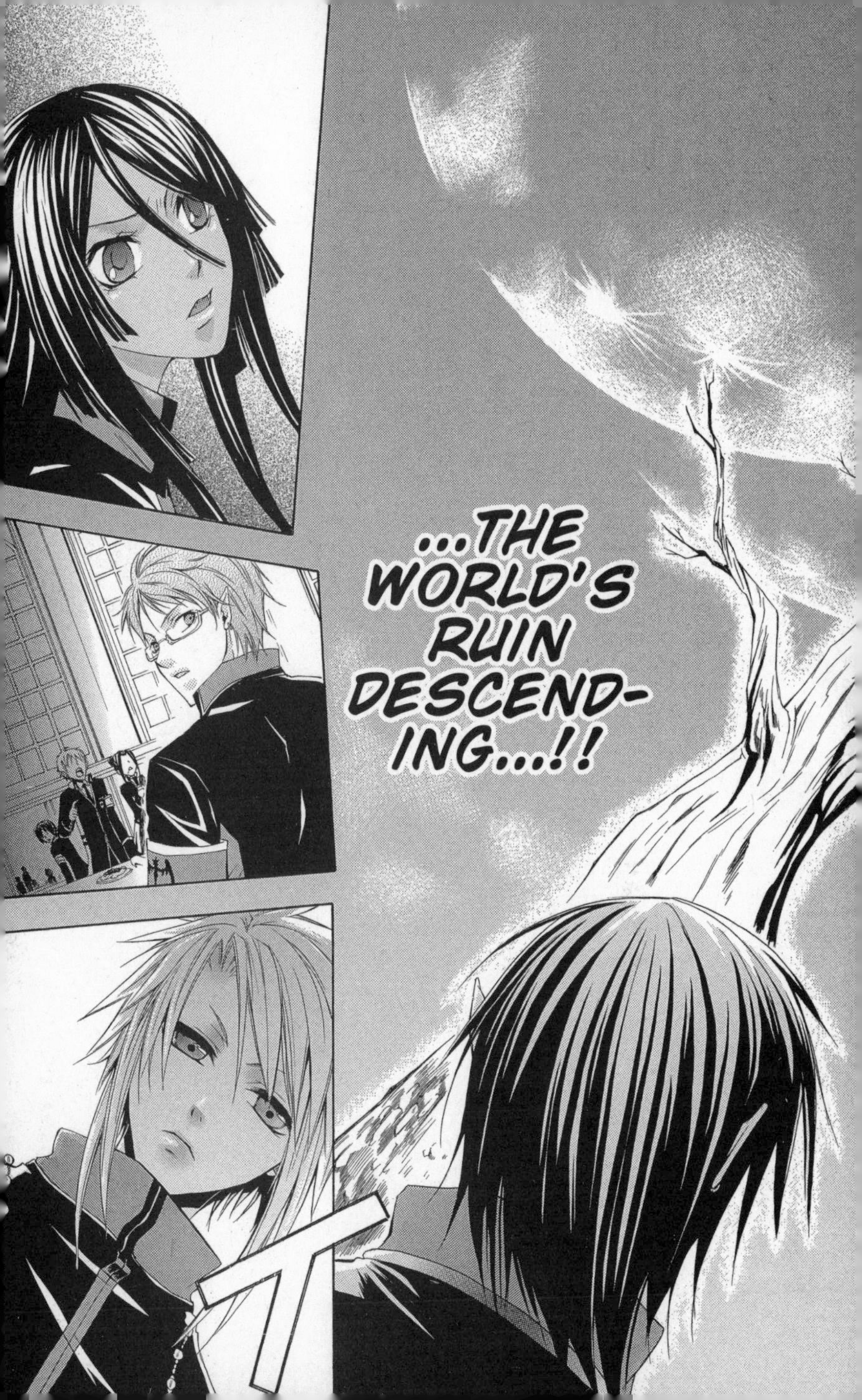
...THE WORLD'S RUIN DESCEND-ING...!!

...SECOND MOON IS EMERGING...!!

A...

!!!

THE NIGHT OF THE TWIN MOONS!!

I'VE ONLY EVER HEARD OLD STORIES ABOUT IT. DON'T TELL ME IT'S REAL...!?

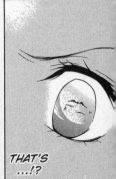
THAT'S...!?

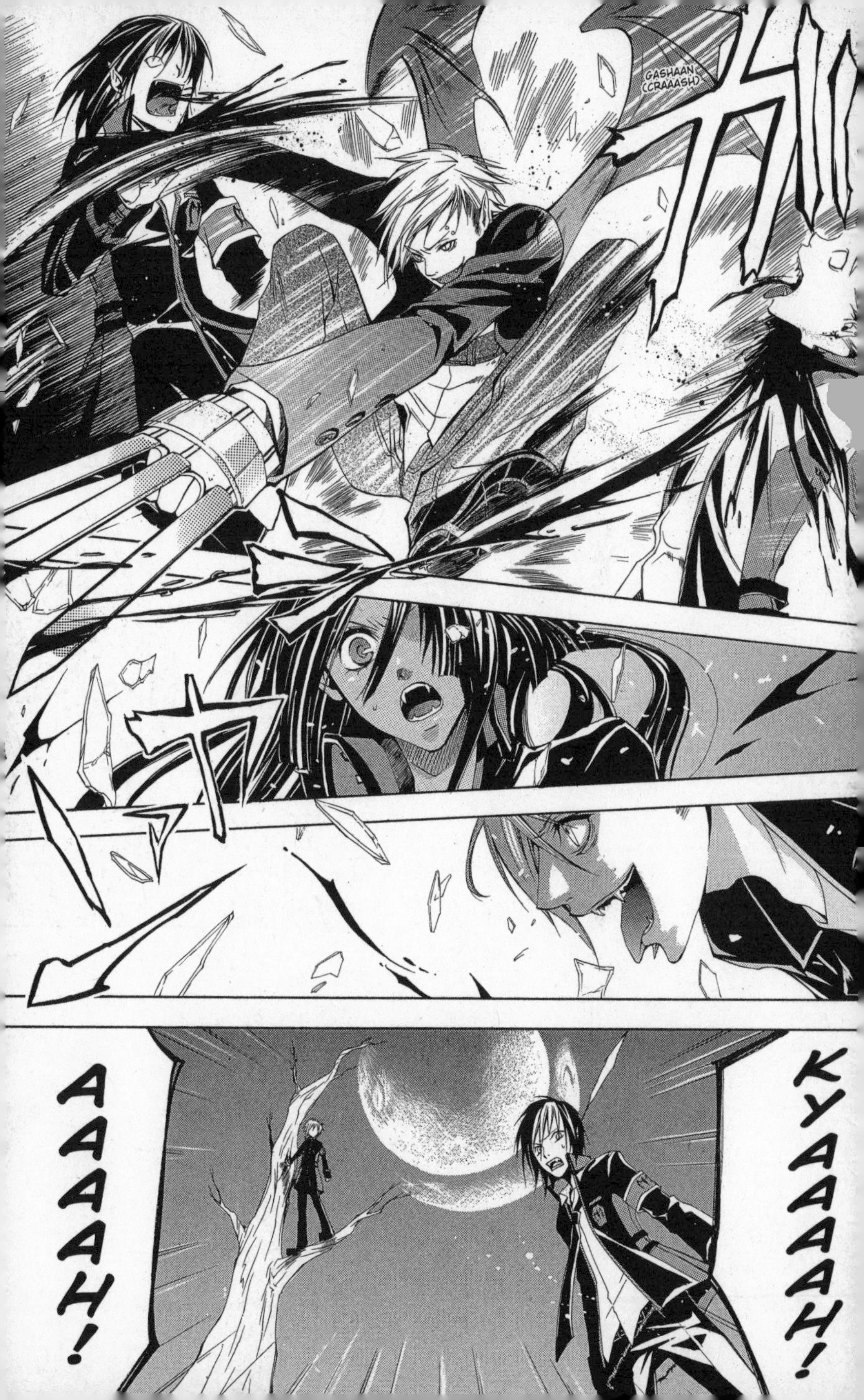
GASHAAN
(CRAAASH)
KYAAAAAAH!
AAAAAH!

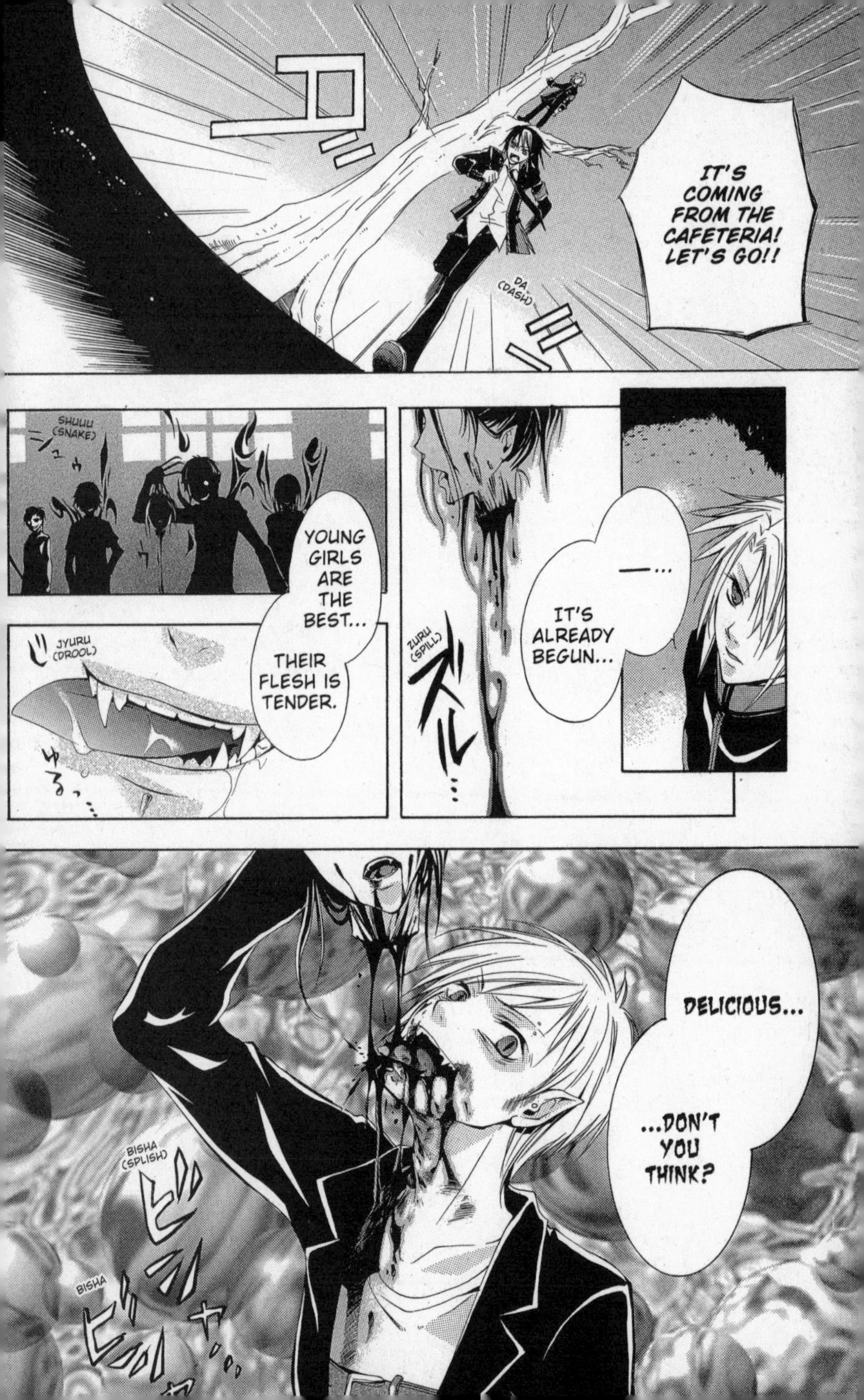
IT'S COMING FROM THE CAFETERIA! LET'S GO!!
DA (DASH)
—...
IT'S ALREADY BEGUN...
ZURU (SPILL)
SHUUU (SNAKE)
YOUNG GIRLS ARE THE BEST...
THEIR FLESH IS TENDER.
JYURU (DROOL)
DELICIOUS...
...DON'T YOU THINK?
BISHA (SPLISH)
BISHA

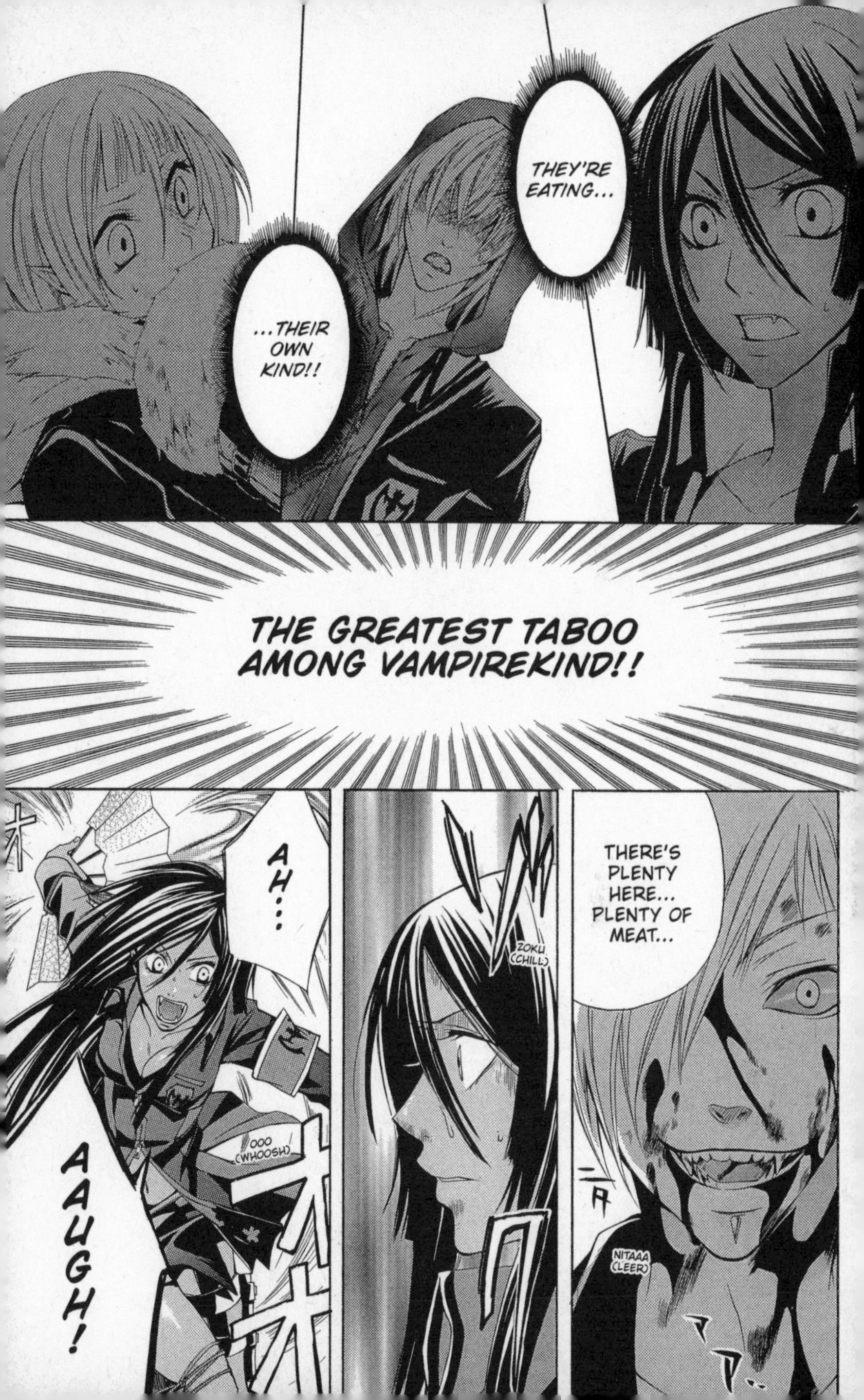
THEY'RE EATING...
...THEIR OWN KIND!!
THE GREATEST TABOO AMONG VAMPIREKIND!!
THERE'S PLENTY HERE... PLENTY OF MEAT...
NITAAA (LEER)
ZOKU (CHILL)
AH...
OOO (WHOOSH)
AAAUGH!

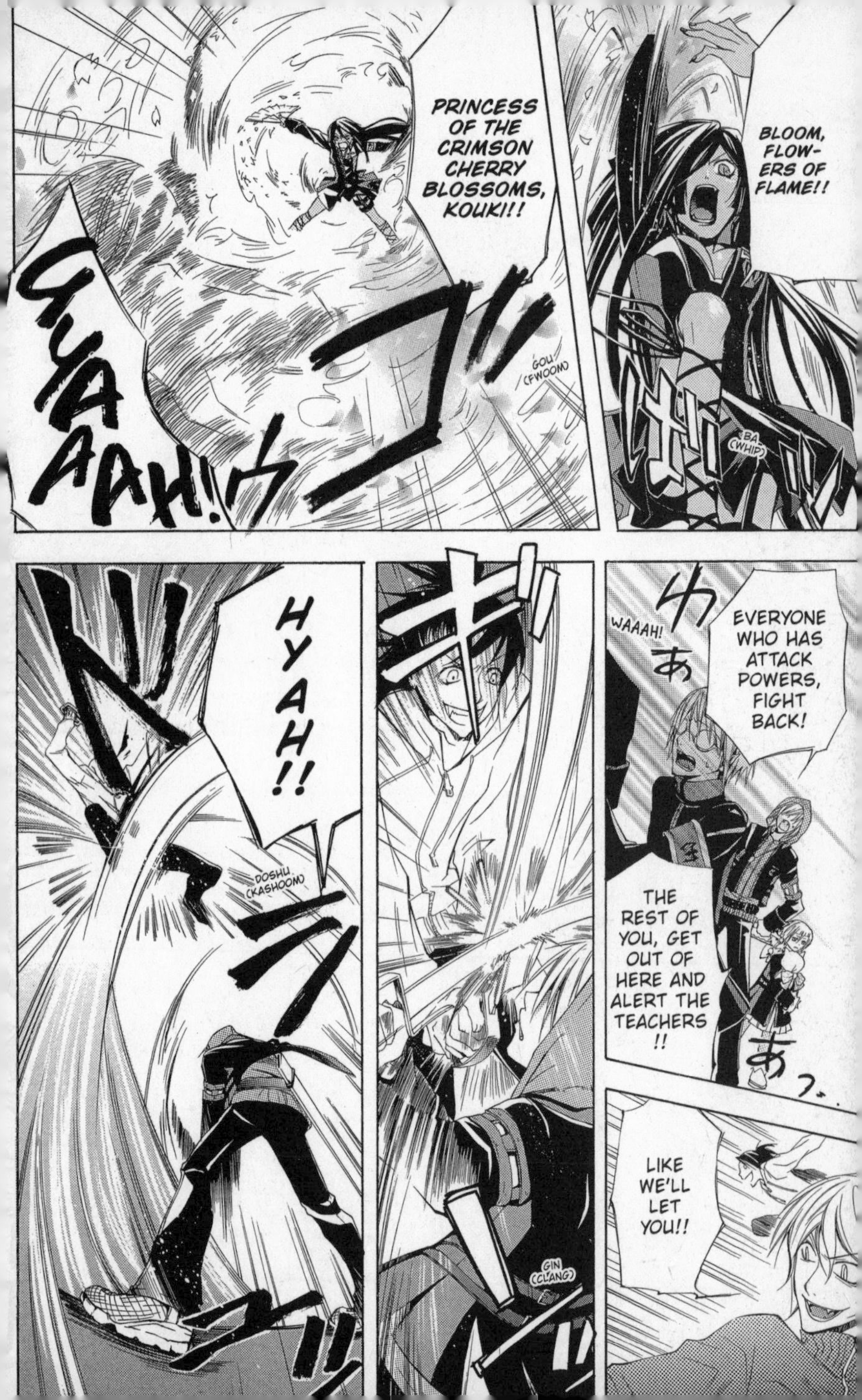

BLOOM, FLOW-ERS OF FLAME!!
BA- (WHIP)
PRINCESS OF THE CRIMSON CHERRY BLOSSOMS, KOUKI!!!
GOU (FWOOM)
UGYAAAH!!
EVERYONE WHO HAS ATTACK POWERS, FIGHT BACK!
WAAAH!
THE REST OF YOU, GET OUT OF HERE AND ALERT THE TEACHERS!!
LIKE WE'LL LET YOU!!
GIN (CLANG)
HYAH!!
DOSHU (KASHOOM)

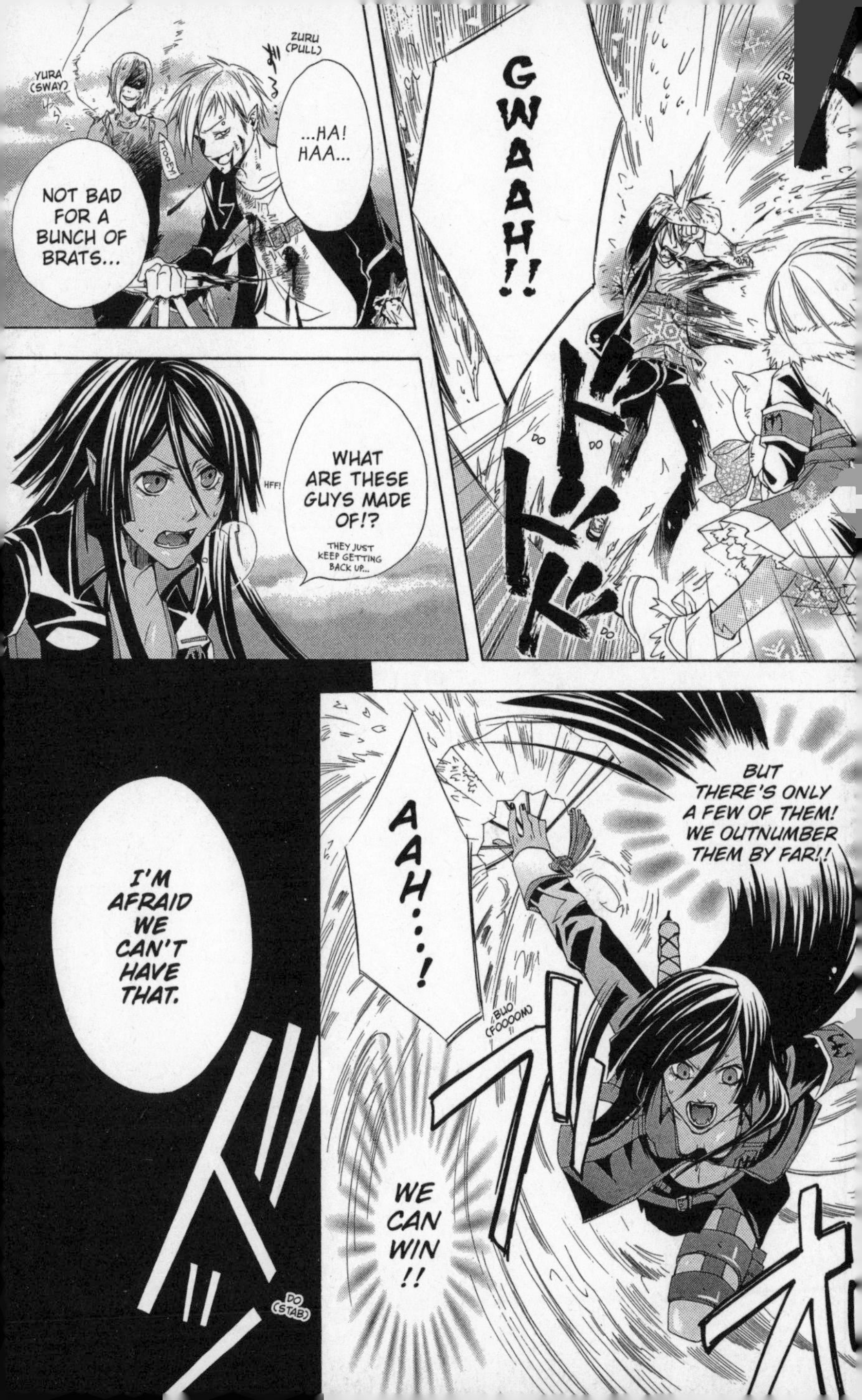
GWAAH!!
DO
DO
DO
ZURU (PULL)
...HA! HAA...
YURA (SWAY)
PTOOEY!
NOT BAD FOR A BUNCH OF BRATS...
WHAT ARE THESE GUYS MADE OF!?
THEY JUST KEEP GETTING BACK UP...
HFF!
BUT THERE'S ONLY A FEW OF THEM! WE OUTNUMBER THEM BY FAR!!
AAH...!
BUO (FOOOOM)
WE CAN WIN!!
I'M AFRAID WE CAN'T HAVE THAT.
DO (STAB)

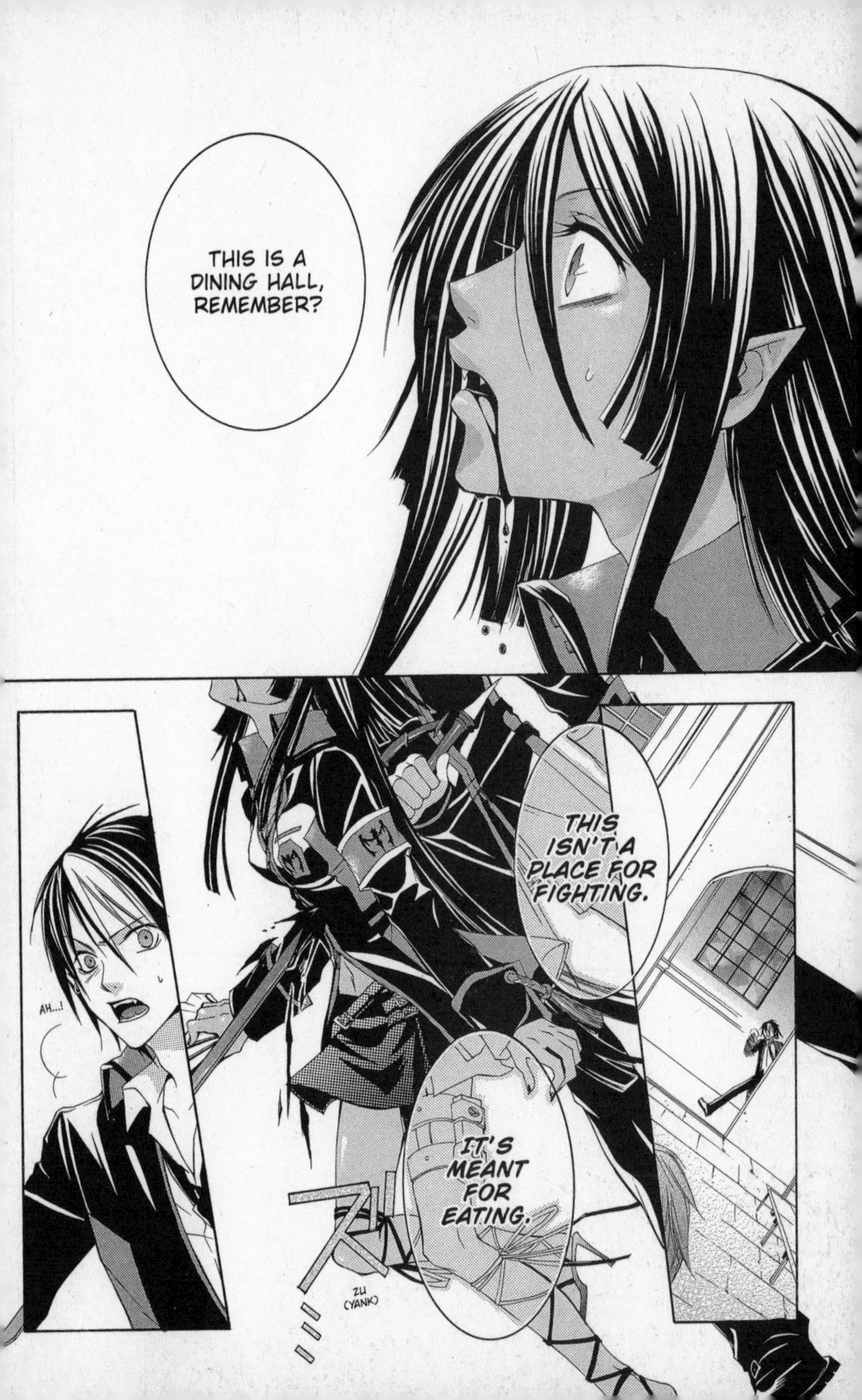
THIS IS A DINING HALL, REMEMBER?
THIS ISN'T A PLACE FOR FIGHTING.
IT'S MEANT FOR EATING.
ZU (YANK)
AH...!

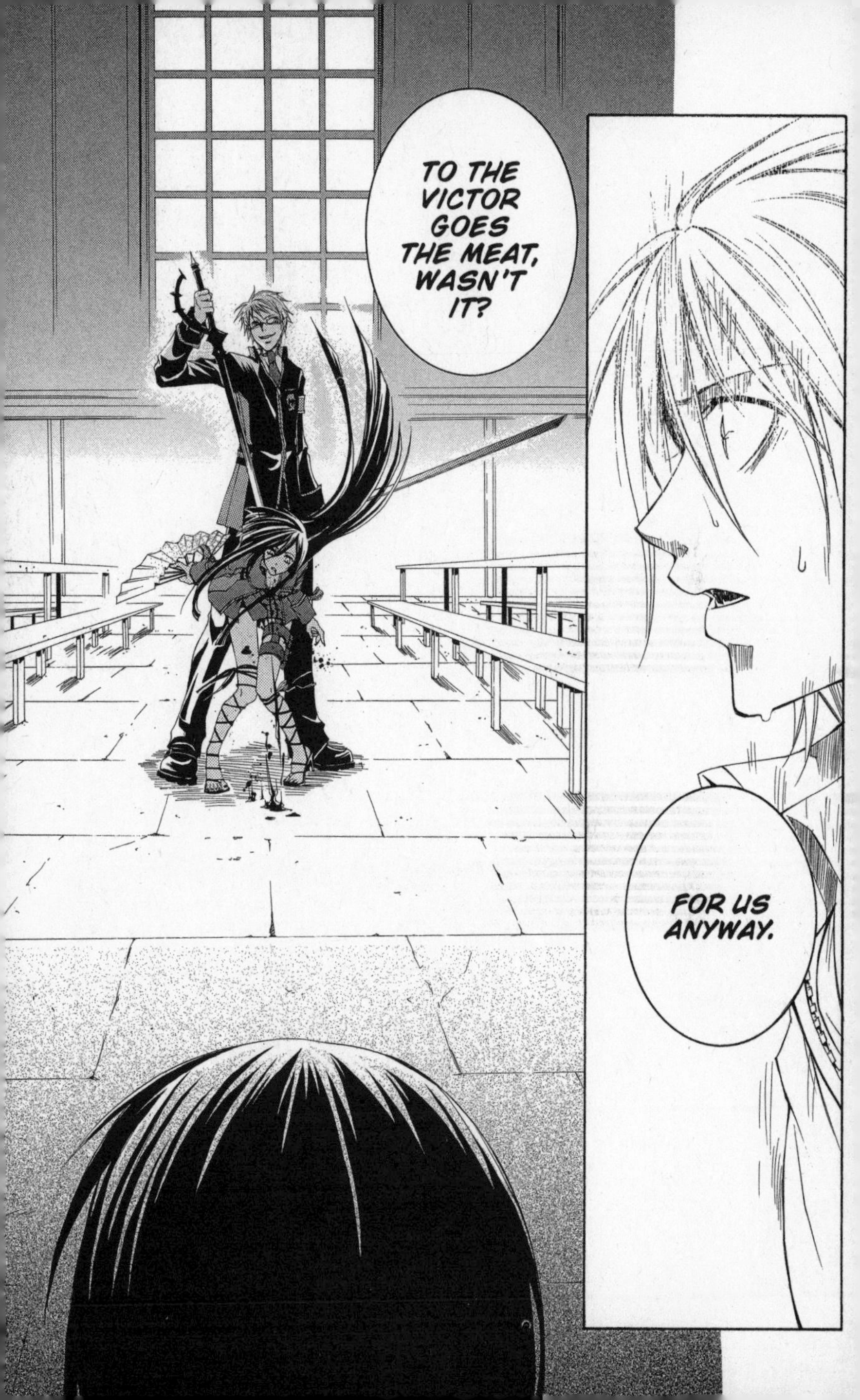
TO THE VICTOR GOES THE MEAT, WASN'T IT?
FOR US ANYWAY.

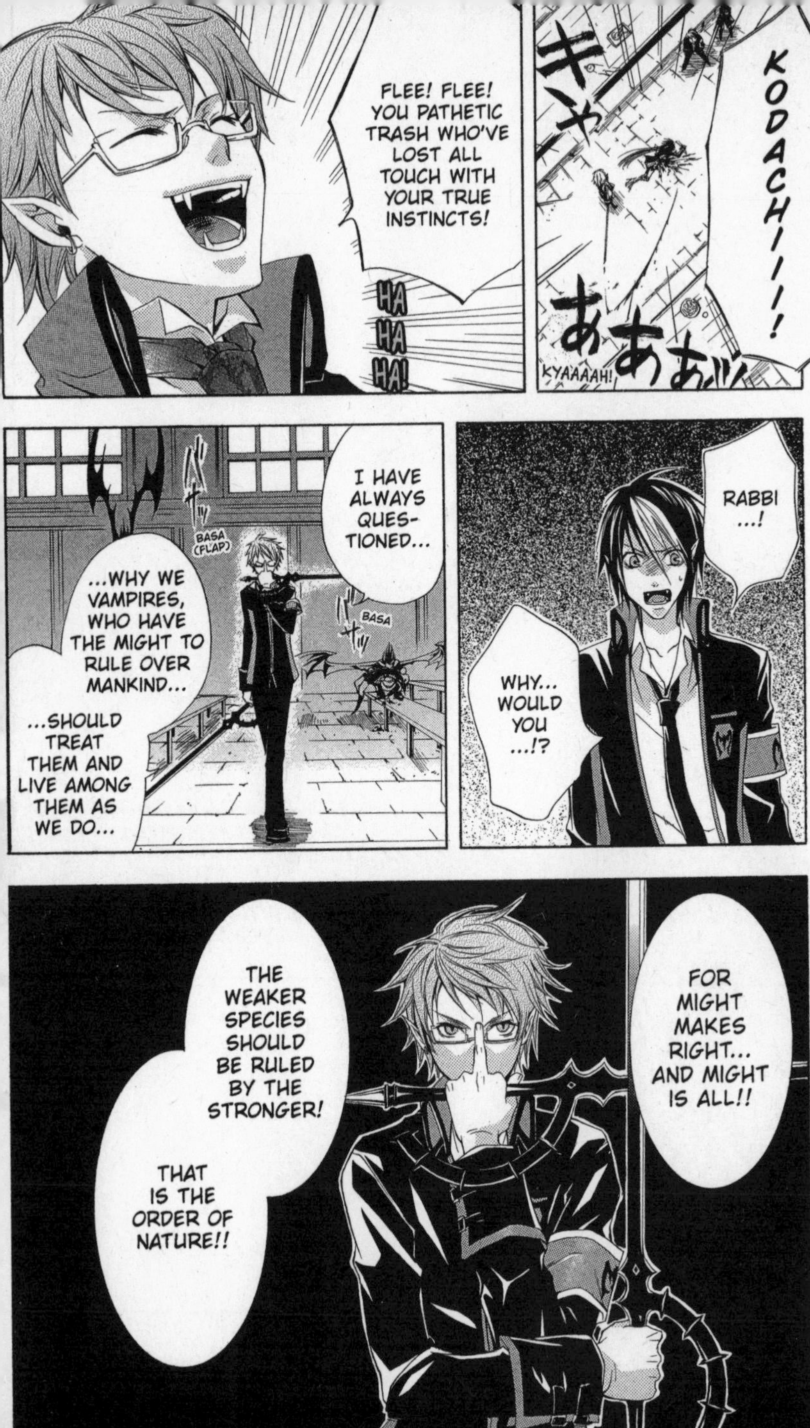
KODACHI!!!!
キャー
ああああ
KYAAAAH!
FLEE! FLEE! YOU PATHETIC TRASH WHO'VE LOST ALL TOUCH WITH YOUR TRUE INSTINCTS!
HA HA HA!
RABBI ...!
WHY... WOULD YOU ...!?
I HAVE ALWAYS QUES-TIONED...
バサッ
BASA (FLAP)
...WHY WE VAMPIRES, WHO HAVE THE MIGHT TO RULE OVER MANKIND...
バサッ
BASA
...SHOULD TREAT THEM AND LIVE AMONG THEM AS WE DO...
FOR MIGHT MAKES RIGHT... AND MIGHT IS ALL!!
THE WEAKER SPECIES SHOULD BE RULED BY THE STRONGER!
THAT IS THE ORDER OF NATURE!!

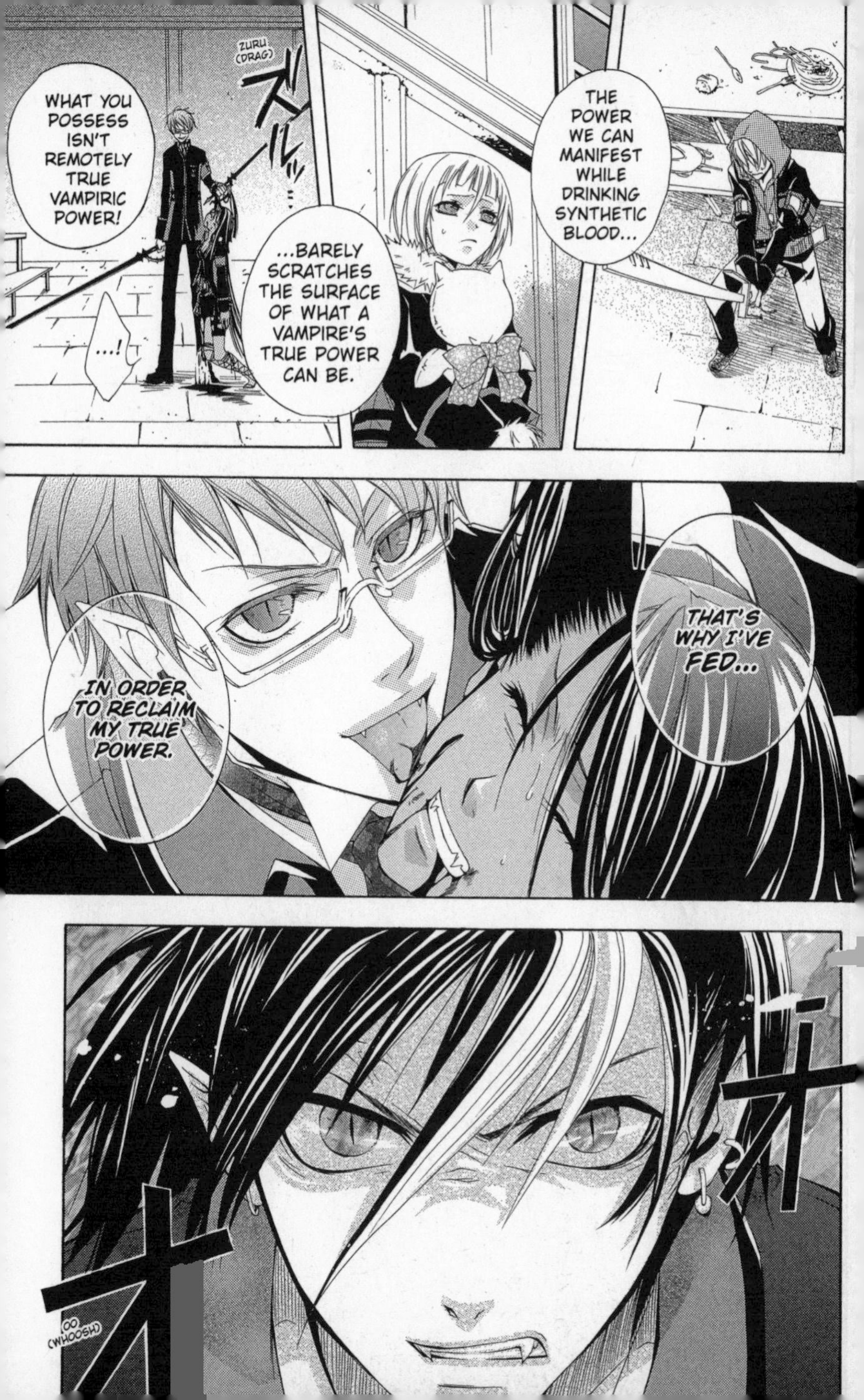
THE POWER WE CAN MANIFEST WHILE DRINKING SYNTHETIC BLOOD...
...BARELY SCRATCHES THE SURFACE OF WHAT A VAMPIRE'S TRUE POWER CAN BE.
ZURU (DRAG)
WHAT YOU POSSESS ISN'T REMOTELY TRUE VAMPIRIC POWER!
...!
THAT'S WHY I'VE FED...
IN ORDER TO RECLAIM MY TRUE POWER.
OO (WHOOSH)

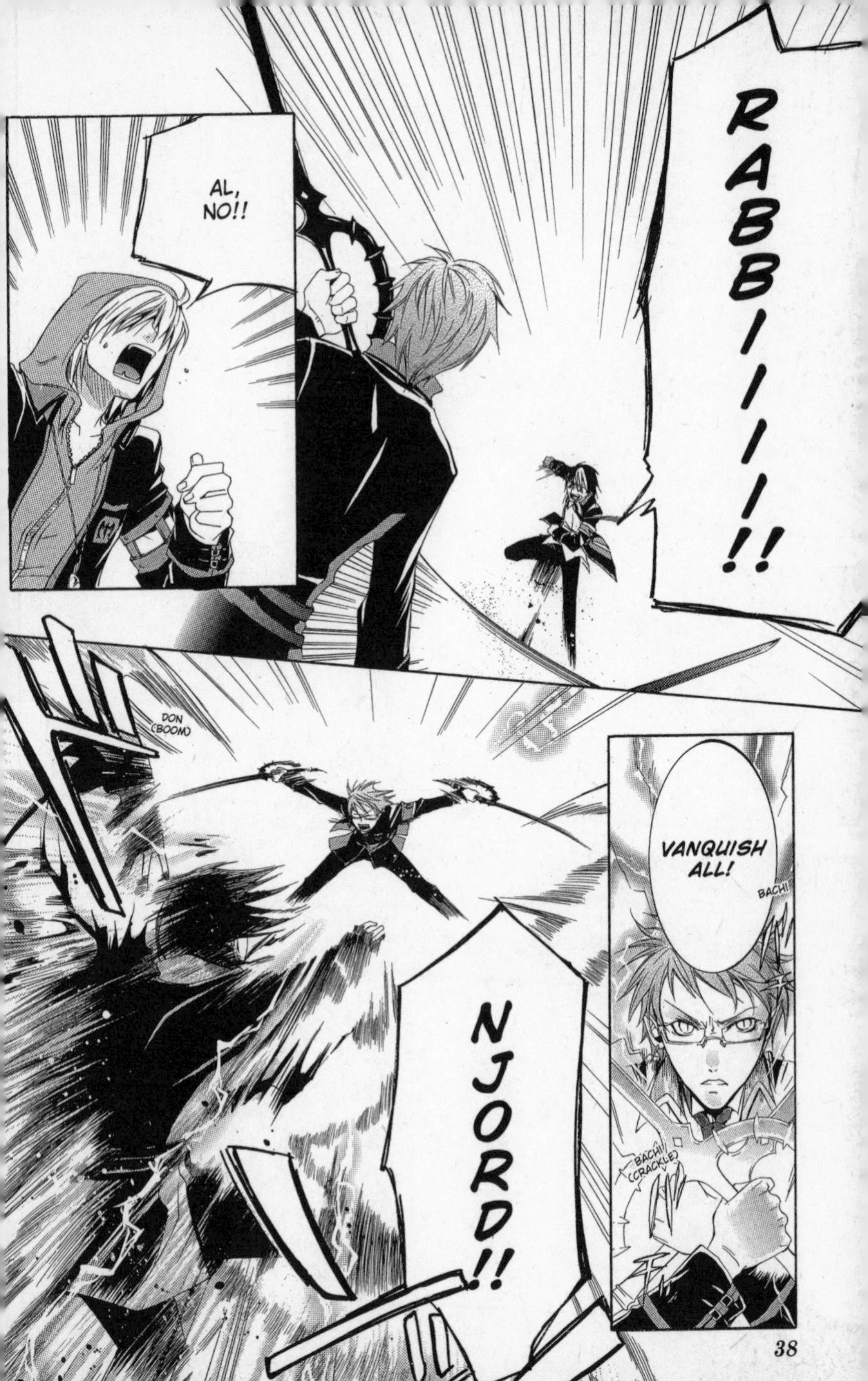
RABBIIII!!
AL, NO!!
VANQUISH ALL!
BACHI
BACHI (CRACKLE)
NJORD!!
DON (BOOM)

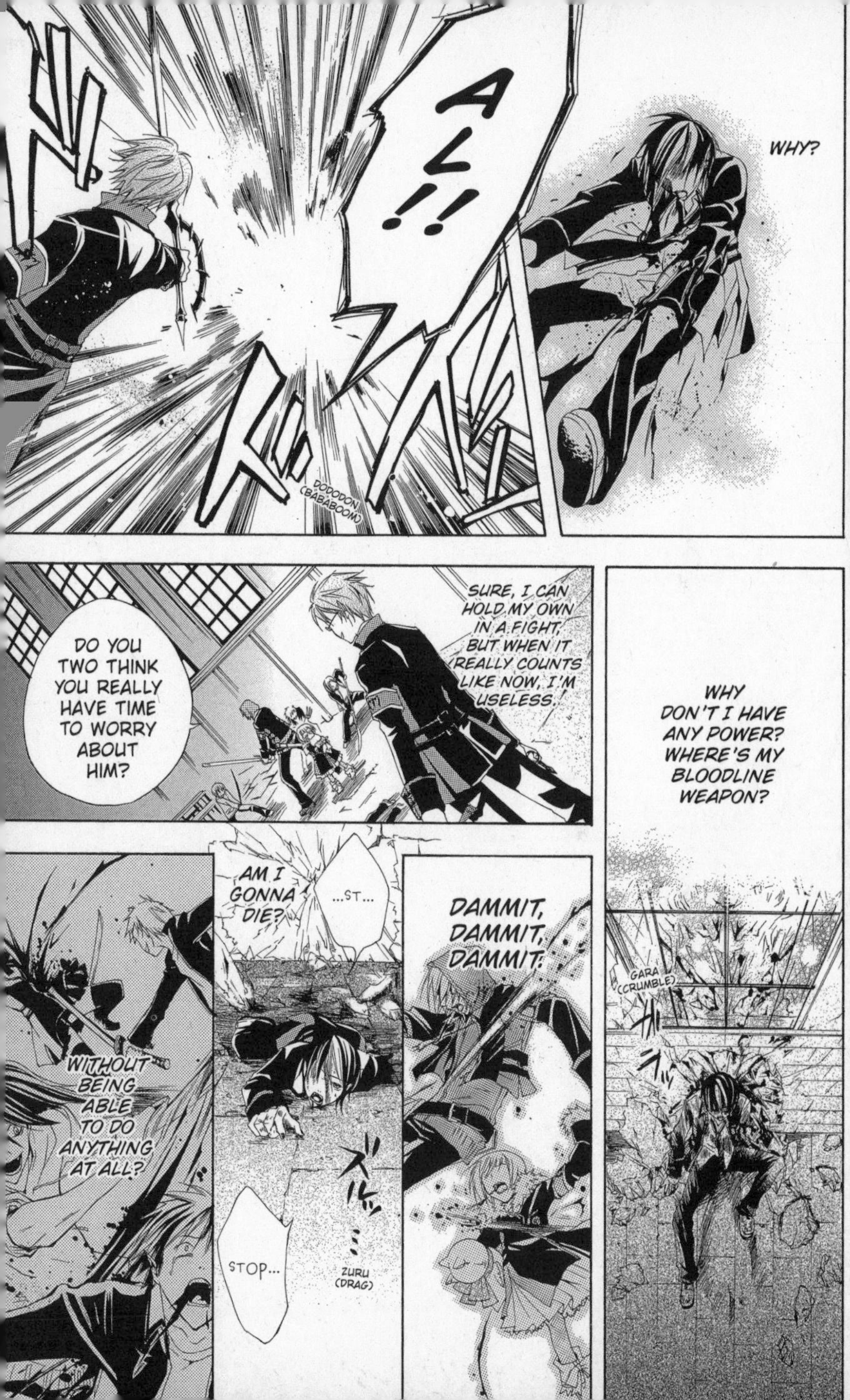
WHY?
AL!!
DODODON (BABABOOM)
WHY DON'T I HAVE ANY POWER? WHERE'S MY BLOODLINE WEAPON?
GARA (CRUMBLE)
SURE, I CAN HOLD MY OWN IN A FIGHT, BUT WHEN IT REALLY COUNTS LIKE NOW, I'M USELESS.
DO YOU TWO THINK YOU REALLY HAVE TIME TO WORRY ABOUT HIM?
DAMMIT, DAMMIT, DAMMIT.
...ST...
AM I GONNA DIE?
ZURU (DRAG)
STOP...
WITHOUT BEING ABLE TO DO ANYTHING AT ALL?

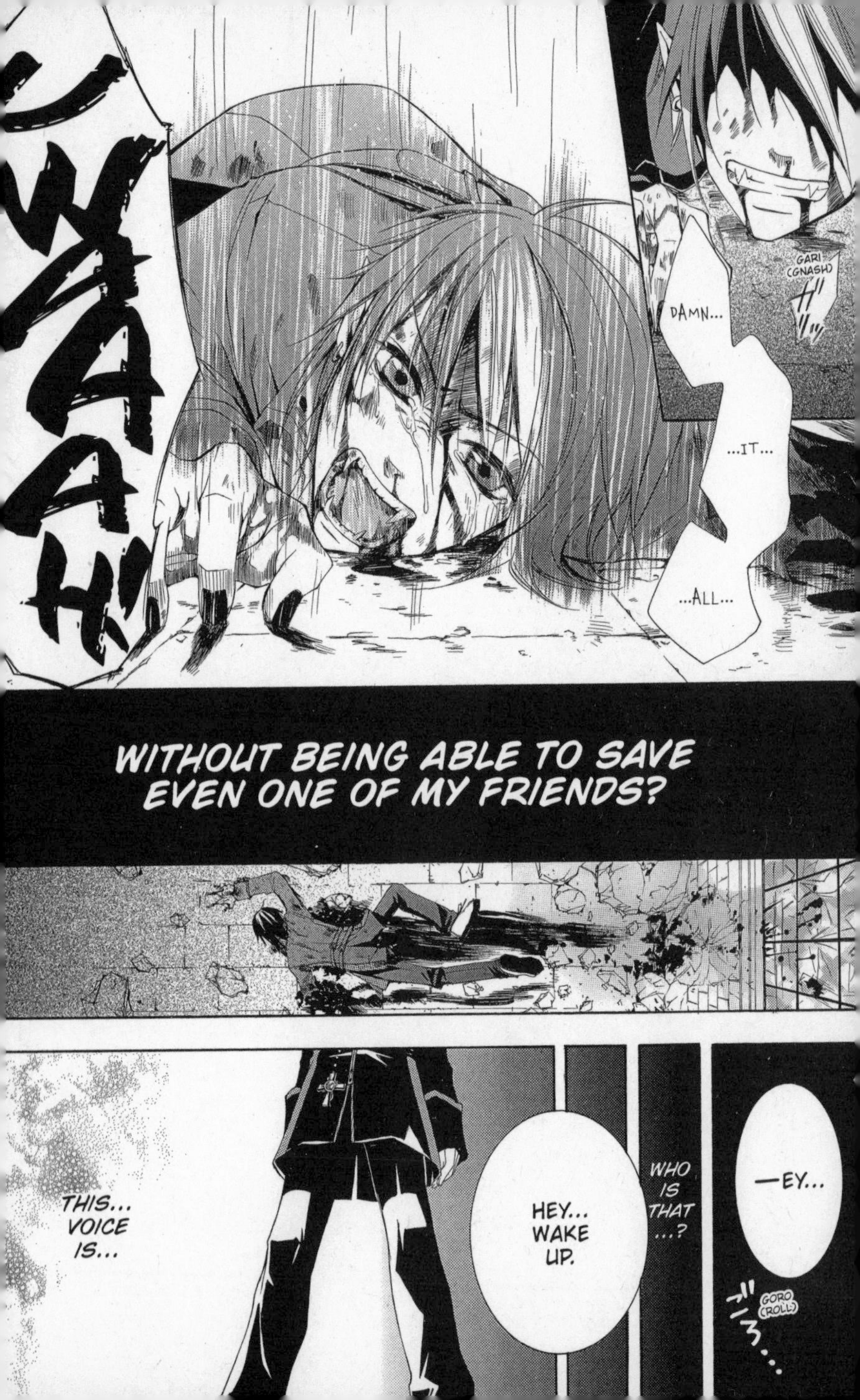
GARI (GNASH)
DAMN...
...IT...
...ALL...
WITHOUT BEING ABLE TO SAVE EVEN ONE OF MY FRIENDS?
—EY...
GORO (ROLL)
WHO IS THAT ...?
HEY... WAKE UP.
THIS... VOICE IS...

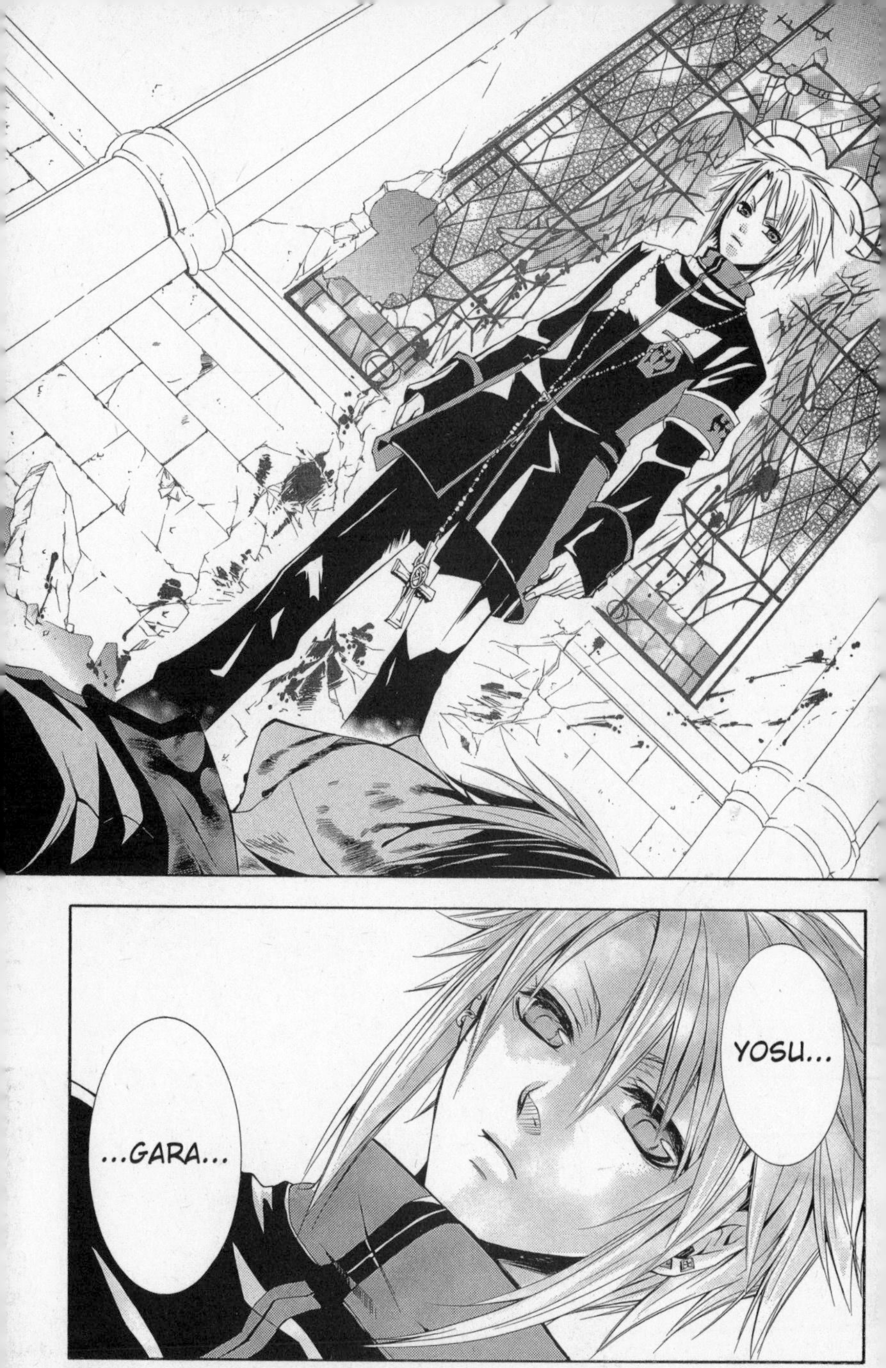
YOSU...
...GARA...

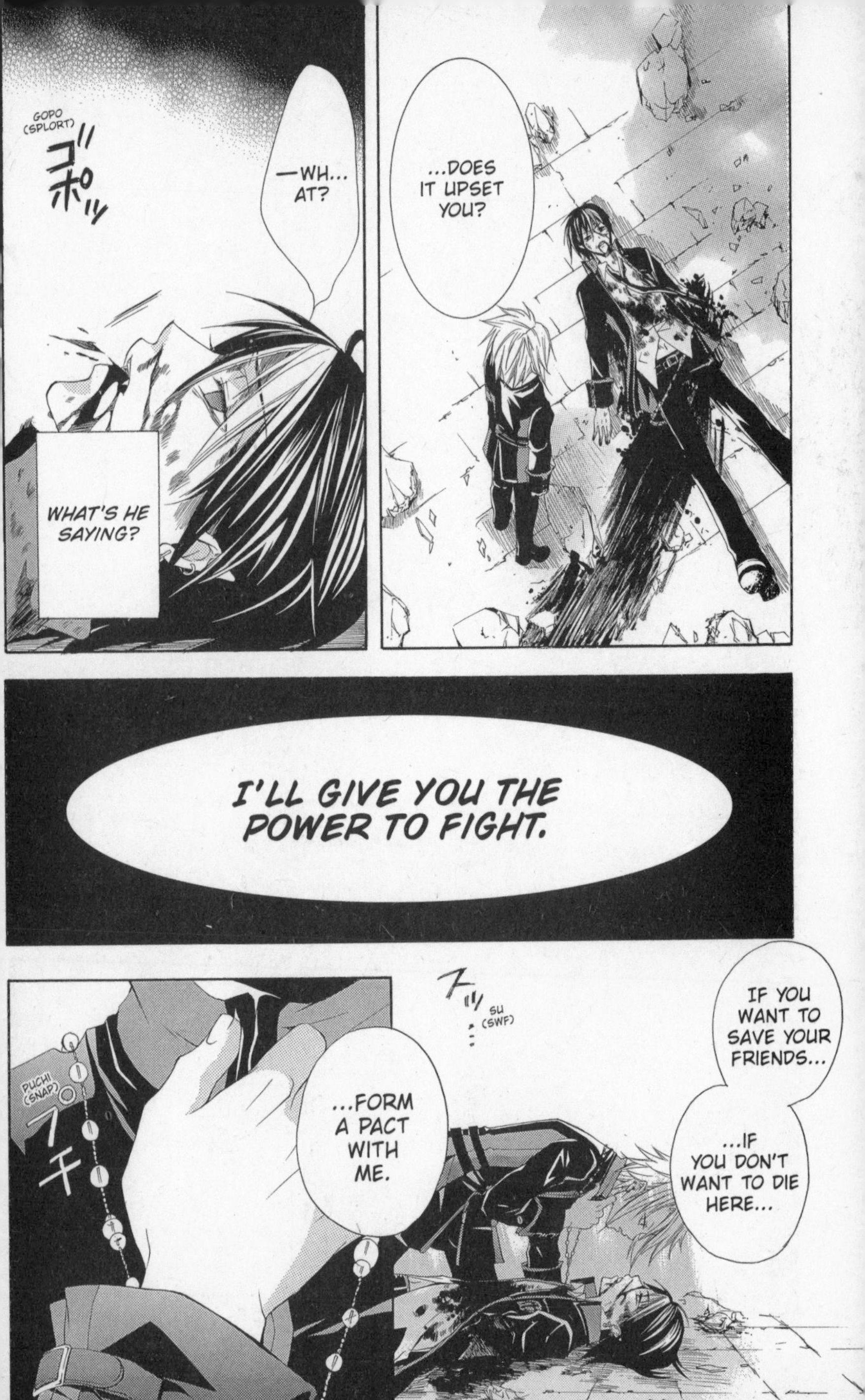
...DOES IT UPSET YOU?
—WH... AT?
ゴポッ
GOPO (SPLORT)
WHAT'S HE SAYING?
I'LL GIVE YOU THE POWER TO FIGHT.
IF YOU WANT TO SAVE YOUR FRIENDS...
...IF YOU DON'T WANT TO DIE HERE...
スッ
SU (SWF)
...FORM A PACT WITH ME.
プチ
PUCHI (SNAP)

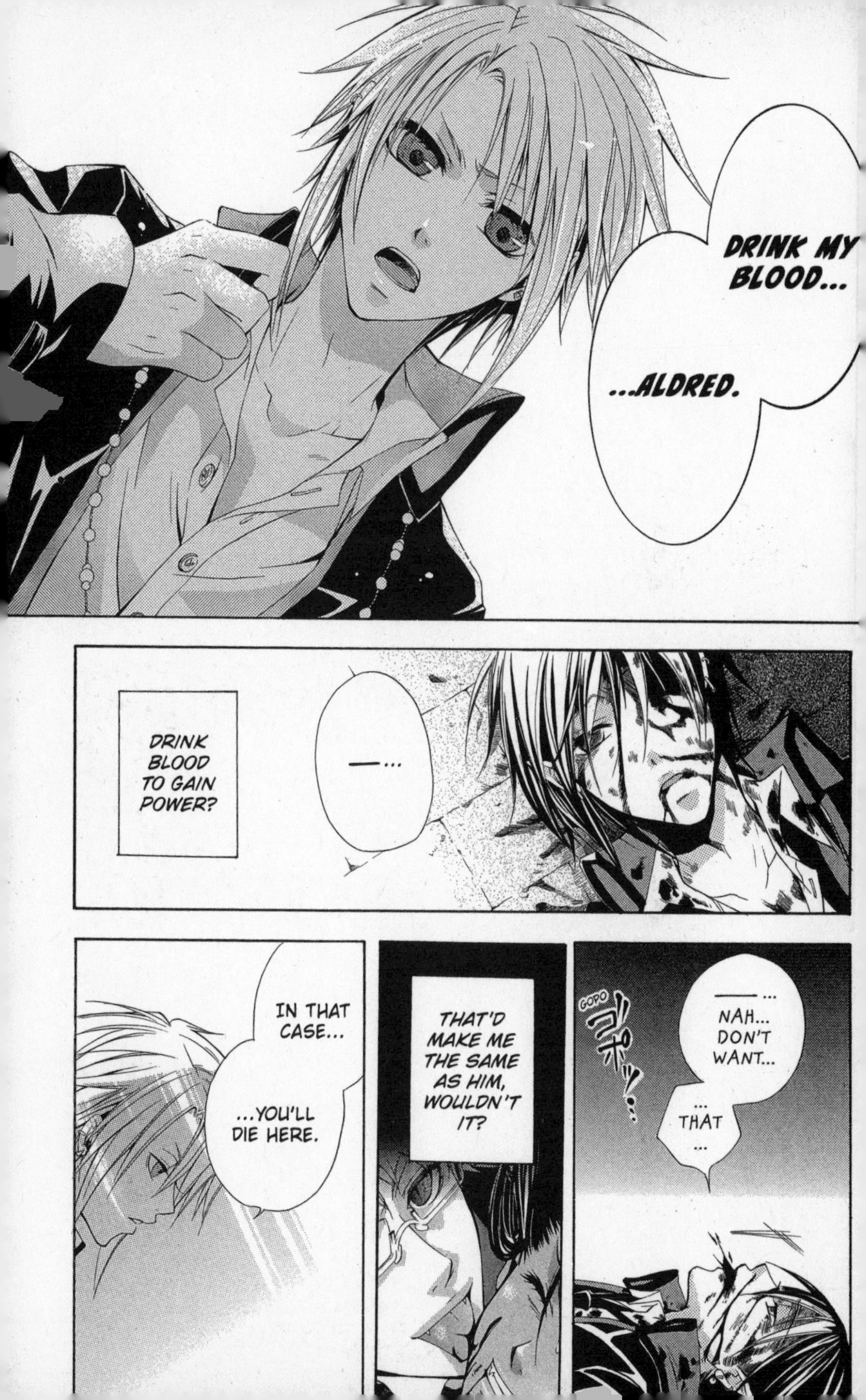
DRINK MY BLOOD...
...ALDRED.
—...
DRINK BLOOD TO GAIN POWER?
—...
NAH... DON'T WANT...
...THAT...
GOPO
THAT'D MAKE ME THE SAME AS HIM, WOULDN'T IT?
IN THAT CASE...
...YOU'LL DIE HERE.

—BUT
...!!

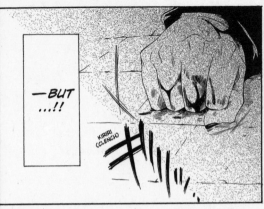

KIRIRI
(CLENCH)

BUT...

GYU
(CLENCH)

ARGH, DAMMIT ALL TO HELL.

WHO
CARES
WHAT I
TURN
INTO!!?

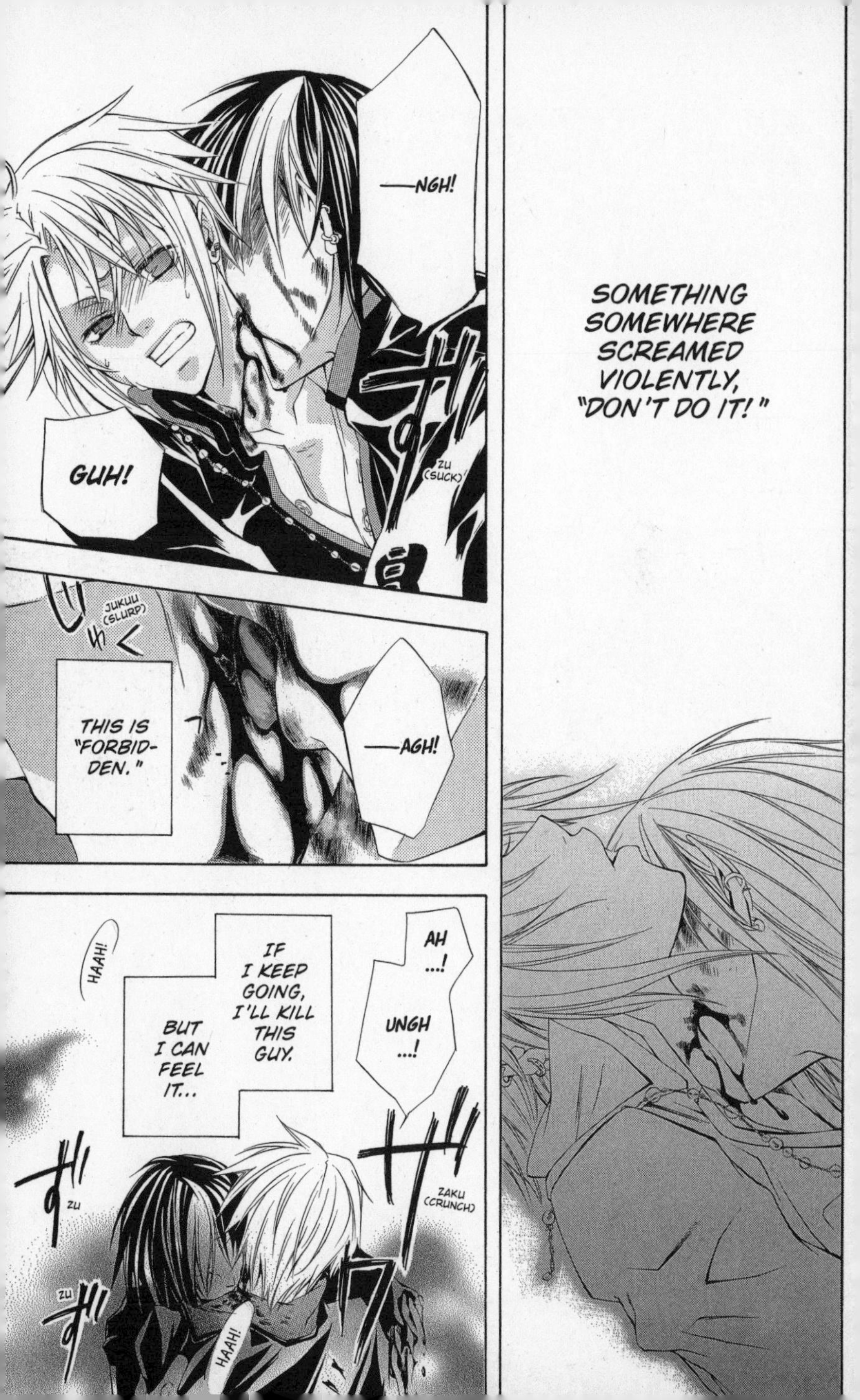
SOMETHING SOMEWHERE SCREAMED VIOLENTLY, "DON'T DO IT!"
—NGH!
ZU (SUCK)
GUH!
JUKUU (SLURP)
—AGH!
THIS IS "FORBID-DEN."
AH ...! UNGH ...!
IF I KEEP GOING, I'LL KILL THIS GUY.
BUT I CAN FEEL IT...
HAAH!
ZAKU (CRUNCH)
ZU
ZU
HAAH!

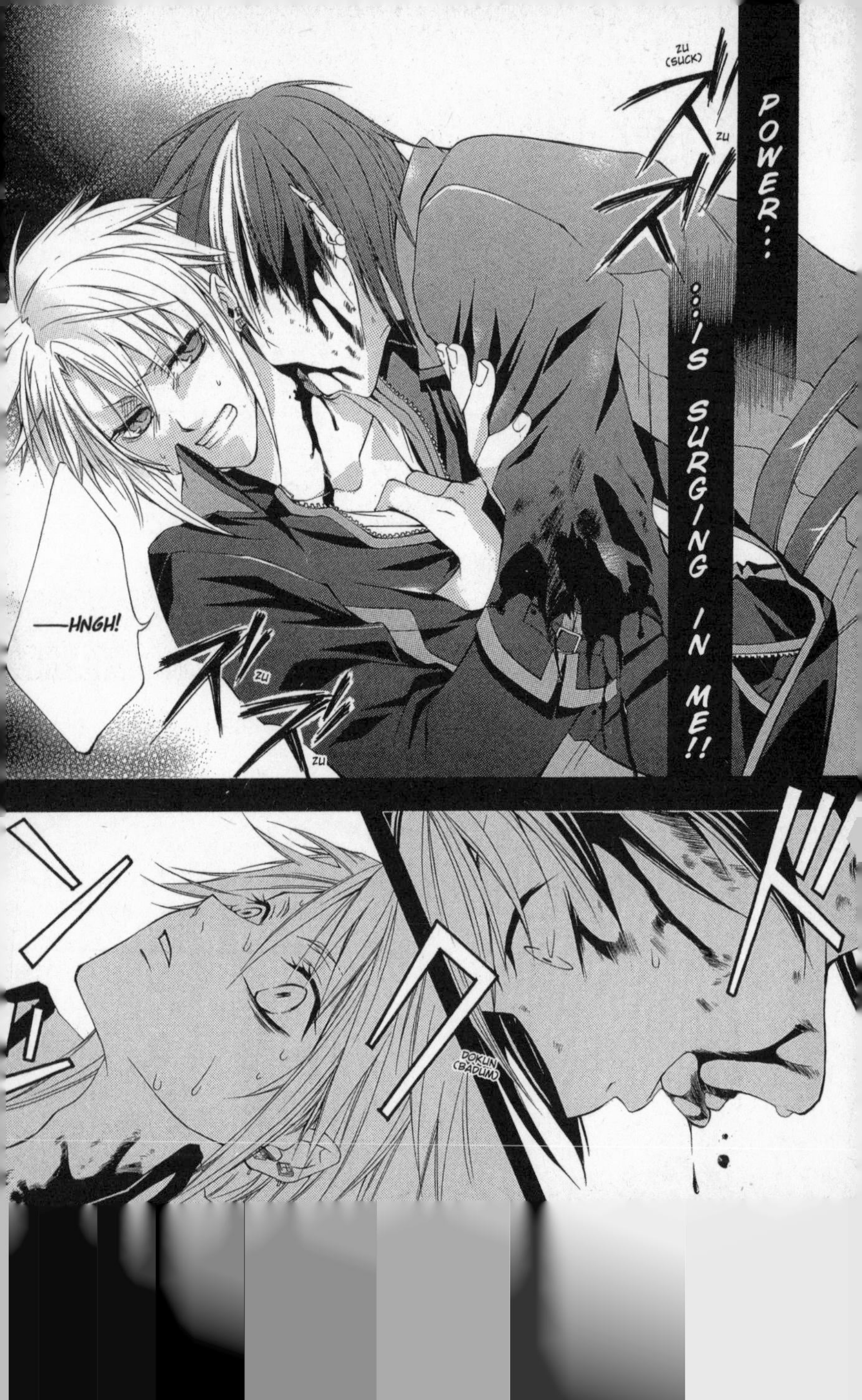
POWER...
ZU (SUCK)
ZU
...IS SURGING IN ME!!
ZU
ZU
—HNGH!
DOKUN (BADUM)

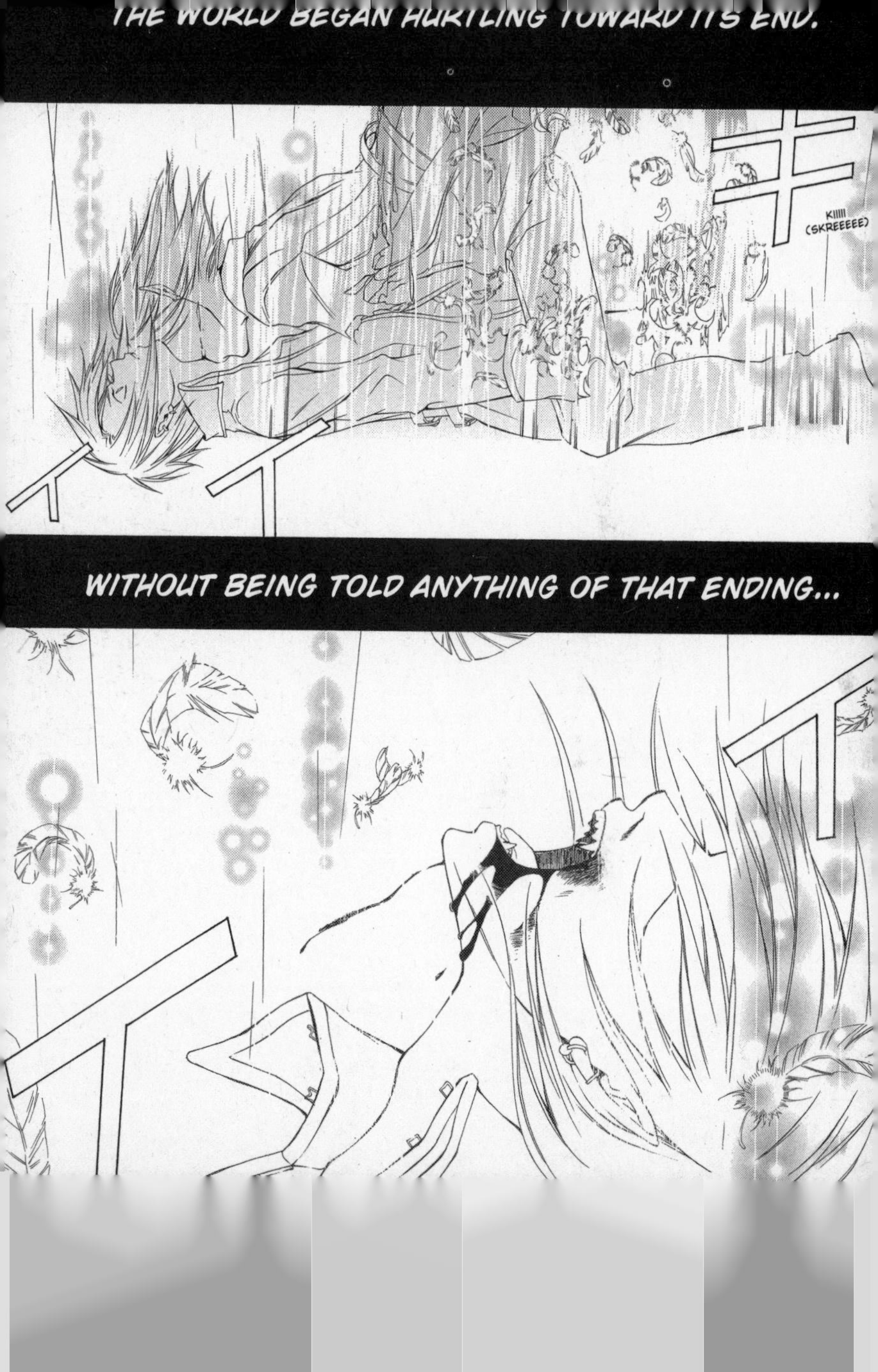
THE WORLD BEGAN HURTLING TOWARD ITS END.
KIIII (SKREEEEE)
WITHOUT BEING TOLD ANYTHING OF THAT ENDING...

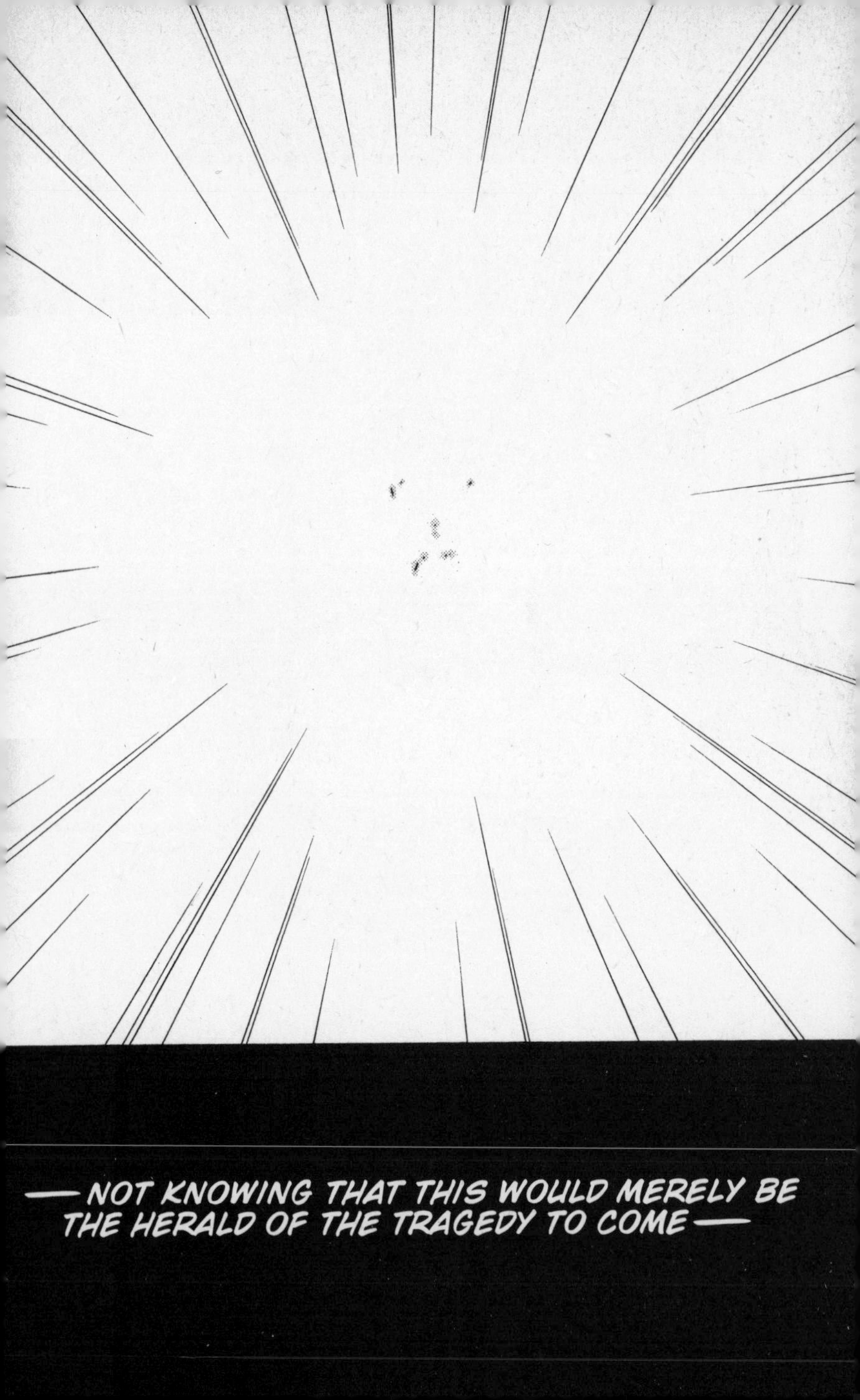
—NOT KNOWING THAT THIS WOULD MERELY BE THE HERALD OF THE TRAGEDY TO COME—

IF I WERE ASKED TO PUT A NAME TO THAT FEELING,

I CAN'T IMAGINE WHAT IT WOULD BE.

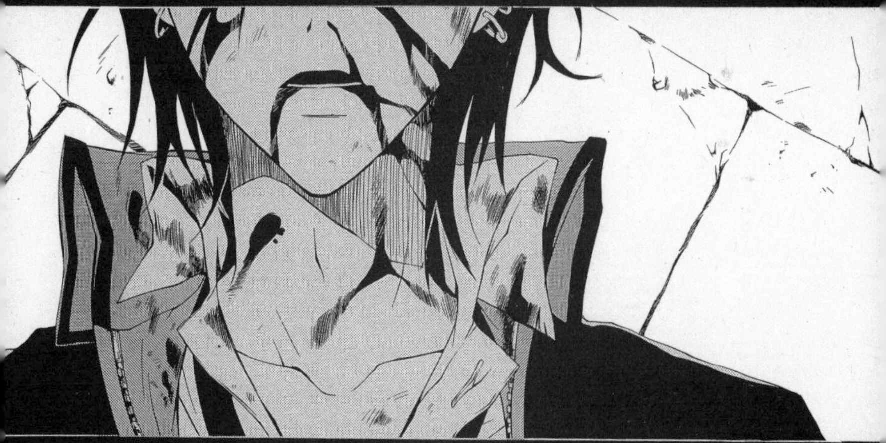

I FELT LIKE A FLEA THAT HAD LEAPED INTO HELLFIRE OF ITS OWN ACCORD...

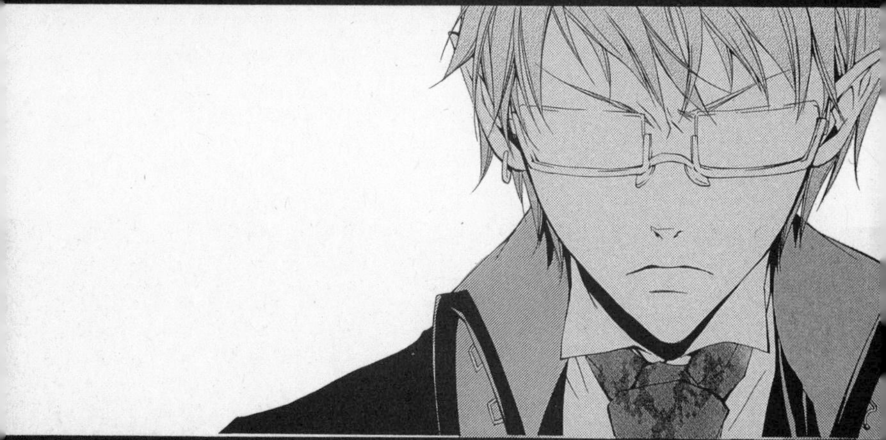

...AND EVEN AS IT LET ITSELF BURN, CONTINUED MADLY FORWARD ON ITS PATH—

BUT TELL ME...
WHO WOULD LOOK UPON THAT...

2nd Cry : Good-bye, My Friends...and My Dear Enemy

...AND LAUGH AND CALL IT "FOLLY"?

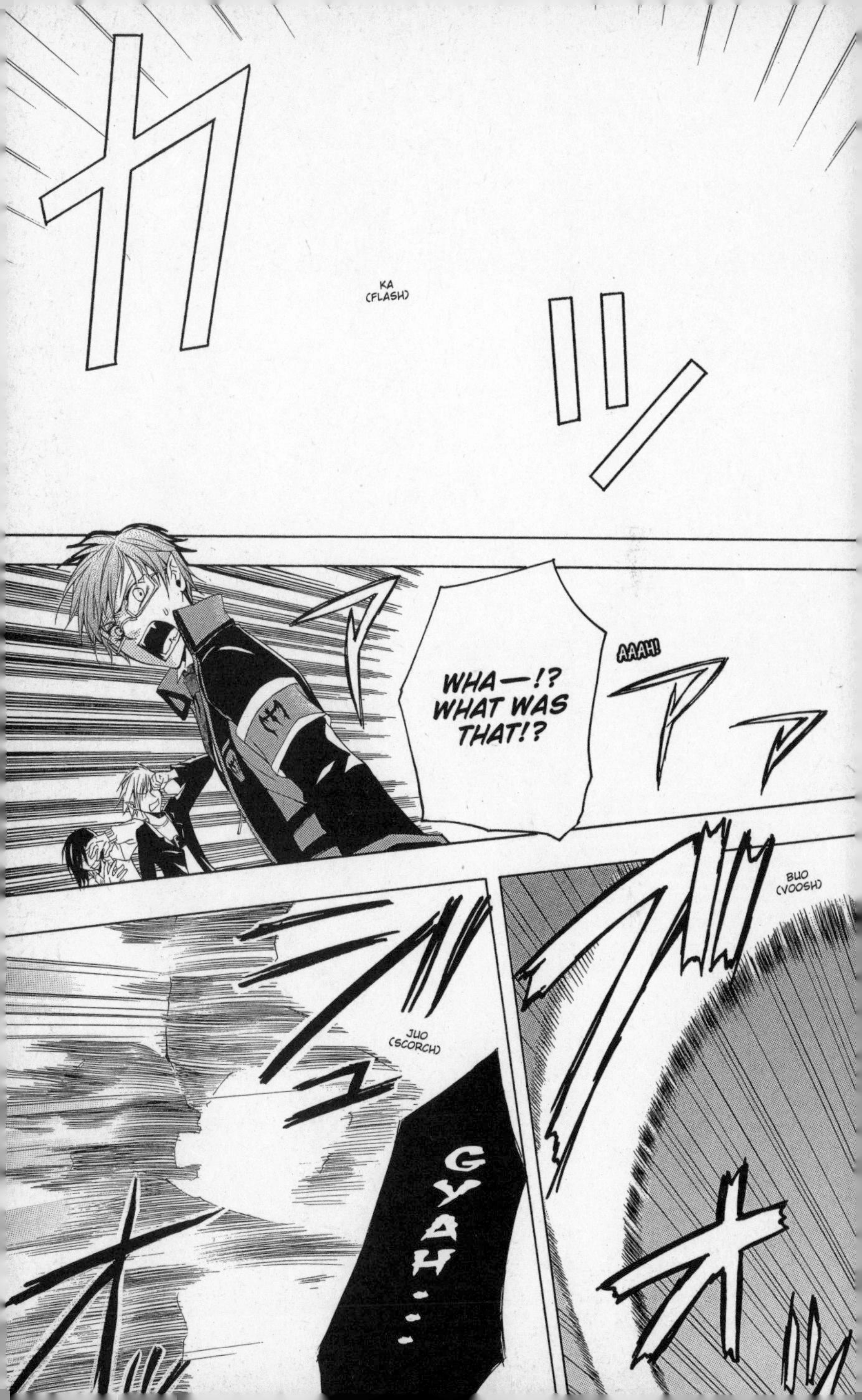
KA
(FLASH)
AAAH!
WHA—!? WHAT WAS THAT!?
BUO
(VOOSH)
JUO
(SCORCH)
GYAH...

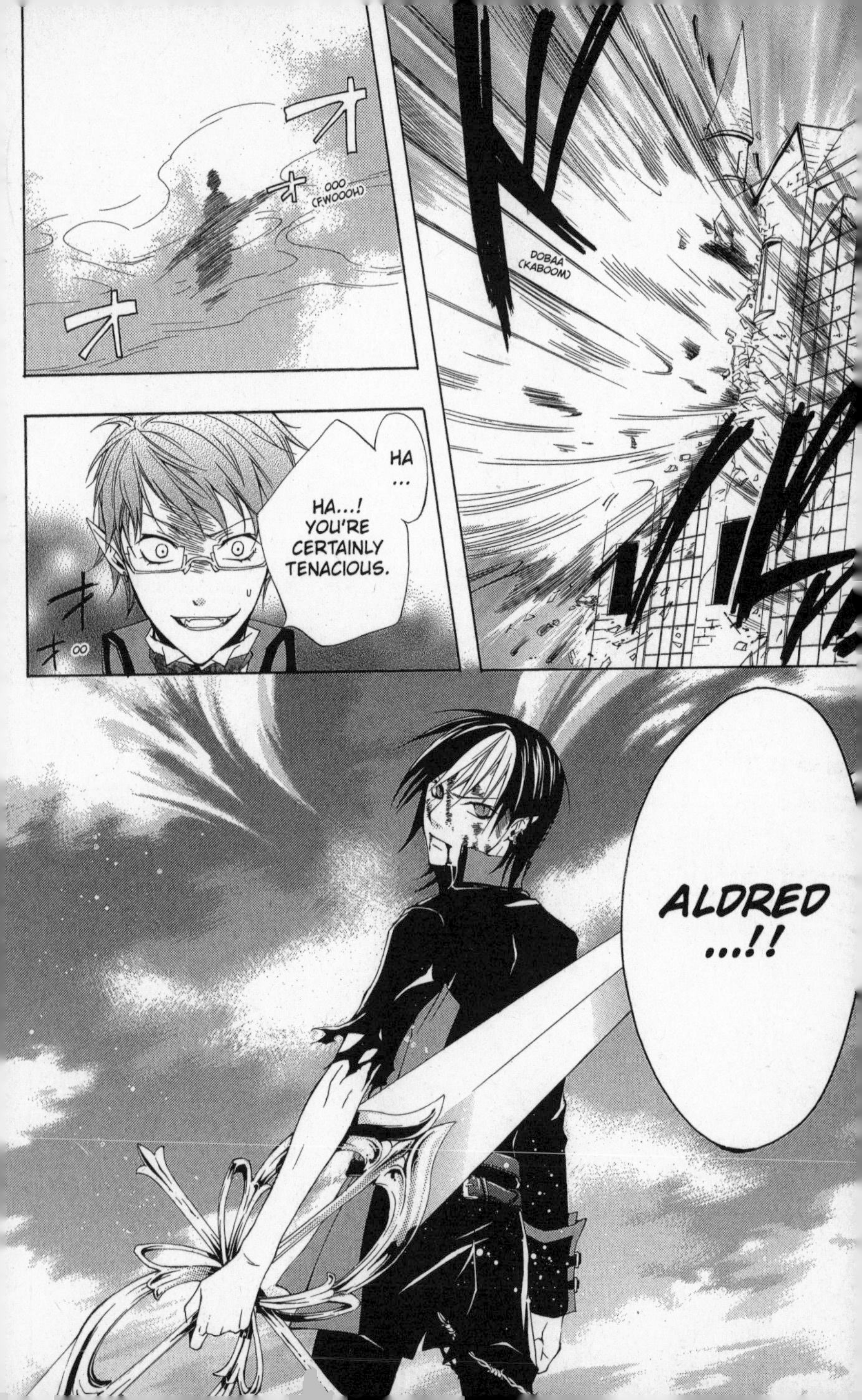
DOBAA (KABOOM)
OOO (FWOOOH)
HA ...
HA...! YOU'RE CERTAINLY TENACIOUS.
ALDRED ...!!

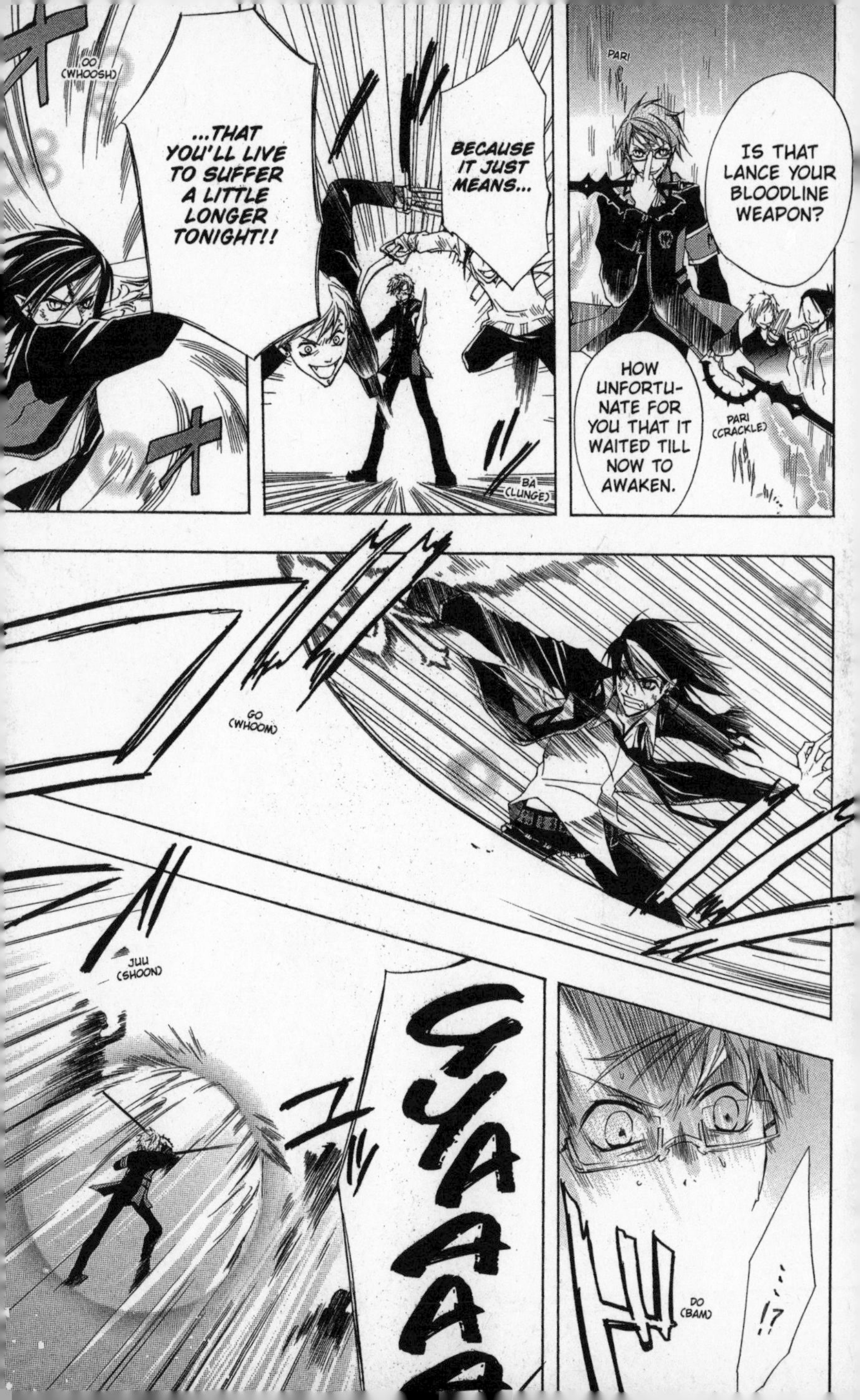
PARI
IS THAT LANCE YOUR BLOODLINE WEAPON?
HOW UNFORTUNATE FOR YOU THAT IT WAITED TILL NOW TO AWAKEN.
PARI (CRACKLE)
BECAUSE IT JUST MEANS...
BA (LUNGE)
...THAT YOU'LL LIVE TO SUFFER A LITTLE LONGER TONIGHT!!
OO (WHOOSH)
GO (WHOOM)
...!?
DO (BAM)
GYAAAA
JUU (SHOON)

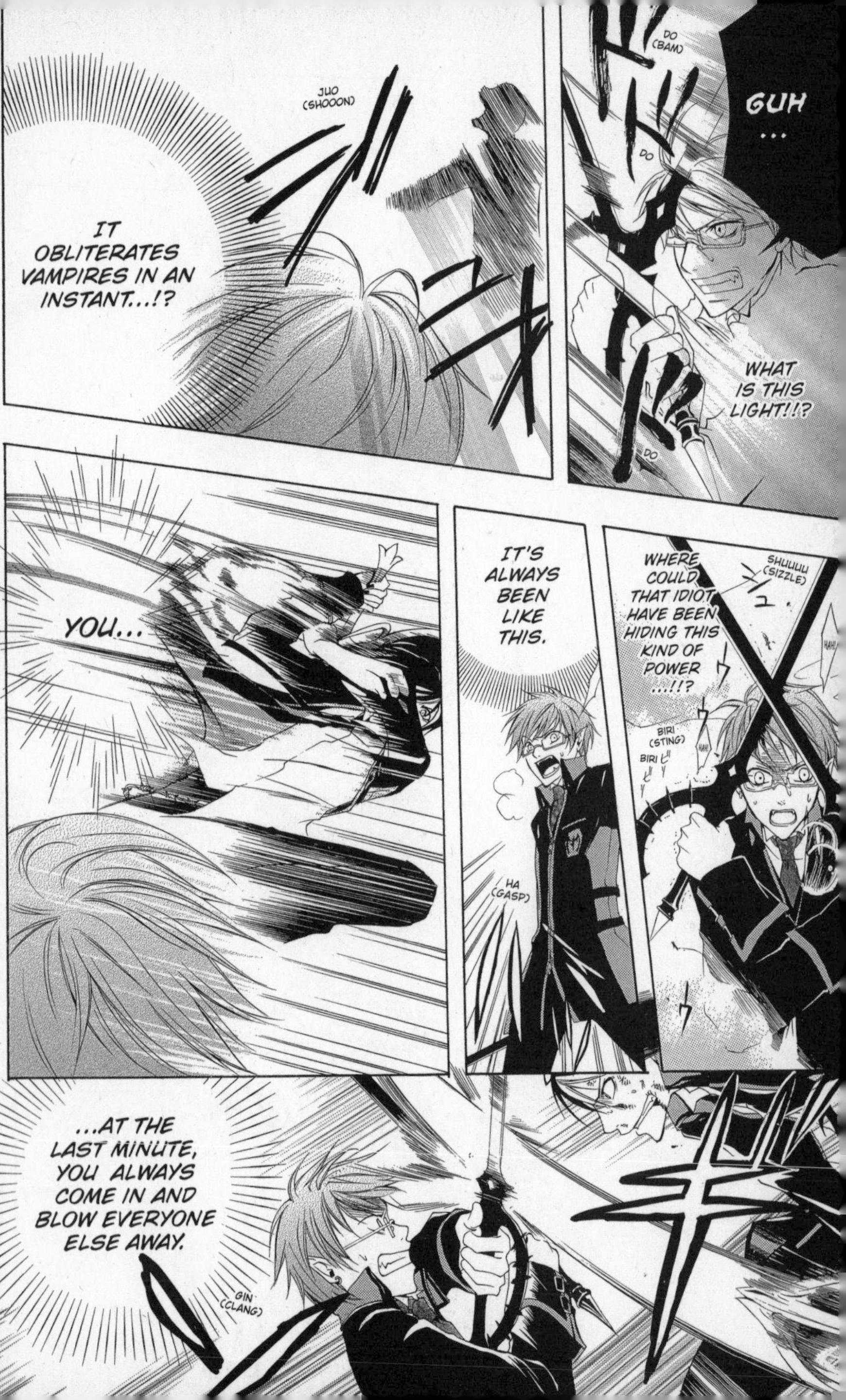
DO
(BAM)
GUH
...
DO
WHAT IS THIS LIGHT!!?
DO
JUO
(SHOOON)
IT OBLITERATES VAMPIRES IN AN INSTANT...!?
SHUUUU
(SIZZLE)
WHERE COULD THAT IDIOT HAVE BEEN HIDING THIS KIND OF POWER ...!!?
HAH!
BIRI
(STING)
BIRI
HAH!
IT'S ALWAYS BEEN LIKE THIS.
HA
(GASP)
YOU...
...AT THE LAST MINUTE, YOU ALWAYS COME IN AND BLOW EVERYONE ELSE AWAY.
GIN
(CLANG)

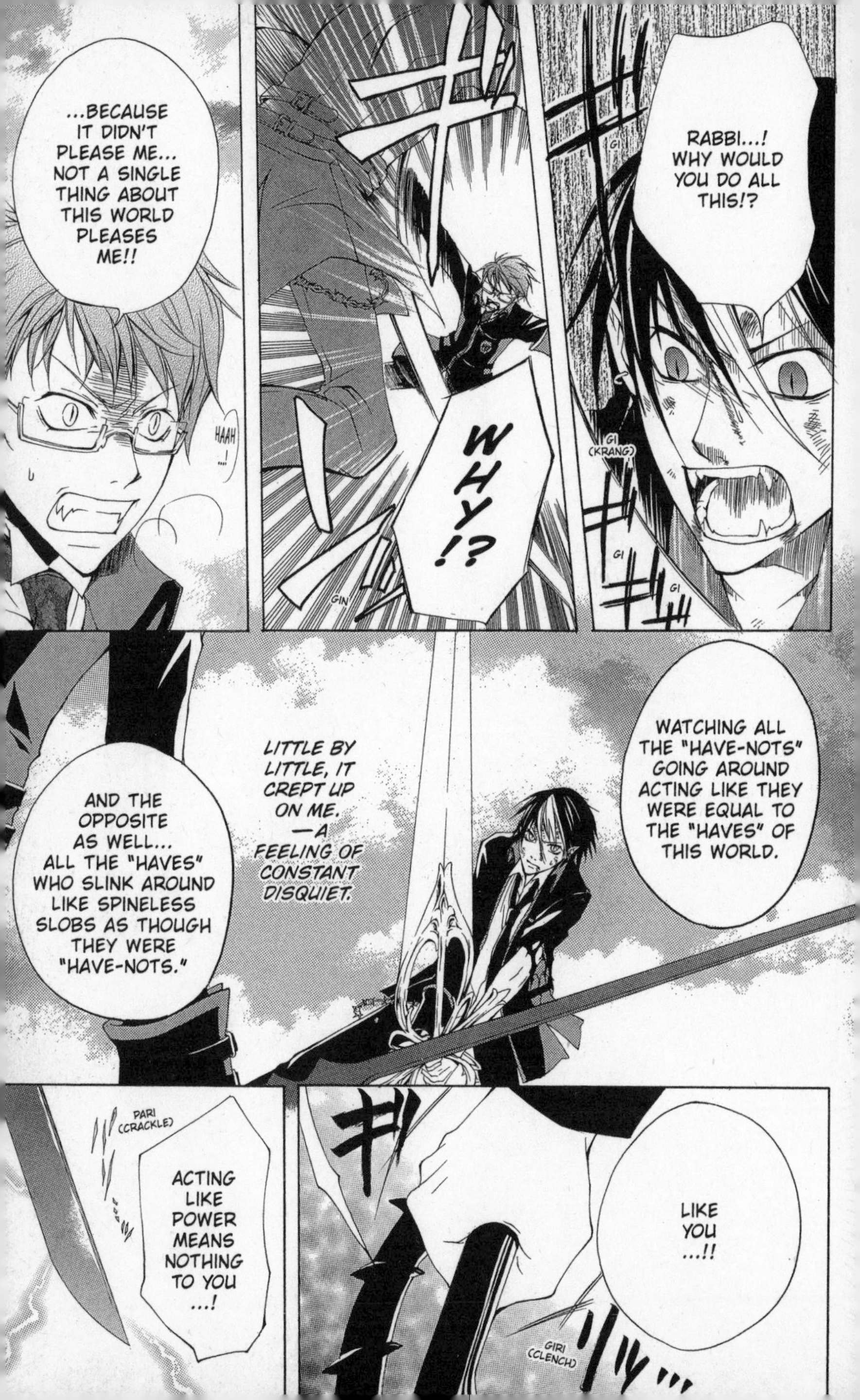
RABBI...! WHY WOULD YOU DO ALL THIS!?
GI
GI (KRANG)
GI
GI
WHY!?
GIN
...BECAUSE IT DIDN'T PLEASE ME... NOT A SINGLE THING ABOUT THIS WORLD PLEASES ME!!
HAAH ...!
WATCHING ALL THE "HAVE-NOTS" GOING AROUND ACTING LIKE THEY WERE EQUAL TO THE "HAVES" OF THIS WORLD.
LITTLE BY LITTLE, IT CREPT UP ON ME. —A FEELING OF CONSTANT DISQUIET.
AND THE OPPOSITE AS WELL... ALL THE "HAVES" WHO SLINK AROUND LIKE SPINELESS SLOBS AS THOUGH THEY WERE "HAVE-NOTS."
LIKE YOU ...!!
GIRI (CLENCH)
PARI (CRACKLE)
ACTING LIKE POWER MEANS NOTHING TO YOU ...!

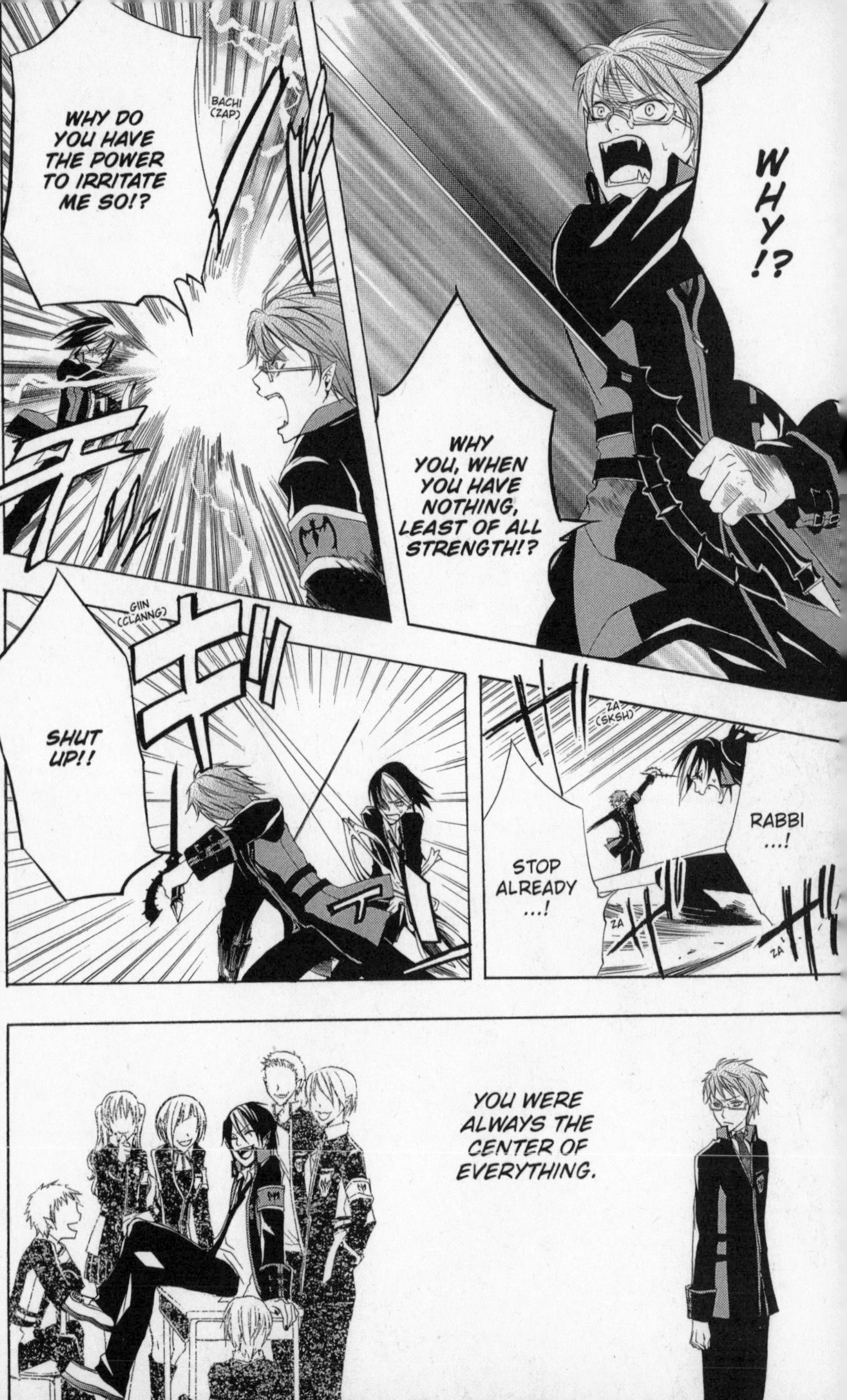
WHY!?
WHY YOU, WHEN YOU HAVE NOTHING, LEAST OF ALL STRENGTH!?
BACHI (ZAP)
WHY DO YOU HAVE THE POWER TO IRRITATE ME SO!?
ZA (SKSH)
RABBI ...!
STOP ALREADY ...!
ZA
ZA
GIIN (CLANNG)
SHUT UP!!
YOU WERE ALWAYS THE CENTER OF EVERYTHING.

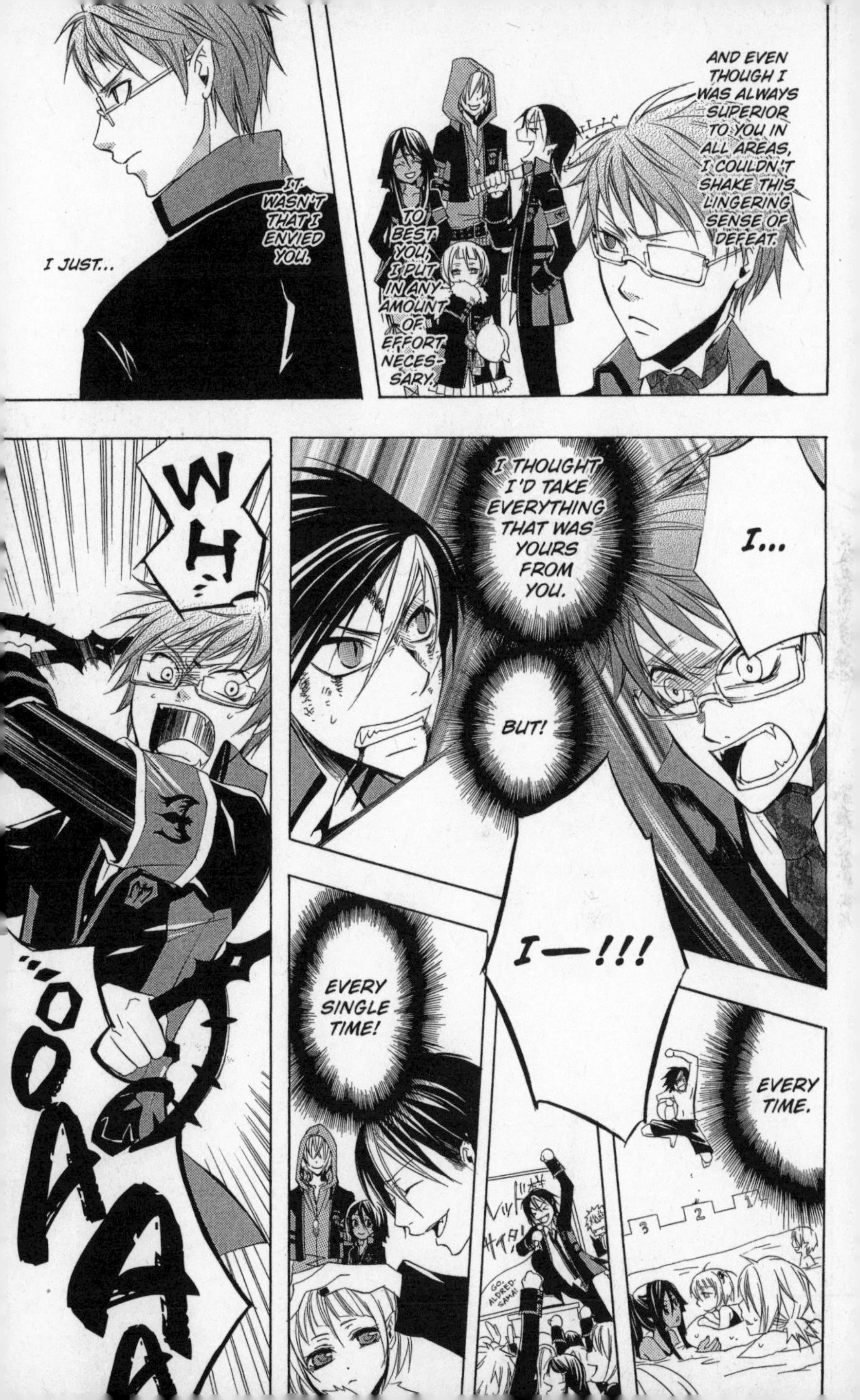
AND EVEN THOUGH I WAS ALWAYS SUPERIOR TO YOU IN ALL AREAS, I COULDN'T SHAKE THIS LINGERING SENSE OF DEFEAT.
TO BEST YOU, I PUT IN ANY AMOUNT OF EFFORT NECESSARY.
IT WASN'T THAT I ENVIED YOU.
I JUST...
I...
I THOUGHT I'D TAKE EVERYTHING THAT WAS YOURS FROM YOU.
BUT!
I—!!!
EVERY TIME.
GO, ALDRED-SAMA!
EVERY SINGLE TIME!
WH
OOAAAA

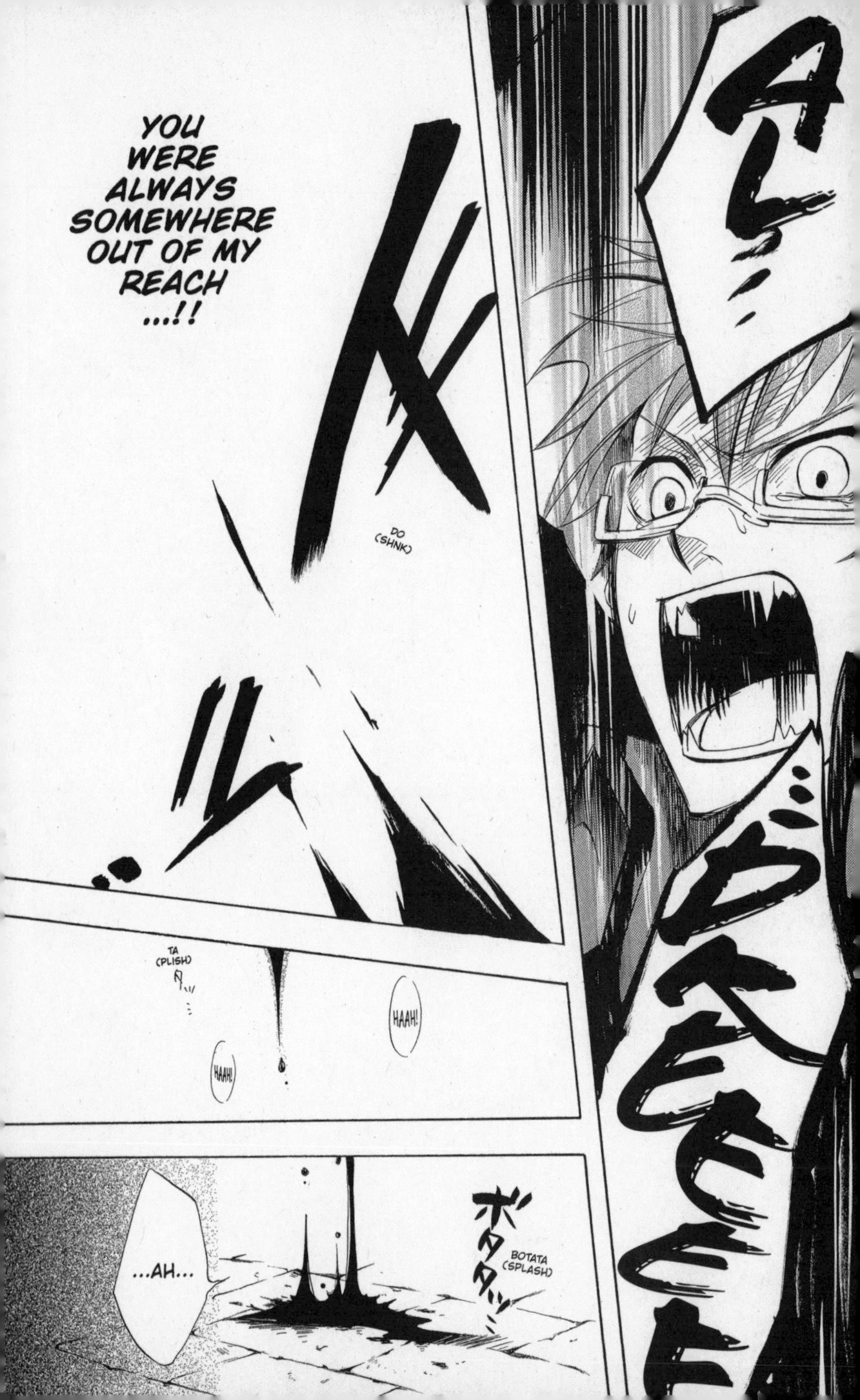
YOU WERE ALWAYS SOMEWHERE OUT OF MY REACH ...!!
DO (SHNK)
HAAH!
HAAH!
TA (PLISH)
BOTATA (SPLASH)
...AH...

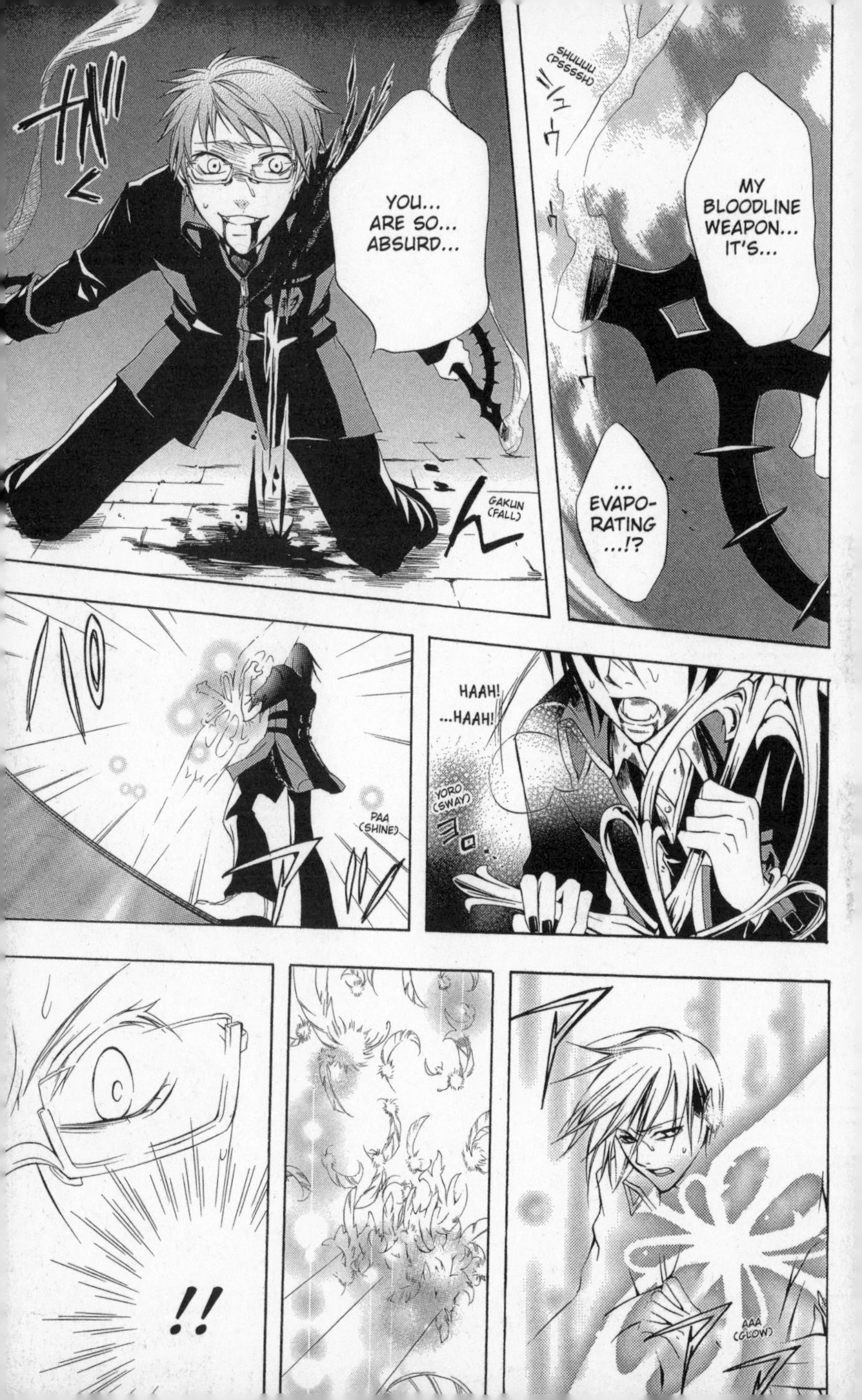
SHUUUUN (PSSSSH)
MY BLOODLINE WEAPON... IT'S...
...EVAPO-RATING ...!?
YOU... ARE SO... ABSURD...
GAKUN (FALL)
HAAH! ...HAAH!
YORO (SWAY)
PAA (SHINE)
AAA (GLOW)
!!

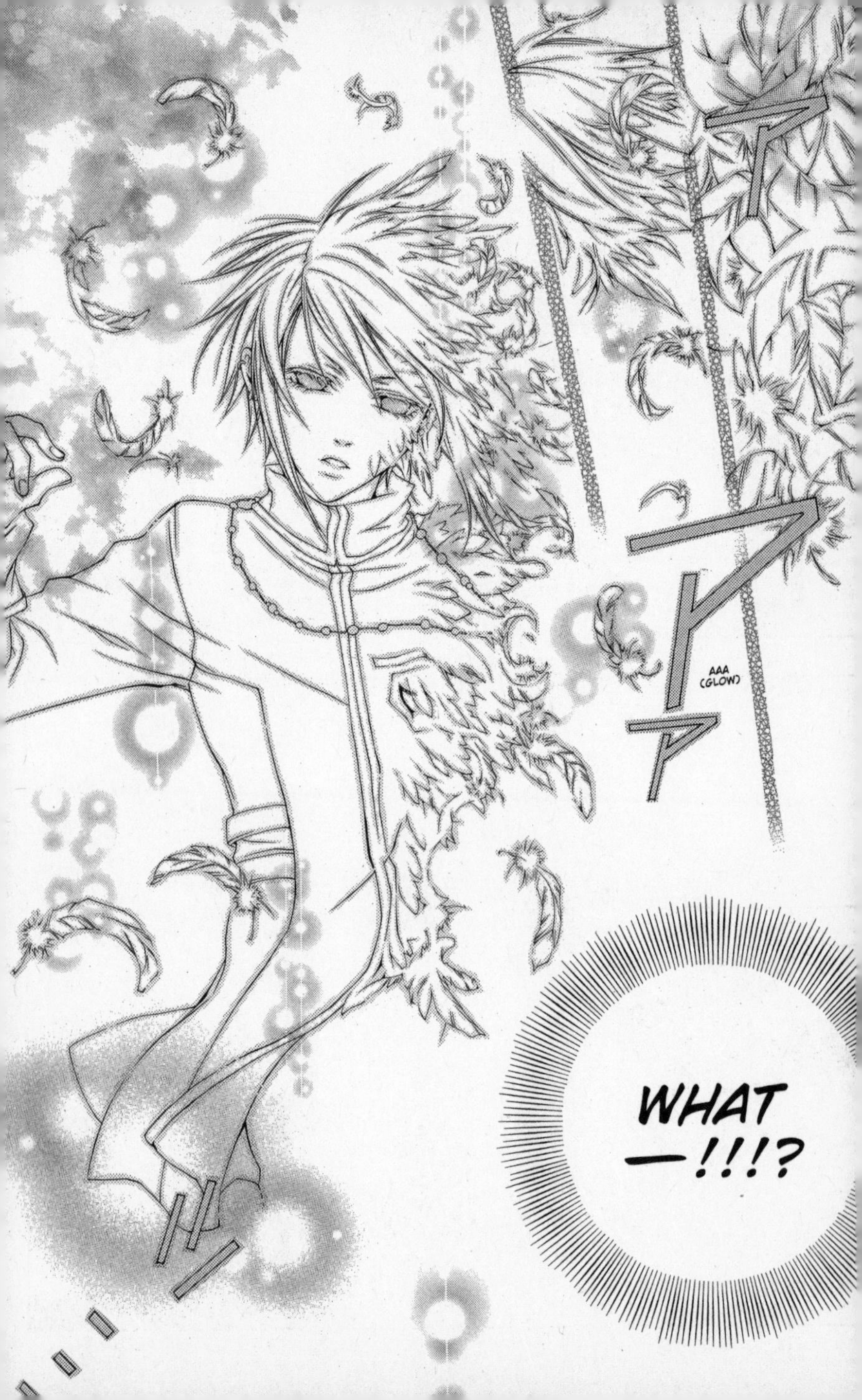
AAA (GLOW)
WHAT—!!!?

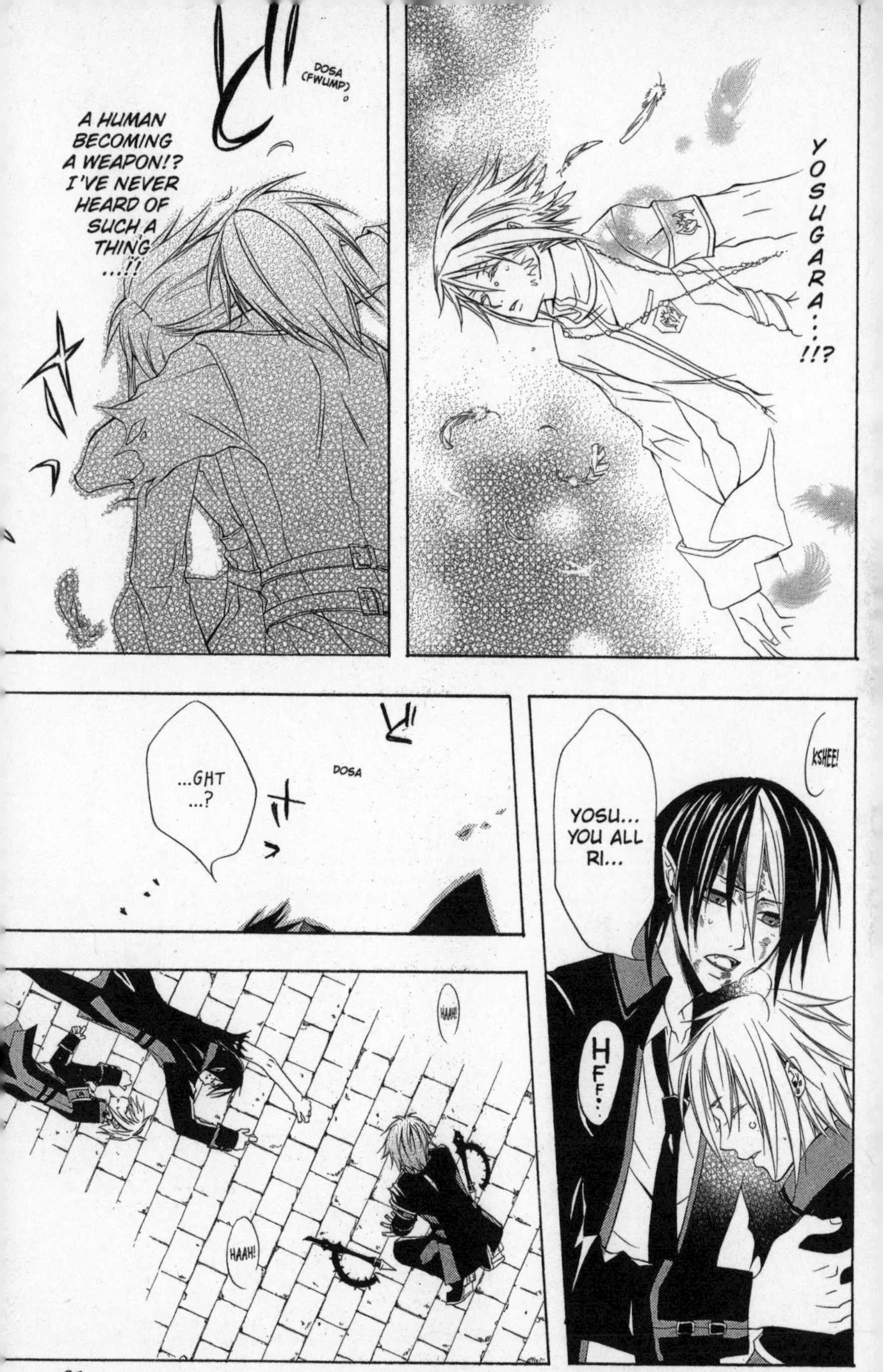
YOSUGARA...!!?
DOSA (FWUMP)
A HUMAN BECOMING A WEAPON!? I'VE NEVER HEARD OF SUCH A THING...!!
KSHEE!
YOSU... YOU ALL RI...
HFF...
DOSA
...GHT ...?
HAAH!
HAAH!

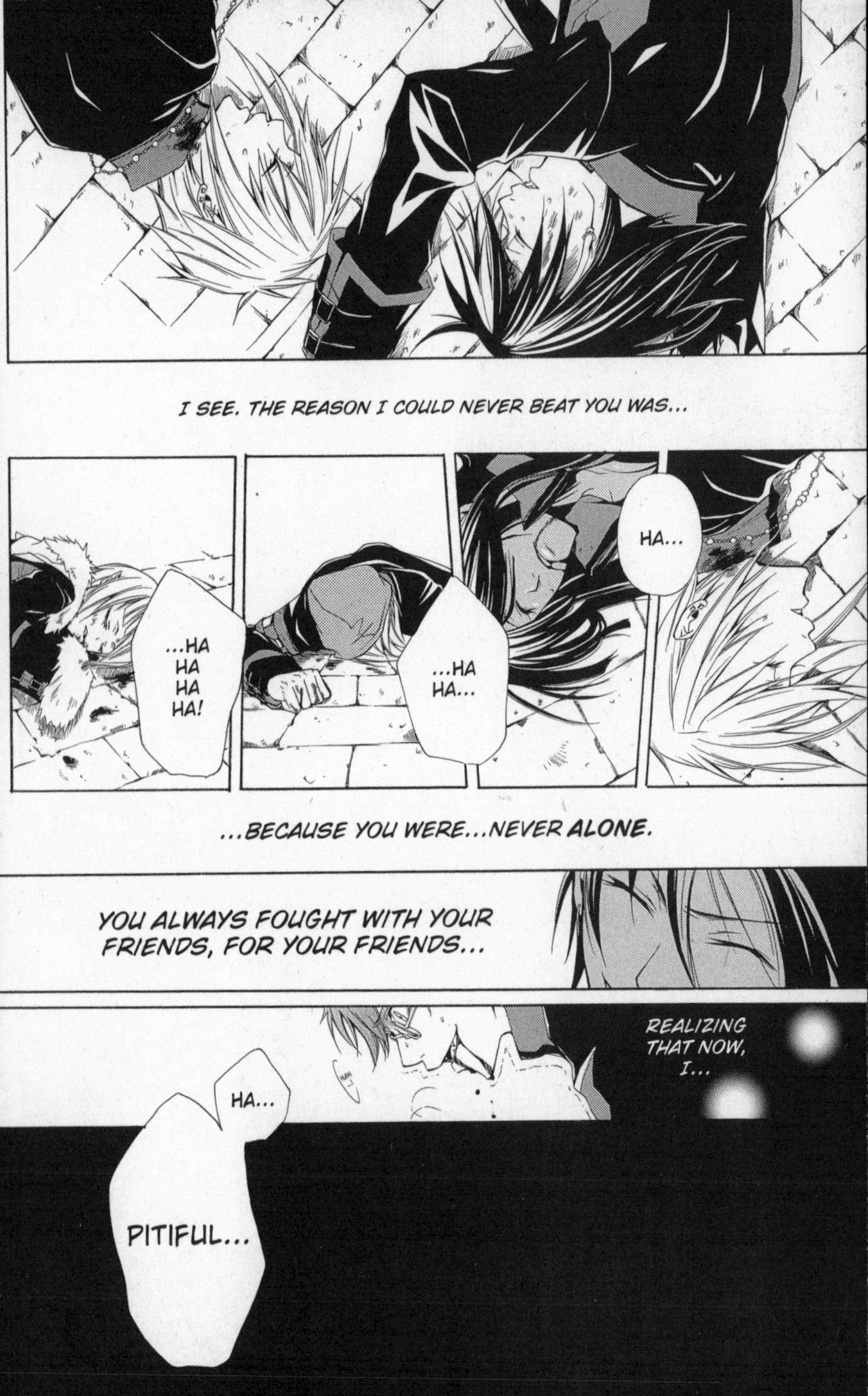
I SEE. THE REASON I COULD NEVER BEAT YOU WAS...
HA...
...HA HA...
...HA HA HA HA!
...BECAUSE YOU WERE...NEVER ALONE.
YOU ALWAYS FOUGHT WITH YOUR FRIENDS, FOR YOUR FRIENDS...
REALIZING THAT NOW, I...
HA...
PITIFUL...

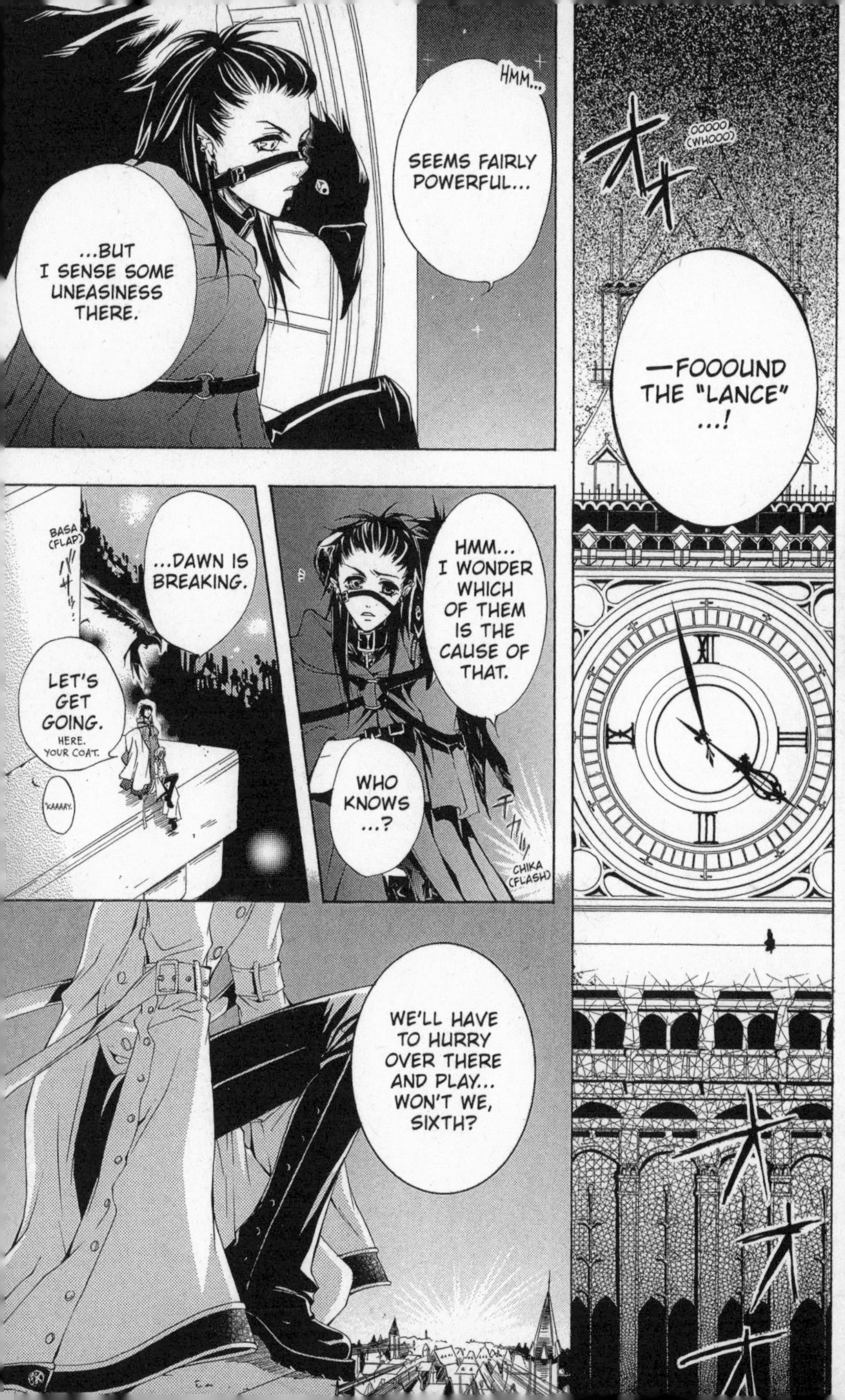
OOOOO (WHOOO)
—FOOOUND THE "LANCE" ...!
HMM...
SEEMS FAIRLY POWERFUL...
...BUT I SENSE SOME UNEASINESS THERE.
HMM... I WONDER WHICH OF THEM IS THE CAUSE OF THAT.
WHO KNOWS ...?
CHIKA (FLASH)
...DAWN IS BREAKING.
BASA (FLAP)
LET'S GET GOING.
HERE. YOUR COAT.
*KAAARY.
WE'LL HAVE TO HURRY OVER THERE AND PLAY... WON'T WE, SIXTH?

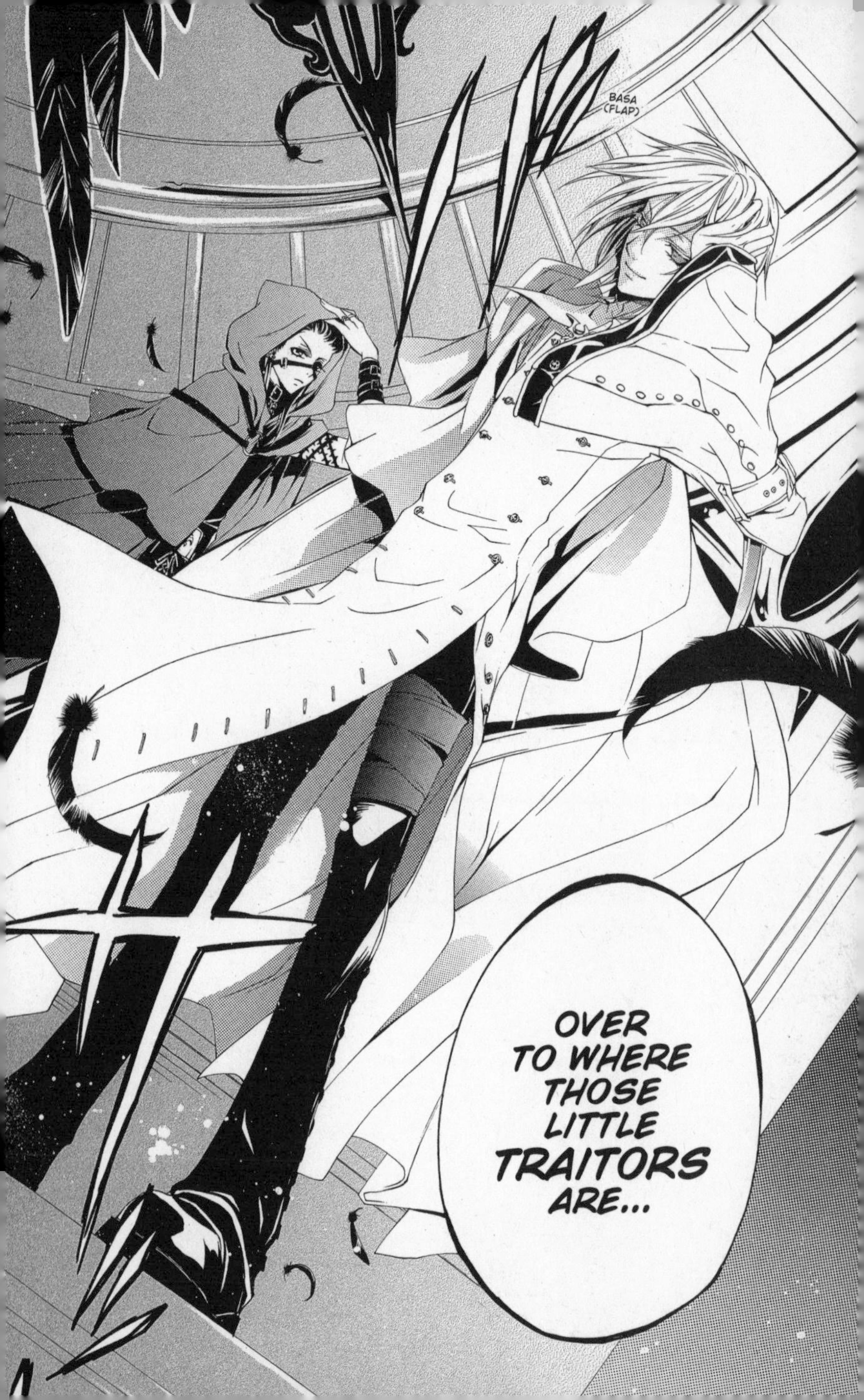
BASA
(FLAP)
OVER TO WHERE THOSE LITTLE TRAITORS ARE...

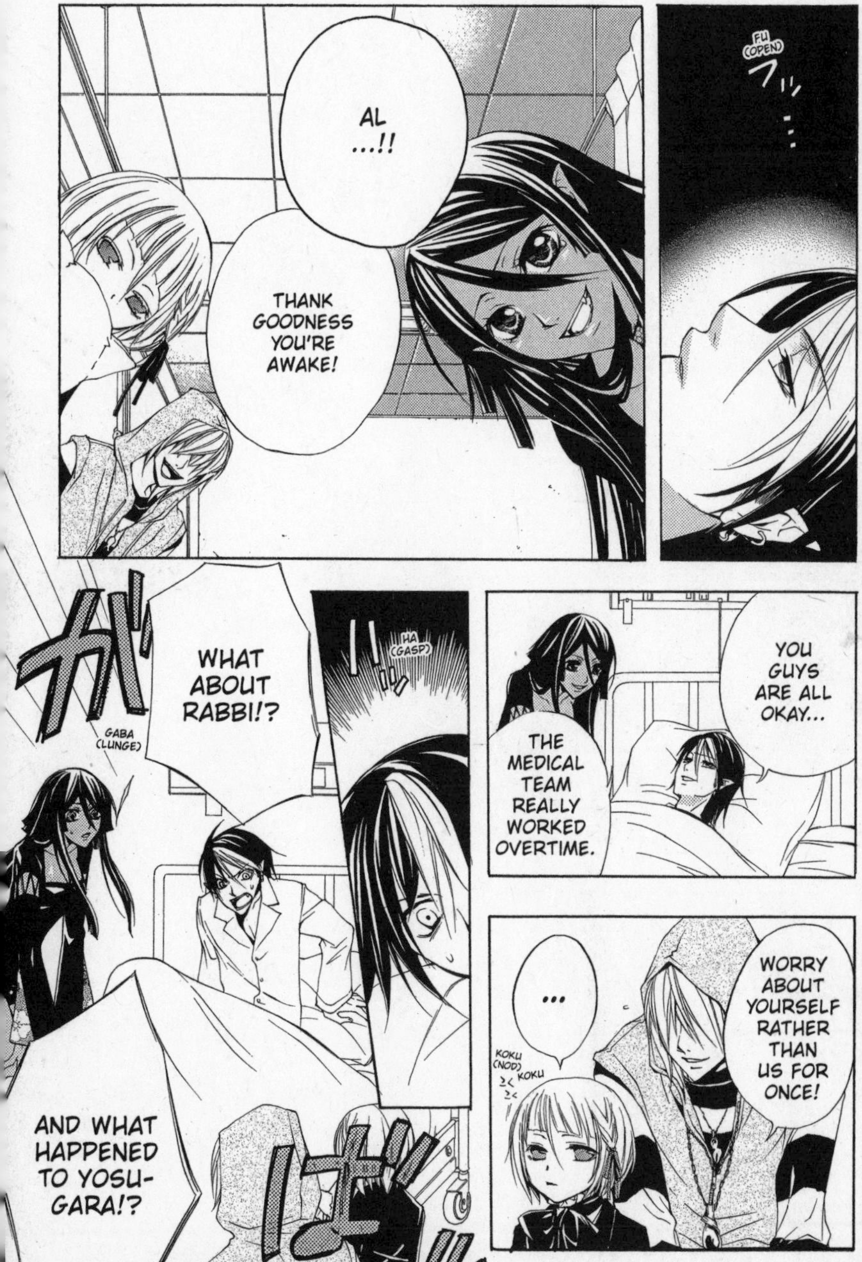
FU (OPEN)
AL ...!!
THANK GOODNESS YOU'RE AWAKE!
YOU GUYS ARE ALL OKAY...
THE MEDICAL TEAM REALLY WORKED OVERTIME.
WORRY ABOUT YOURSELF RATHER THAN US FOR ONCE!
...
KOKU (NOD) KOKU
HA (GASP)
WHAT ABOUT RABBI!?
GABA (LUNGE)
AND WHAT HAPPENED TO YOSU-GARA!?

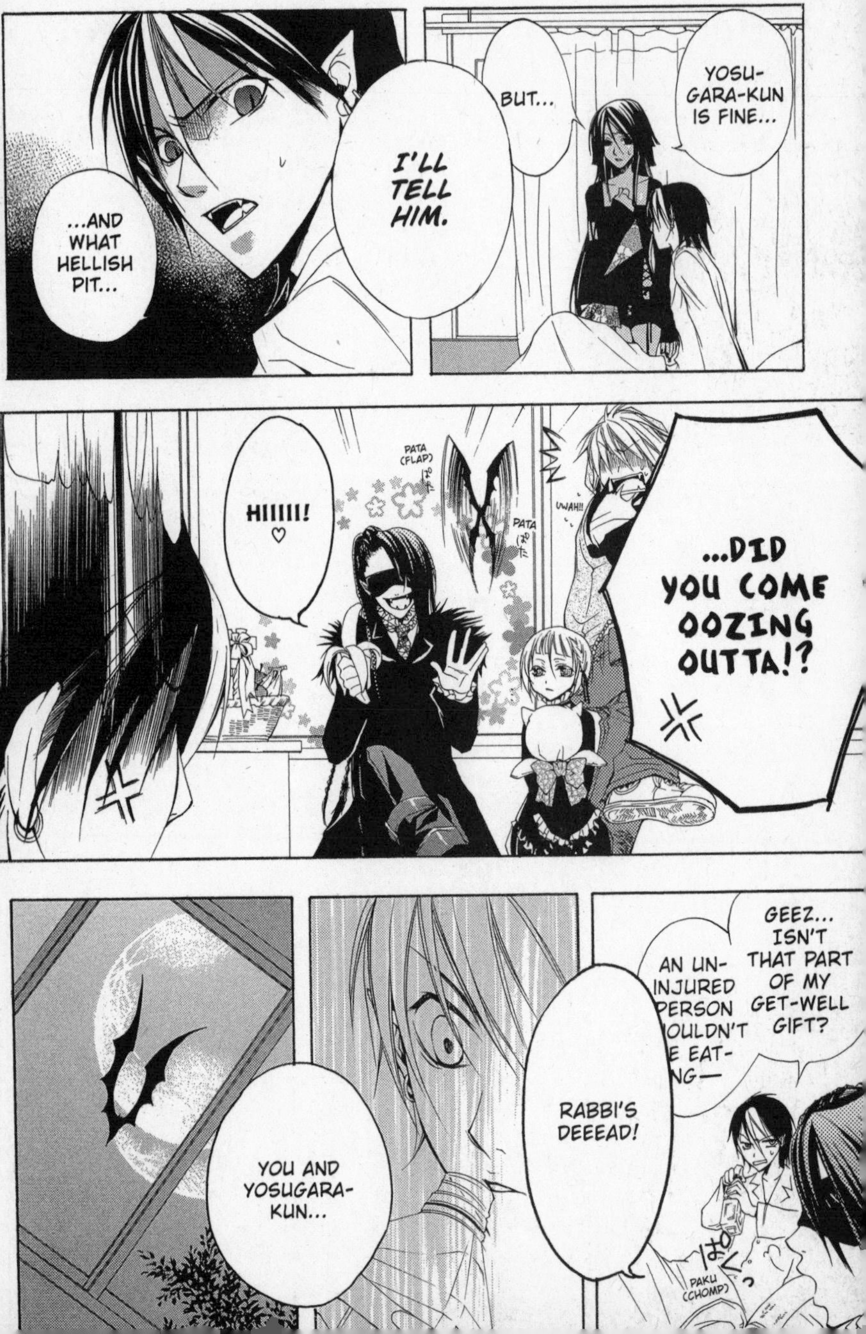
YOSU-GARA-KUN IS FINE...
BUT...
I'LL TELL HIM.
...AND WHAT HELLISH PIT...
...DID YOU COME OOZING OUTTA!?
UWAH!!
PATA (FLAP) ぱた
PATA ぱた
HIIIII! ♡
GEEZ... ISN'T THAT PART OF MY GET-WELL GIFT?
AN UN-INJURED PERSON OULDN'T E EAT-NG—
PAKU (CHOMP) ぱくっ
RABBI'S DEEEAD!
YOU AND YOSUGARA-KUN...

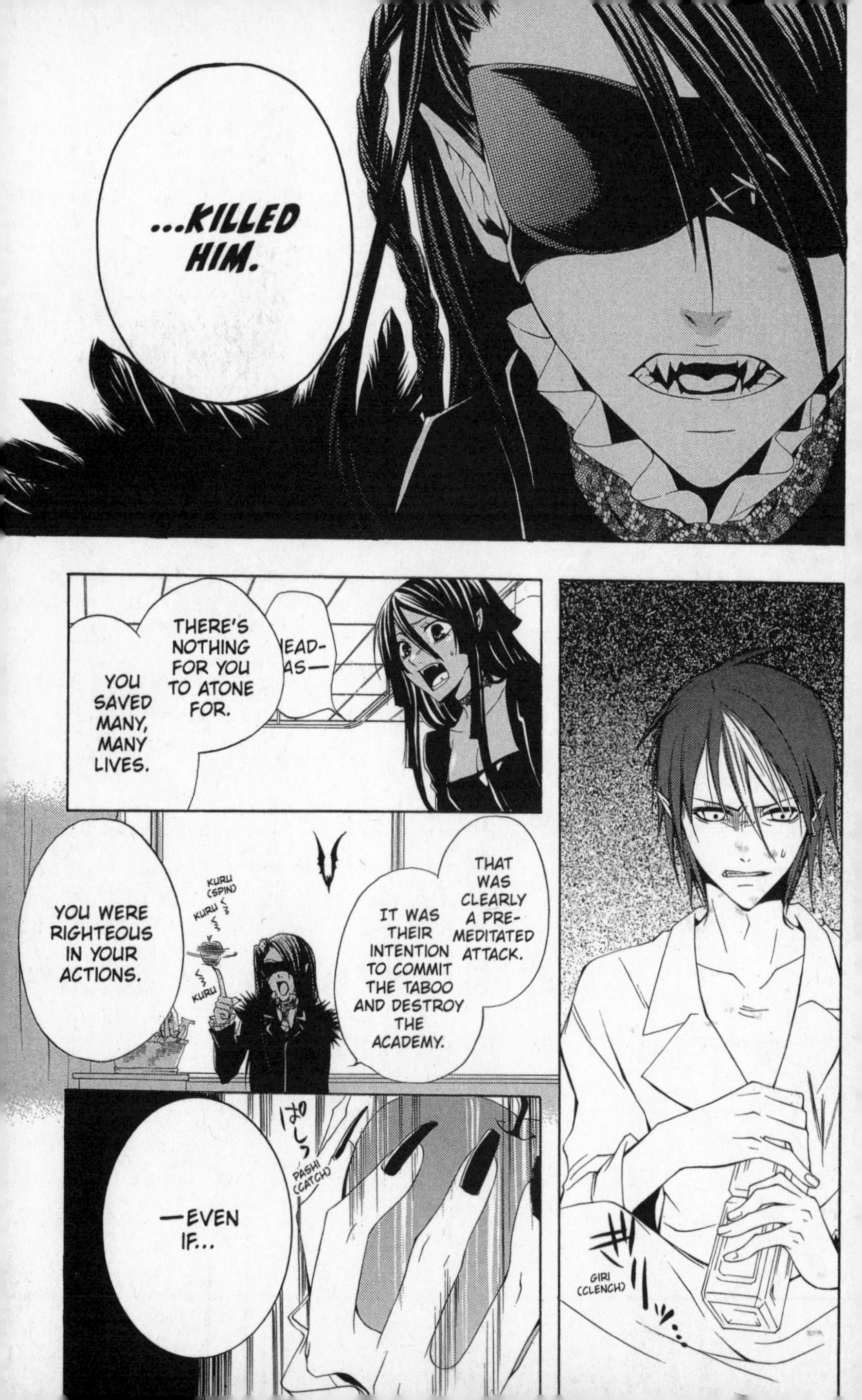
...KILLED HIM.
GIRI (CLENCH)
HEAD- AS—
THERE'S NOTHING FOR YOU TO ATONE FOR.
YOU SAVED MANY, MANY LIVES.
THAT WAS CLEARLY A PRE-MEDITATED ATTACK.
IT WAS THEIR INTENTION TO COMMIT THE TABOO AND DESTROY THE ACADEMY.
KURU (SPIN)
KURU
KURU
YOU WERE RIGHTEOUS IN YOUR ACTIONS.
PASHI (CATCH)
—EVEN IF...

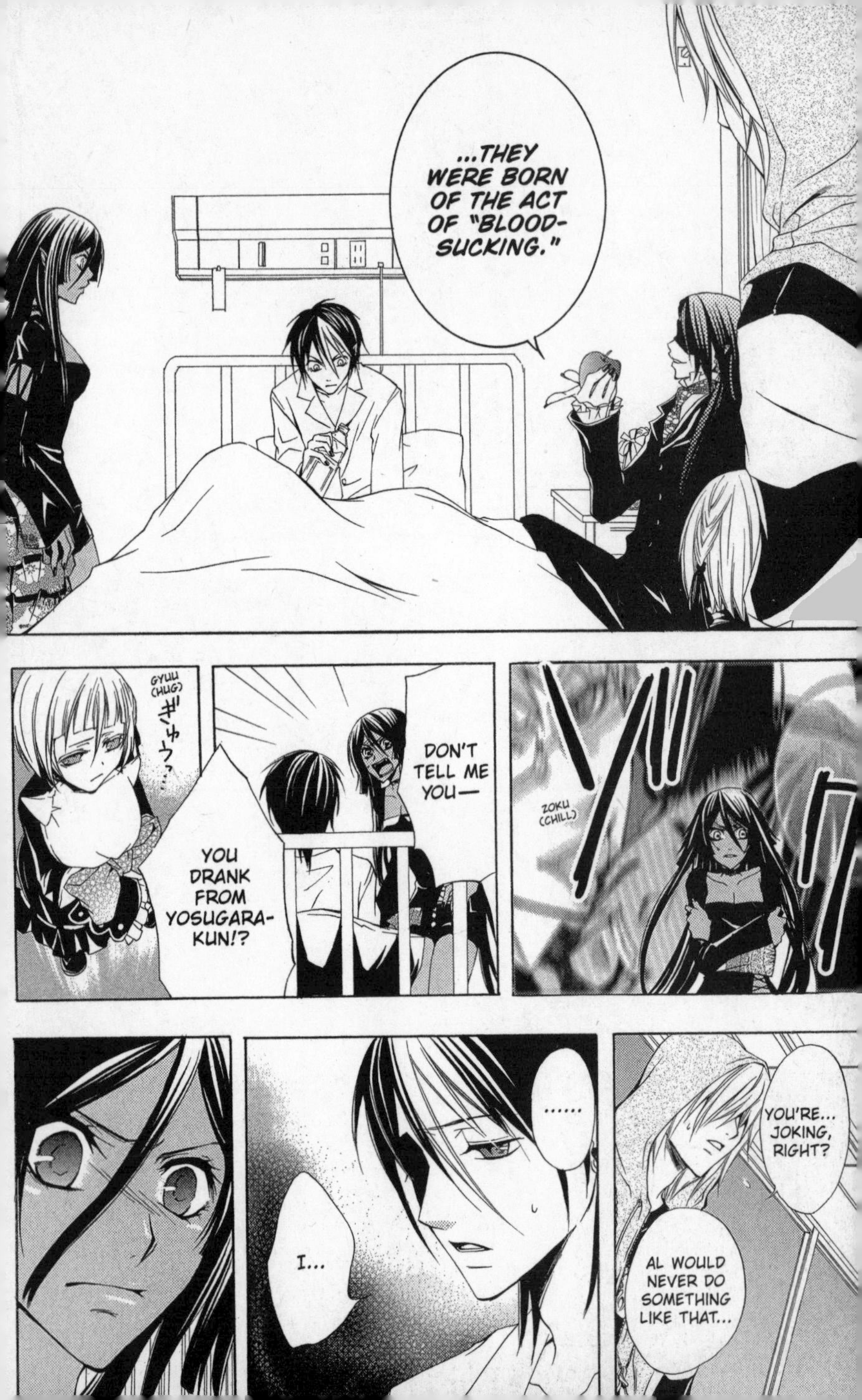
...THEY WERE BORN OF THE ACT OF "BLOOD-SUCKING."
ZOKU (CHILL)
DON'T TELL ME YOU—
YOU DRANK FROM YOSUGARA-KUN!?
GYUU (HUG)
YOU'RE... JOKING, RIGHT?
AL WOULD NEVER DO SOMETHING LIKE THAT...
......
I...

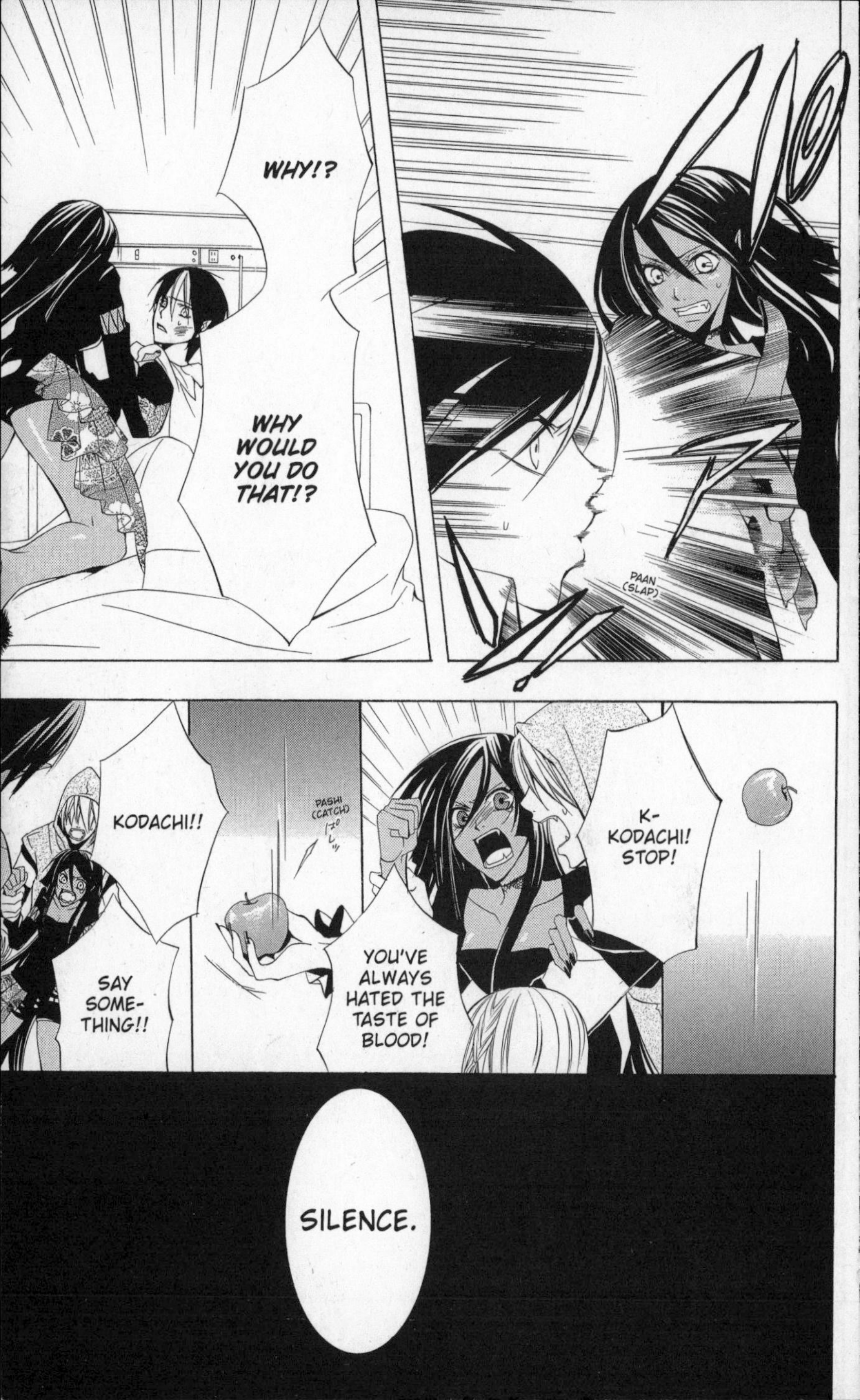
PAAN (SLAP)
WHY!?
WHY WOULD YOU DO THAT!?
K-KODACHI! STOP!
YOU'VE ALWAYS HATED THE TASTE OF BLOOD!
PASHI (CATCH)
KODACHI!!
SAY SOMETHING!!
SILENCE.

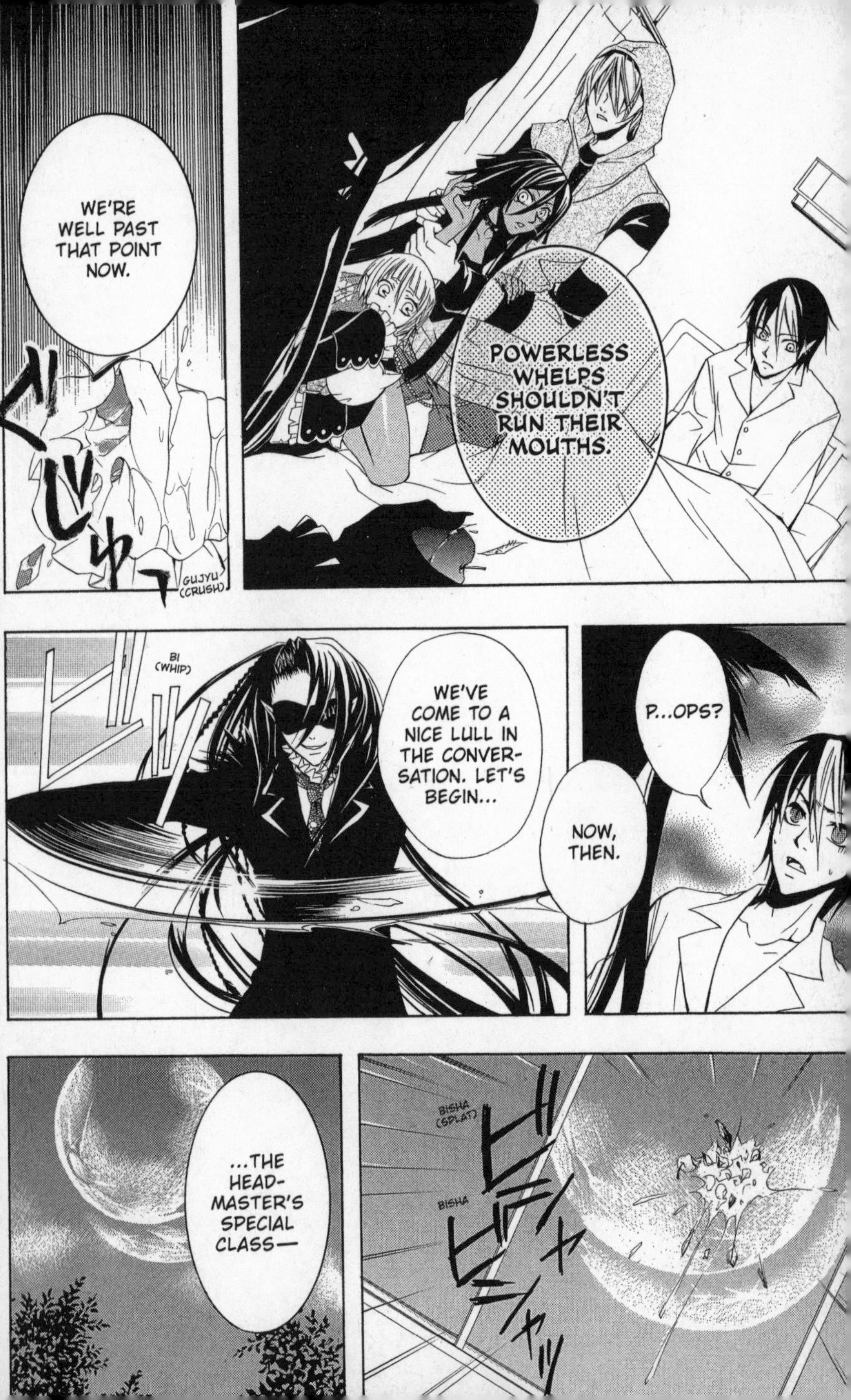
POWERLESS WHELPS SHOULDN'T RUN THEIR MOUTHS.
WE'RE WELL PAST THAT POINT NOW.
GUJYU (CRUSH)
P...OPS?
NOW, THEN.
BI (WHIP)
WE'VE COME TO A NICE LULL IN THE CONVER-SATION. LET'S BEGIN...
BISHA (SPLAT)
BISHA
...THE HEAD-MASTER'S SPECIAL CLASS—

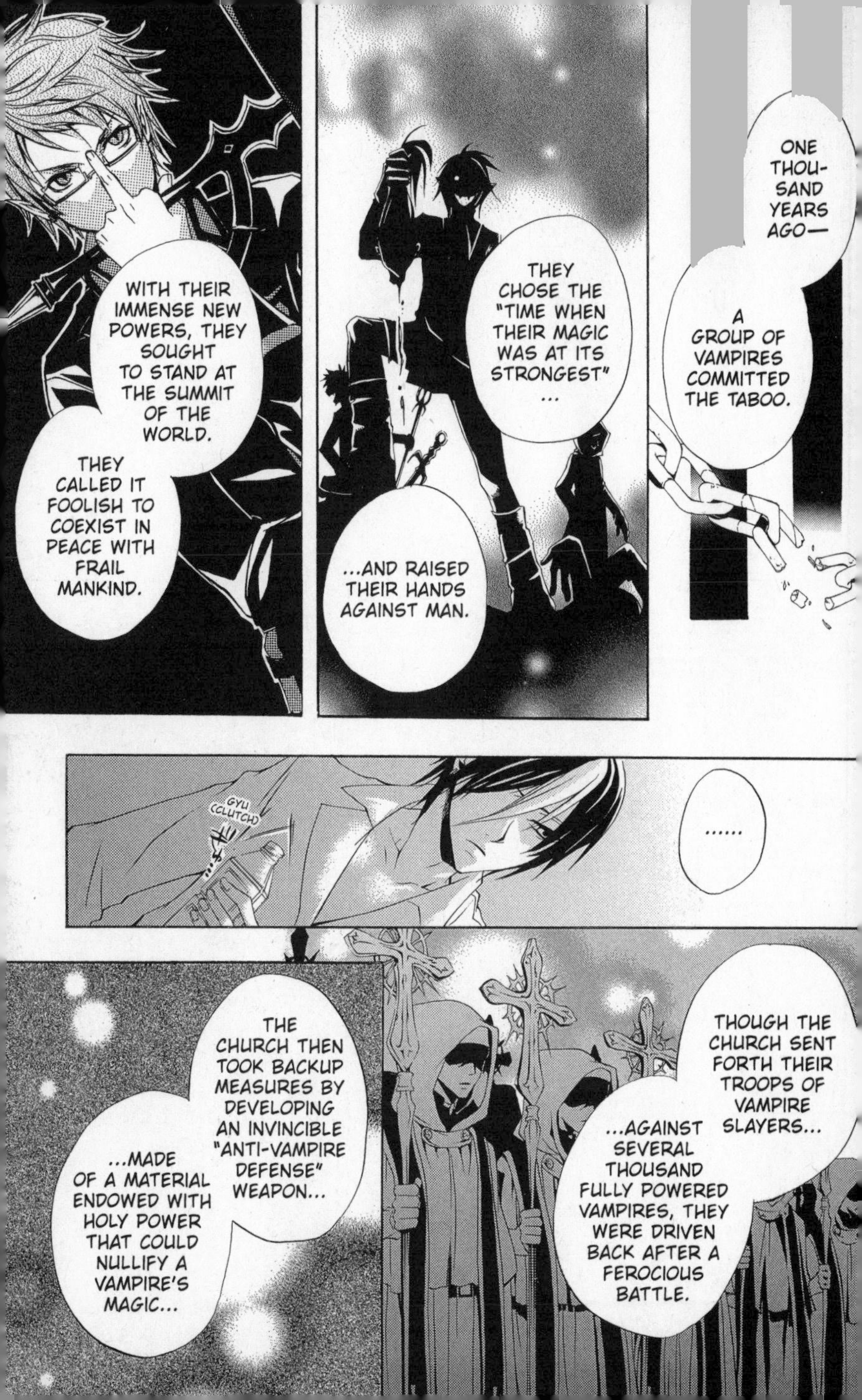
ONE THOUSAND YEARS AGO—
A GROUP OF VAMPIRES COMMITTED THE TABOO.
THEY CHOSE THE "TIME WHEN THEIR MAGIC WAS AT ITS STRONGEST" ...
...AND RAISED THEIR HANDS AGAINST MAN.
WITH THEIR IMMENSE NEW POWERS, THEY SOUGHT TO STAND AT THE SUMMIT OF THE WORLD.
THEY CALLED IT FOOLISH TO COEXIST IN PEACE WITH FRAIL MANKIND.
......
GYU (CLUTCH)
THOUGH THE CHURCH SENT FORTH THEIR TROOPS OF VAMPIRE SLAYERS...
...AGAINST SEVERAL THOUSAND FULLY POWERED VAMPIRES, THEY WERE DRIVEN BACK AFTER A FEROCIOUS BATTLE.
THE CHURCH THEN TOOK BACKUP MEASURES BY DEVELOPING AN INVINCIBLE "ANTI-VAMPIRE DEFENSE" WEAPON...
...MADE OF A MATERIAL ENDOWED WITH HOLY POWER THAT COULD NULLIFY A VAMPIRE'S MAGIC...

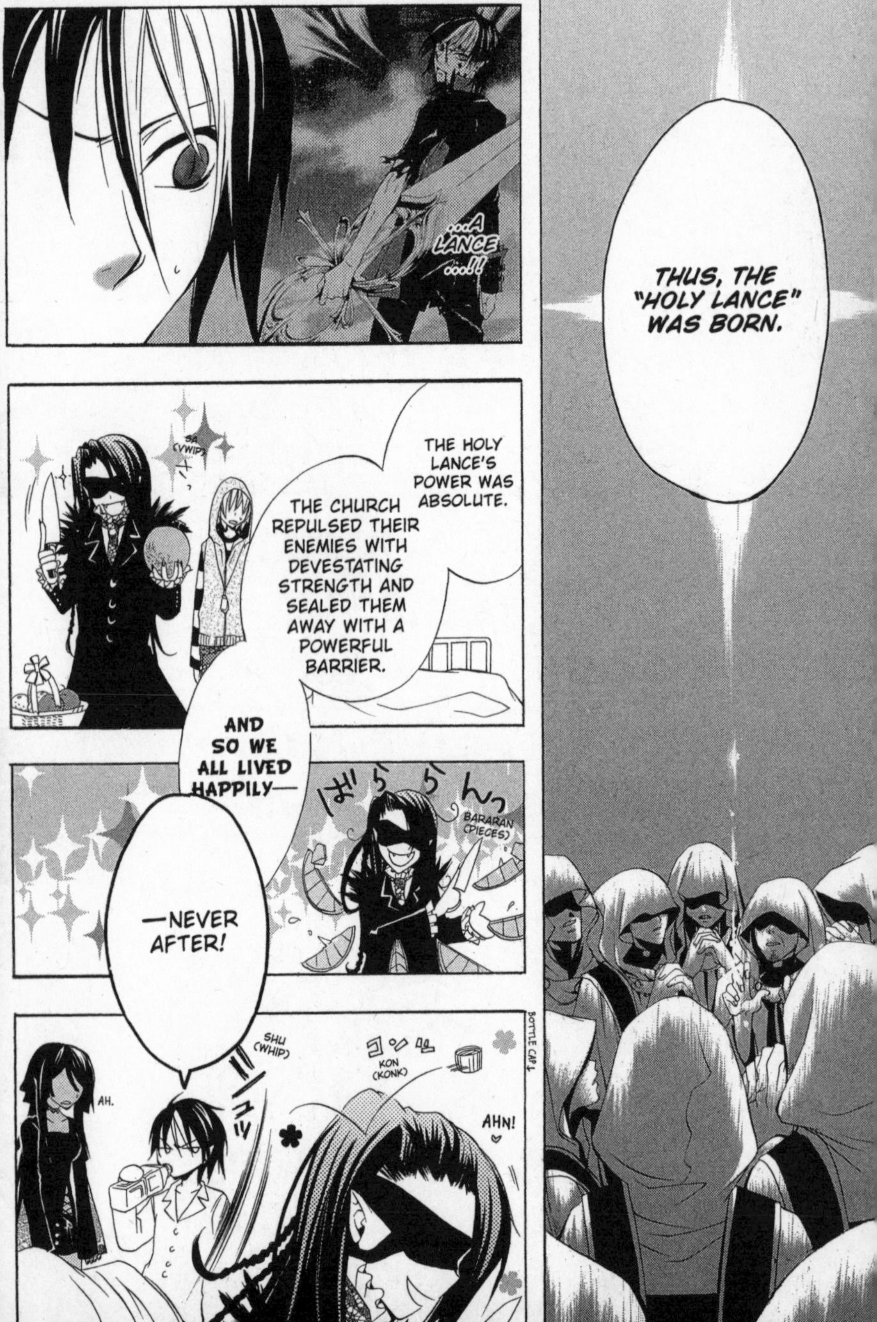
THUS, THE "HOLY LANCE" WAS BORN.
...A LANCE ...!!
SA (VWIP)
THE HOLY LANCE'S POWER WAS ABSOLUTE.
THE CHURCH REPULSED THEIR ENEMIES WITH DEVESTATING STRENGTH AND SEALED THEM AWAY WITH A POWERFUL BARRIER.
AND SO WE ALL LIVED HAPPILY—
ばららんっ
BARARAN (PIECES)
—NEVER AFTER!
SHU (WHIP)
KON (KONK)
BOTTLE CAP
AH.
AHN!

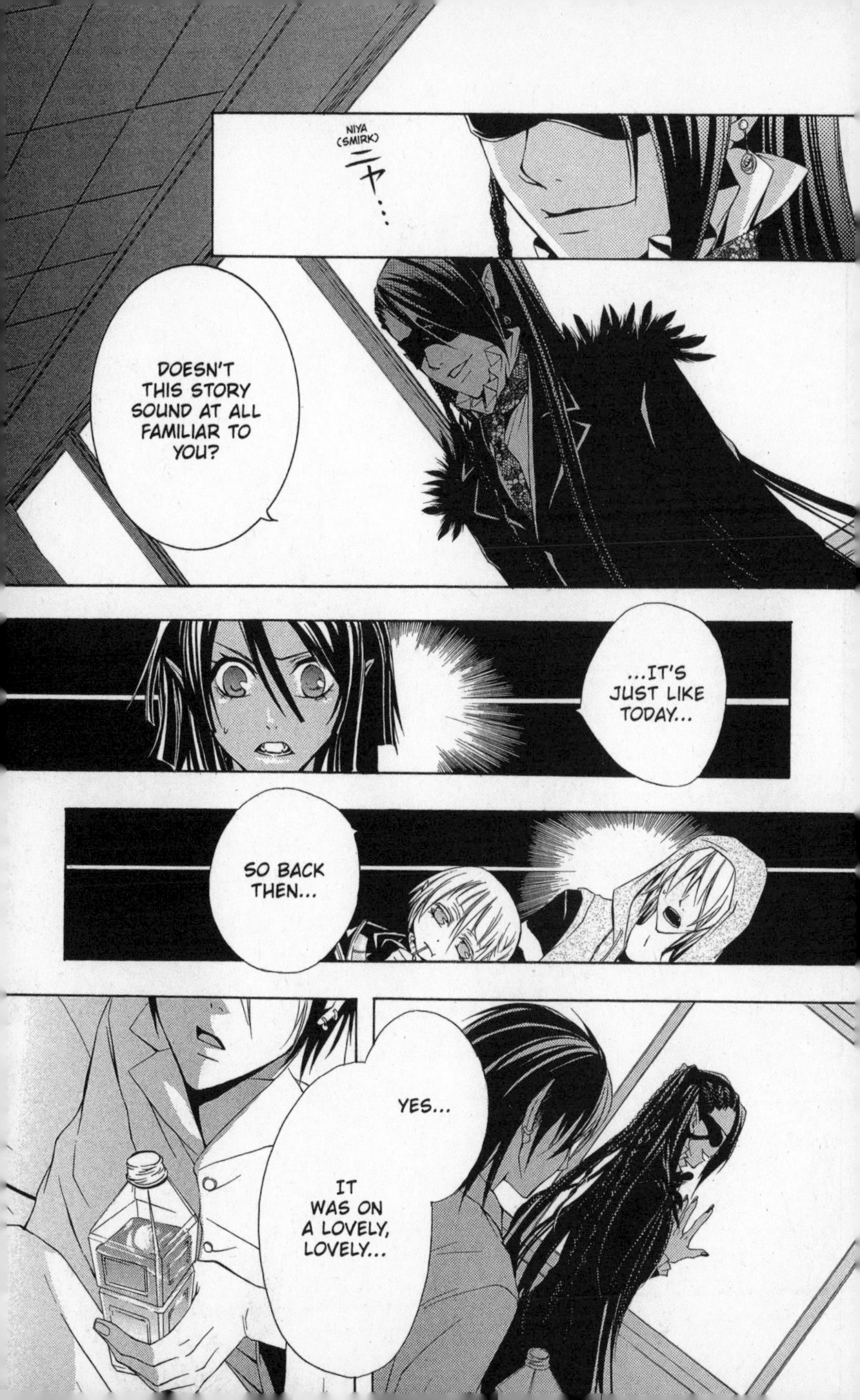
NIYA (SMIRK)
ニヤ…
DOESN'T THIS STORY SOUND AT ALL FAMILIAR TO YOU?
...IT'S JUST LIKE TODAY...
SO BACK THEN...
YES...
IT WAS ON A LOVELY, LOVELY...

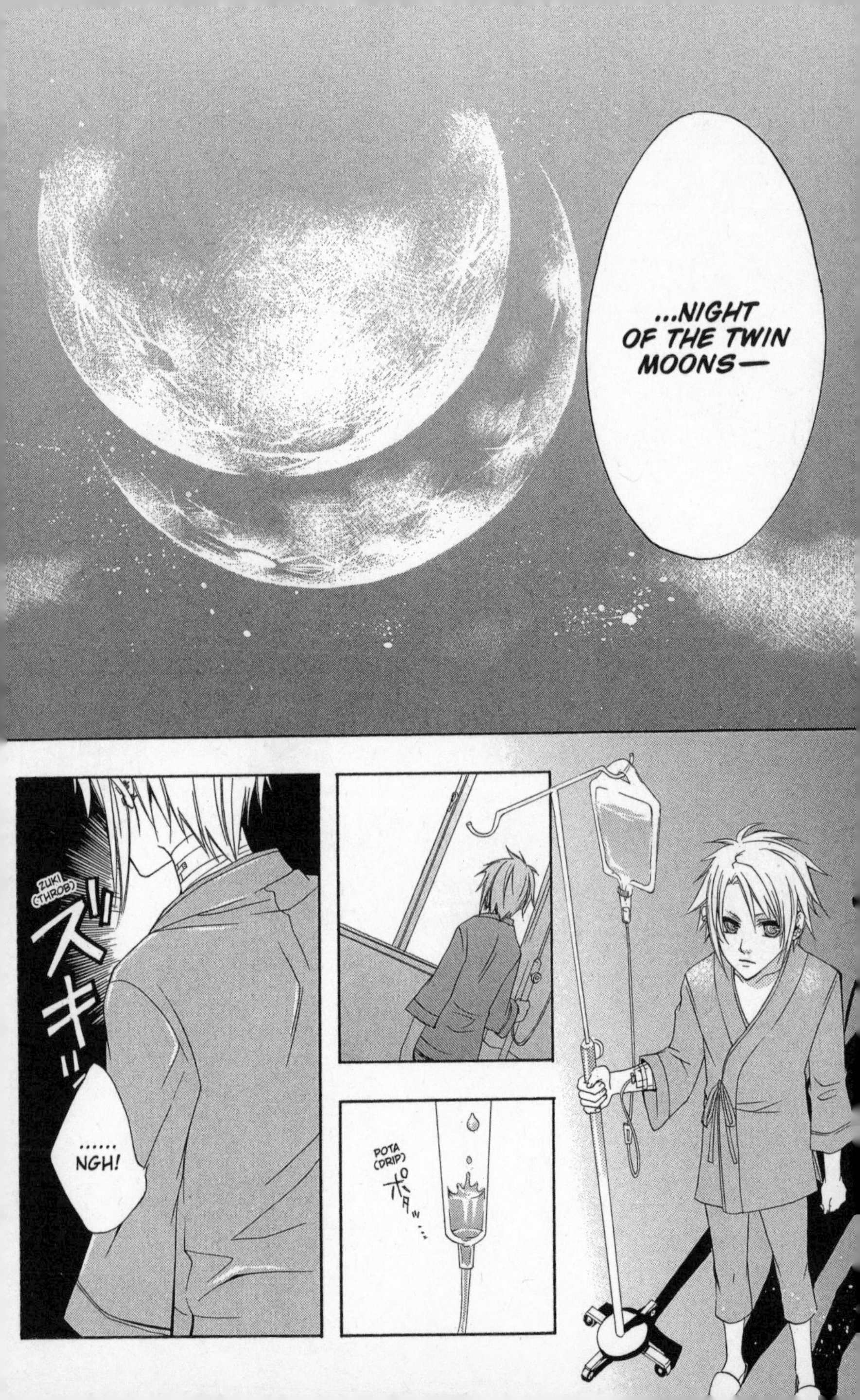
...NIGHT OF THE TWIN MOONS—
POTA (DRIP)
ZUKI (THROB)
......NGH!

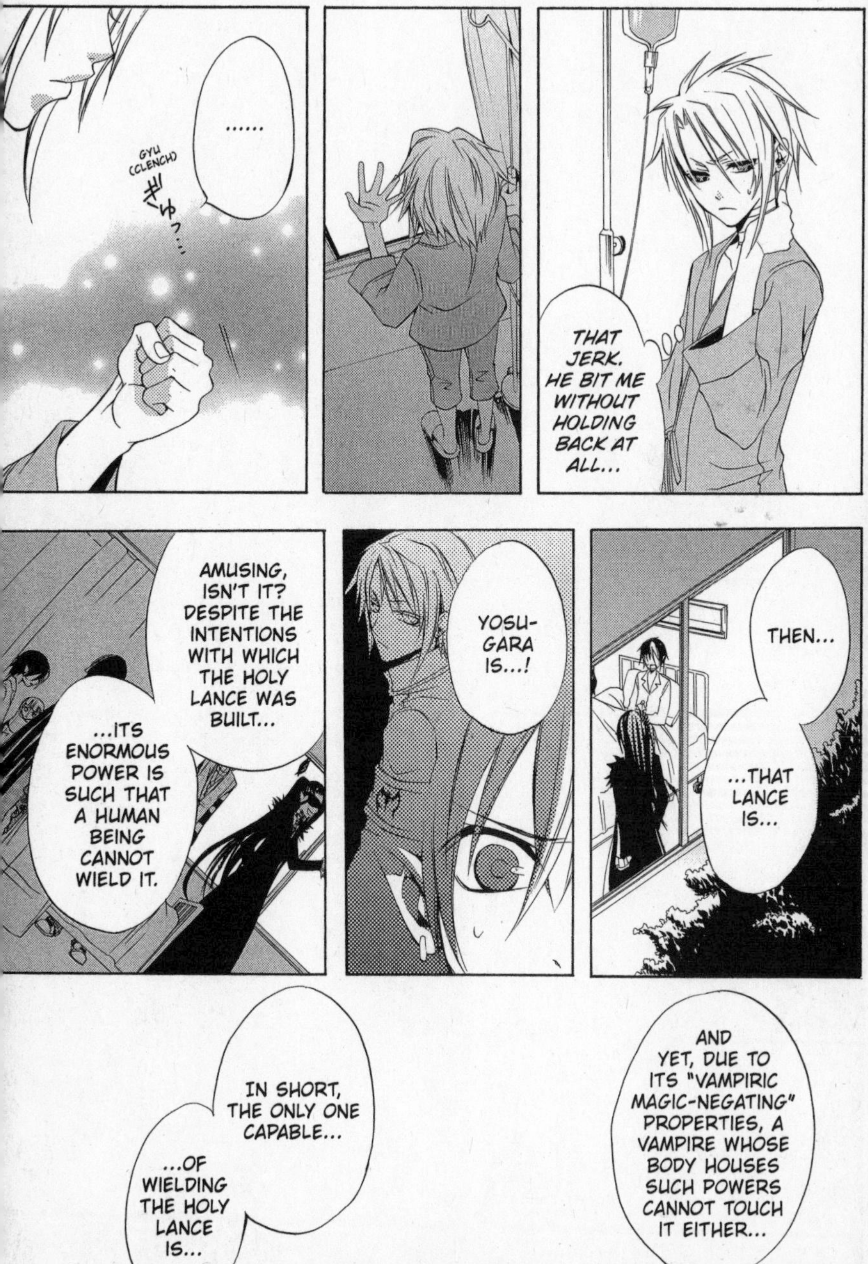
THAT JERK. HE BIT ME WITHOUT HOLDING BACK AT ALL...
......
GYU (CLENCH)
ぎゅっ…
THEN...
...THAT LANCE IS...
YOSU-GARA IS...!
AMUSING, ISN'T IT? DESPITE THE INTENTIONS WITH WHICH THE HOLY LANCE WAS BUILT...
...ITS ENORMOUS POWER IS SUCH THAT A HUMAN BEING CANNOT WIELD IT.
AND YET, DUE TO ITS "VAMPIRIC MAGIC-NEGATING" PROPERTIES, A VAMPIRE WHOSE BODY HOUSES SUCH POWERS CANNOT TOUCH IT EITHER...
IN SHORT, THE ONLY ONE CAPABLE...
...OF WIELDING THE HOLY LANCE IS...

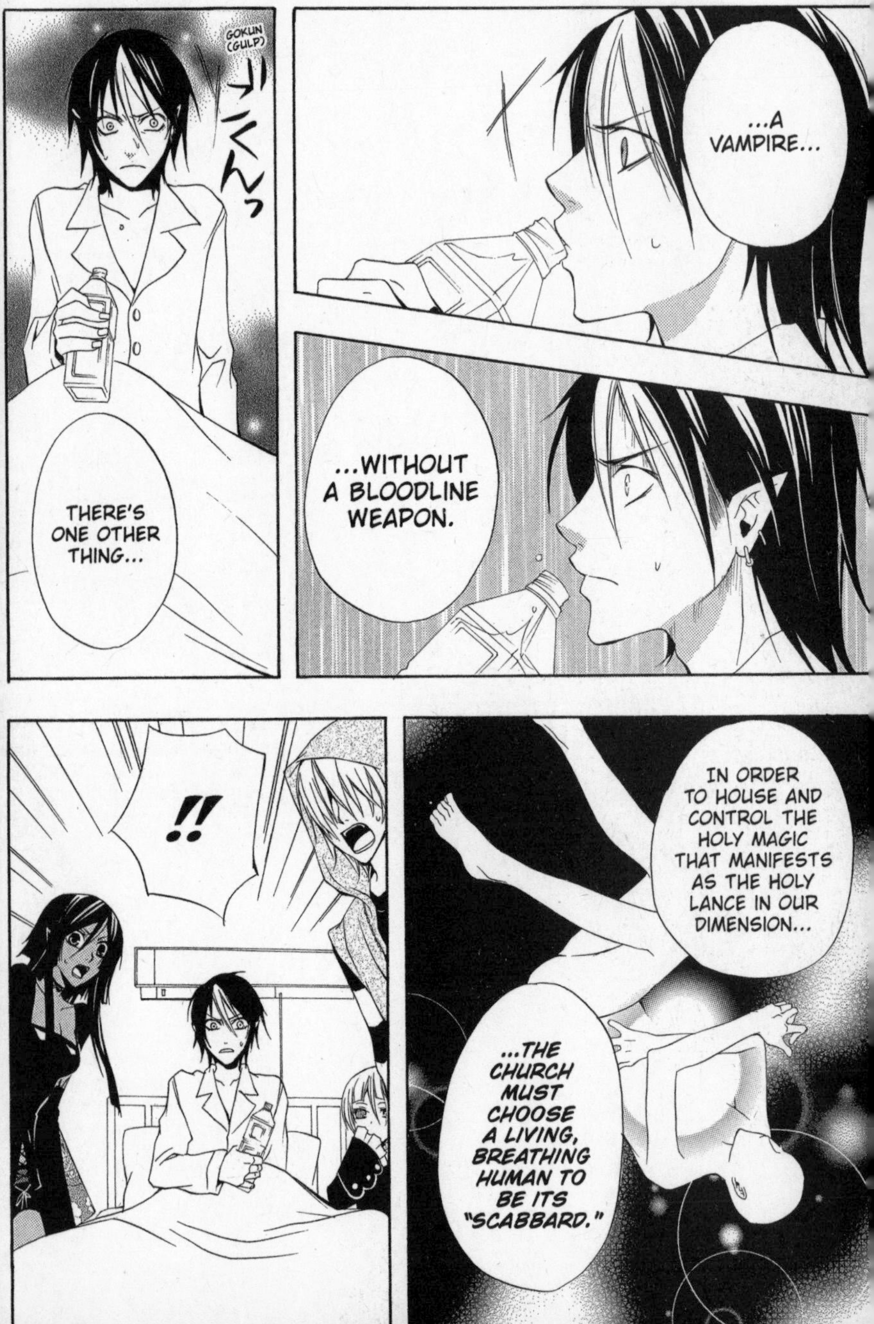
...A VAMPIRE...
...WITHOUT A BLOODLINE WEAPON.
ごくんっ
GOKUN (GULP)
THERE'S ONE OTHER THING...
IN ORDER TO HOUSE AND CONTROL THE HOLY MAGIC THAT MANIFESTS AS THE HOLY LANCE IN OUR DIMENSION...
...THE CHURCH MUST CHOOSE A LIVING, BREATHING HUMAN TO BE ITS "SCABBARD."
!!

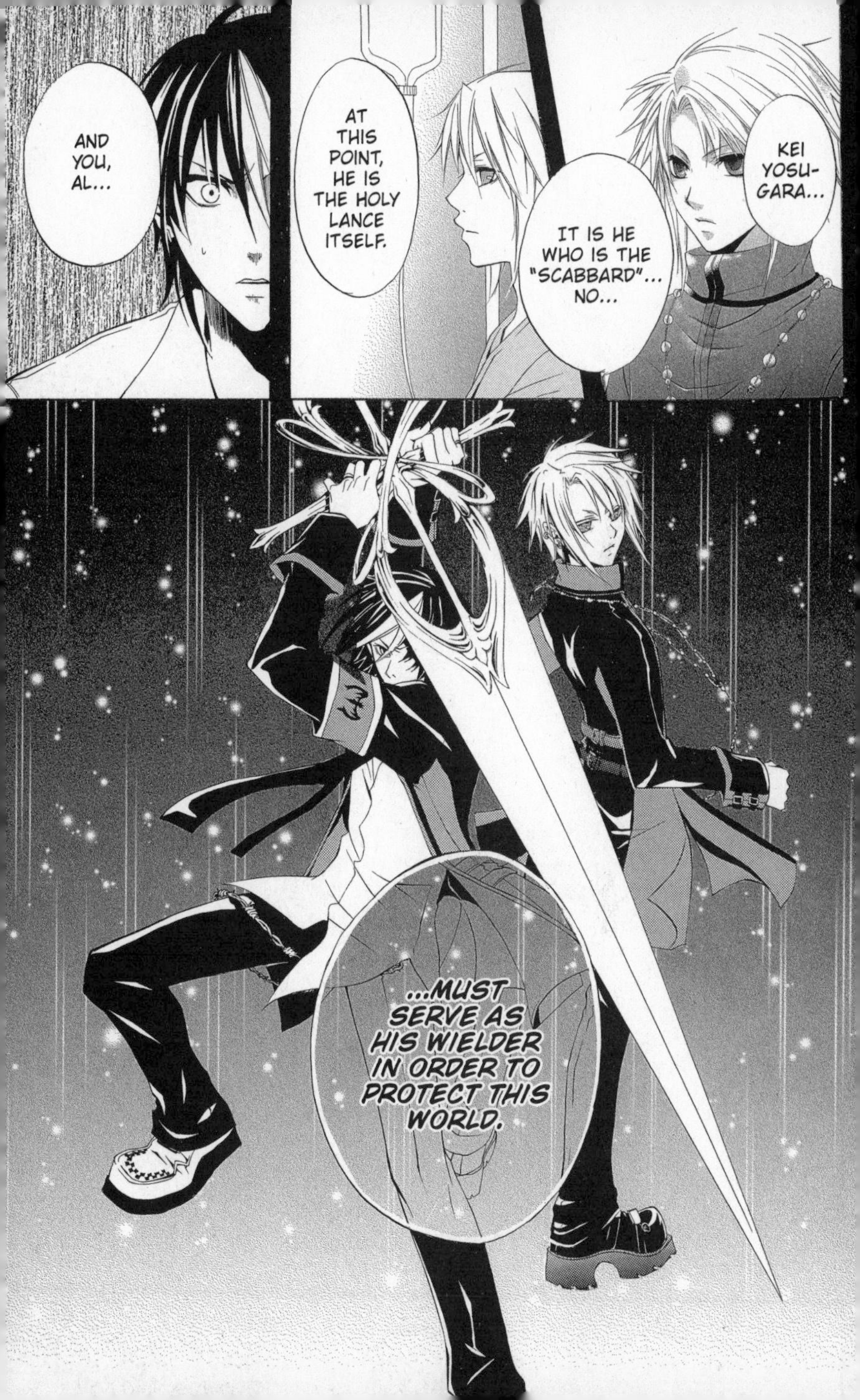
KEI YOSU-GARA...
IT IS HE WHO IS THE "SCABBARD"... NO...
AT THIS POINT, HE IS THE HOLY LANCE ITSELF.
AND YOU, AL...
...MUST SERVE AS HIS WIELDER IN ORDER TO PROTECT THIS WORLD.

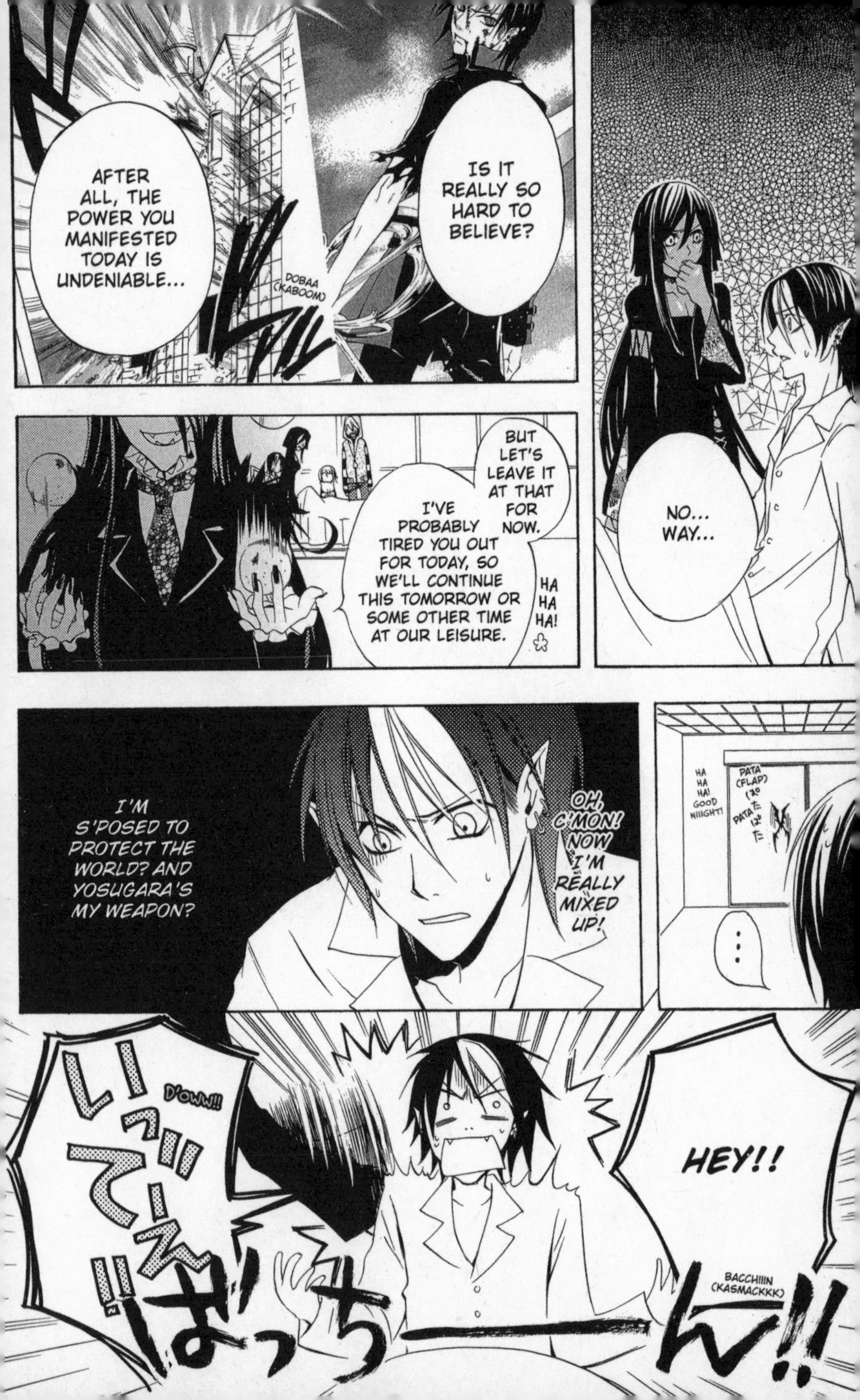
NO... WAY...
IS IT REALLY SO HARD TO BELIEVE?
AFTER ALL, THE POWER YOU MANIFESTED TODAY IS UNDENIABLE...
DOBAA (KABOOM)
BUT LET'S LEAVE IT AT THAT FOR NOW.
I'VE PROBABLY TIRED YOU OUT FOR TODAY, SO WE'LL CONTINUE THIS TOMORROW OR SOME OTHER TIME AT OUR LEISURE.
HA HA HA!
HA HA HA! GOOD NIIIGHT!
PATA (FLAP)
PATA
...
OH, C'MON! NOW I'M REALLY MIXED UP!
I'M S'POSED TO PROTECT THE WORLD? AND YOSUGARA'S MY WEAPON?
HEY!!
BACCHIIIN (KASMACKKK)
ばっちーーん!!
いってーー!!
D'OWW!!

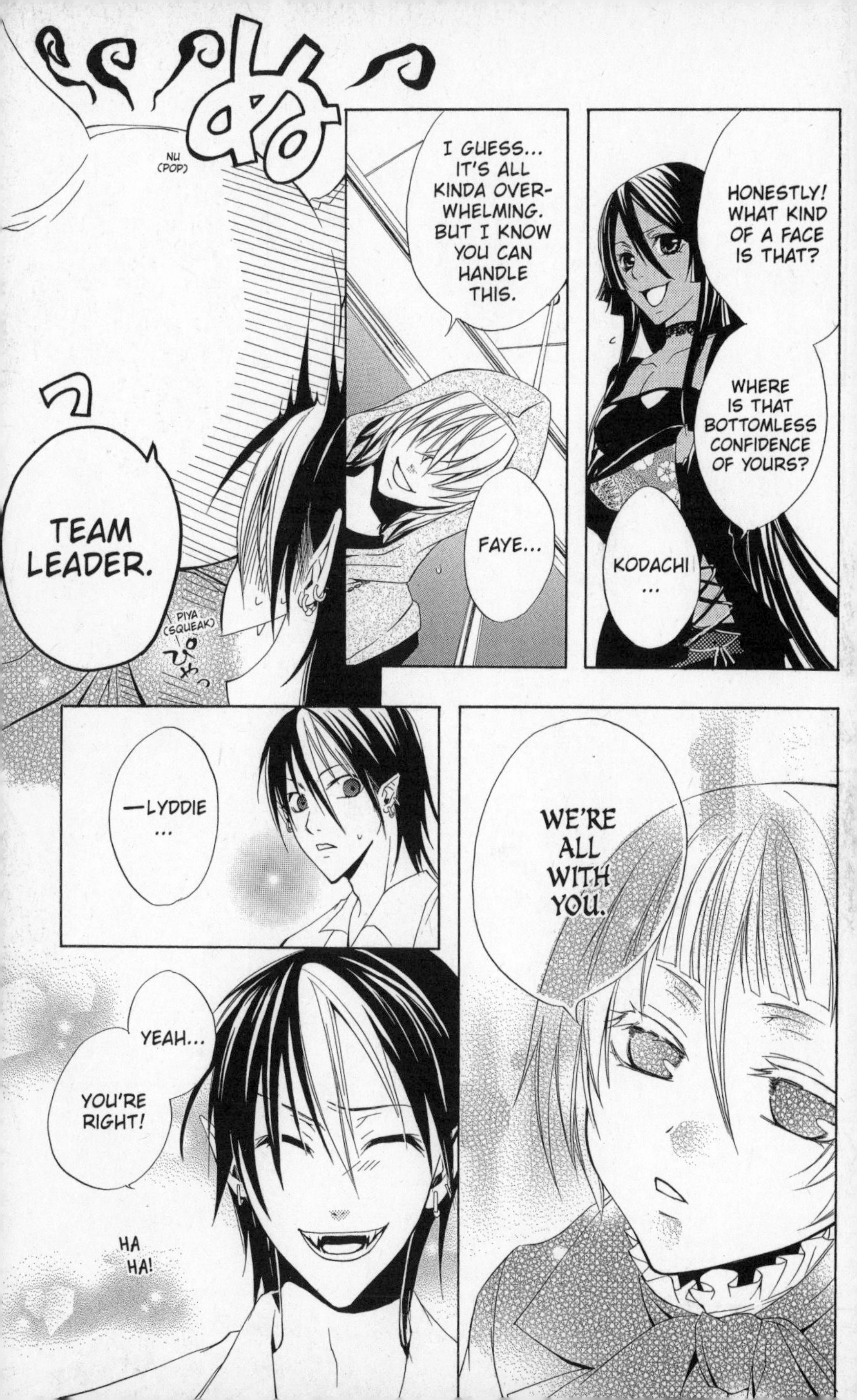
HONESTLY! WHAT KIND OF A FACE IS THAT?
WHERE IS THAT BOTTOMLESS CONFIDENCE OF YOURS?
KODACHI ...
I GUESS... IT'S ALL KINDA OVER-WHELMING. BUT I KNOW YOU CAN HANDLE THIS.
FAYE...
NU (POP)
TEAM LEADER.
PIYA (SQUEAK)
WE'RE ALL WITH YOU.
—LYDDIE ...
YEAH...
YOU'RE RIGHT!
HA HA!

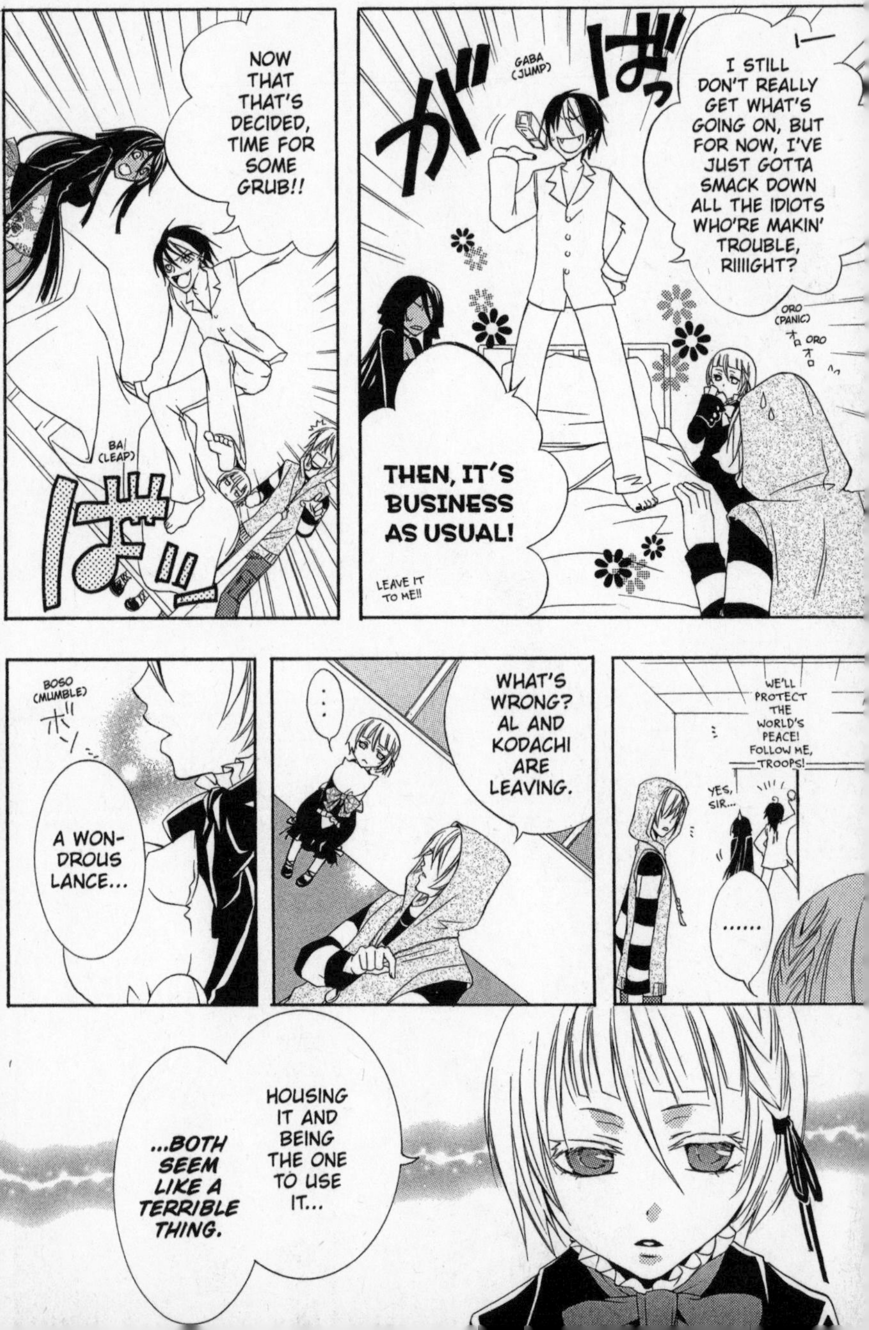
GABA (JUMP)
I STILL DON'T REALLY GET WHAT'S GOING ON, BUT FOR NOW, I'VE JUST GOTTA SMACK DOWN ALL THE IDIOTS WHO'RE MAKIN' TROUBLE, RIIIGHT?
ORO (PANIC)
THEN, IT'S BUSINESS AS USUAL!
LEAVE IT TO ME!!
NOW THAT THAT'S DECIDED, TIME FOR SOME GRUB!!
BA (LEAP)
WE'LL PROTECT THE WORLD'S PEACE! FOLLOW ME, TROOPS!
YES, SIR...
......
...
WHAT'S WRONG? AL AND KODACHI ARE LEAVING.
BOSO (MUMBLE)
A WON-DROUS LANCE...
HOUSING IT AND BEING THE ONE TO USE IT...
...BOTH SEEM LIKE A TERRIBLE THING.

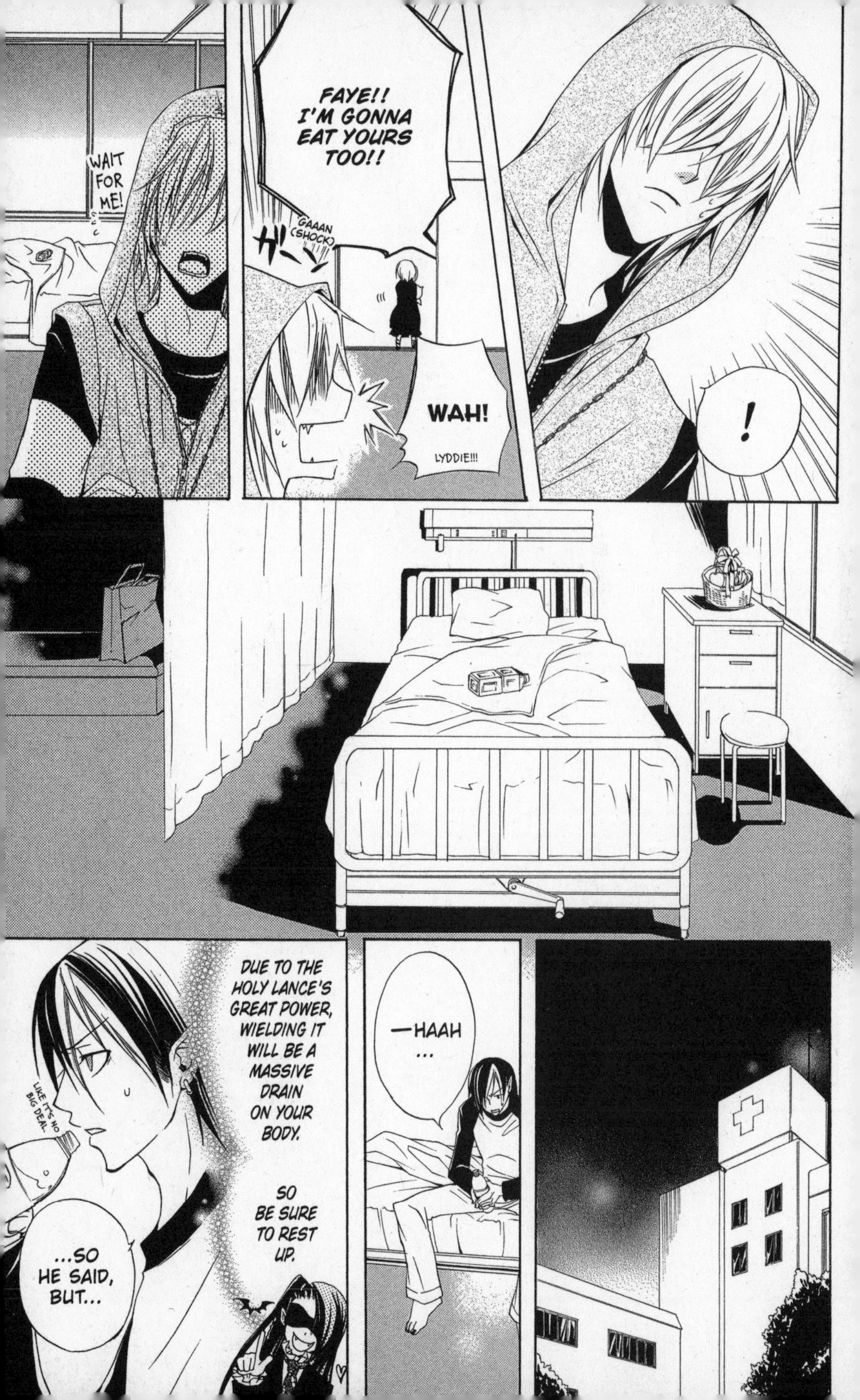
!
FAYE!! I'M GONNA EAT YOURS TOO!!
GAAAN (SHOCK)
WAH!
LYDDIE!!!
WAIT FOR ME!
—HAAH ...
DUE TO THE HOLY LANCE'S GREAT POWER, WIELDING IT WILL BE A MASSIVE DRAIN ON YOUR BODY.
SO BE SURE TO REST UP.
...SO HE SAID, BUT...
LIKE IT'S NO BIG DEAL.

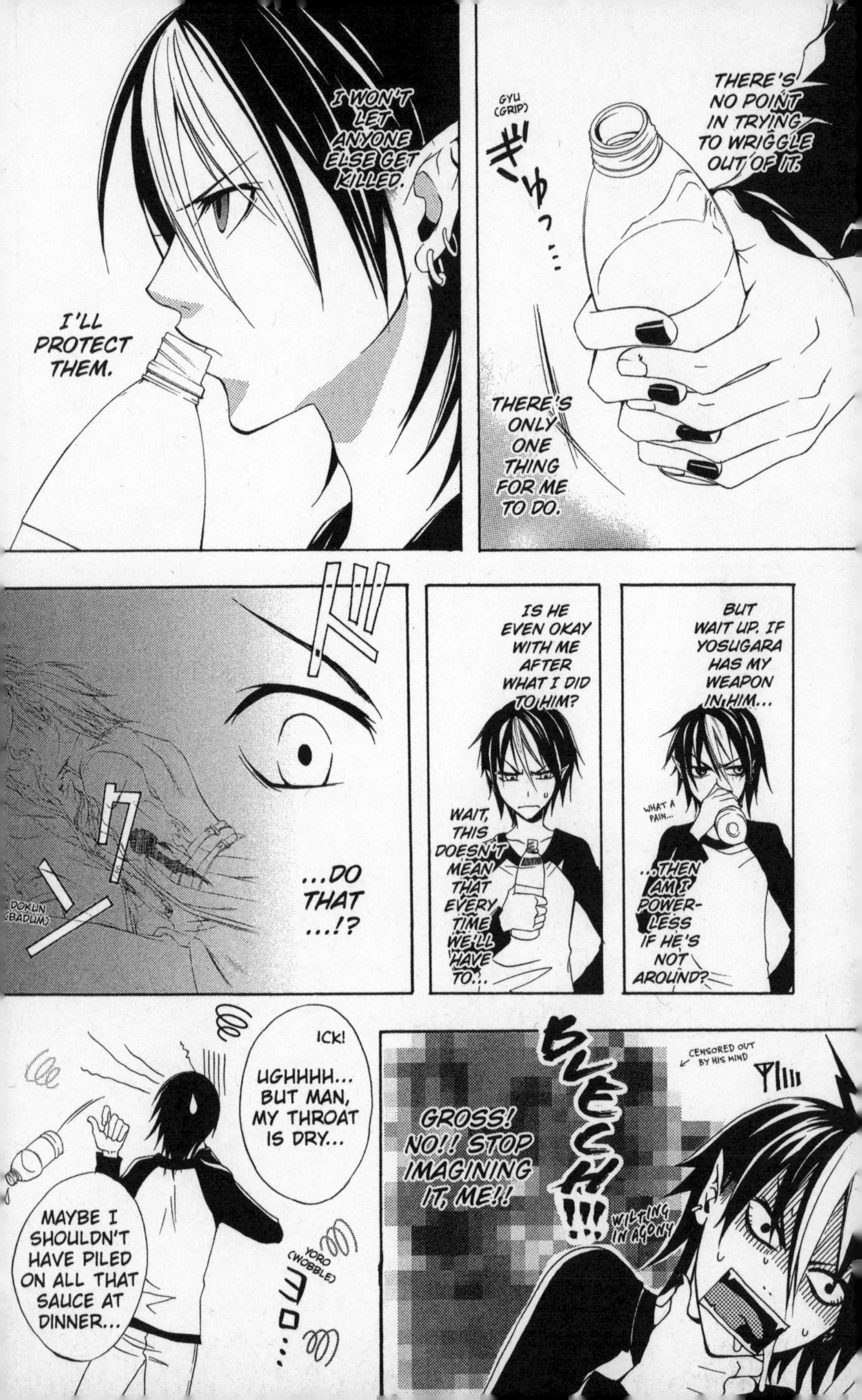
THERE'S NO POINT IN TRYING TO WRIGGLE OUT OF IT.
GYU (GRIP)
THERE'S ONLY ONE THING FOR ME TO DO.
I WON'T LET ANYONE ELSE GET KILLED.
I'LL PROTECT THEM.
BUT WAIT UP. IF YOSUGARA HAS MY WEAPON IN HIM...
WHAT A PAIN...
...THEN AM I POWERLESS IF HE'S NOT AROUND?
IS HE EVEN OKAY WITH ME AFTER WHAT I DID TO HIM?
WAIT, THIS DOESN'T MEAN THAT EVERY TIME WE'LL HAVE TO...
...DO THAT ...!?
DOKUN (BADUM)
CENSORED OUT BY HIS MIND
BLECH!!!
GROSS! NO!! STOP IMAGINING IT, ME!!
WILTING IN AGONY
ICK!
UGHHHH... BUT MAN, MY THROAT IS DRY...
MAYBE I SHOULDN'T HAVE PILED ON ALL THAT SAUCE AT DINNER...
YORO (WOBBLE)

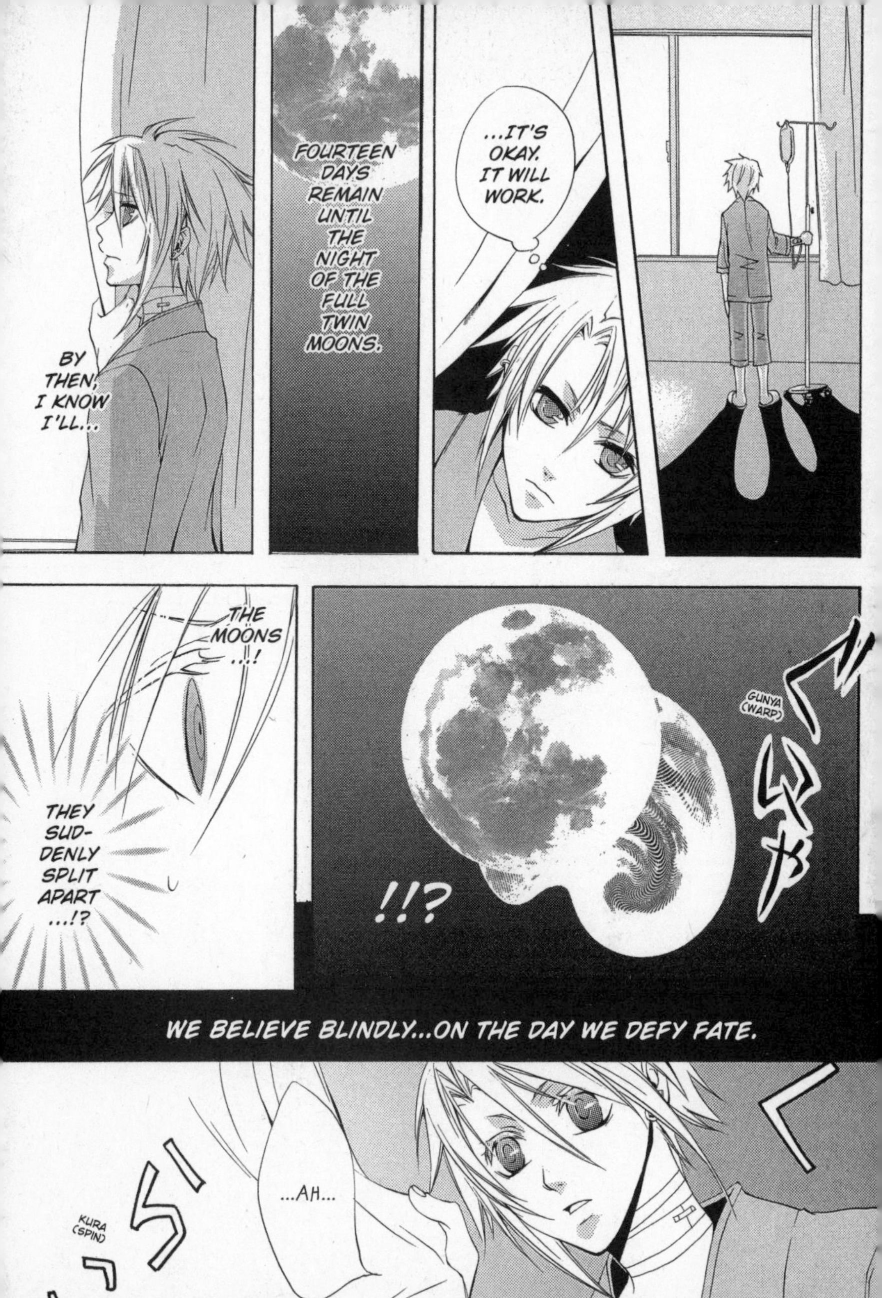
...IT'S OKAY. IT WILL WORK.
FOURTEEN DAYS REMAIN UNTIL THE NIGHT OF THE FULL TWIN MOONS.
BY THEN, I KNOW I'LL...
GUNYA (WARP)
!!?
THE MOONS...!
THEY SUD-DENLY SPLIT APART...!?
WE BELIEVE BLINDLY...ON THE DAY WE DEFY FATE.
...AH...
KURA (SPIN)

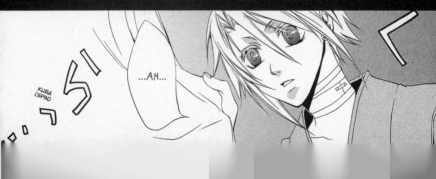

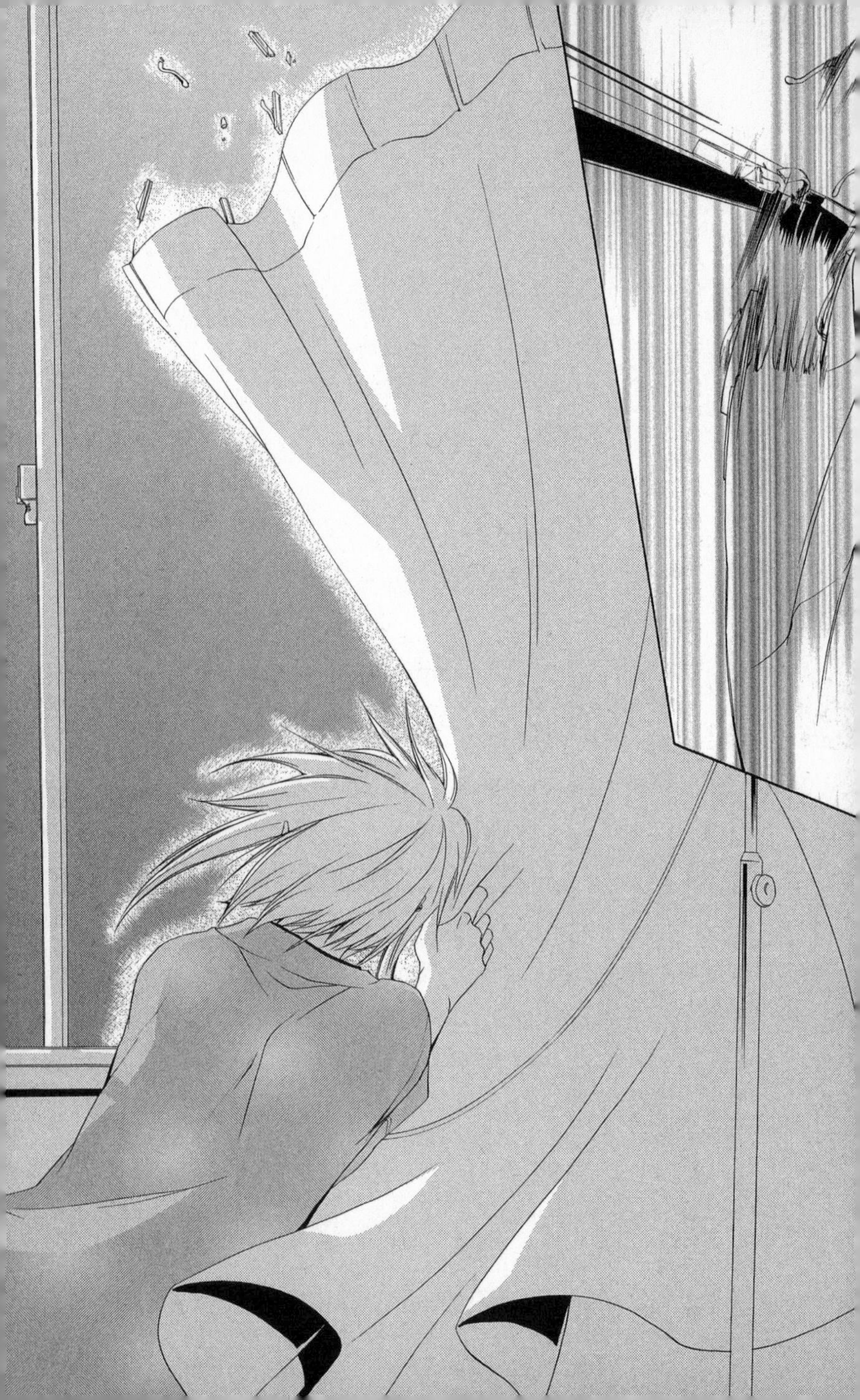

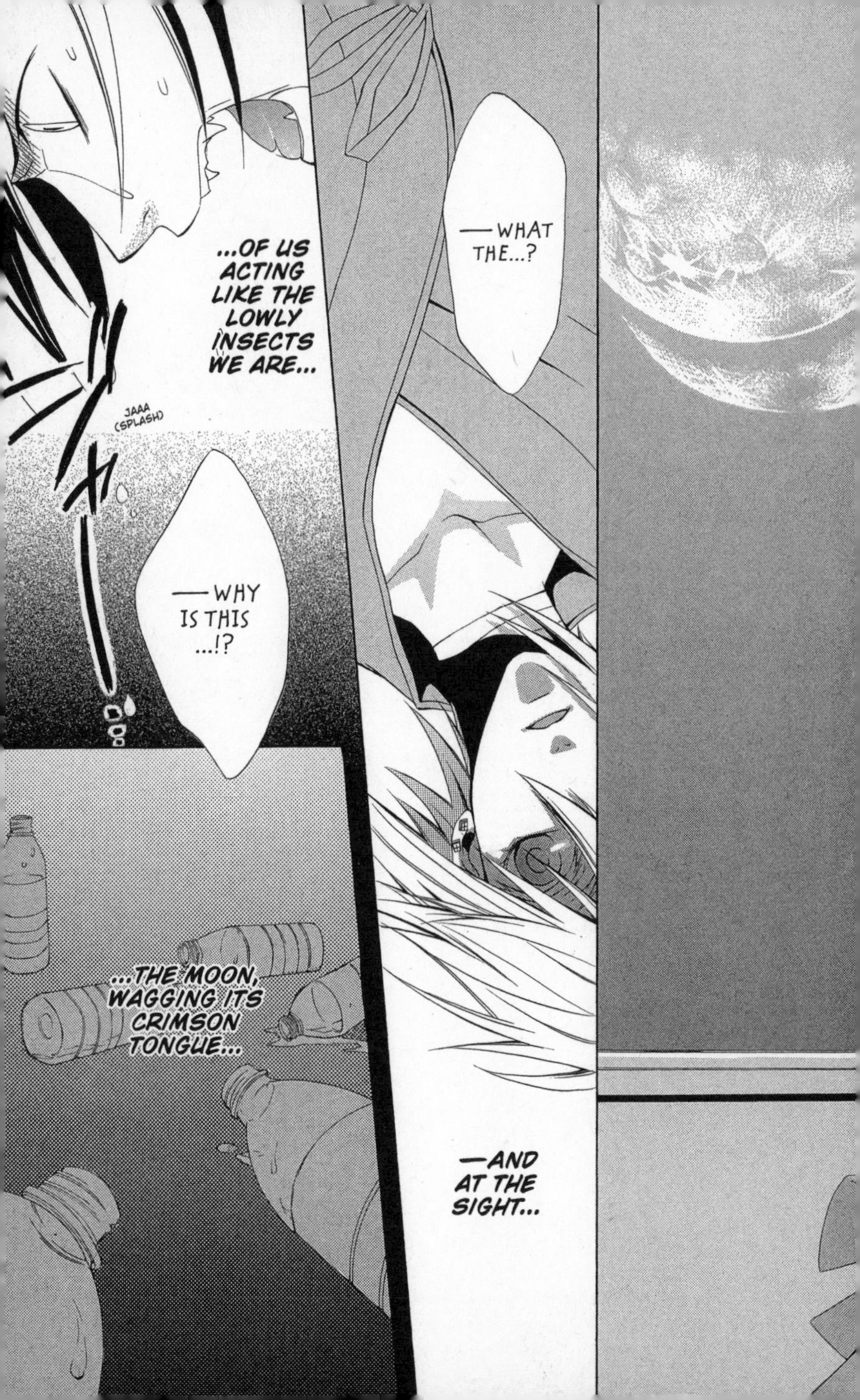
—WHAT THE...?
—AND AT THE SIGHT...
...OF US ACTING LIKE THE LOWLY INSECTS WE ARE...
JAAA (SPLASH)
—WHY IS THIS ...!?
...THE MOON, WAGGING ITS CRIMSON TONGUE...

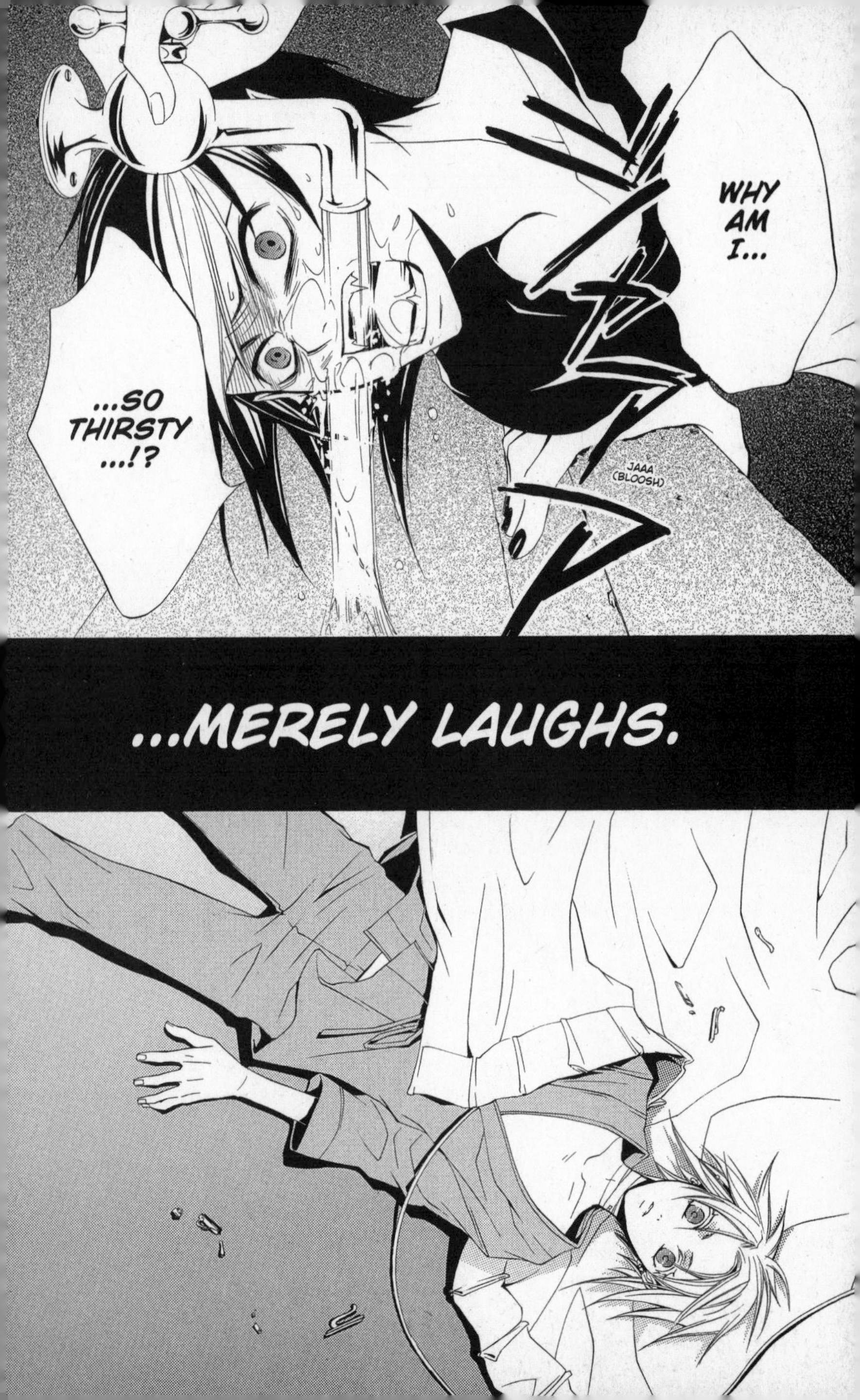
WHY AM I...
...SO THIRSTY ...!?
JAAA (BLOOSH)
...MERELY LAUGHS.

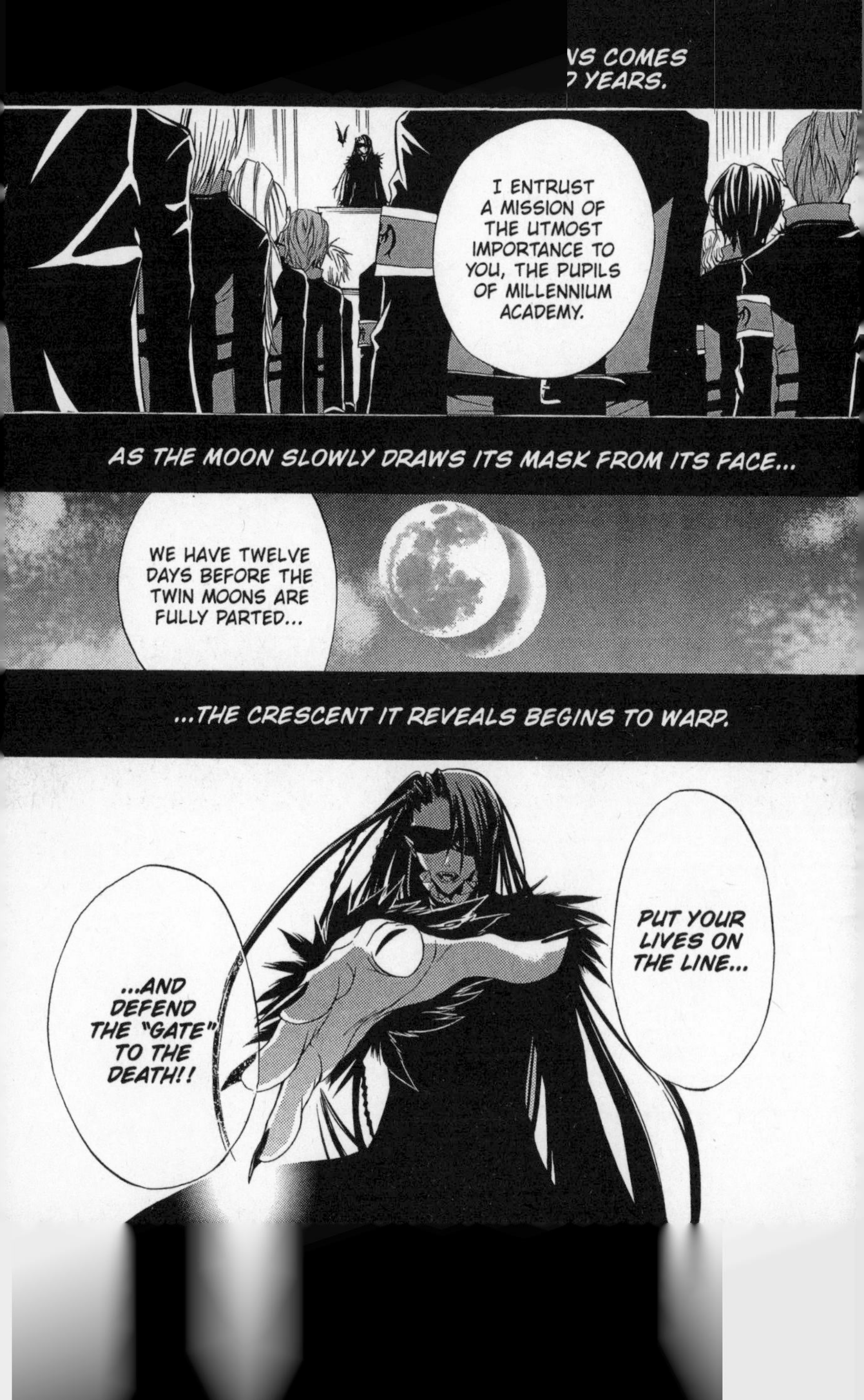
COMES
YEARS.
I ENTRUST A MISSION OF THE UTMOST IMPORTANCE TO YOU, THE PUPILS OF MILLENNIUM ACADEMY.
AS THE MOON SLOWLY DRAWS ITS MASK FROM ITS FACE...
WE HAVE TWELVE DAYS BEFORE THE TWIN MOONS ARE FULLY PARTED...
...THE CRESCENT IT REVEALS BEGINS TO WARP.
PUT YOUR LIVES ON THE LINE...
...AND DEFEND THE "GATE" TO THE DEATH!!

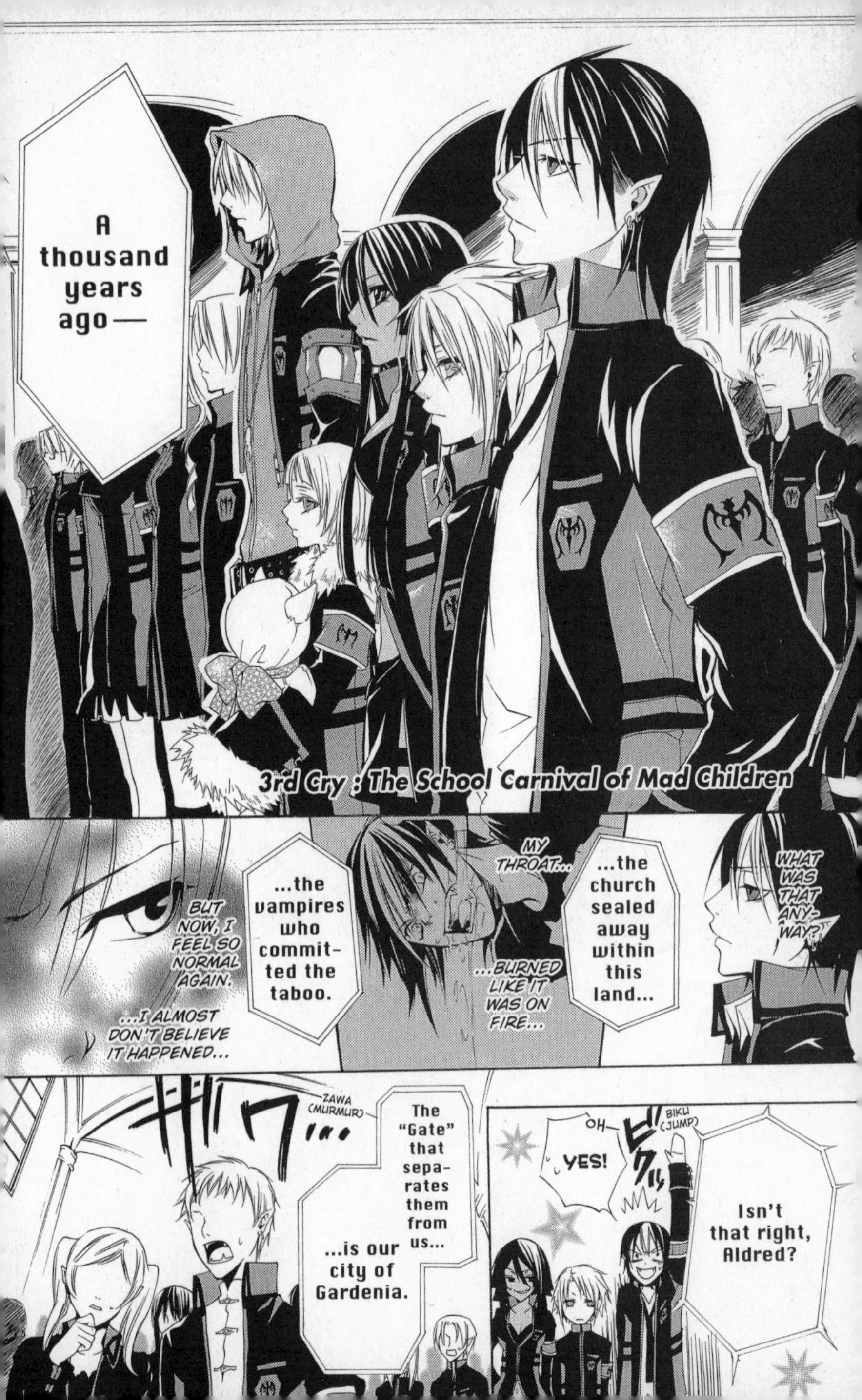
A thousand years ago—
3rd Cry : The School Carnival of Mad Children
WHAT WAS THAT ANYWAY?
...the church sealed away within this land...
MY THROAT...
...BURNED LIKE IT WAS ON FIRE...
...the vampires who commit-ted the taboo.
BUT NOW, I FEEL SO NORMAL AGAIN.
...I ALMOST DON'T BELIEVE IT HAPPENED...
Isn't that right, Aldred?
BIKU (JUMP)
OH— YES!
The "Gate" that sepa-rates them from us...
...is our city of Gardenia.
ZAWA (MURMUR)

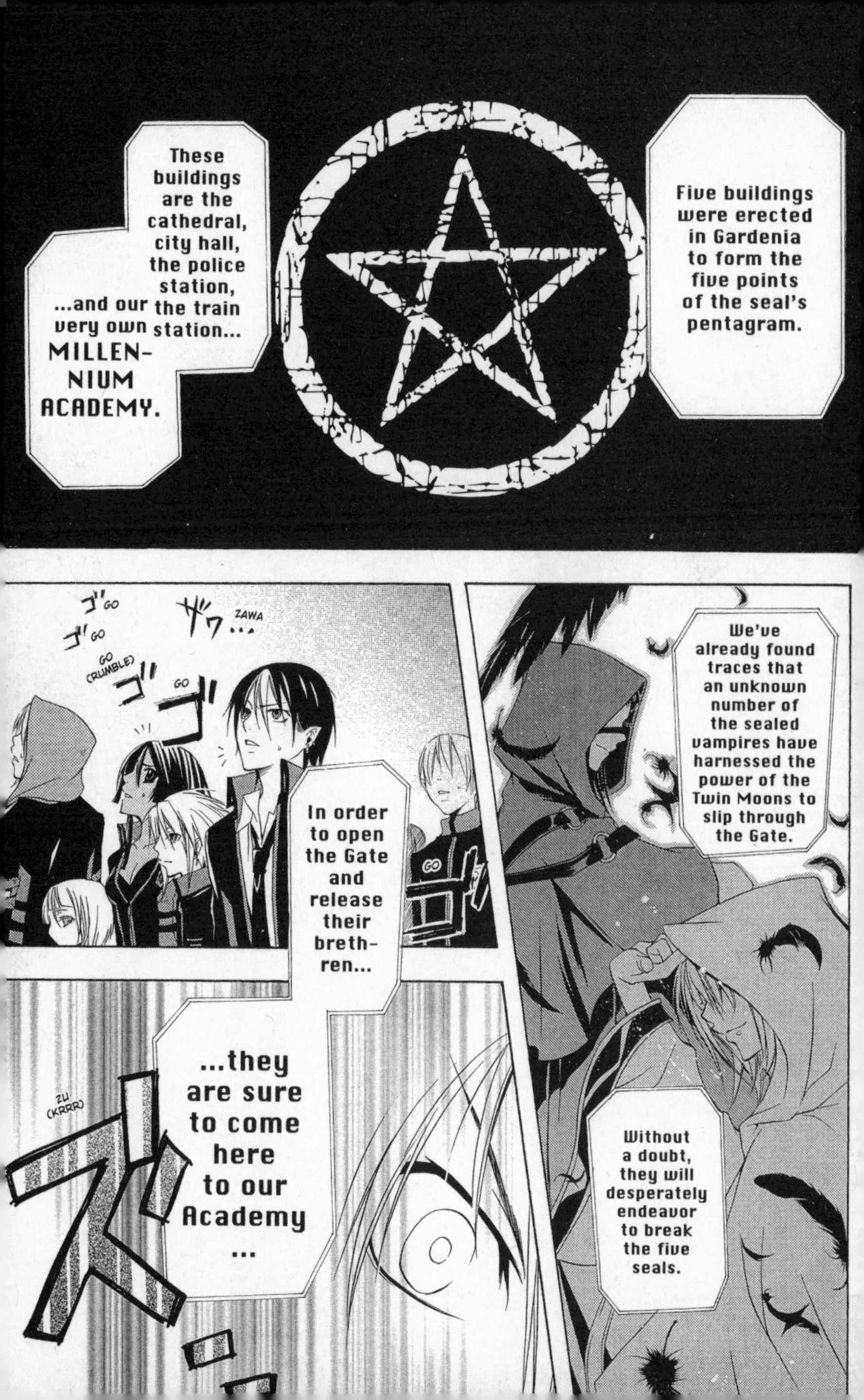
Five buildings were erected in Gardenia to form the five points of the seal's pentagram.
These buildings are the cathedral, city hall, the police station, the train station...
...and our very own MILLEN-NIUM ACADEMY.
We've already found traces that an unknown number of the sealed vampires have harnessed the power of the Twin Moons to slip through the Gate.
Without a doubt, they will desperately endeavor to break the five seals.
ザワ ZAWA...
ゴ GO
ゴ GO
GO (RUMBLE)
ゴゴ GO
In order to open the Gate and release their breth-ren...
ZU (KRRR)
...they are sure to come here to our Academy...

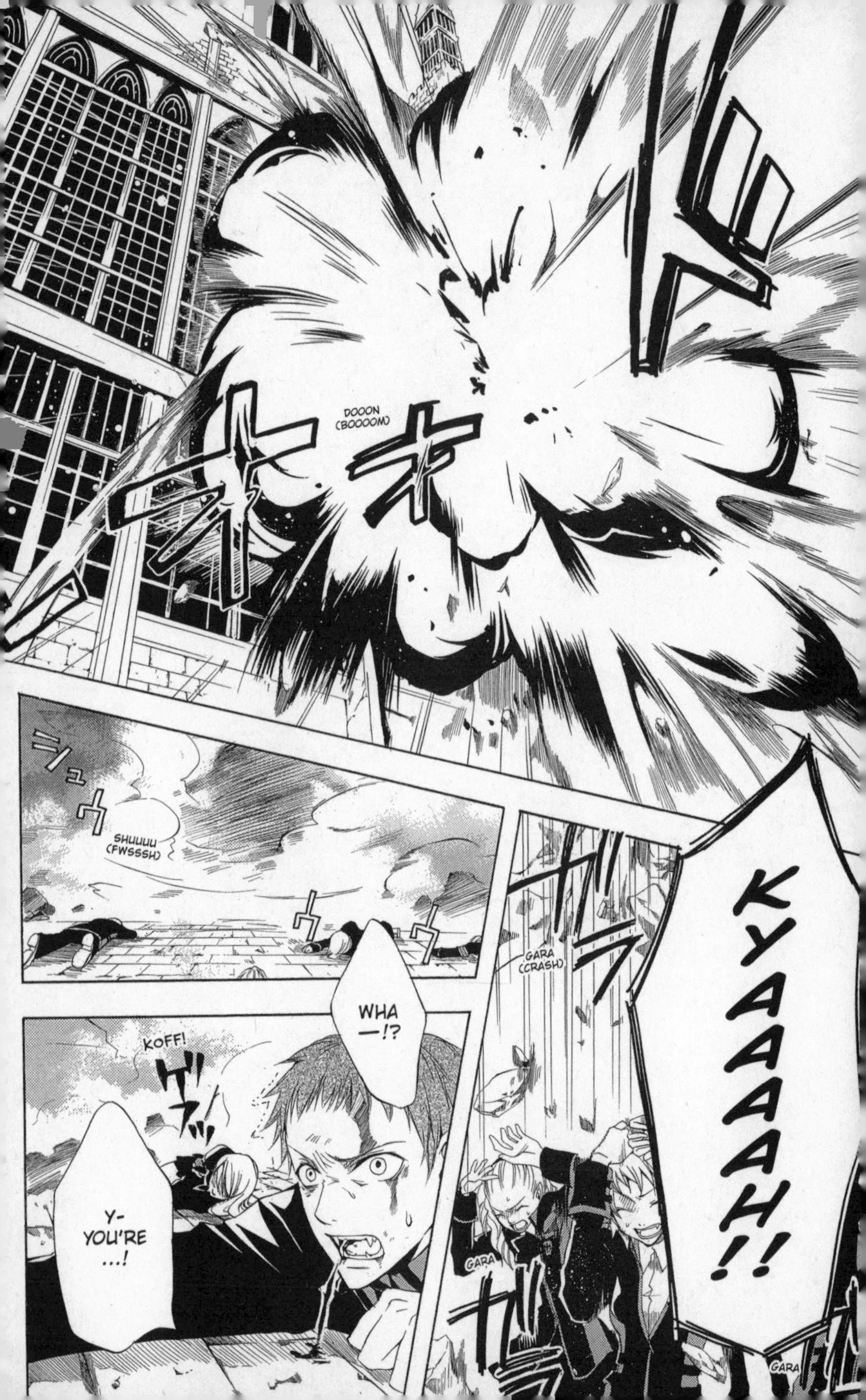
DOOON (BOOOOM)
KYAAAAAH!!
GARA (CRASH)
GARA
GARA
SHUUUU (FWSSSH)
WHA —!?
KOFF!
Y-YOU'RE ...!

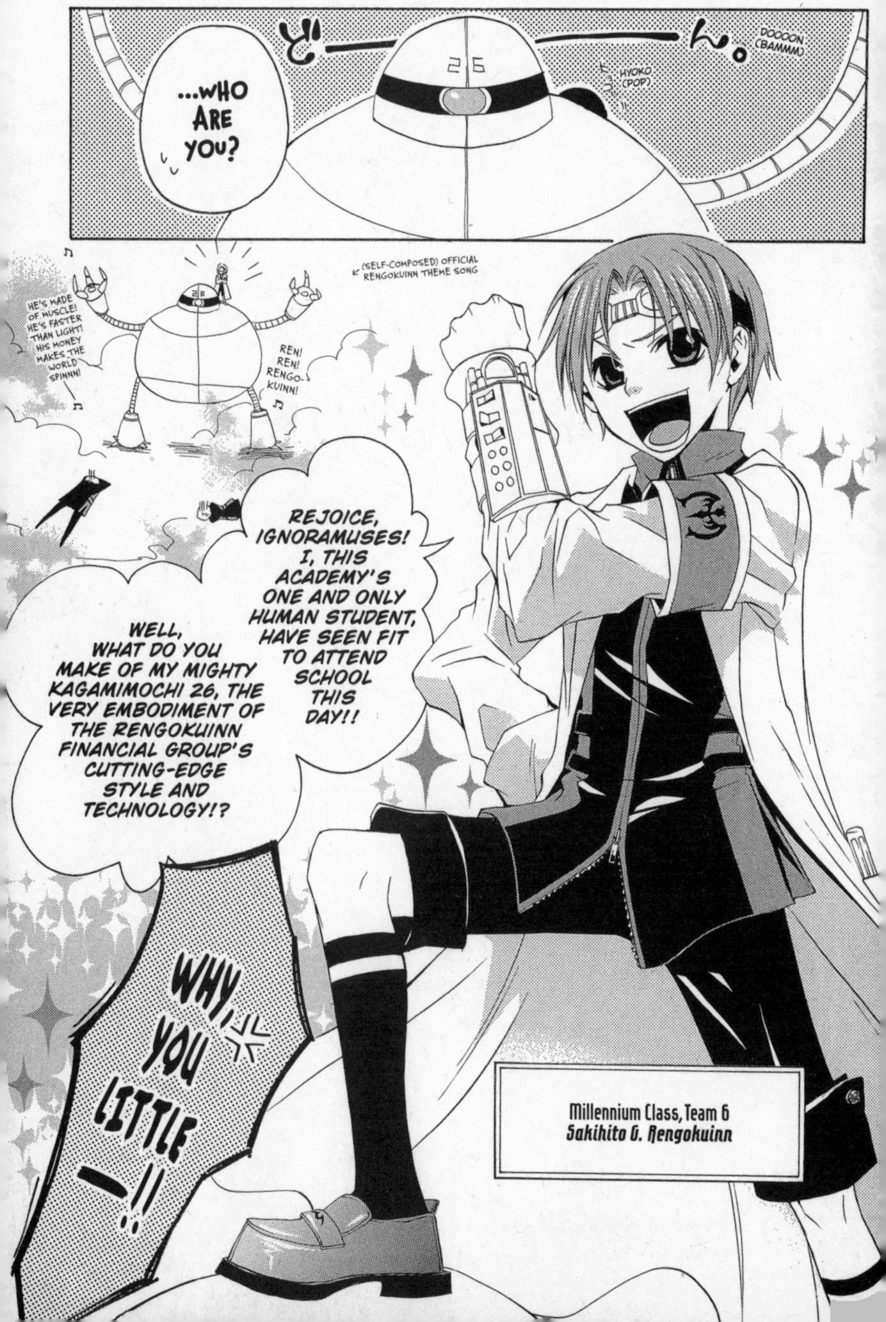
DOOOON (BAMMM)
HYOKO (POP)
...WHO ARE YOU?
(SELF-COMPOSED) OFFICIAL RENGOKUINN THEME SONG
REN! REN! RENGO-KUINN!
HE'S MADE OF MUSCLE! HE'S FASTER THAN LIGHT! HIS MONEY MAKES THE WORLD SPINNN!
REJOICE, IGNORAMUSES! I, THIS ACADEMY'S ONE AND ONLY HUMAN STUDENT, HAVE SEEN FIT TO ATTEND SCHOOL THIS DAY!!
WELL, WHAT DO YOU MAKE OF MY MIGHTY KAGAMIMOCHI 26, THE VERY EMBODIMENT OF THE RENGOKUINN FINANCIAL GROUP'S CUTTING-EDGE STYLE AND TECHNOLOGY!?
Millennium Class, Team 6
Sakihito G. Rengokuinn
WHY, YOU LITTLE—!!

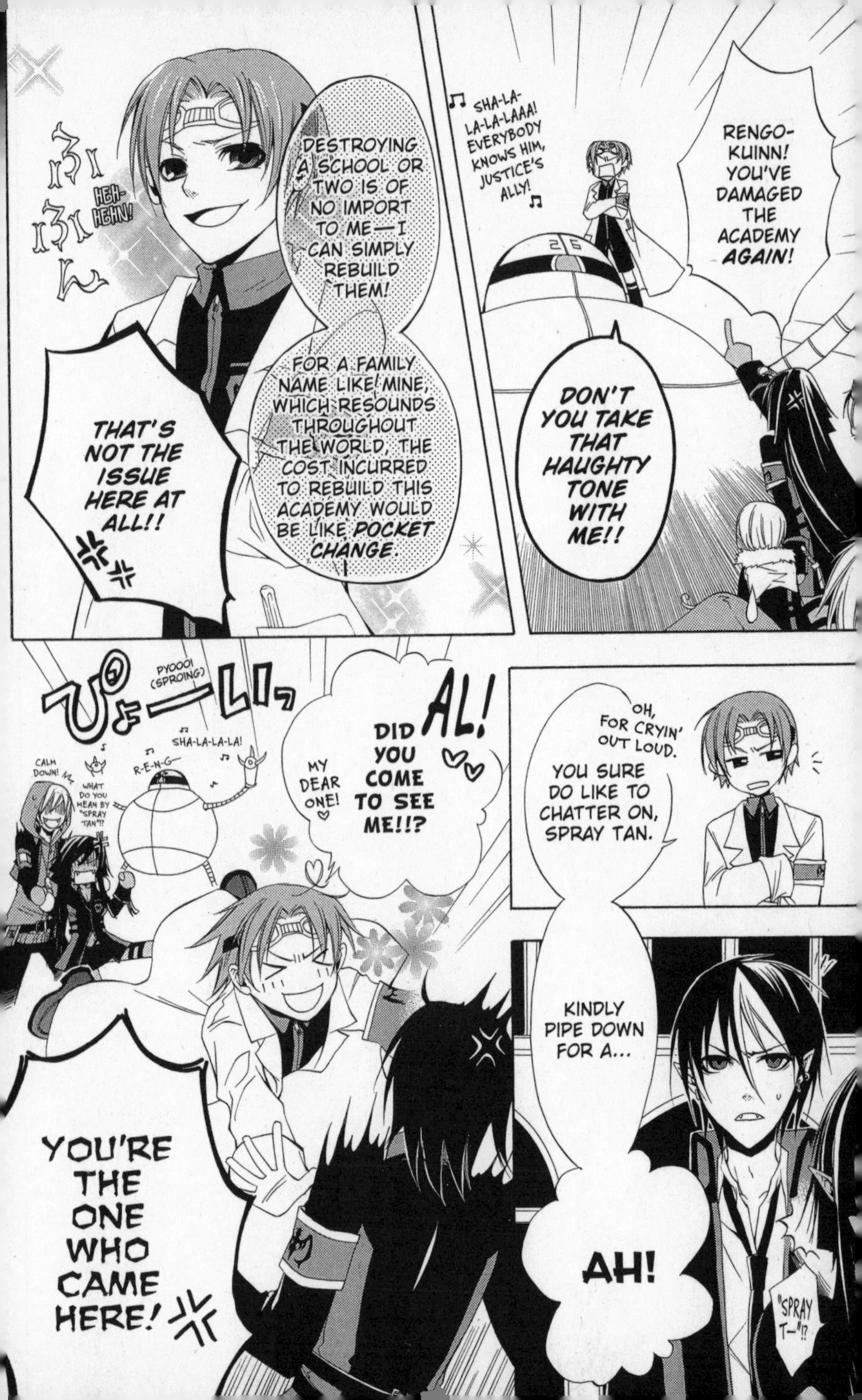
RENGO-KUINN! YOU'VE DAMAGED THE ACADEMY AGAIN!
SHA-LA-LA-LA-LAAA! EVERYBODY KNOWS HIM, JUSTICE'S ALLY!
DON'T YOU TAKE THAT HAUGHTY TONE WITH ME!!
DESTROYING A SCHOOL OR TWO IS OF NO IMPORT TO ME—I CAN SIMPLY REBUILD THEM!
HEH-HEHN!
FOR A FAMILY NAME LIKE MINE, WHICH RESOUNDS THROUGHOUT THE WORLD, THE COST INCURRED TO REBUILD THIS ACADEMY WOULD BE LIKE POCKET CHANGE.
THAT'S NOT THE ISSUE HERE AT ALL!!
OH, FOR CRYIN' OUT LOUD.
YOU SURE DO LIKE TO CHATTER ON, SPRAY TAN.
KINDLY PIPE DOWN FOR A...
AH!
"SPRAY T—"!?
PYOOOI (SPROING)
AL!
DID YOU COME TO SEE ME!!?
MY DEAR ONE!
SHA-LA-LA-LA!
R-E-N-G-
CALM DOWN!
WHAT DO YOU MEAN BY "SPRAY TAN"?!
YOU'RE THE ONE WHO CAME HERE!

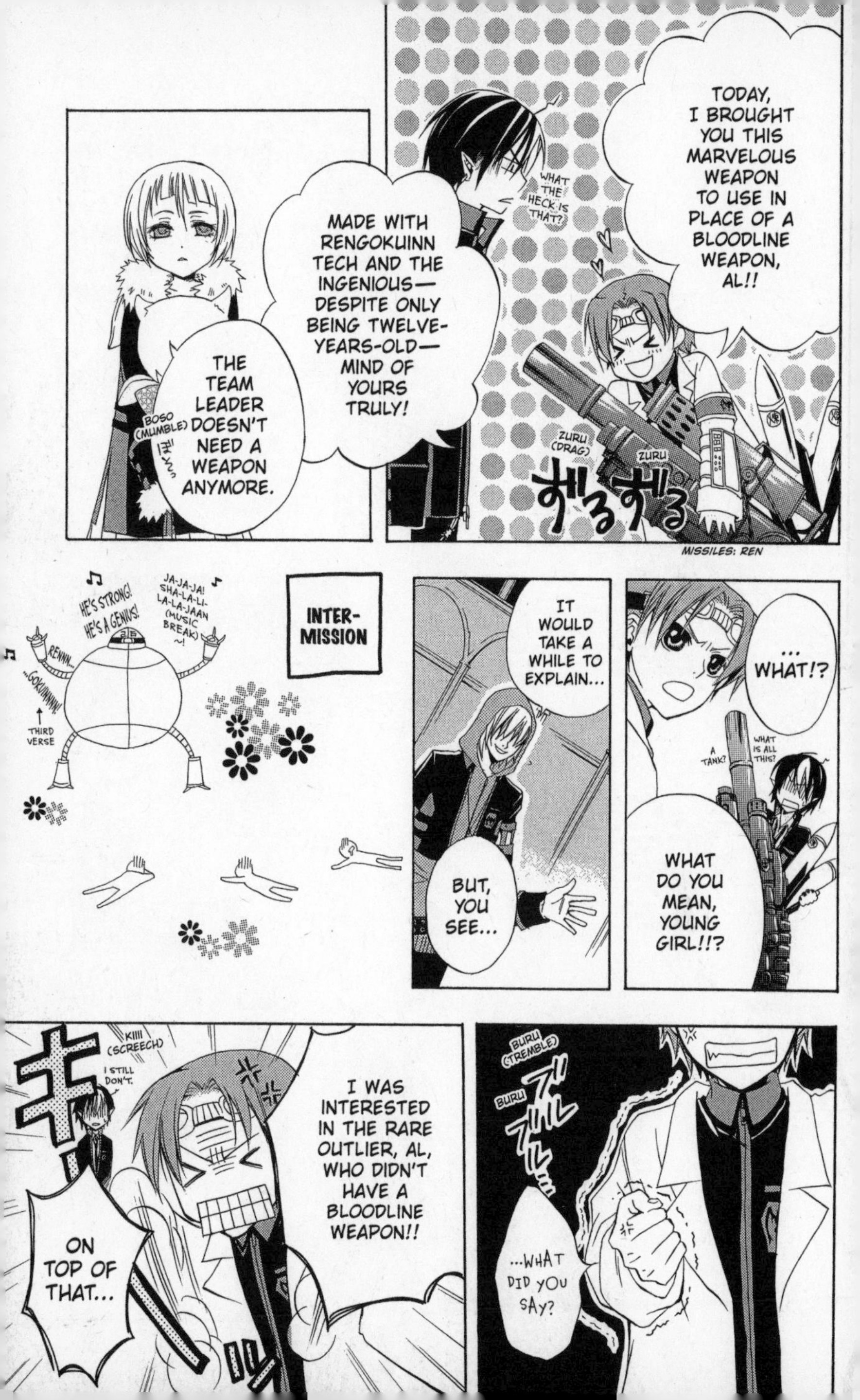
TODAY, I BROUGHT YOU THIS MARVELOUS WEAPON TO USE IN PLACE OF A BLOODLINE WEAPON, AL!!
WHAT THE HECK IS THAT?
ZURU (DRAG)
ZURU
MISSILES: REN
MADE WITH RENGOKUINN TECH AND THE INGENIOUS—DESPITE ONLY BEING TWELVE-YEARS-OLD—MIND OF YOURS TRULY!
BOSO (MUMBLE)
THE TEAM LEADER DOESN'T NEED A WEAPON ANYMORE.
... WHAT!?
WHAT IS ALL THIS?
A TANK?
WHAT DO YOU MEAN, YOUNG GIRL!!?
IT WOULD TAKE A WHILE TO EXPLAIN...
BUT, YOU SEE...
INTER-MISSION
JA-JA-JA! SHA-LA-LI-LA-LA-JAAN (MUSIC BREAK) ~!
HE'S STRONG! HE'S A GENIUS!
RENNN... GOKUINNNN!!
THIRD VERSE
BURU (TREMBLE)
BURU
...WHAT DID YOU SAY?
KIIII (SCREECH)
I STILL DON'T.
I WAS INTERESTED IN THE RARE OUTLIER, AL, WHO DIDN'T HAVE A BLOODLINE WEAPON!!
ON TOP OF THAT...

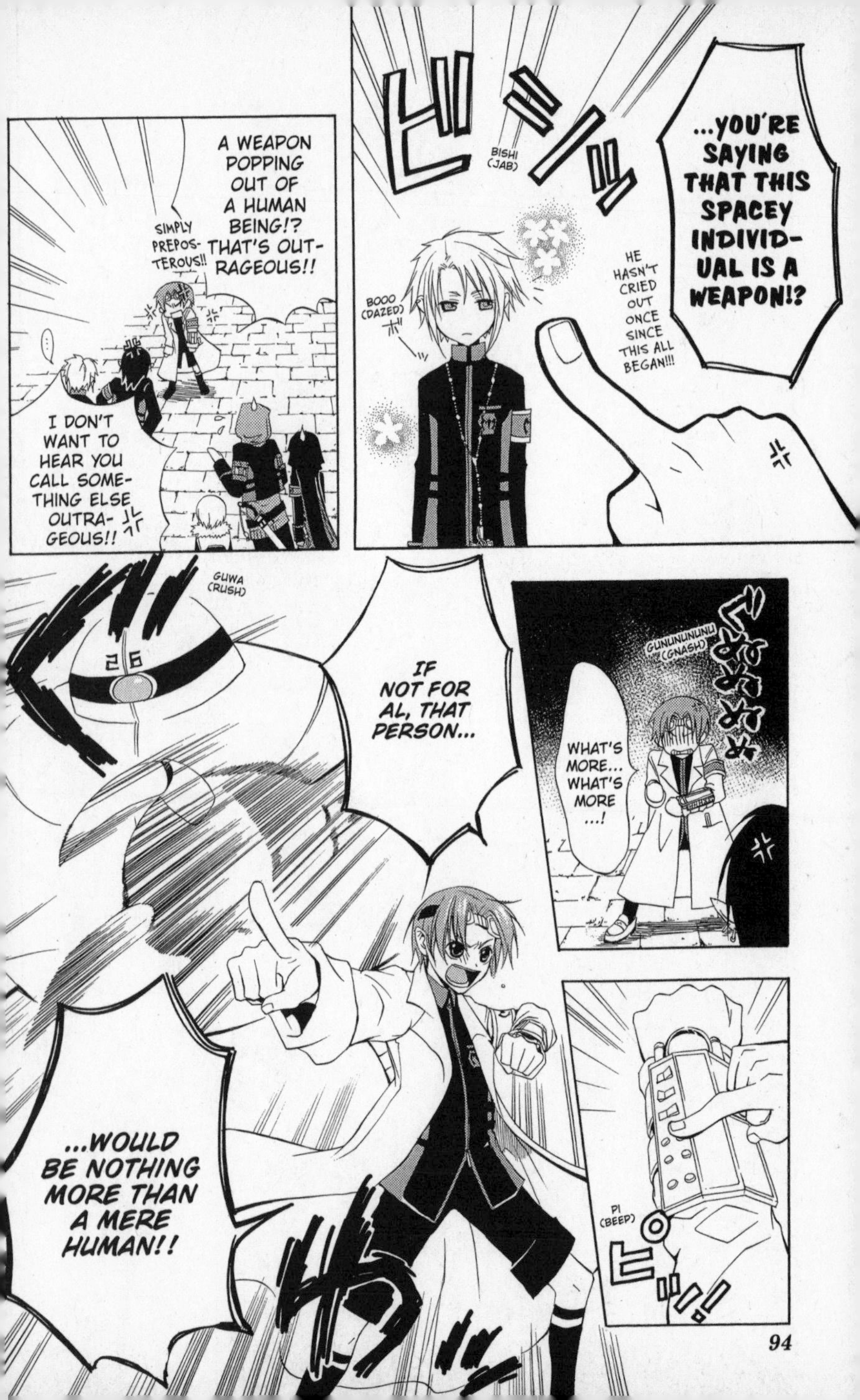
BISHI (JAB)
...YOU'RE SAYING THAT THIS SPACEY INDIVIDUAL IS A WEAPON!?
HE HASN'T CRIED OUT ONCE SINCE THIS ALL BEGAN!!!
BOOO (DAZED)
A WEAPON POPPING OUT OF A HUMAN BEING!? THAT'S OUTRAGEOUS!!
SIMPLY PREPOSTEROUS!!
...
I DON'T WANT TO HEAR YOU CALL SOMETHING ELSE OUTRAGEOUS!!
GUNUNUNUNU (GNASH)
WHAT'S MORE... WHAT'S MORE ...!
PI (BEEP)
GUWA (RUSH)
IF NOT FOR AL, THAT PERSON...
...WOULD BE NOTHING MORE THAN A MERE HUMAN!!

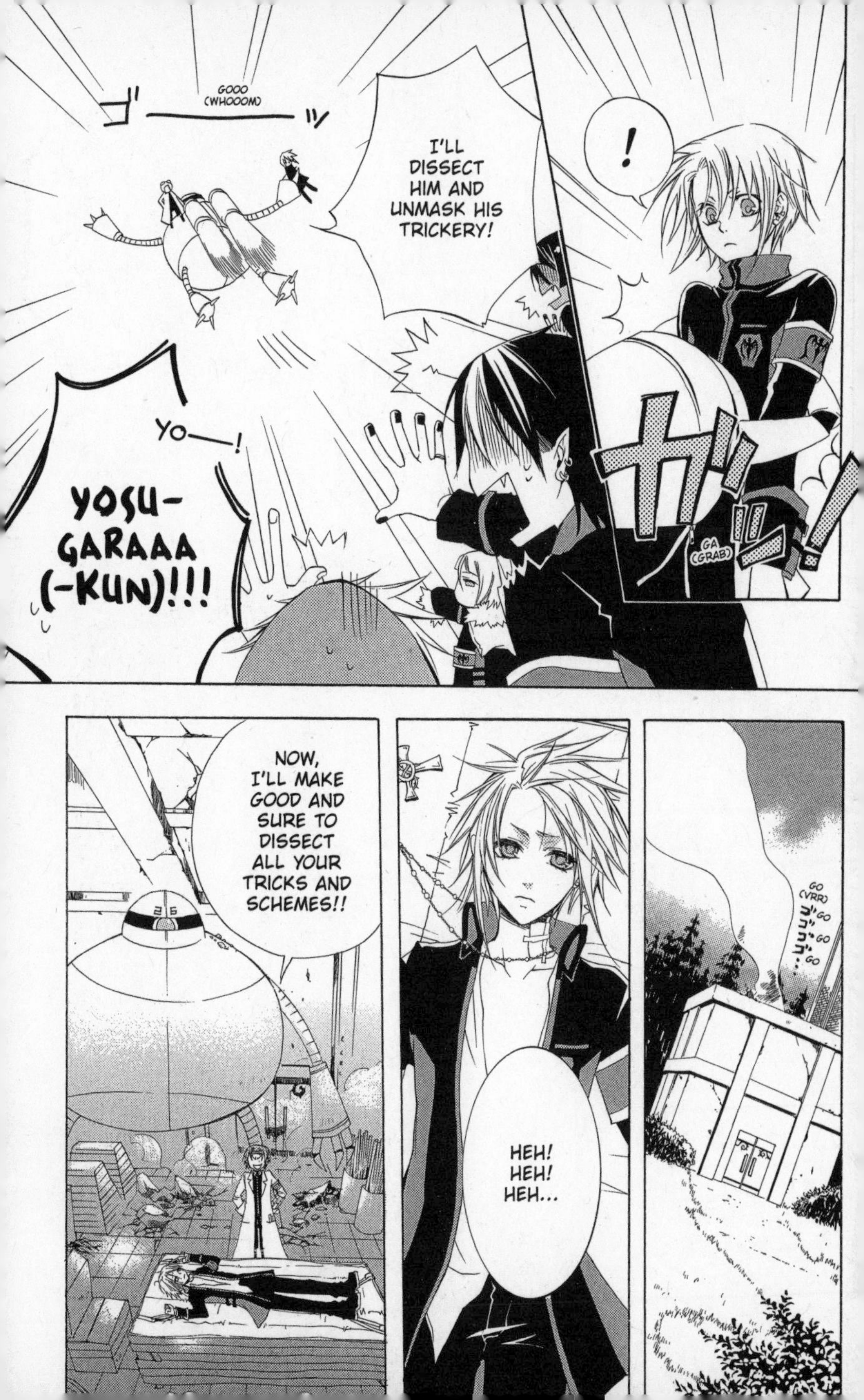
!
GA (GRAB)
GOOO (WHOOOM)
I'LL DISSECT HIM AND UNMASK HIS TRICKERY!
YO—!
YOSU-GARAAA (-KUN)!!!
GO (VRR) GO GO GO...
HEH! HEH! HEH...
NOW, I'LL MAKE GOOD AND SURE TO DISSECT ALL YOUR TRICKS AND SCHEMES!!

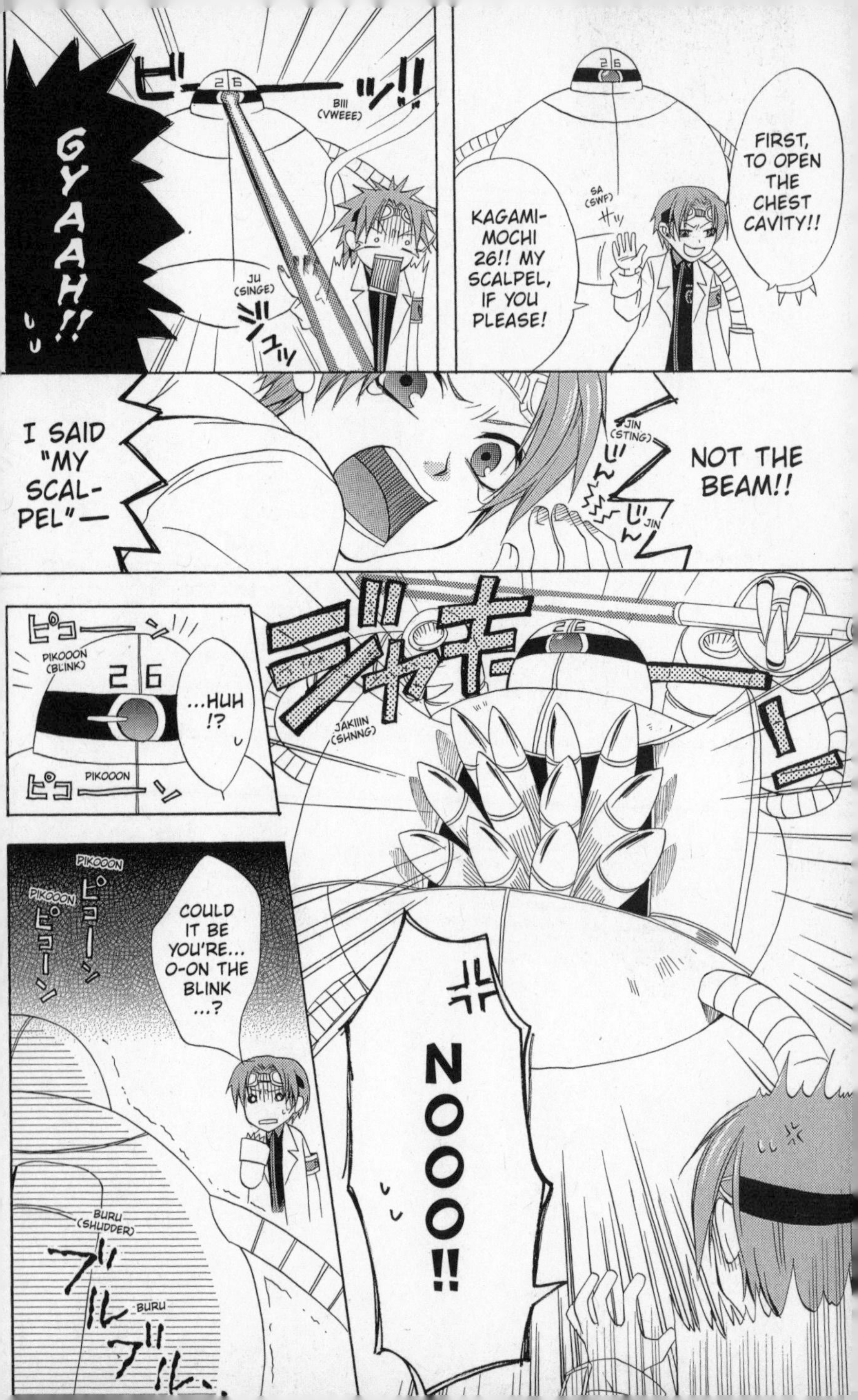
FIRST, TO OPEN THE CHEST CAVITY!!
SA (SWF)
KAGAMI-MOCHI 26!! MY SCALPEL, IF YOU PLEASE!
BIII (VWEEE)
GYAAAH!!
JU (SINGE)
I SAID "MY SCAL-PEL"—
NOT THE BEAM!!
JIN (STING)
JIN
JAKIIIN (SHNNG)
PIKOOON (BLINK)
...HUH!?
PIKOOON
NOOOO!!
PIKOOON
PIKOOON
COULD IT BE YOU'RE... O-ON THE BLINK ...?
BURU (SHUDDER)
BURU

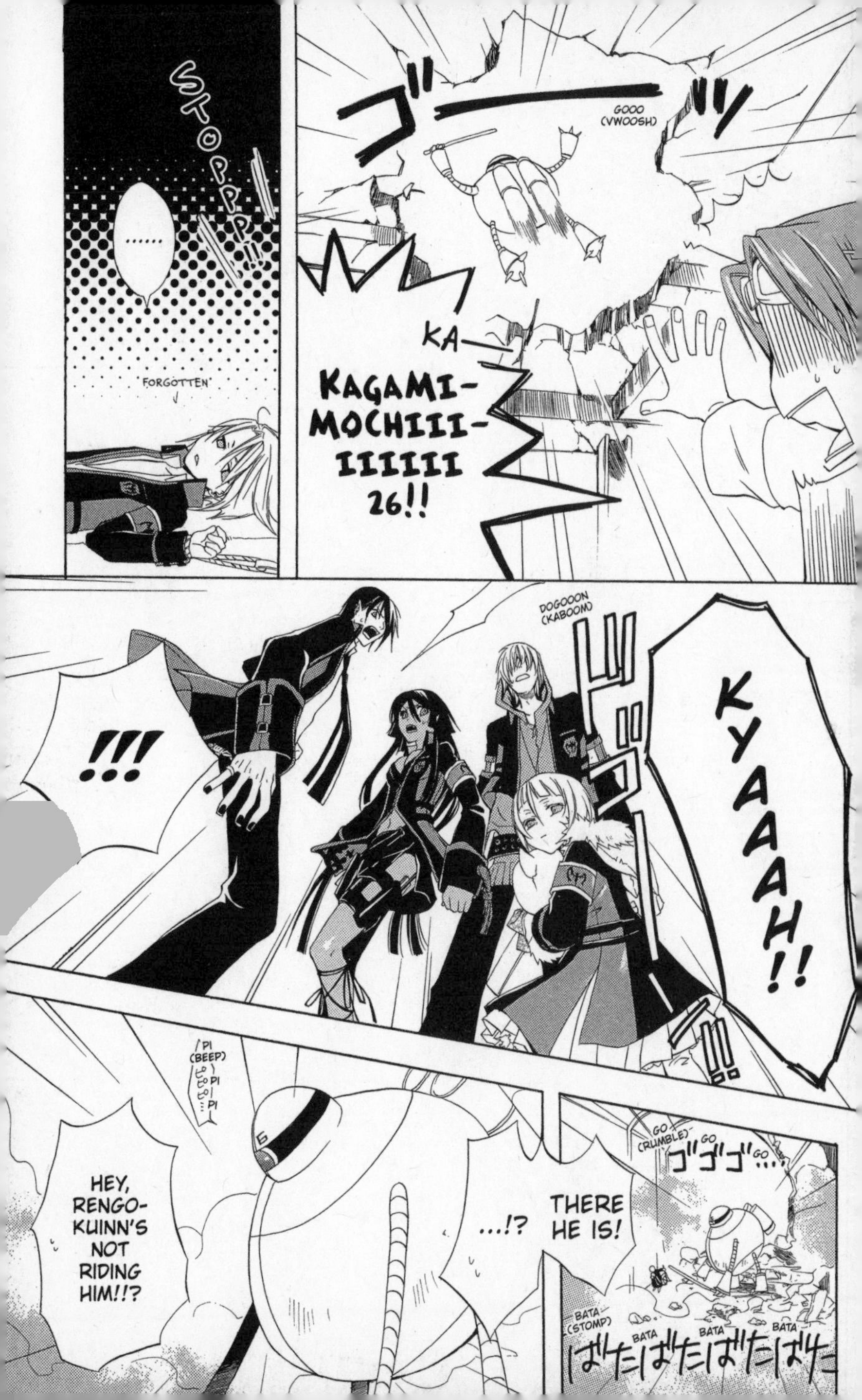
GOOO (VWOOSH)
ゴーーッ
KA—
KAGAMI-MOCHIII-IIIIII 26!!
STOPPP!!
......
FORGOTTEN
DOGOOON (KABOOM)
ドゴーン!!
KYAAAH!!
!!!
GO (RUMBLE) GO GO...
ゴゴゴ...
THERE HE IS!
BATA (STOMP) BATA BATA BATA
ばたばたばたばた
PI (BEEP) PI PI
ピピピ...
...!?
HEY, RENGO-KUINN'S NOT RIDING HIM!!?

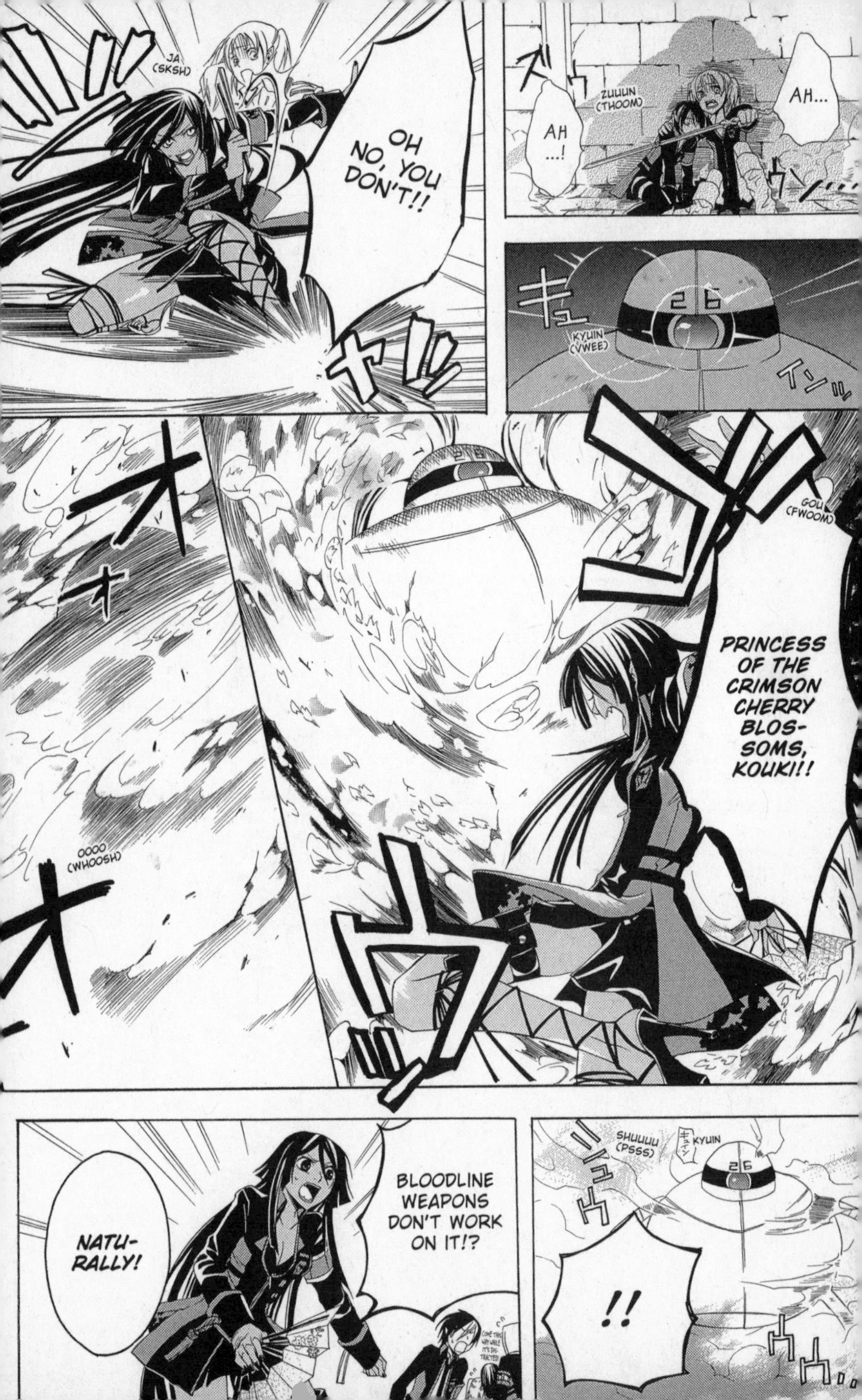
AH...
ZUUUN (THOOM)
AH ...!
KYUIN (VWEE)
JA (SKSH)
OH NO, YOU DON'T!!
GOU (FWOOM)
PRINCESS OF THE CRIMSON CHERRY BLOS-SOMS, KOUKI!!
OOOO (WHOOSH)
SHUUUU (PSSS)
KYUIN
!!
BLOODLINE WEAPONS DON'T WORK ON IT!?
NATU-RALLY!
COME THIS WAY WHILE IT'S DIS-TRACTED!

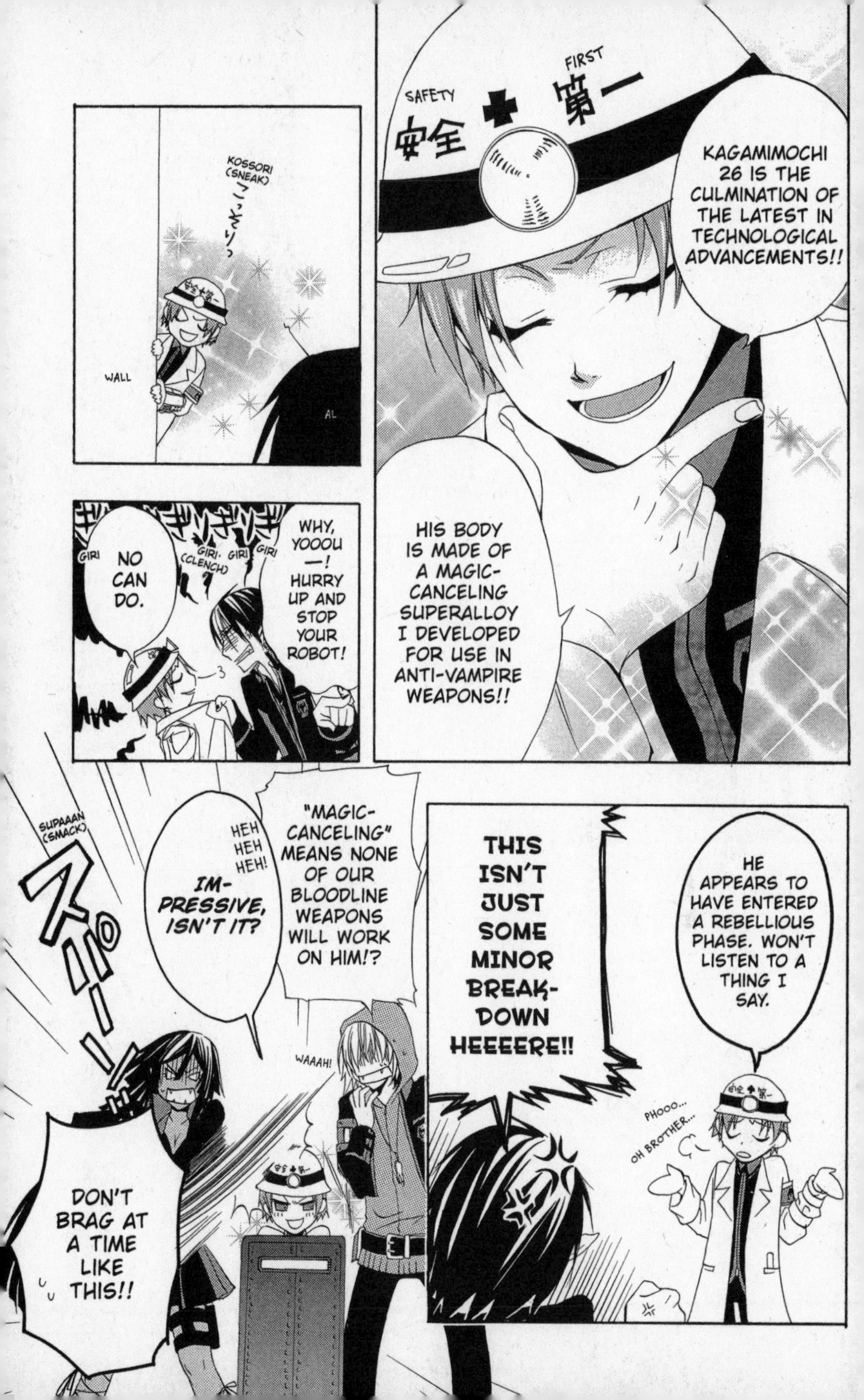

FIRST
SAFETY
KAGAMIMOCHI 26 IS THE CULMINATION OF THE LATEST IN TECHNOLOGICAL ADVANCEMENTS!!
HIS BODY IS MADE OF A MAGIC-CANCELING SUPERALLOY I DEVELOPED FOR USE IN ANTI-VAMPIRE WEAPONS!!
KOSSORI (SNEAK)
WALL
AL
WHY, YOOOU—! HURRY UP AND STOP YOUR ROBOT!
GIRI GIRI (CLENCH) GIRI GIRI
NO CAN DO.
HE APPEARS TO HAVE ENTERED A REBELLIOUS PHASE. WON'T LISTEN TO A THING I SAY.
PHOOO... OH BROTHER...
THIS ISN'T JUST SOME MINOR BREAK-DOWN HEEEEERE!!
"MAGIC-CANCELING" MEANS NONE OF OUR BLOODLINE WEAPONS WILL WORK ON HIM!?
HEH HEH HEH! IM-PRESSIVE, ISN'T IT?
WAAAH!
SUPAAAN (SMACK)
DON'T BRAG AT A TIME LIKE THIS!!

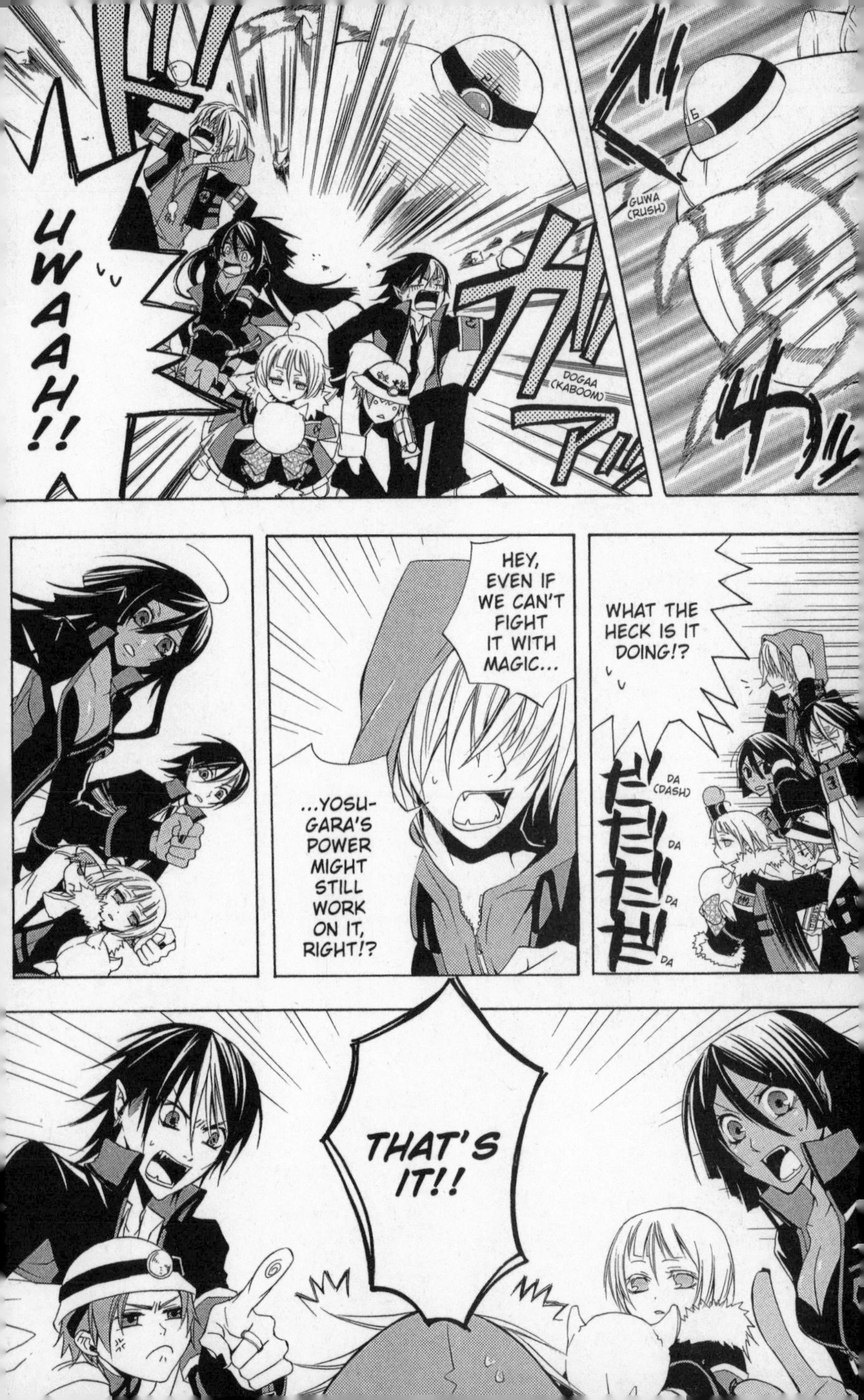
GUWA (RUSH)
DOGAA (KABOOM)
UWAAAH!!
WHAT THE HECK IS IT DOING!?
DA (DASH) DA DA DA
HEY, EVEN IF WE CAN'T FIGHT IT WITH MAGIC...
...YOSU-GARA'S POWER MIGHT STILL WORK ON IT, RIGHT!?
THAT'S IT!!

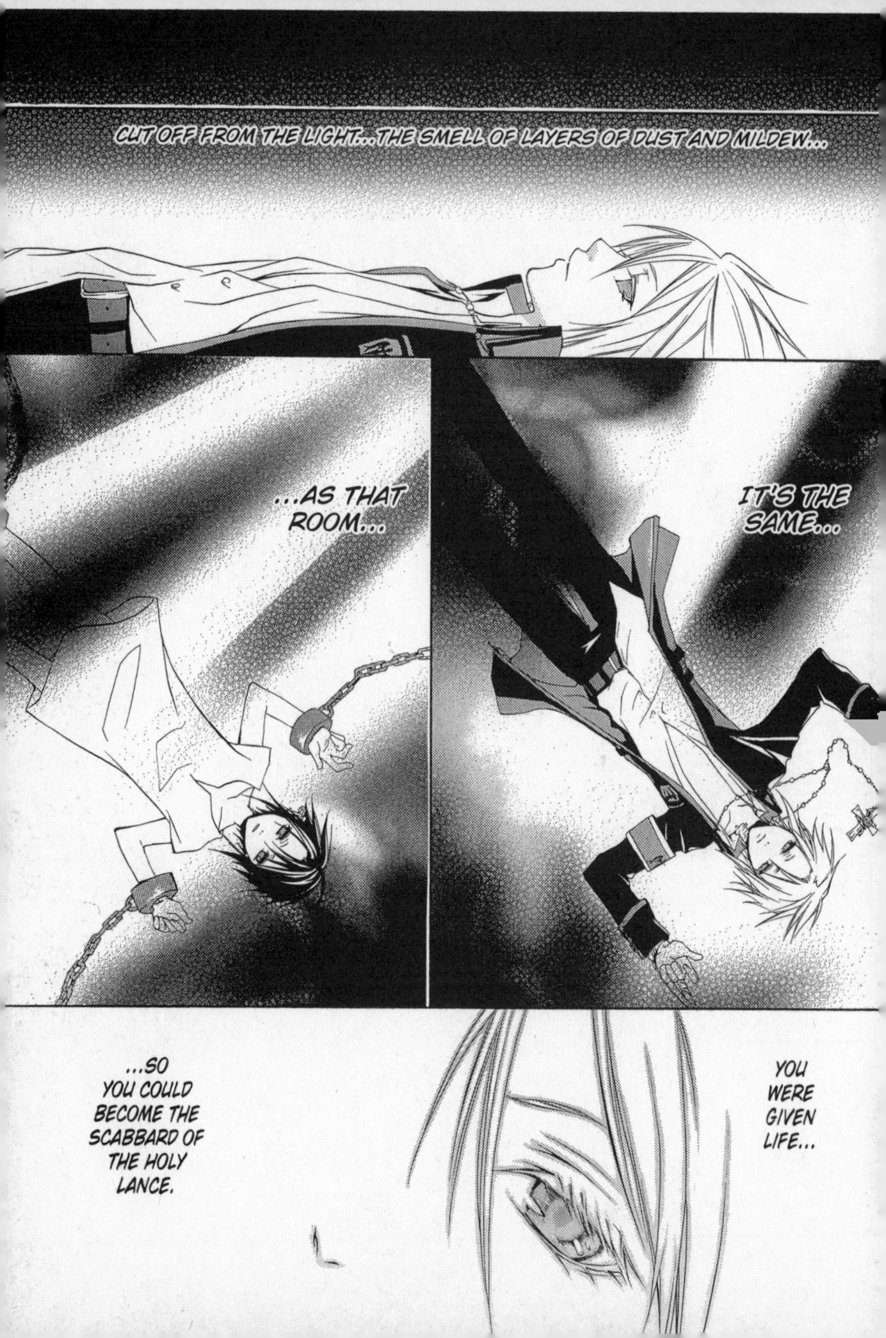
CUT OFF FROM THE LIGHT...THE SMELL OF LAYERS OF DUST AND MILDEW...
IT'S THE SAME...
...AS THAT ROOM...
YOU WERE GIVEN LIFE...
...SO YOU COULD BECOME THE SCABBARD OF THE HOLY LANCE.

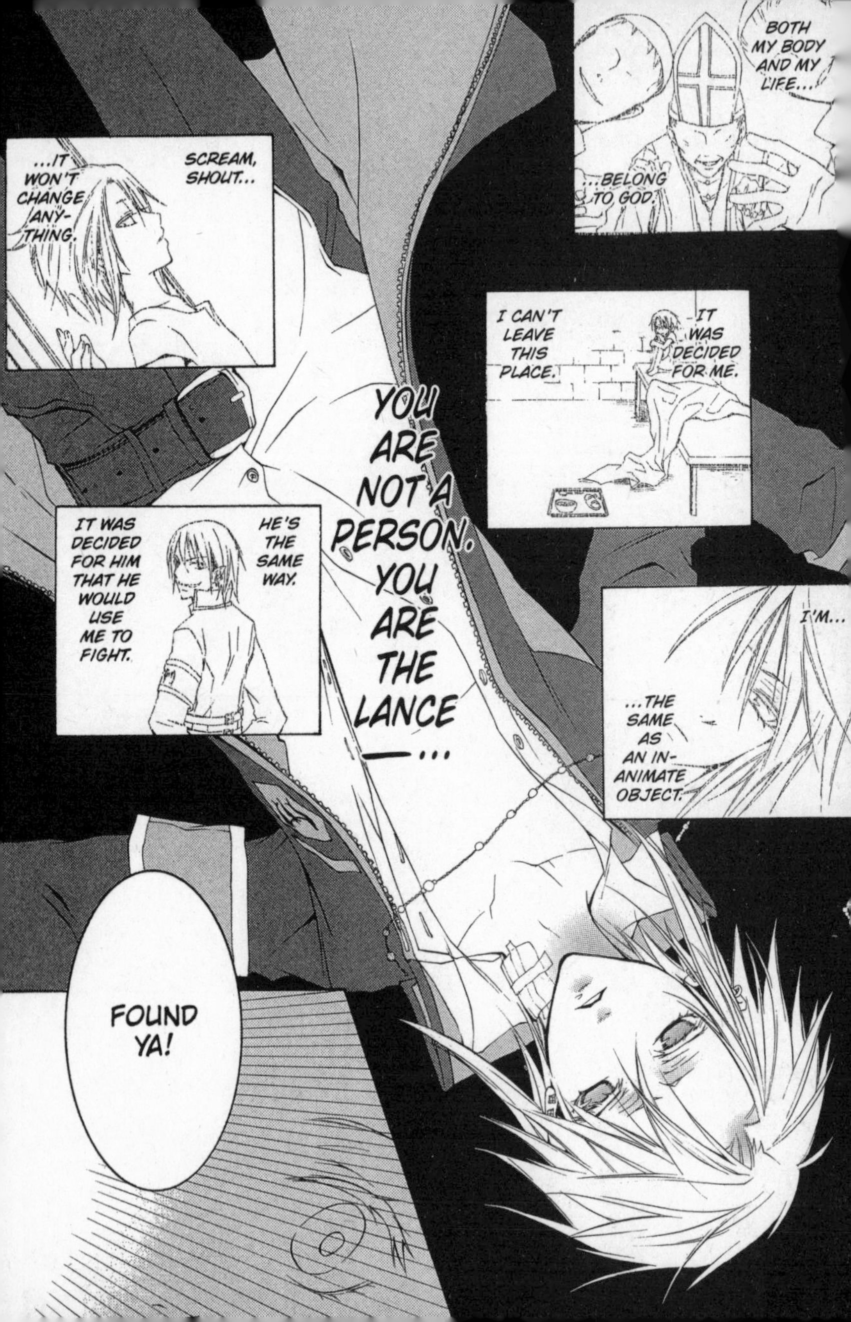
BOTH MY BODY AND MY LIFE...
...BELONG TO GOD.
SCREAM, SHOUT...
...IT WON'T CHANGE ANYTHING.
IT WAS DECIDED FOR ME.
I CAN'T LEAVE THIS PLACE.
HE'S THE SAME WAY.
IT WAS DECIDED FOR HIM THAT HE WOULD USE ME TO FIGHT.
YOU ARE NOT A PERSON. YOU ARE THE LANCE—...
I'M...
...THE SAME AS AN INANIMATE OBJECT.
FOUND YA!

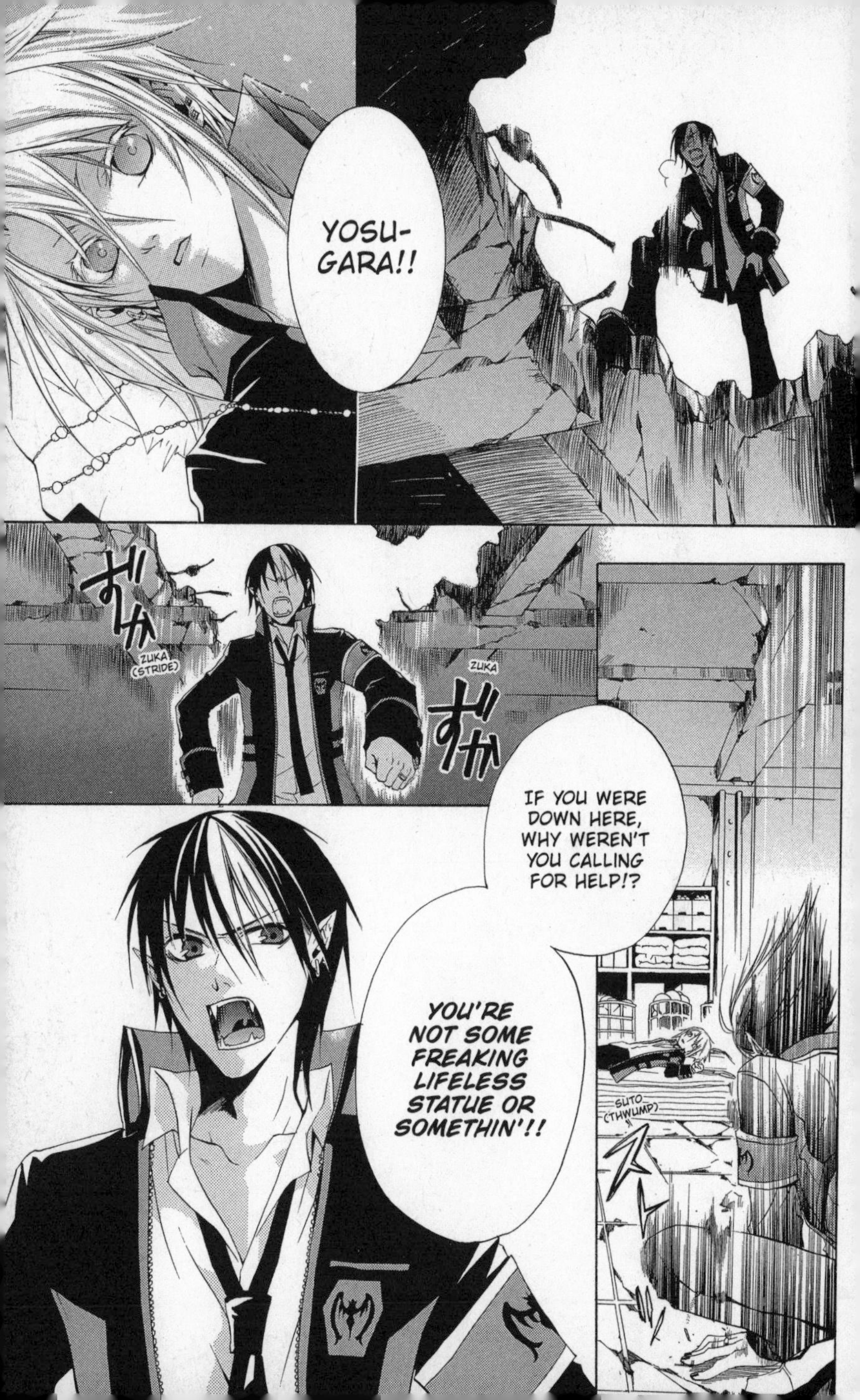
YOSU-GARA!!
ZUKA
ずか
ZUKA (STRIDE)
ずか
SUTO (THWUMP)
IF YOU WERE DOWN HERE, WHY WEREN'T YOU CALLING FOR HELP!?
YOU'RE NOT SOME FREAKING LIFELESS STATUE OR SOMETHIN'!!

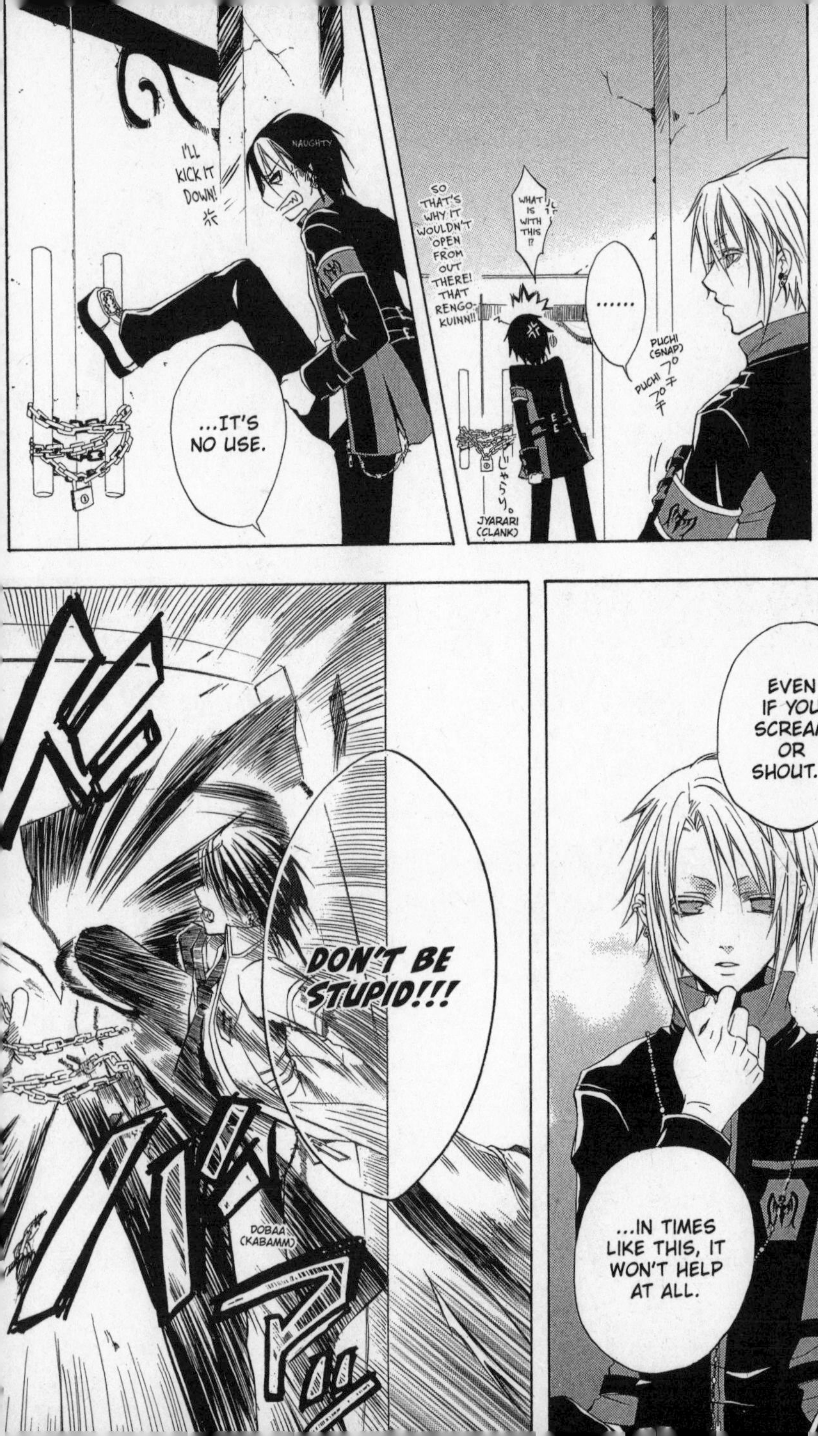
WHAT IS WITH THIS!?
SO THAT'S WHY IT WOULDN'T OPEN FROM OUT THERE! THAT RENGO-KUINN!!
......
PUCHI (SNAP) PUCHI
じゃらり。
JYARARI (CLANK)
NAUGHTY
I'LL KICK IT DOWN!
...IT'S NO USE.
EVEN IF YOU SCREAM OR SHOUT...
...IN TIMES LIKE THIS, IT WON'T HELP AT ALL.
DON'T BE STUPID!!!
DOBAA (KABAMM)

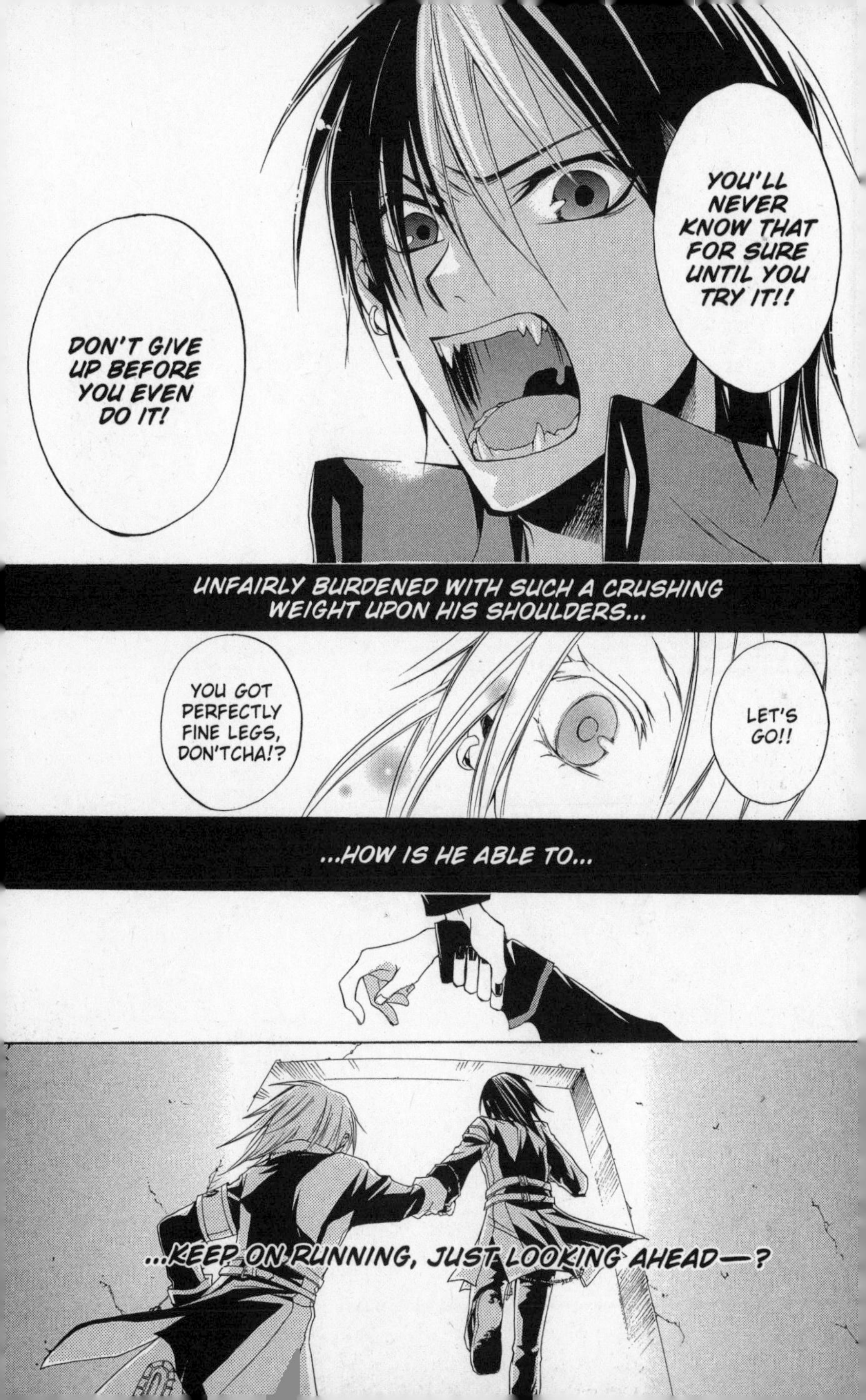
YOU'LL NEVER KNOW THAT FOR SURE UNTIL YOU TRY IT!!
DON'T GIVE UP BEFORE YOU EVEN DO IT!
UNFAIRLY BURDENED WITH SUCH A CRUSHING WEIGHT UPON HIS SHOULDERS...
LET'S GO!!
YOU GOT PERFECTLY FINE LEGS, DON'TCHA!?
...HOW IS HE ABLE TO...
...KEEP ON RUNNING, JUST LOOKING AHEAD—?

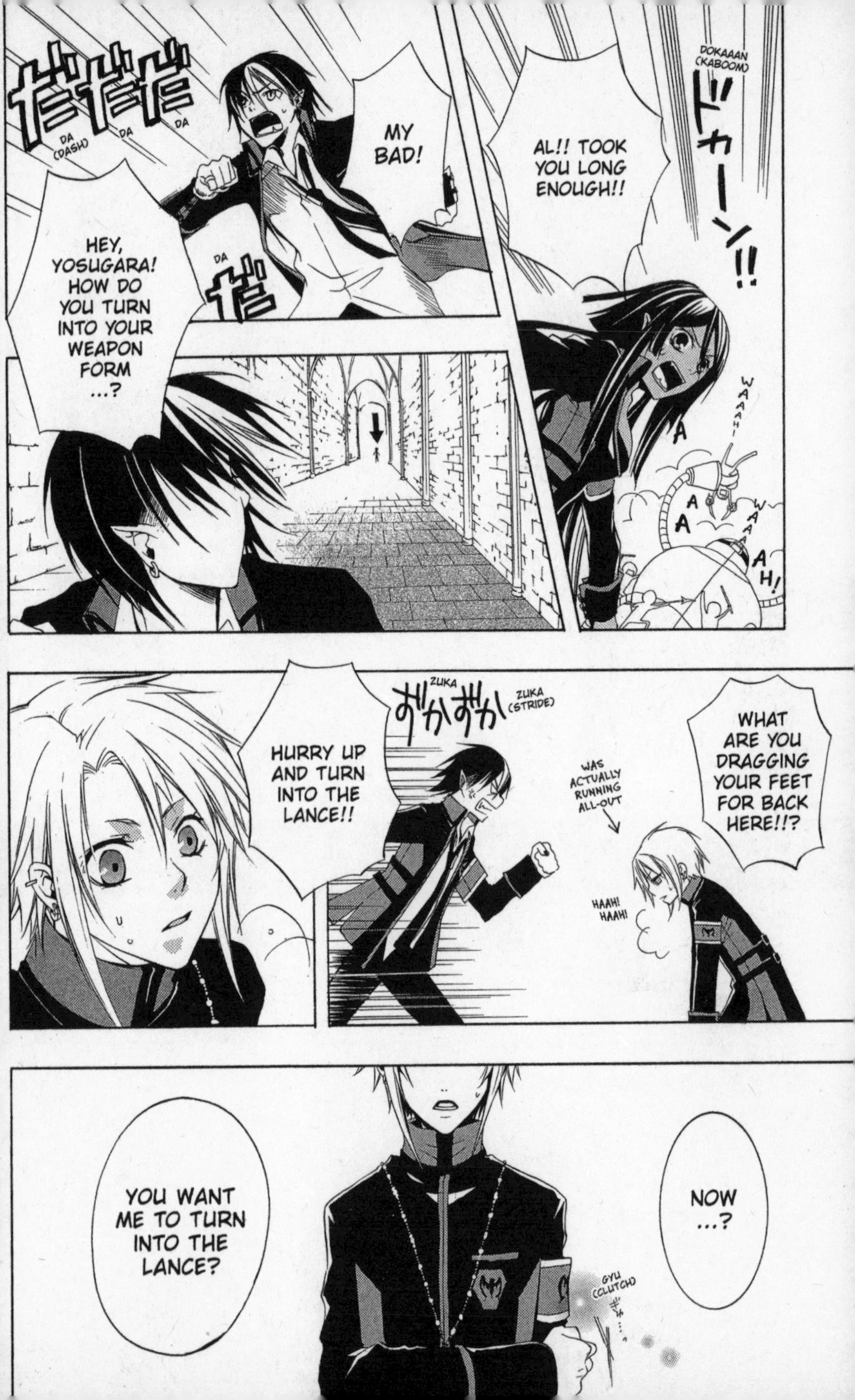

DOKAAAN (KABOOM)
ドカーン!!
AL!! TOOK YOU LONG ENOUGH!!
WAAAH!
AAA
WAAAAH!
MY BAD!
だだだ
DA (DASH) DA DA
DA
だ
HEY, YOSUGARA! HOW DO YOU TURN INTO YOUR WEAPON FORM ...?
WHAT ARE YOU DRAGGING YOUR FEET FOR BACK HERE!!?
WAS ACTUALLY RUNNING ALL-OUT
HAAH! HAAH!
ずかずか
ZUKA ZUKA (STRIDE)
HURRY UP AND TURN INTO THE LANCE!!
NOW ...?
YOU WANT ME TO TURN INTO THE LANCE?
GYU (CLUTCH)
ぎゅ…

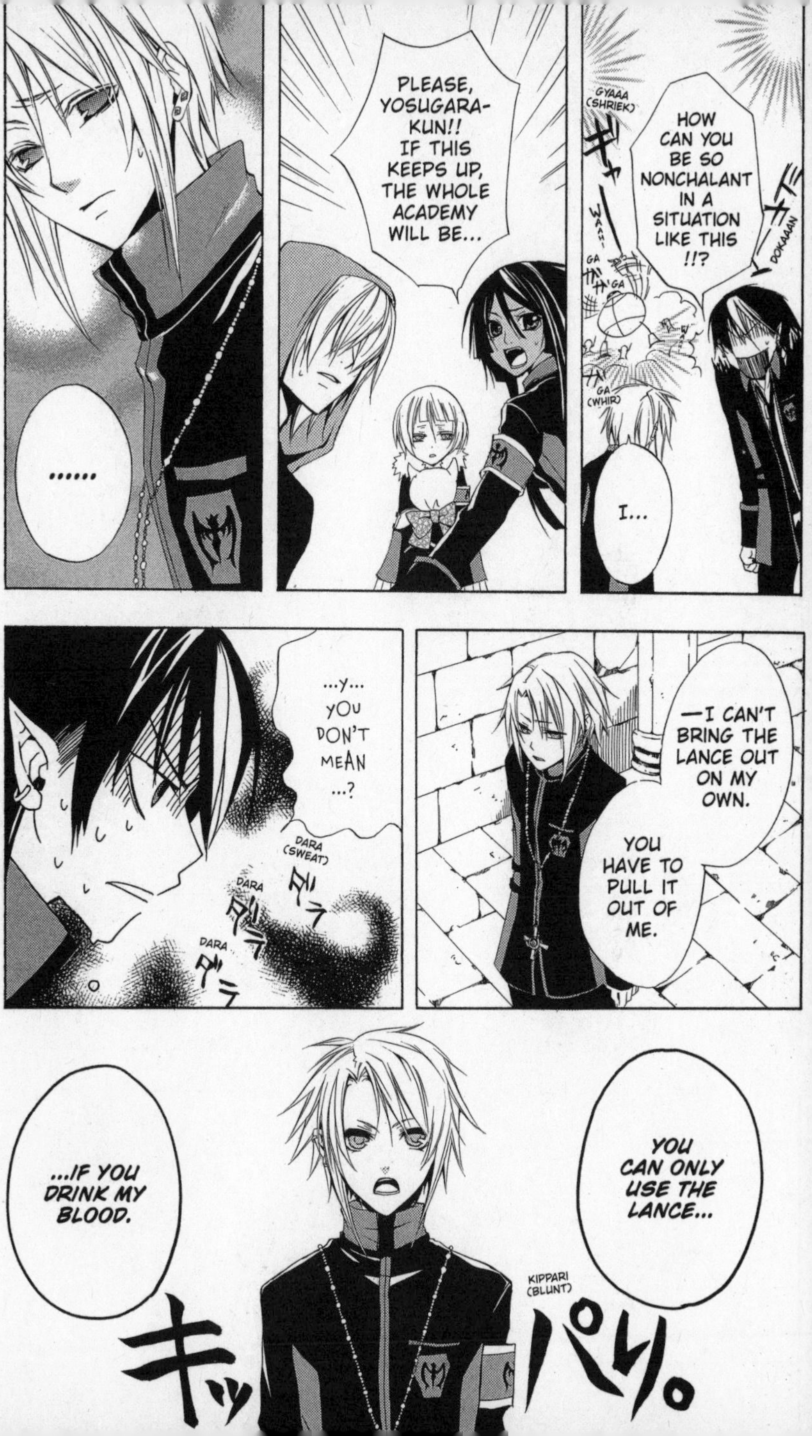
GYAAA (SHRIEK)
HOW CAN YOU BE SO NONCHALANT IN A SITUATION LIKE THIS!!?
DOKAAAN
WAAH!
GA
GA
GA (WHIR)
I...
PLEASE, YOSUGARA-KUN!! IF THIS KEEPS UP, THE WHOLE ACADEMY WILL BE...
......
—I CAN'T BRING THE LANCE OUT ON MY OWN.
YOU HAVE TO PULL IT OUT OF ME.
...Y... YOU DON'T MEAN ...?
DARA (SWEAT)
DARA
DARA
YOU CAN ONLY USE THE LANCE...
KIPPARI (BLUNT)
...IF YOU DRINK MY BLOOD.

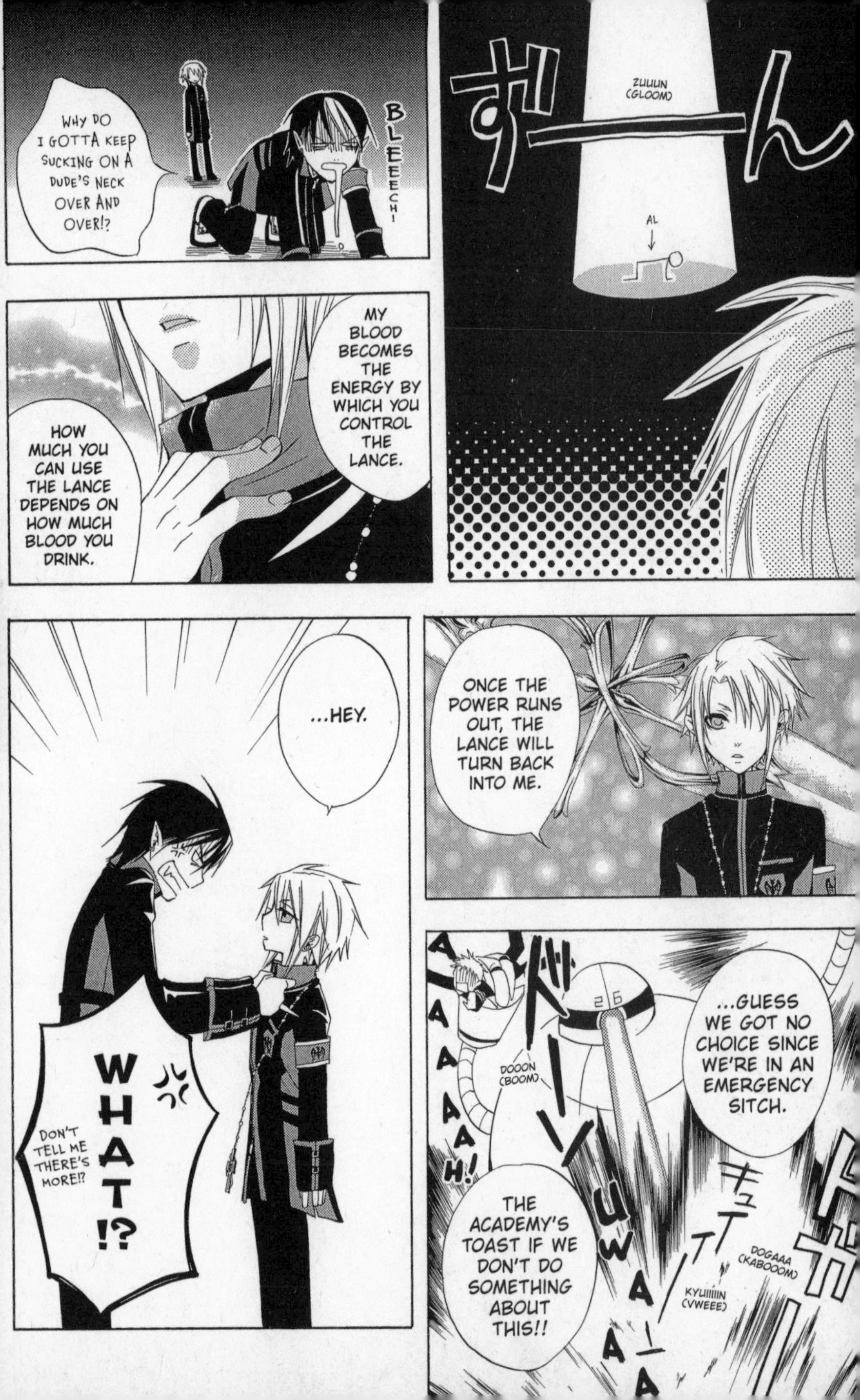
ZUUUN (GLOOM)
AL
WHY DO I GOTTA KEEP SUCKING ON A DUDE'S NECK OVER AND OVER!?
BLEEECH!
MY BLOOD BECOMES THE ENERGY BY WHICH YOU CONTROL THE LANCE.
HOW MUCH YOU CAN USE THE LANCE DEPENDS ON HOW MUCH BLOOD YOU DRINK.
ONCE THE POWER RUNS OUT, THE LANCE WILL TURN BACK INTO ME.
AAAAAAAH!
DOOON (BOOM)
...GUESS WE GOT NO CHOICE SINCE WE'RE IN AN EMERGENCY SITCH.
THE ACADEMY'S TOAST IF WE DON'T DO SOMETHING ABOUT THIS!!
KYUIIIIN (VWEEE)
DOGAAA (KABOOOM)
...HEY.
WHAT!?
DON'T TELL ME THERE'S MORE!?

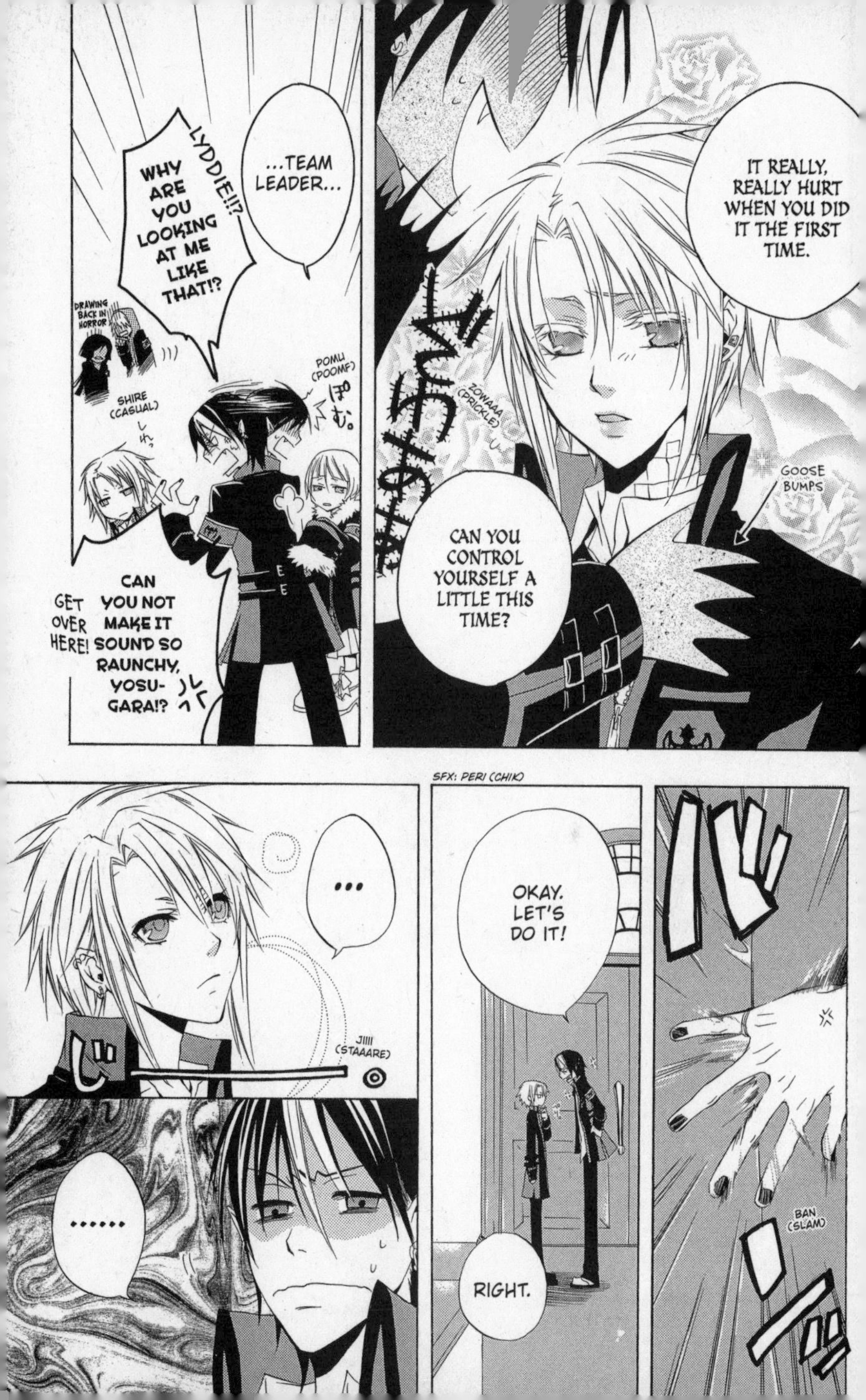
IT REALLY, REALLY HURT WHEN YOU DID IT THE FIRST TIME.
ZOWAAA (PRICKLE)
GOOSE BUMPS
CAN YOU CONTROL YOURSELF A LITTLE THIS TIME?
...TEAM LEADER...
LYDDIE!!?
WHY ARE YOU LOOKING AT ME LIKE THAT!?
POMU (POOMF)
ぽむ。
DRAWING BACK IN HORROR
SHIRE (CASUAL)
CAN YOU NOT MAKE IT SOUND SO RAUNCHY, YOSU-GARA!?
GET OVER HERE!
SFX: PERI (CHIK)
BAN (SLAM)
OKAY. LET'S DO IT!
RIGHT.
...
JIIII (STAAARE)
......

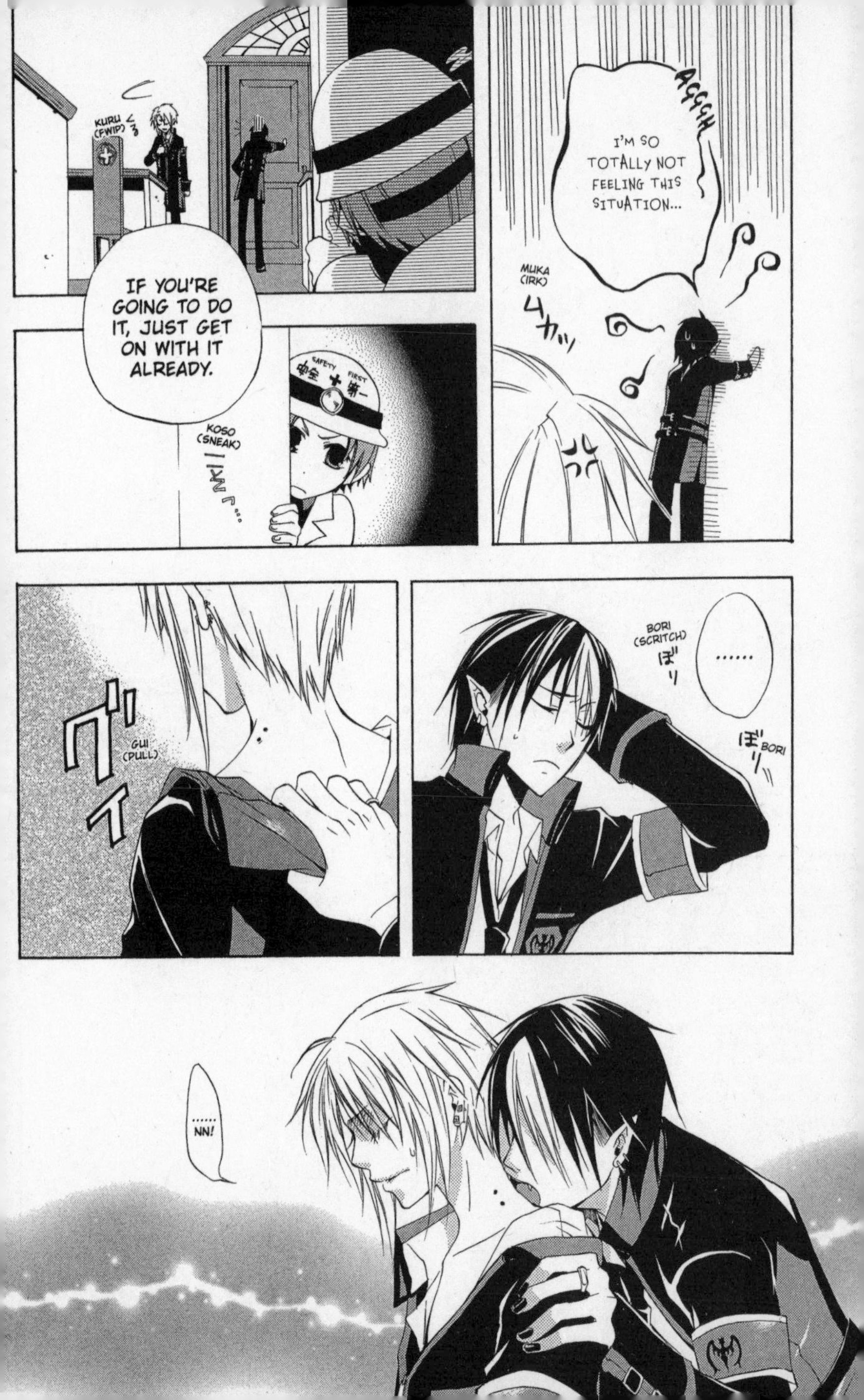

AGGGH
I'M SO TOTALLY NOT FEELING THIS SITUATION...
MUKA (IRK)
ムカッ
KURU (FWIP)
くる
IF YOU'RE GOING TO DO IT, JUST GET ON WITH IT ALREADY.
SAFETY FIRST
安全第一
KOSO (SNEAK)
こそ…
......
BORI (SCRITCH)
ぼり
ぼり BORI
グイ
GUI (PULL)
......
NN!

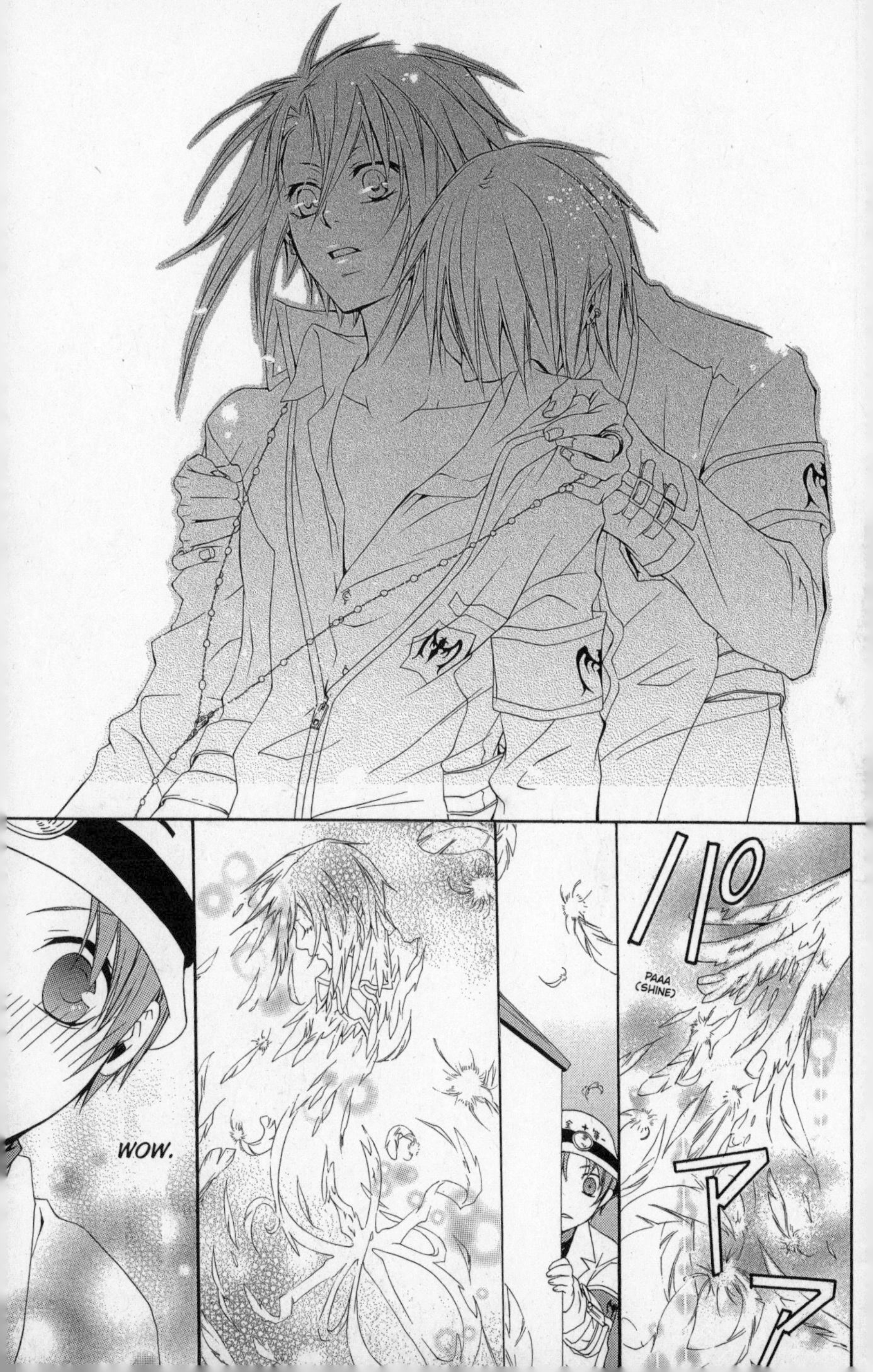
パアア
PAAA (SHINE)
WOW.

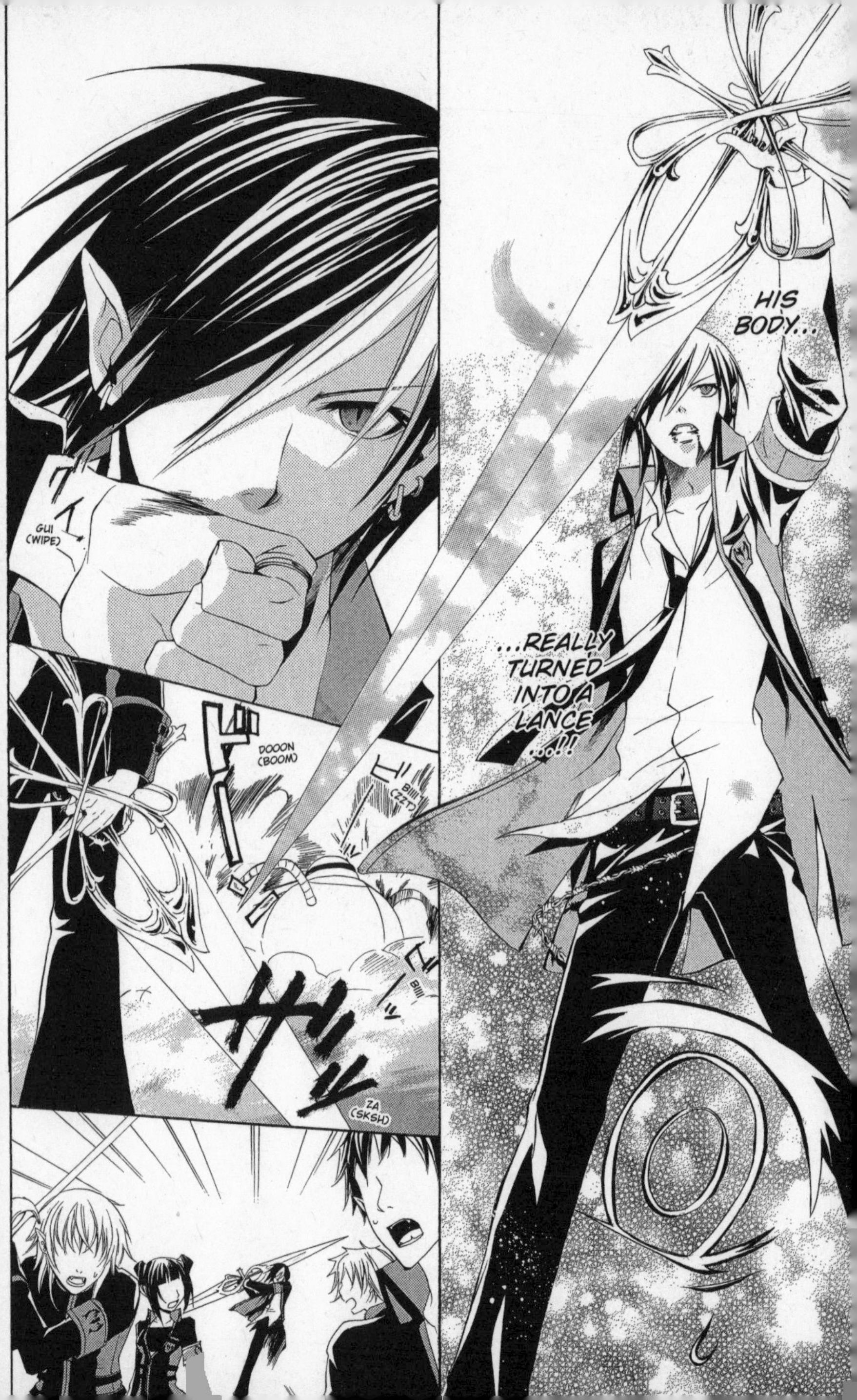
HIS BODY...
...REALLY TURNED INTO A LANCE...!!
GUI (WIPE)
DOOON (BOOM)
BIII (ZZT)
BIII
ZA (SKSH)

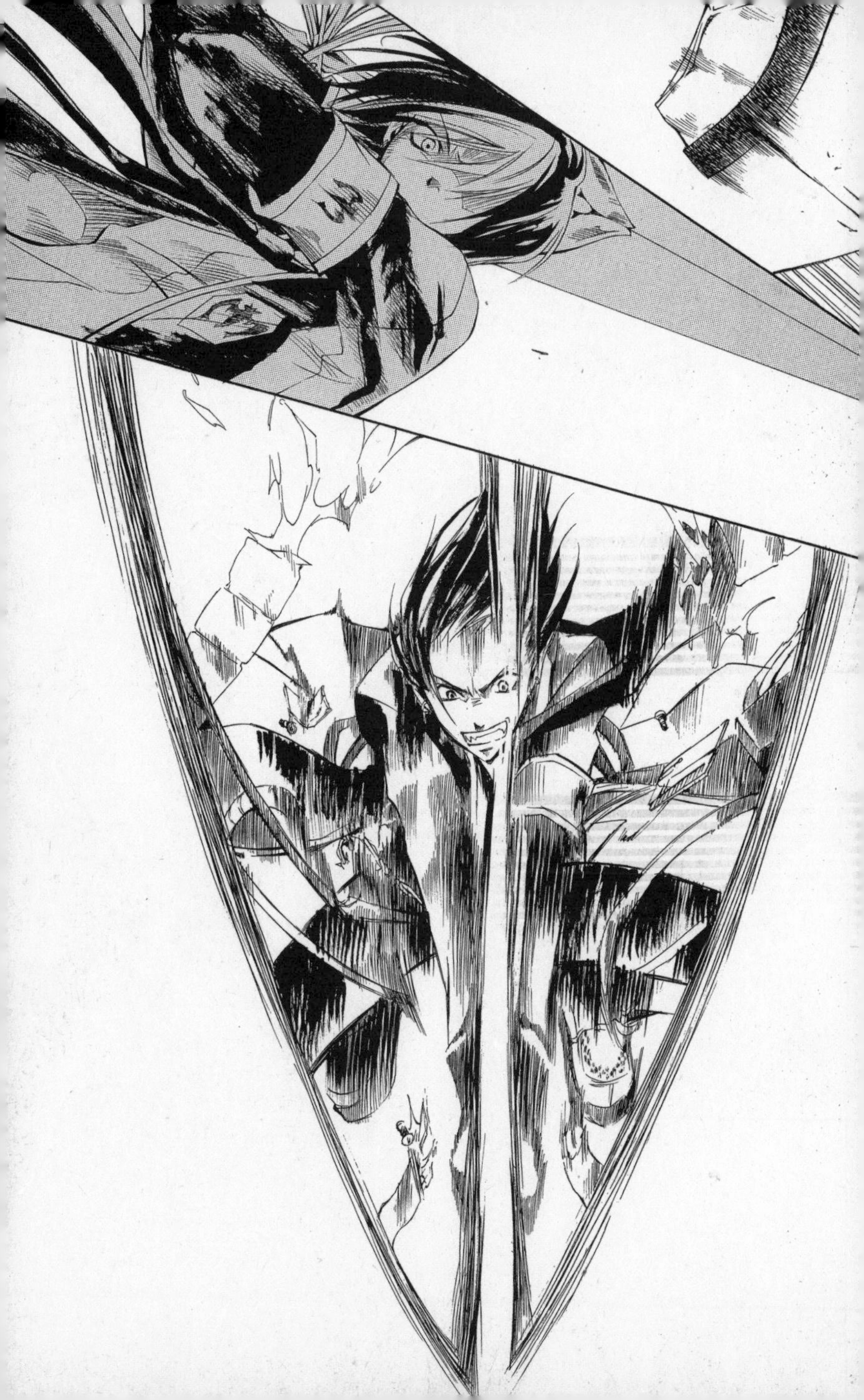

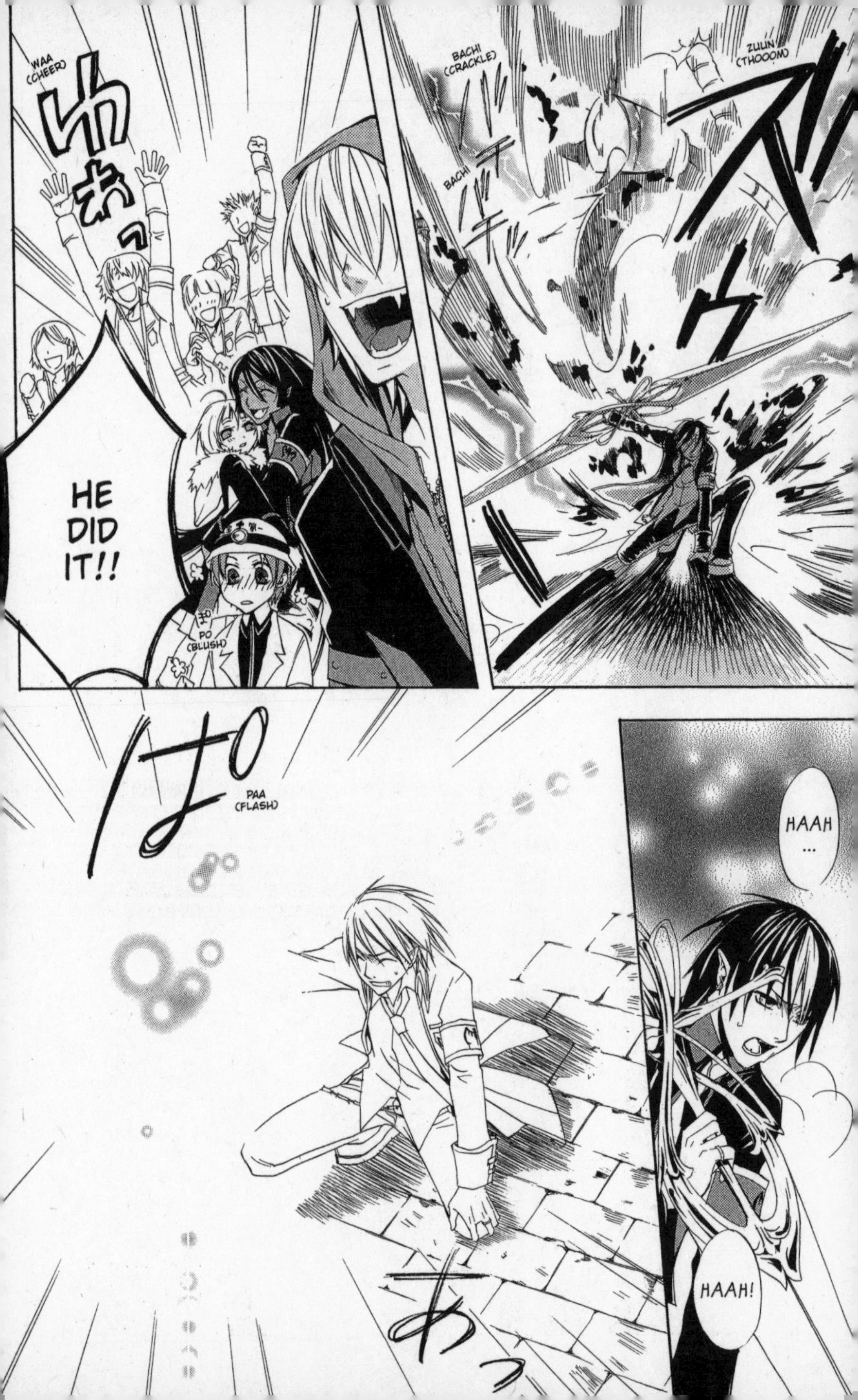
ZUUN (THOOOM)
BACHI (CRACKLE)
BACHI
WAA (CHEER)
HE DID IT!!
PO (BLUSH)
HAAH ...
HAAH!
PAA (FLASH)

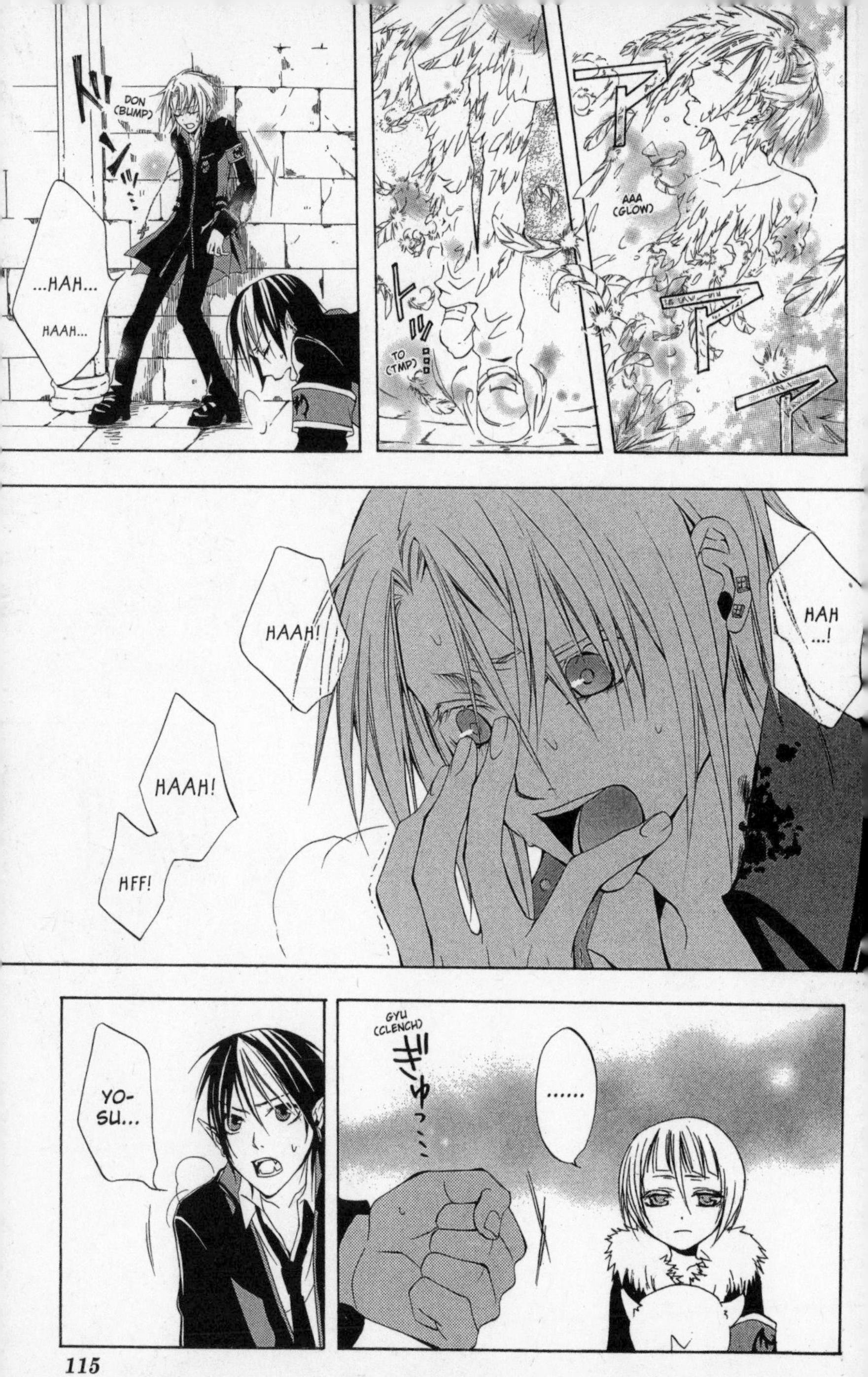
AAA (GLOW)
TO (TMP)
DON (BUMP)
...HAH... HAAH...
HAH ...!
HAAH!
HAAH!
HFF!
GYU (CLENCH)
......
YO-SU...

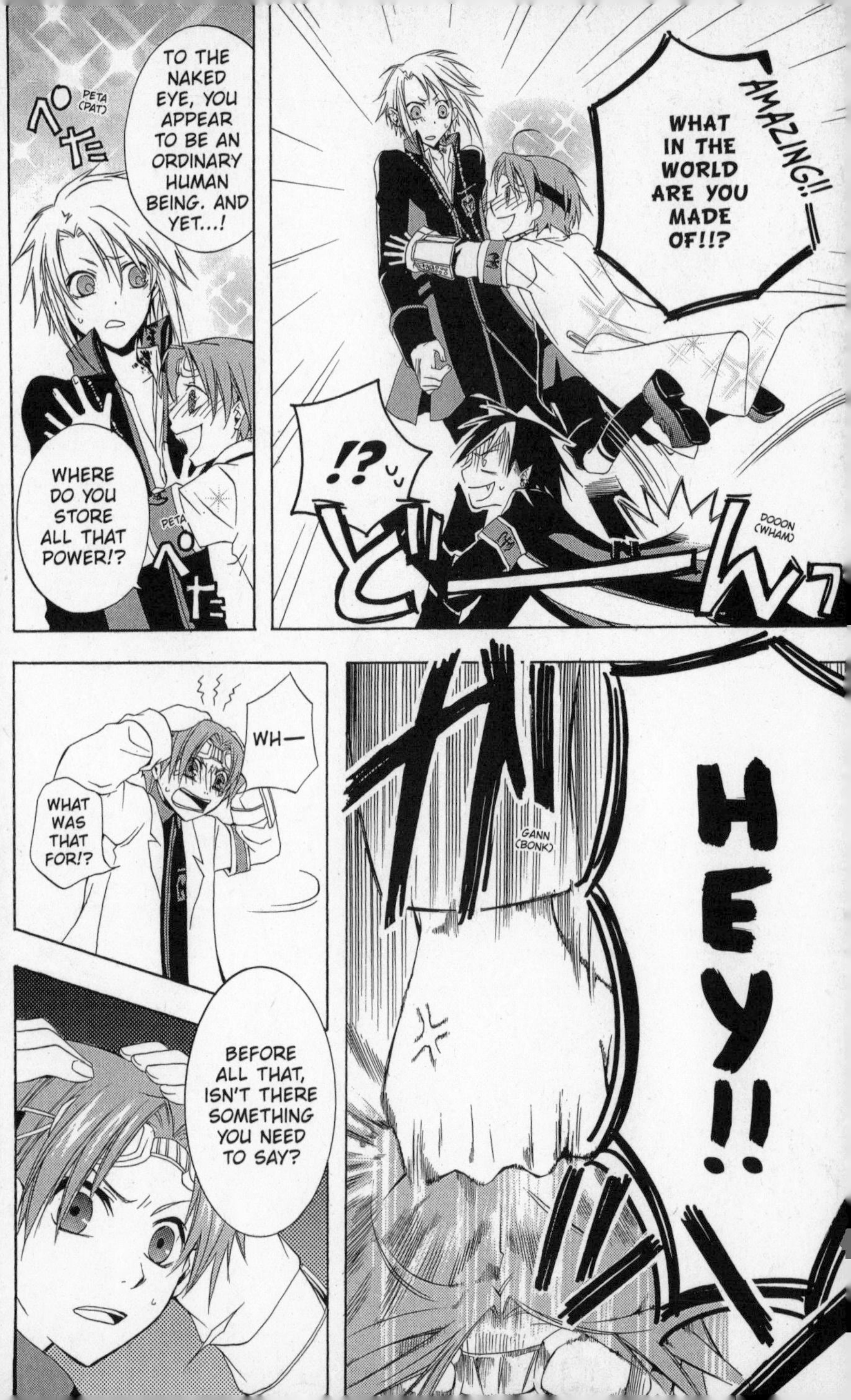
AMAZING!!
WHAT IN THE WORLD ARE YOU MADE OF!!?
DOOON (WHAM)
!?
TO THE NAKED EYE, YOU APPEAR TO BE AN ORDINARY HUMAN BEING. AND YET...!
PETA (PAT)
WHERE DO YOU STORE ALL THAT POWER!?
PETA
HEY!!
GANN (BONK)
WH—
WHAT WAS THAT FOR!?
BEFORE ALL THAT, ISN'T THERE SOMETHING YOU NEED TO SAY?

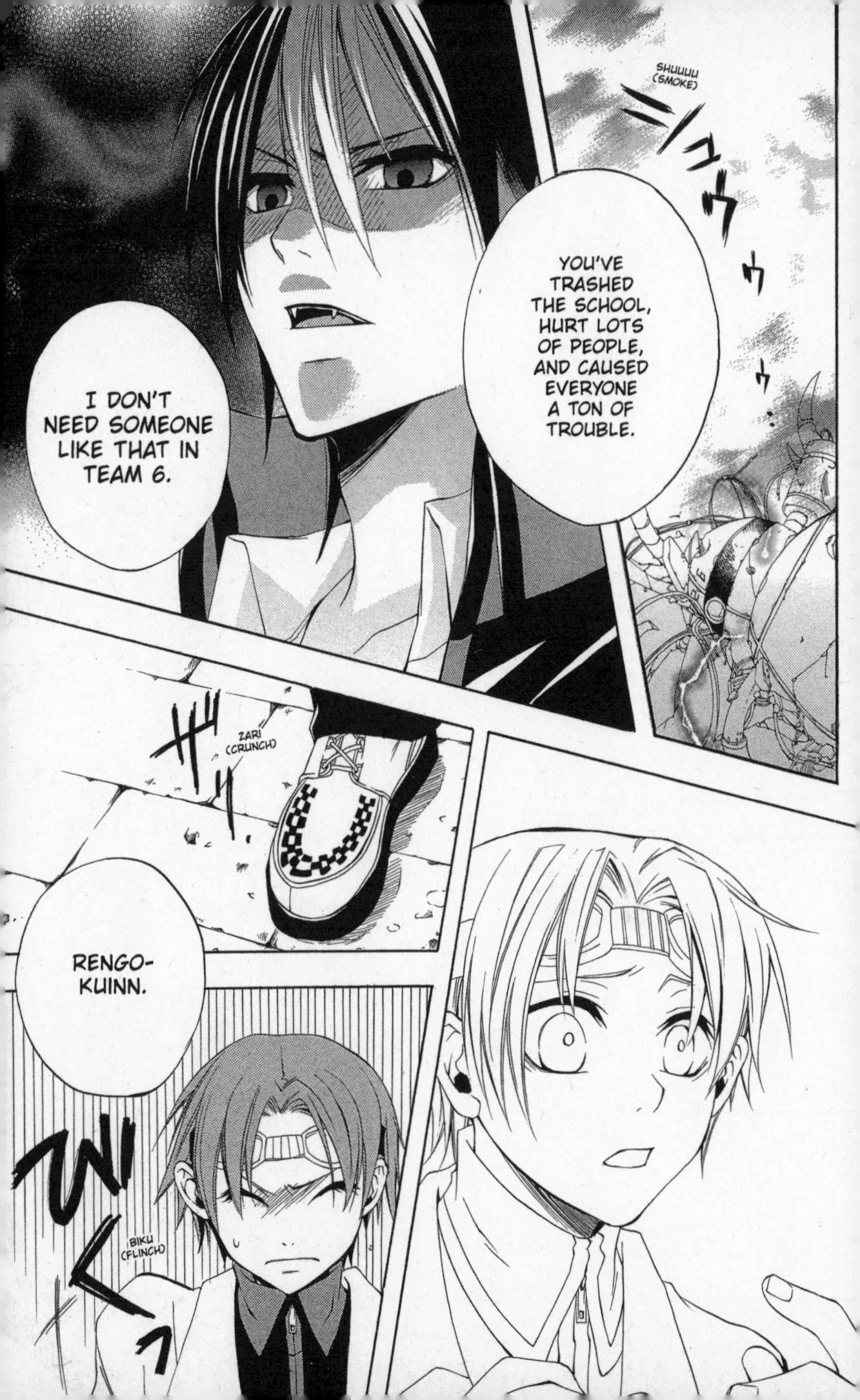
SHUUUU (SMOKE)
YOU'VE TRASHED THE SCHOOL, HURT LOTS OF PEOPLE, AND CAUSED EVERYONE A TON OF TROUBLE.
I DON'T NEED SOMEONE LIKE THAT IN TEAM 6.
ZARI (CRUNCH)
RENGO-KUINN.
BIKU (FLINCH)

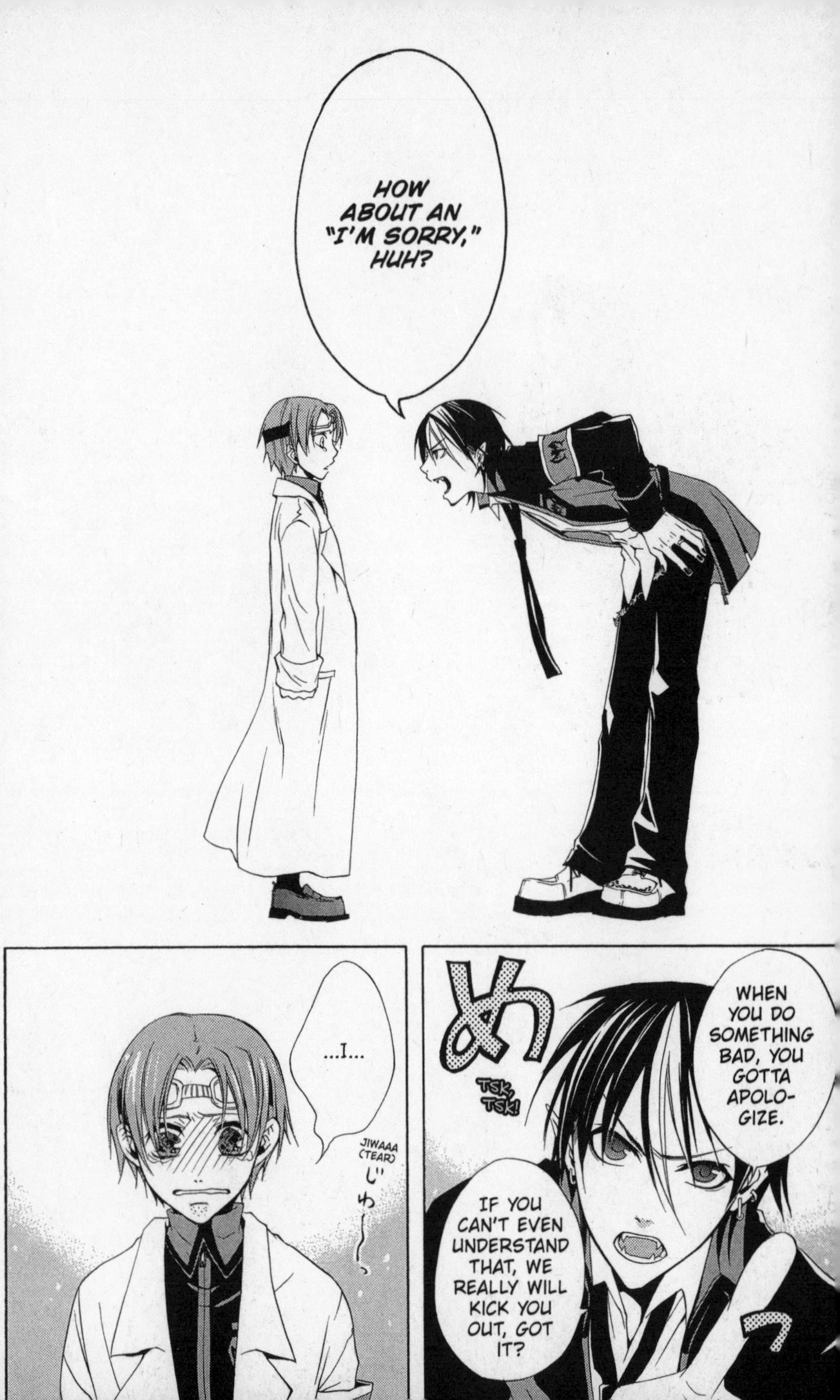
HOW ABOUT AN "I'M SORRY," HUH?
め
TSK, TSK!
WHEN YOU DO SOMETHING BAD, YOU GOTTA APOLOGIZE.
IF YOU CAN'T EVEN UNDERSTAND THAT, WE REALLY WILL KICK YOU OUT, GOT IT?
...I...
JIWAAA (TEAR)
じわ~っ

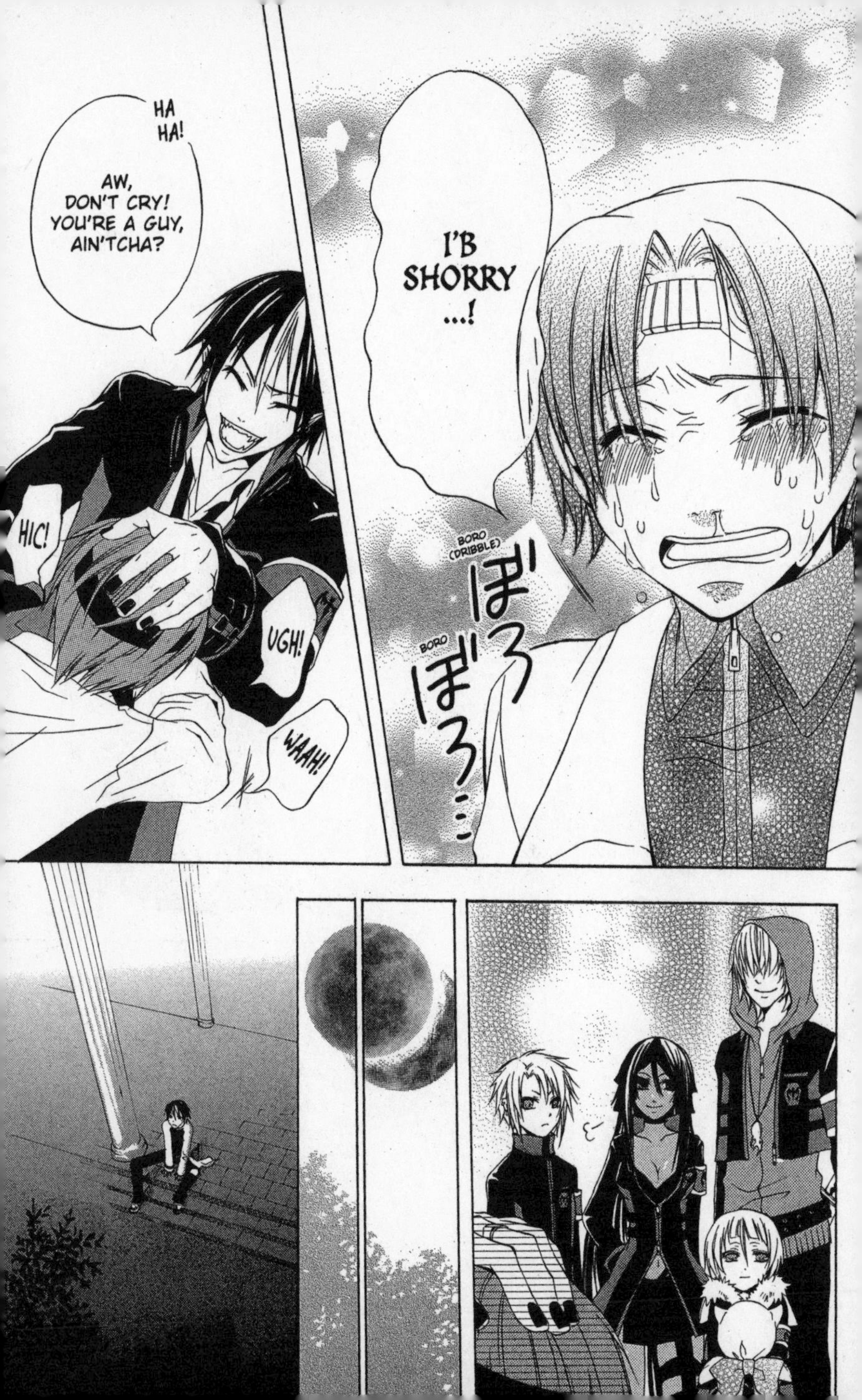

I'B SHORRY ...!
BORO (DRIBBLE)
ぼろ
BORO
ぼろ
HA HA!
AW, DON'T CRY! YOU'RE A GUY, AIN'TCHA?
UGH!
WAAH!
HIC!

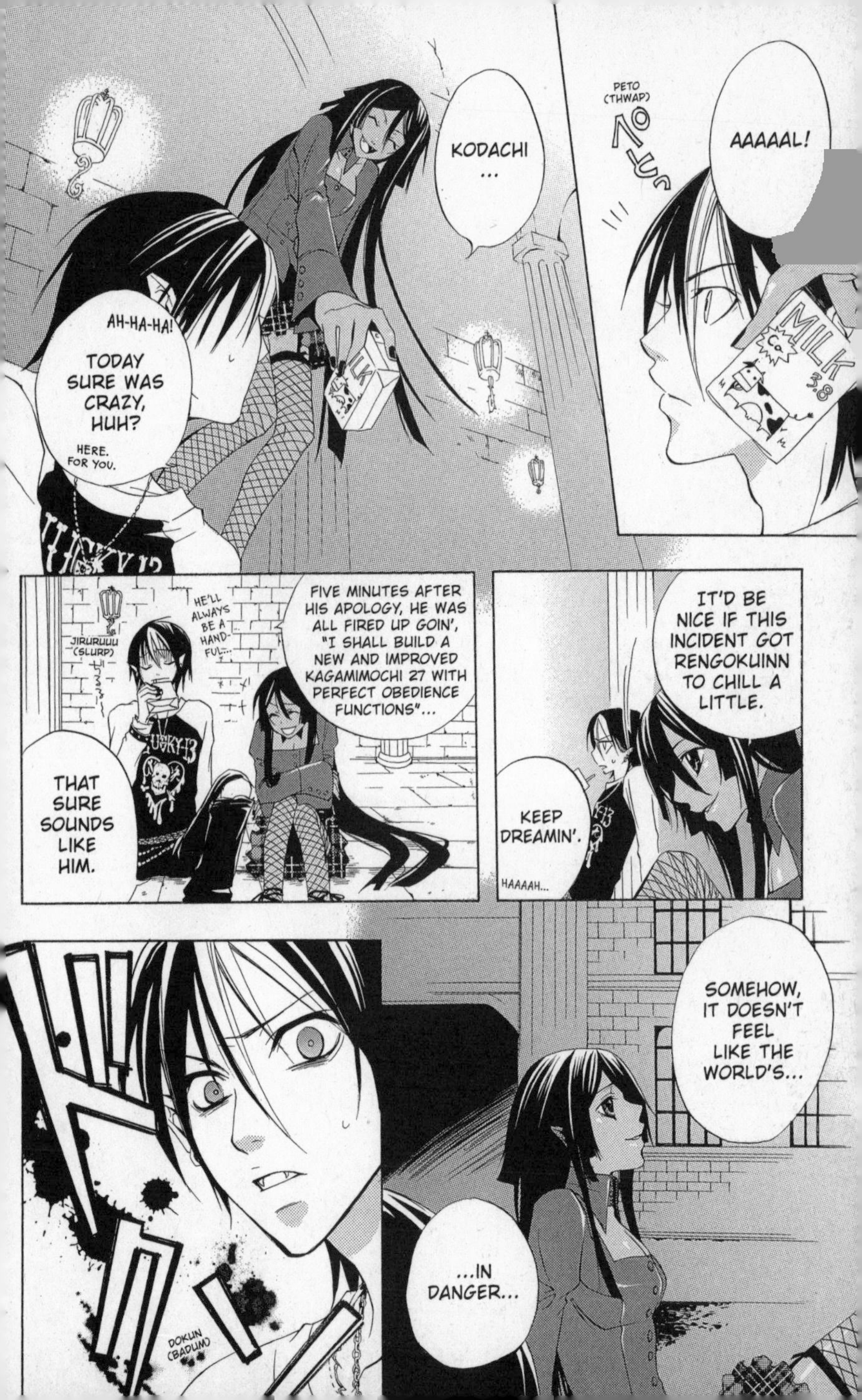
PETO (THWAP)
AAAAAL!
KODACHI ...
AH-HA-HA!
TODAY SURE WAS CRAZY, HUH?
HERE. FOR YOU.
IT'D BE NICE IF THIS INCIDENT GOT RENGOKUINN TO CHILL A LITTLE.
KEEP DREAMIN'.
HAAAAH...
FIVE MINUTES AFTER HIS APOLOGY, HE WAS ALL FIRED UP GOIN', "I SHALL BUILD A NEW AND IMPROVED KAGAMIMOCHI 27 WITH PERFECT OBEDIENCE FUNCTIONS"...
HE'LL ALWAYS BE A HANDFUL...
JIRURUUU (SLURP)
THAT SURE SOUNDS LIKE HIM.
SOMEHOW, IT DOESN'T FEEL LIKE THE WORLD'S...
...IN DANGER...
DOKUN (BADUM)

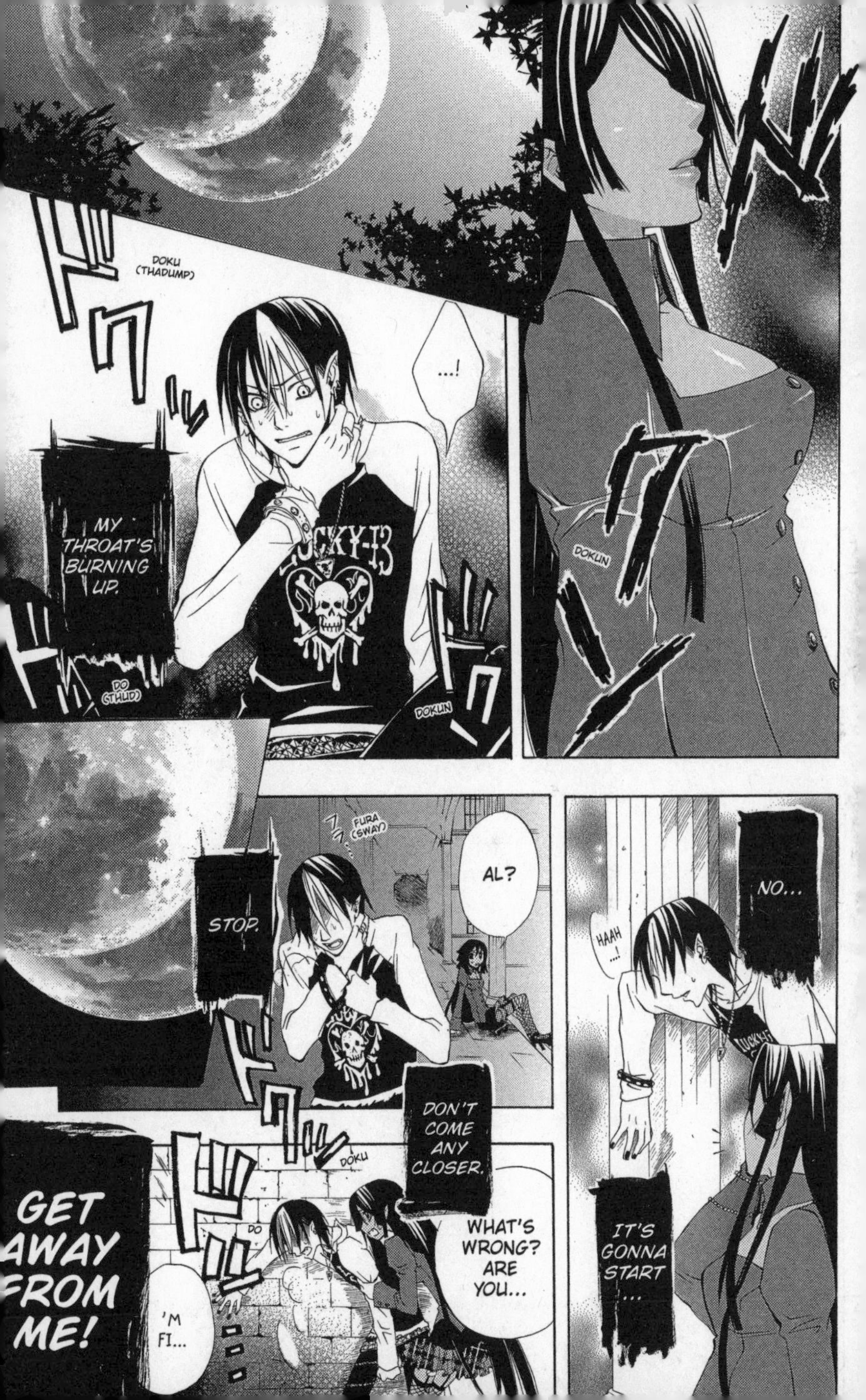
DOKUN
DOKU (THADUMP)
...!
MY THROAT'S BURNING UP.
DO (THUD)
DOKUN
NO...
HAAH...!
IT'S GONNA START...
FURA (SWAY)
AL?
STOP.
DON'T COME ANY CLOSER.
DOKU
WHAT'S WRONG? ARE YOU...
DO
'M FI...
GET AWAY FROM ME!

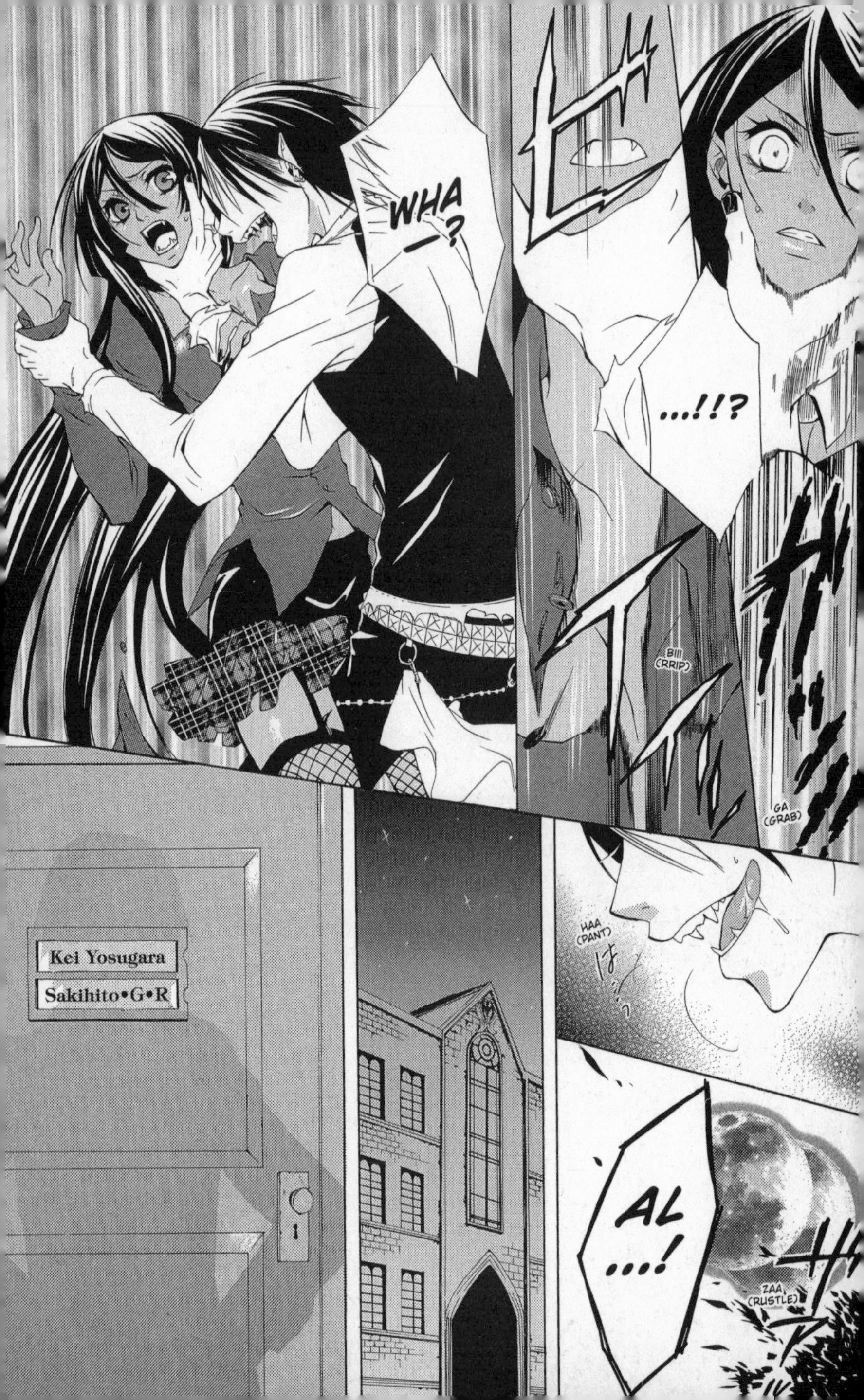
...!!?
BIII (RRIP)
GA (GRAB)
WHA—?
HAA (PANT)
AL...!
ZAA (RUSTLE)
Kei Yosugara
Sakihito•G•R

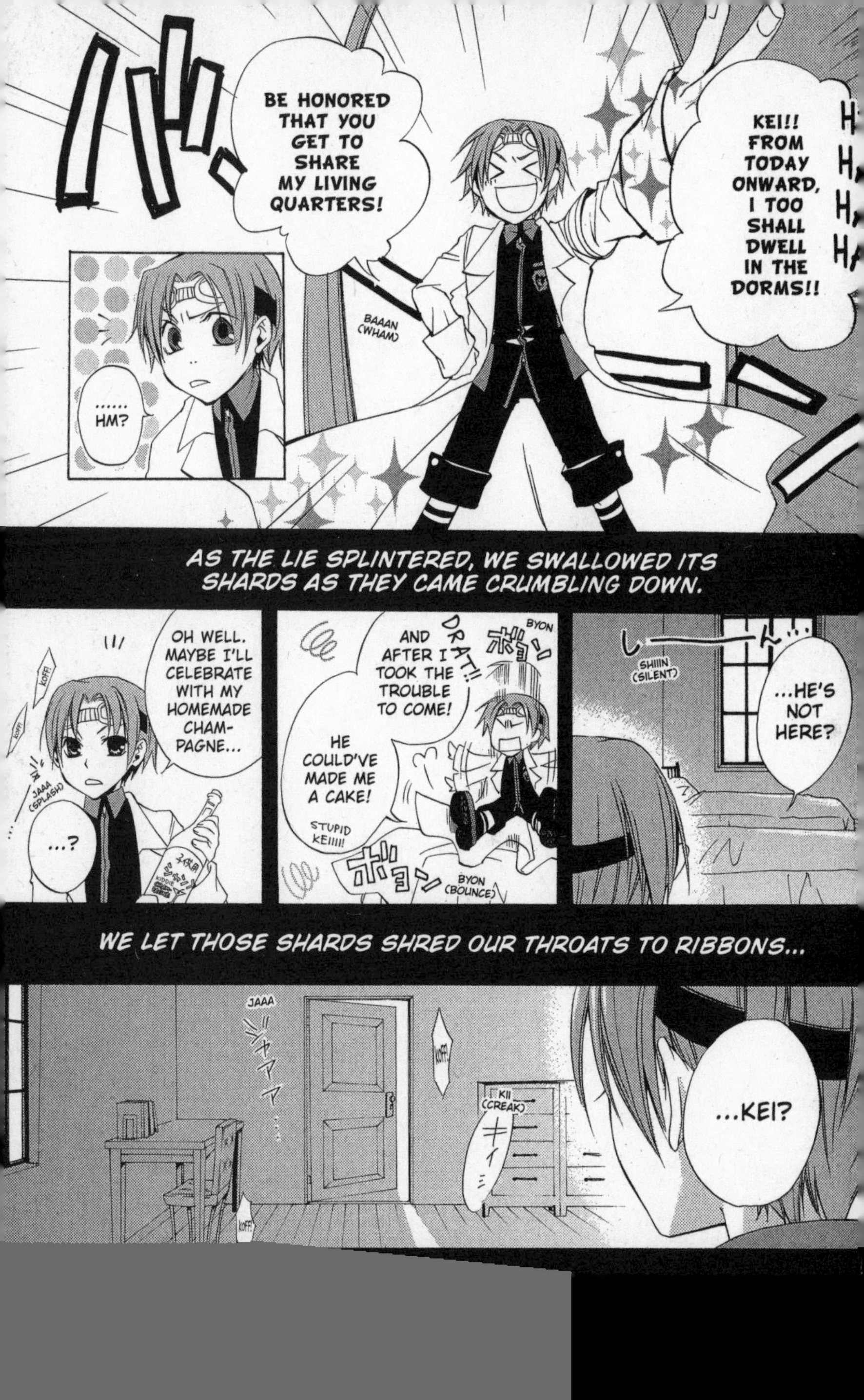
KEI!! FROM TODAY ONWARD, I TOO SHALL DWELL IN THE DORMS!!
HA HA HA HA
BE HONORED THAT YOU GET TO SHARE MY LIVING QUARTERS!
BAAAN (WHAM)
......HM?
AS THE LIE SPLINTERED, WE SWALLOWED ITS SHARDS AS THEY CAME CRUMBLING DOWN.
SHIIN (SILENT)
...HE'S NOT HERE?
BYON
DRAT!!
AND AFTER I TOOK THE TROUBLE TO COME!
HE COULD'VE MADE ME A CAKE!
STUPID KEIIIII!
BYON (BOUNCE)
OH WELL. MAYBE I'LL CELEBRATE WITH MY HOMEMADE CHAMPAGNE...
KOFF!
KOFF!
JAAA (SPLASH)
...?
KIDDIE
WE LET THOSE SHARDS SHRED OUR THROATS TO RIBBONS...
...KEI?
KII (CREAK)
KOFF!
JAAA
KOFF!

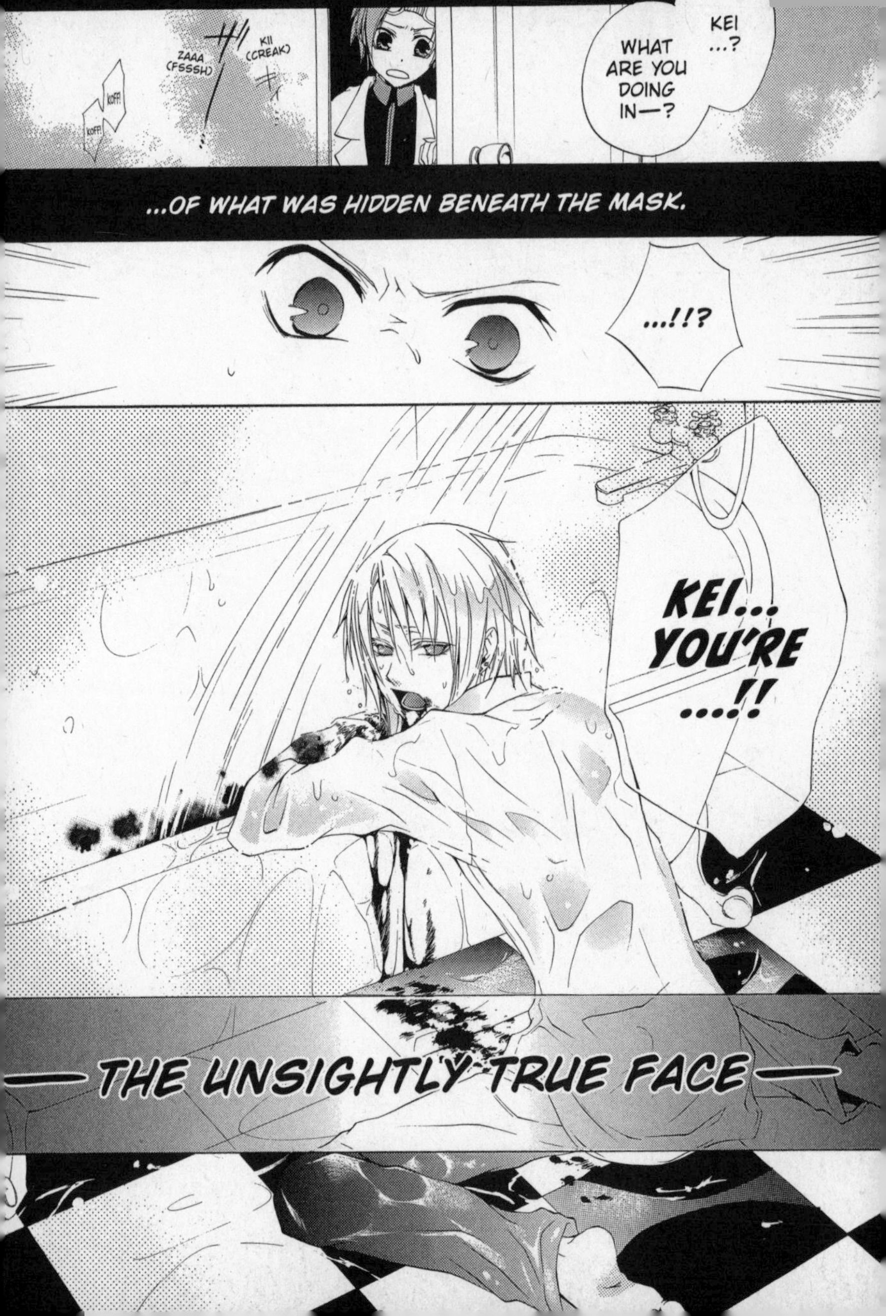
KEI ...?
WHAT ARE YOU DOING IN—?
KII (CREAK)
ZAAA (FSSSH)
KOFF!
KOFF!
...OF WHAT WAS HIDDEN BENEATH THE MASK.
...!!?
KEI... YOU'RE ...!!
—THE UNSIGHTLY TRUE FACE—

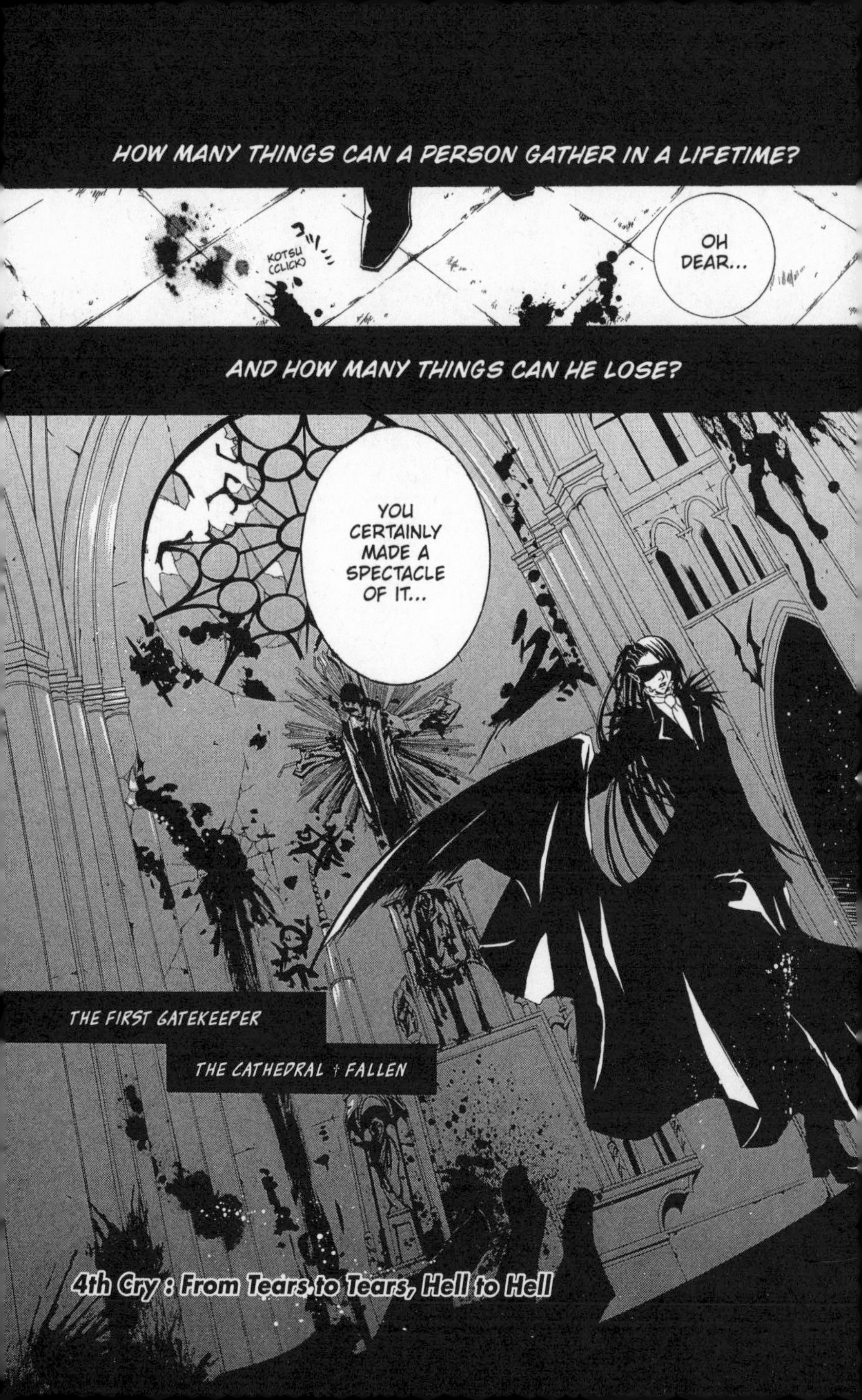
HOW MANY THINGS CAN A PERSON GATHER IN A LIFETIME?
OH DEAR...
KOTSU (CLICK)
AND HOW MANY THINGS CAN HE LOSE?
YOU CERTAINLY MADE A SPECTACLE OF IT...
THE FIRST GATEKEEPER
THE CATHEDRAL † FALLEN
4th Cry : From Tears to Tears, Hell to Hell

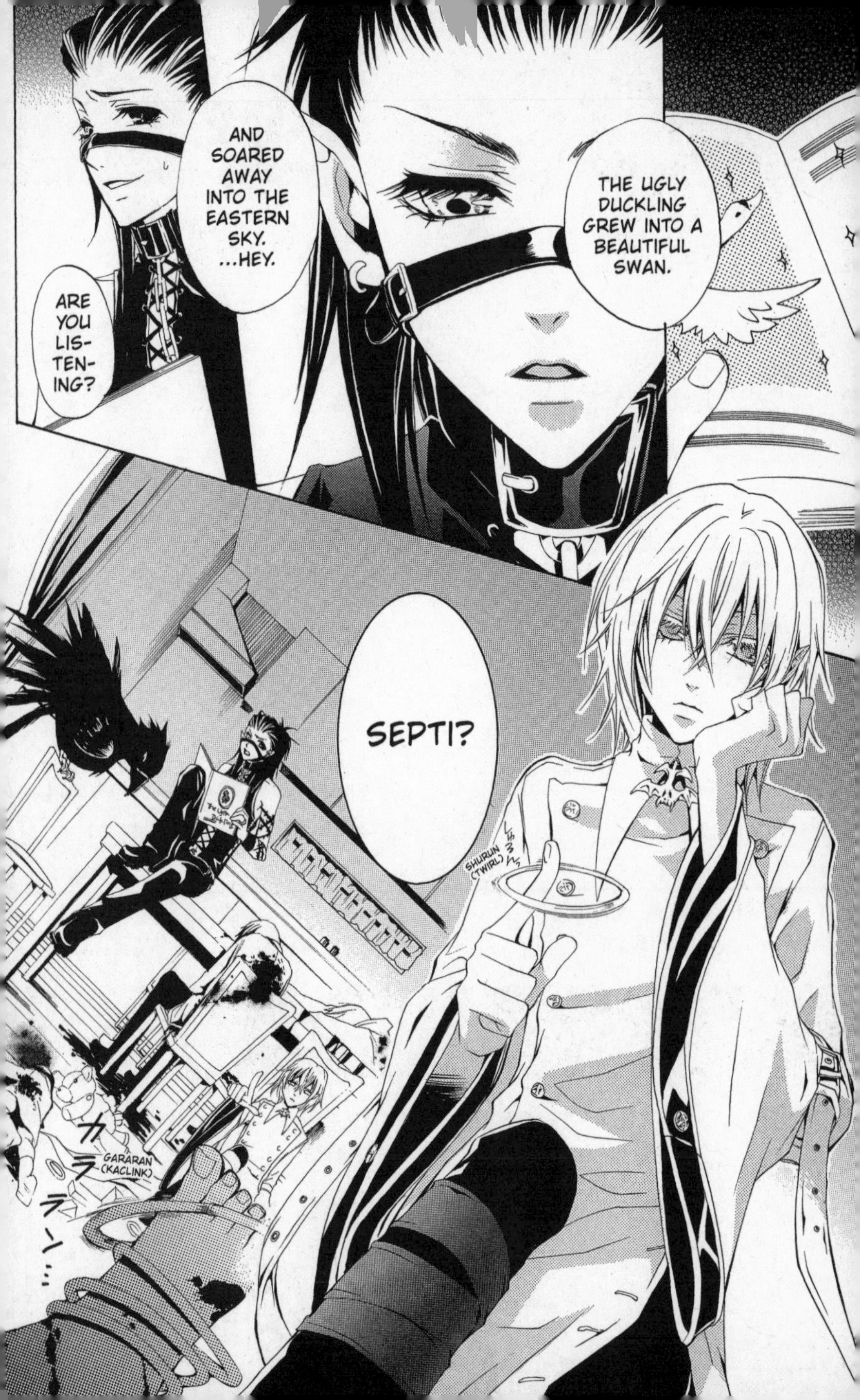
THE UGLY DUCKLING GREW INTO A BEAUTIFUL SWAN.
AND SOARED AWAY INTO THE EASTERN SKY. ...HEY.
ARE YOU LIS-TEN-ING?
SEPTI?
SHURUN (TWIRL)
GARARAN (KACLINK)

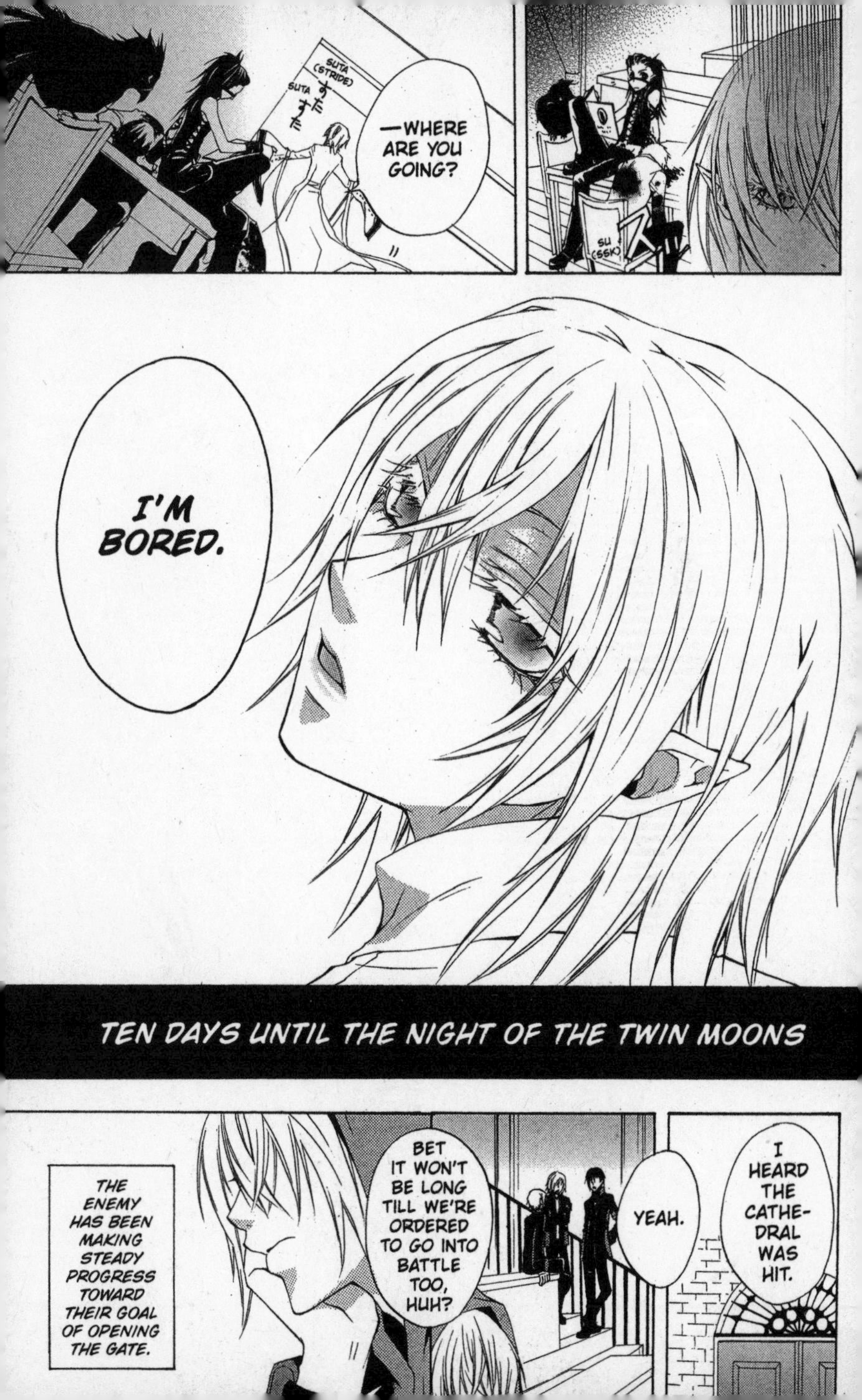
SU (SSK)
SUTA (STRIDE) SUTA
すたすた
—WHERE ARE YOU GOING?
I'M BORED.
TEN DAYS UNTIL THE NIGHT OF THE TWIN MOONS
I HEARD THE CATHEDRAL WAS HIT.
YEAH.
BET IT WON'T BE LONG TILL WE'RE ORDERED TO GO INTO BATTLE TOO, HUH?
THE ENEMY HAS BEEN MAKING STEADY PROGRESS TOWARD THEIR GOAL OF OPENING THE GATE.

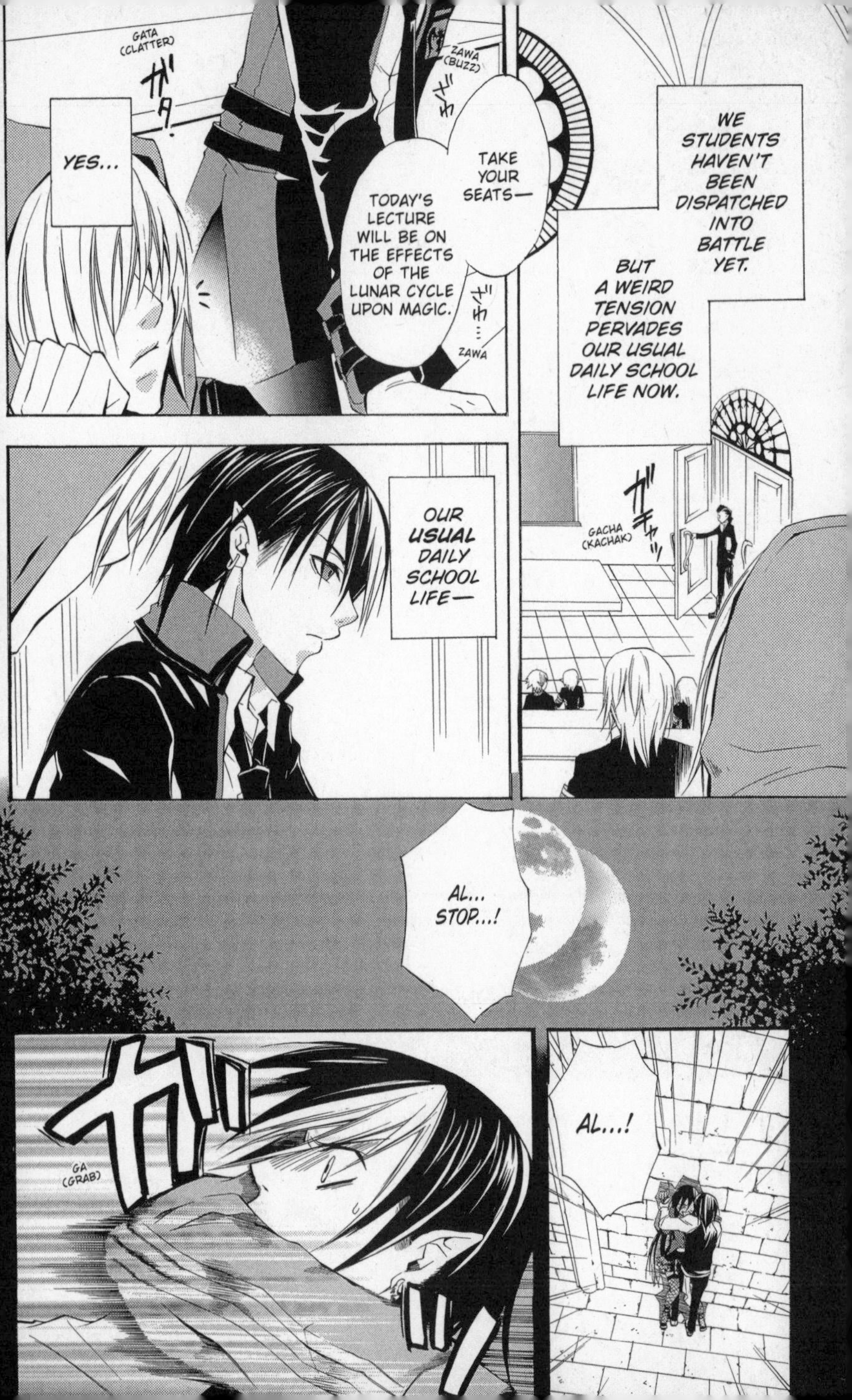
WE STUDENTS HAVEN'T BEEN DISPATCHED INTO BATTLE YET.
BUT A WEIRD TENSION PERVADES OUR USUAL DAILY SCHOOL LIFE NOW.
ZAWA (BUZZ)
TAKE YOUR SEATS—
TODAY'S LECTURE WILL BE ON THE EFFECTS OF THE LUNAR CYCLE UPON MAGIC.
ZAWA
GATA (CLATTER)
YES...
GACHA (KACHAK)
OUR USUAL DAILY SCHOOL LIFE—
AL... STOP...!
AL...!
GA (GRAB)

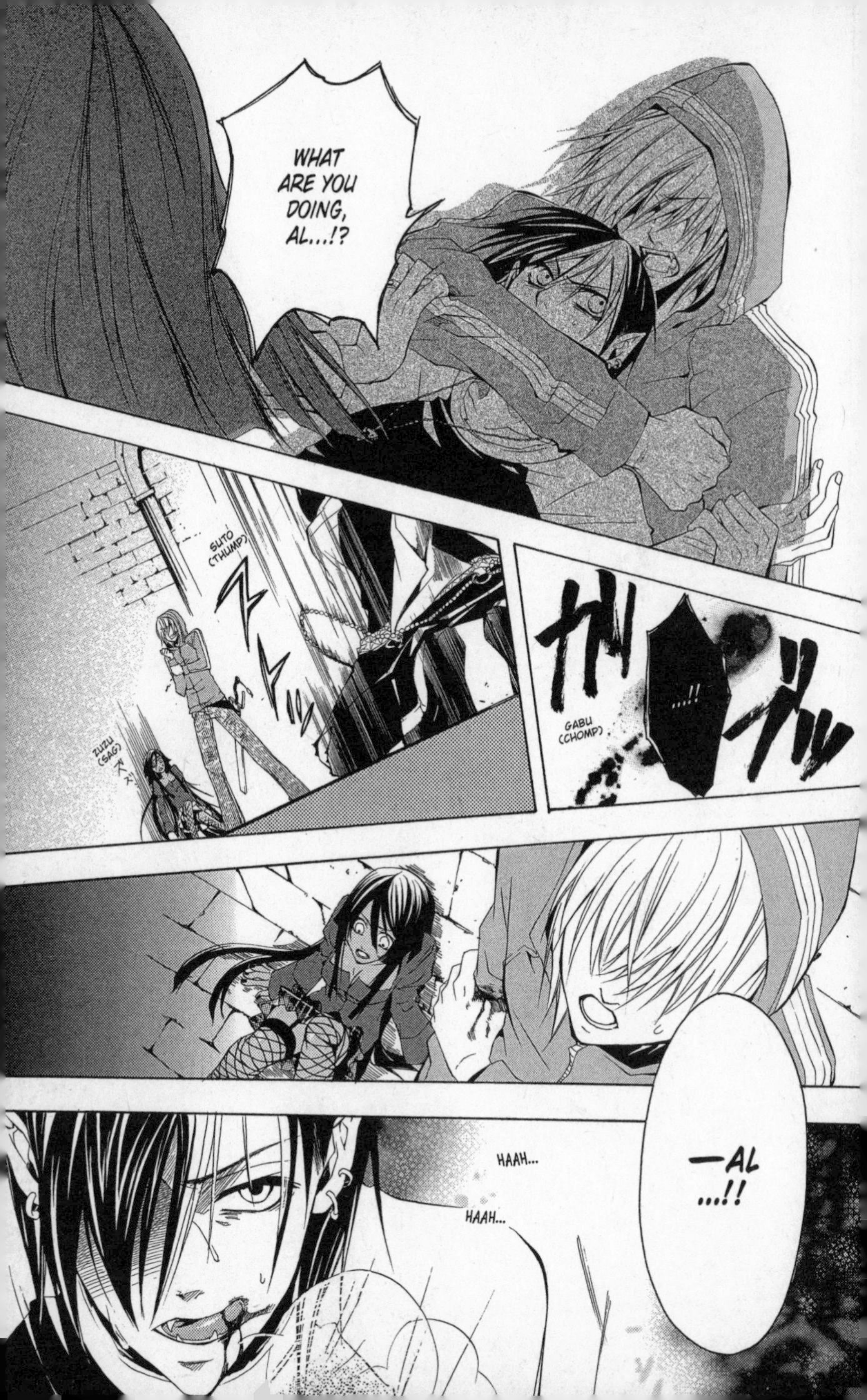
WHAT ARE YOU DOING, AL...!?
GABU (CHOMP)
...!!
SUTO (THUMP)
ZUZU (SAG)
—AL ...!!
HAAH...
HAAH...

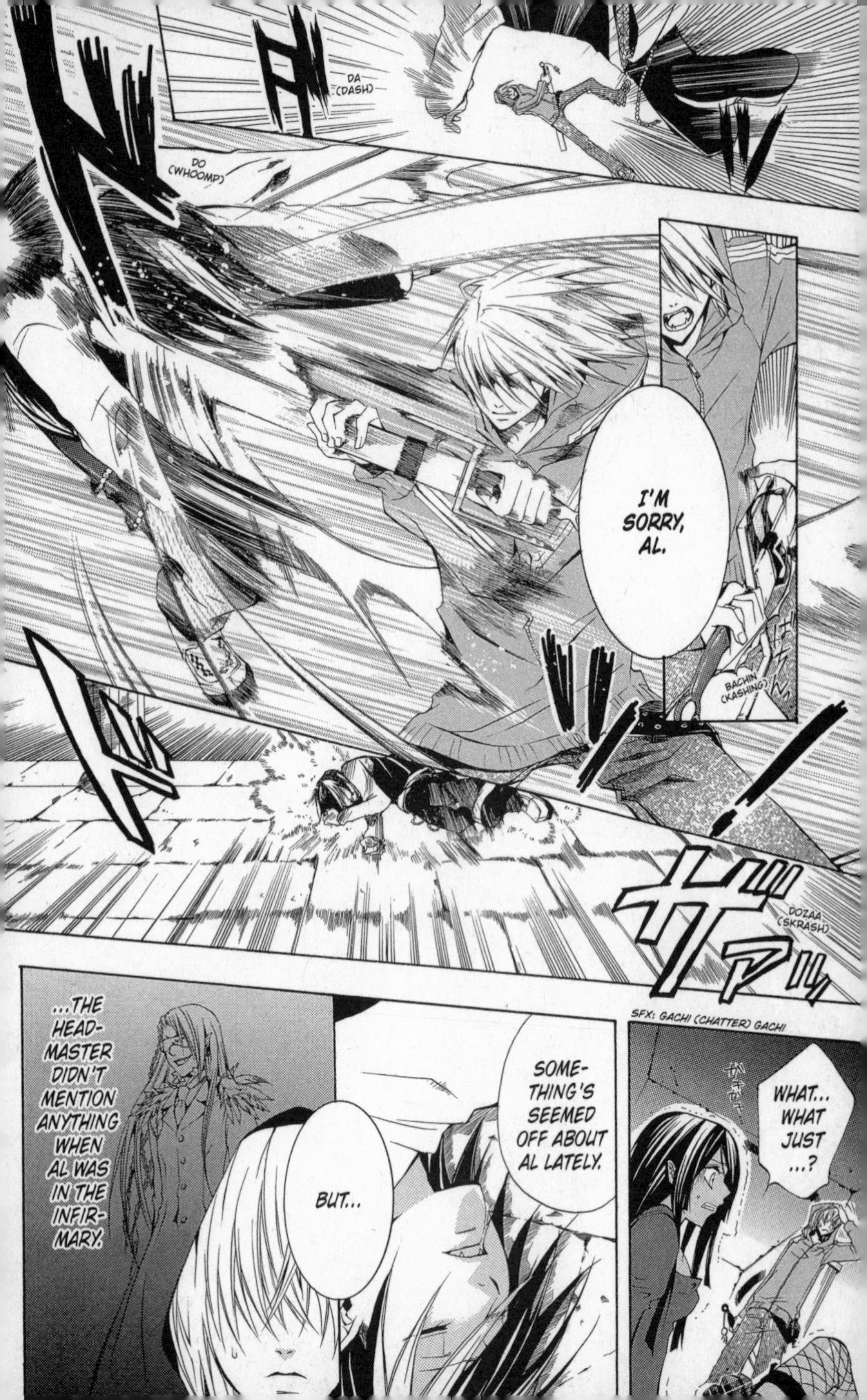
DA (DASH)
DO (WHOOMP)
I'M SORRY, AL.
BACHIN (KASHING)
DOZAA (SKRASH)
SFX: GACHI (CHATTER) GACHI
WHAT... WHAT JUST ...?
SOME-THING'S SEEMED OFF ABOUT AL LATELY.
BUT...
...THE HEAD-MASTER DIDN'T MENTION ANYTHING WHEN AL WAS IN THE INFIR-MARY.

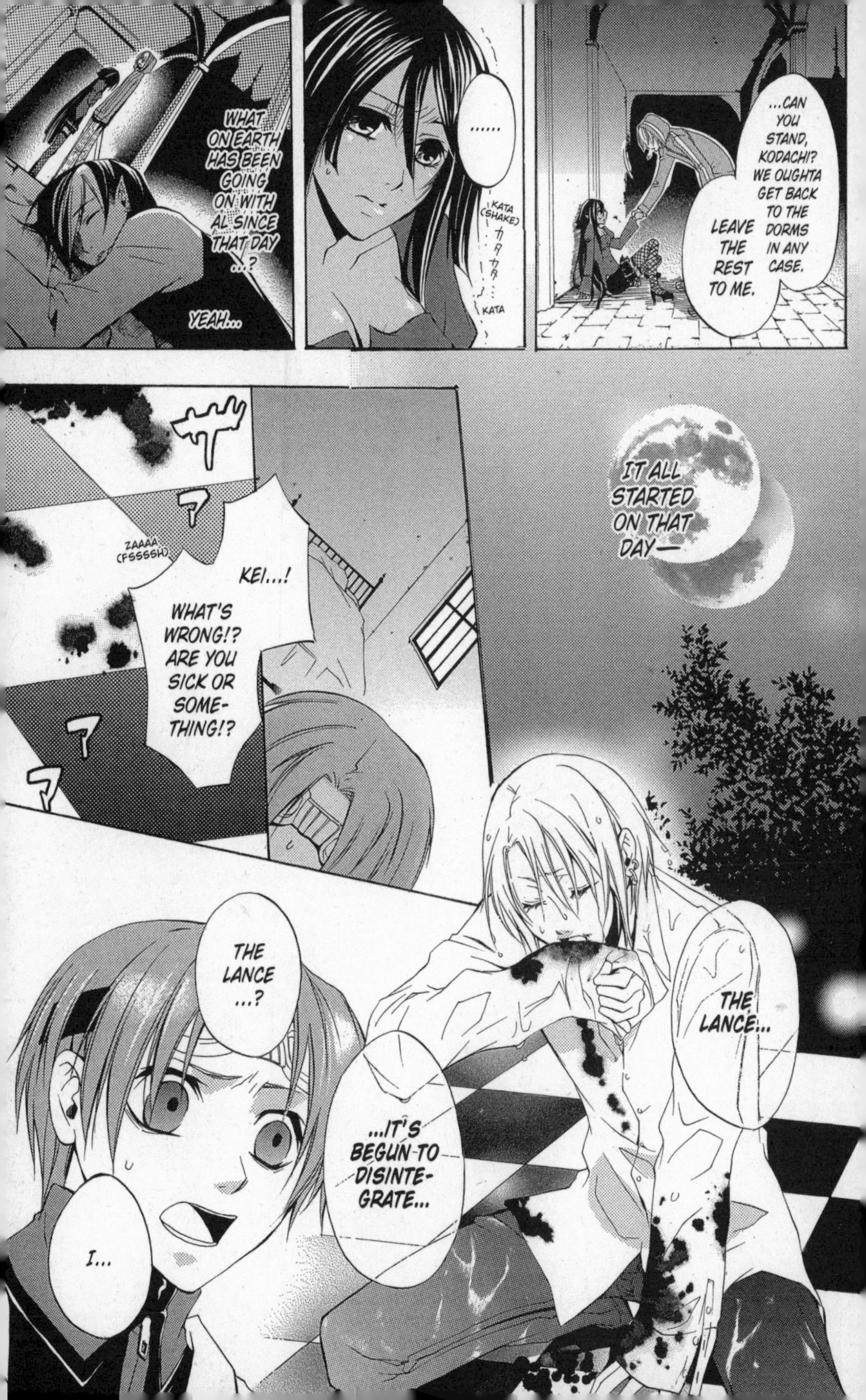
...CAN YOU STAND, KODACHI? WE OUGHTA GET BACK TO THE DORMS IN ANY CASE.
LEAVE THE REST TO ME.
......
KATA (SHAKE)
KATA
WHAT ON EARTH HAS BEEN GOING ON WITH AL SINCE THAT DAY ...?
YEAH...
IT ALL STARTED ON THAT DAY—
ZAAAA (FSSSSH)
KEI...!
WHAT'S WRONG!? ARE YOU SICK OR SOME-THING!?
THE LANCE...
...IT'S BEGUN TO DISINTE-GRATE...
THE LANCE ...?
I...

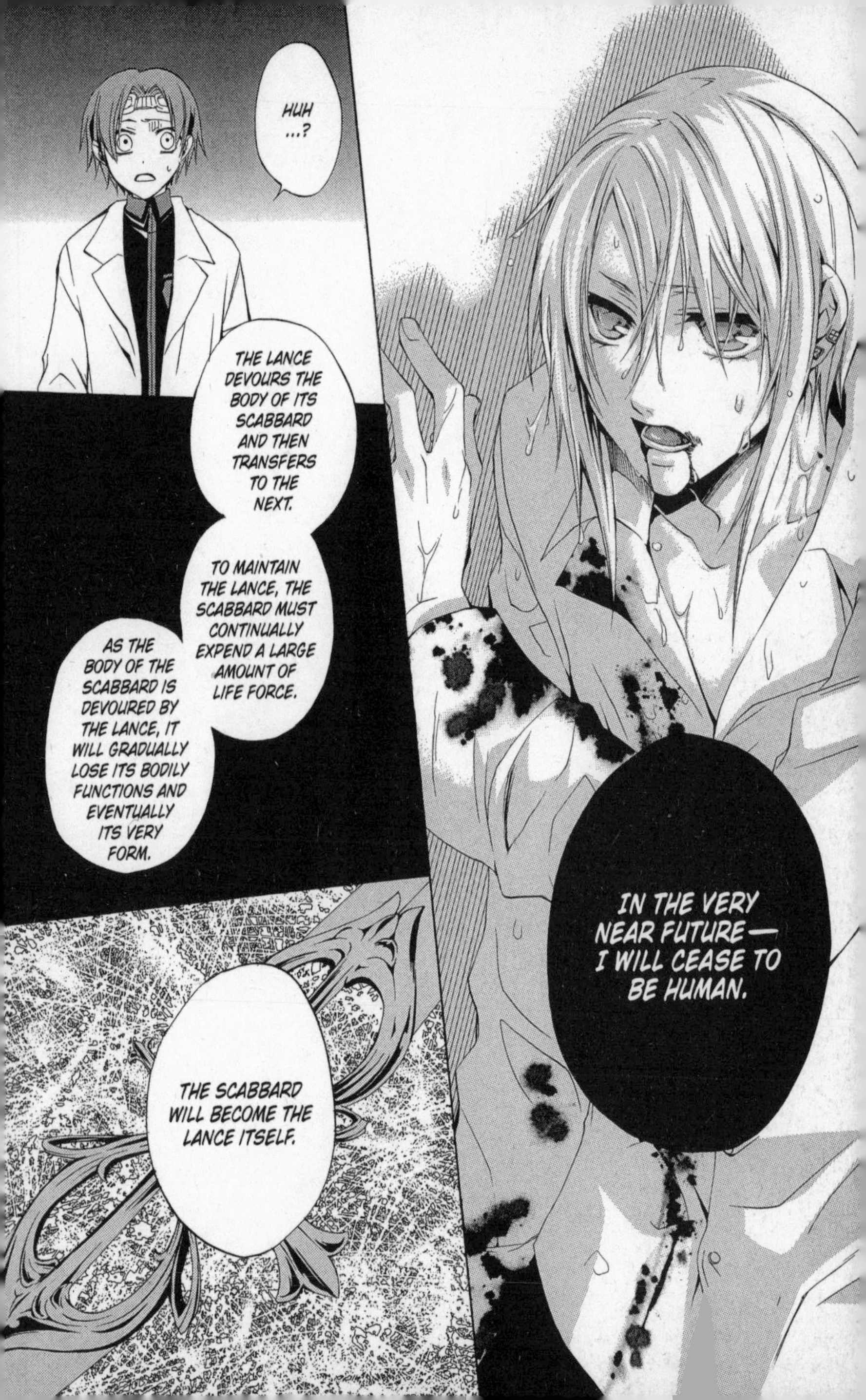

IN THE VERY NEAR FUTURE— I WILL CEASE TO BE HUMAN.
HUH ...?
THE LANCE DEVOURS THE BODY OF ITS SCABBARD AND THEN TRANSFERS TO THE NEXT.
TO MAINTAIN THE LANCE, THE SCABBARD MUST CONTINUALLY EXPEND A LARGE AMOUNT OF LIFE FORCE.
AS THE BODY OF THE SCABBARD IS DEVOURED BY THE LANCE, IT WILL GRADUALLY LOSE ITS BODILY FUNCTIONS AND EVENTUALLY ITS VERY FORM.
THE SCABBARD WILL BECOME THE LANCE ITSELF.

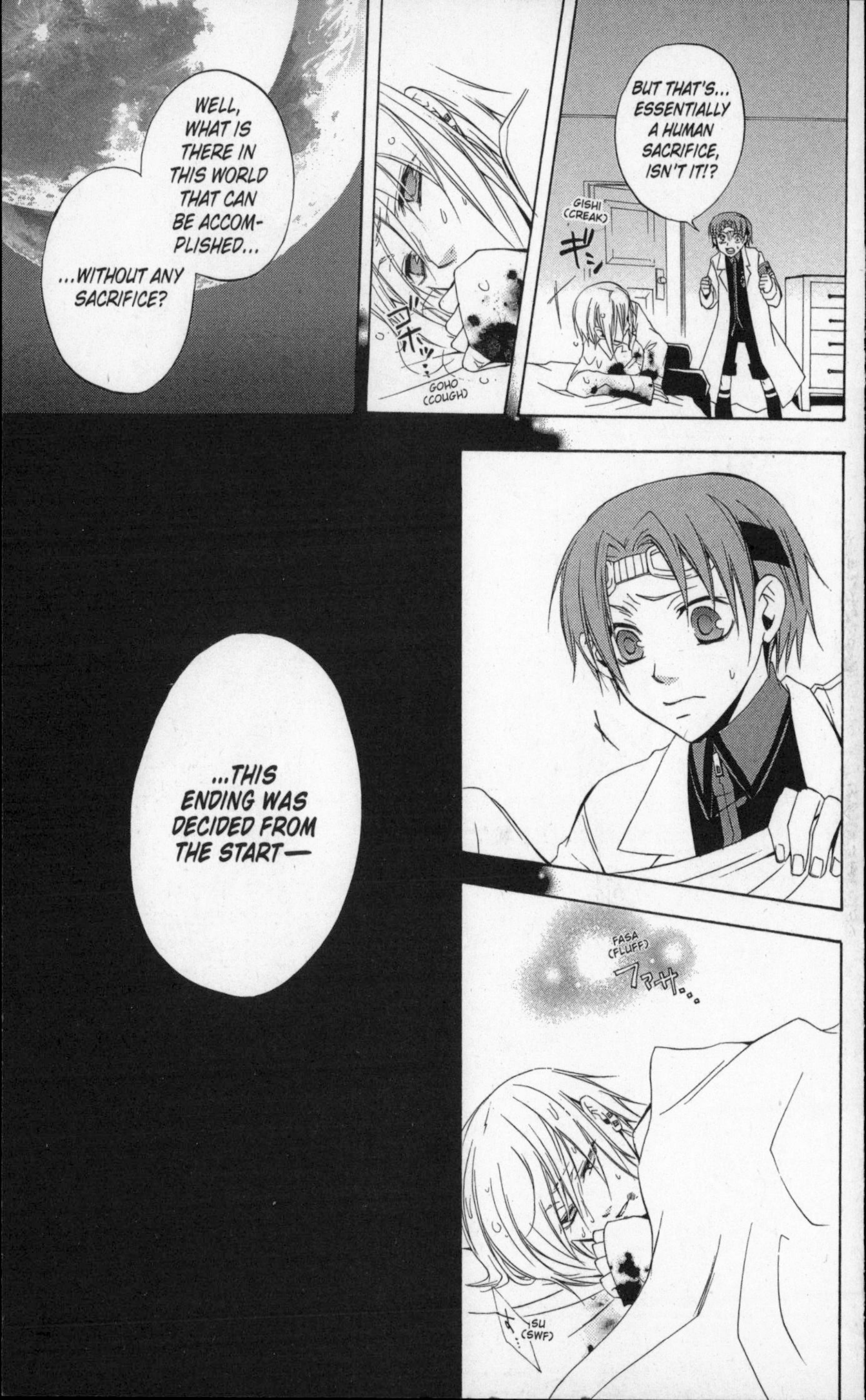
BUT THAT'S... ESSENTIALLY A HUMAN SACRIFICE, ISN'T IT!?
GISHI (CREAK)
GOHO (COUGH)
WELL, WHAT IS THERE IN THIS WORLD THAT CAN BE ACCOMPLISHED...
...WITHOUT ANY SACRIFICE?
FASA (FLUFF)
SU (SWF)
...THIS ENDING WAS DECIDED FROM THE START—

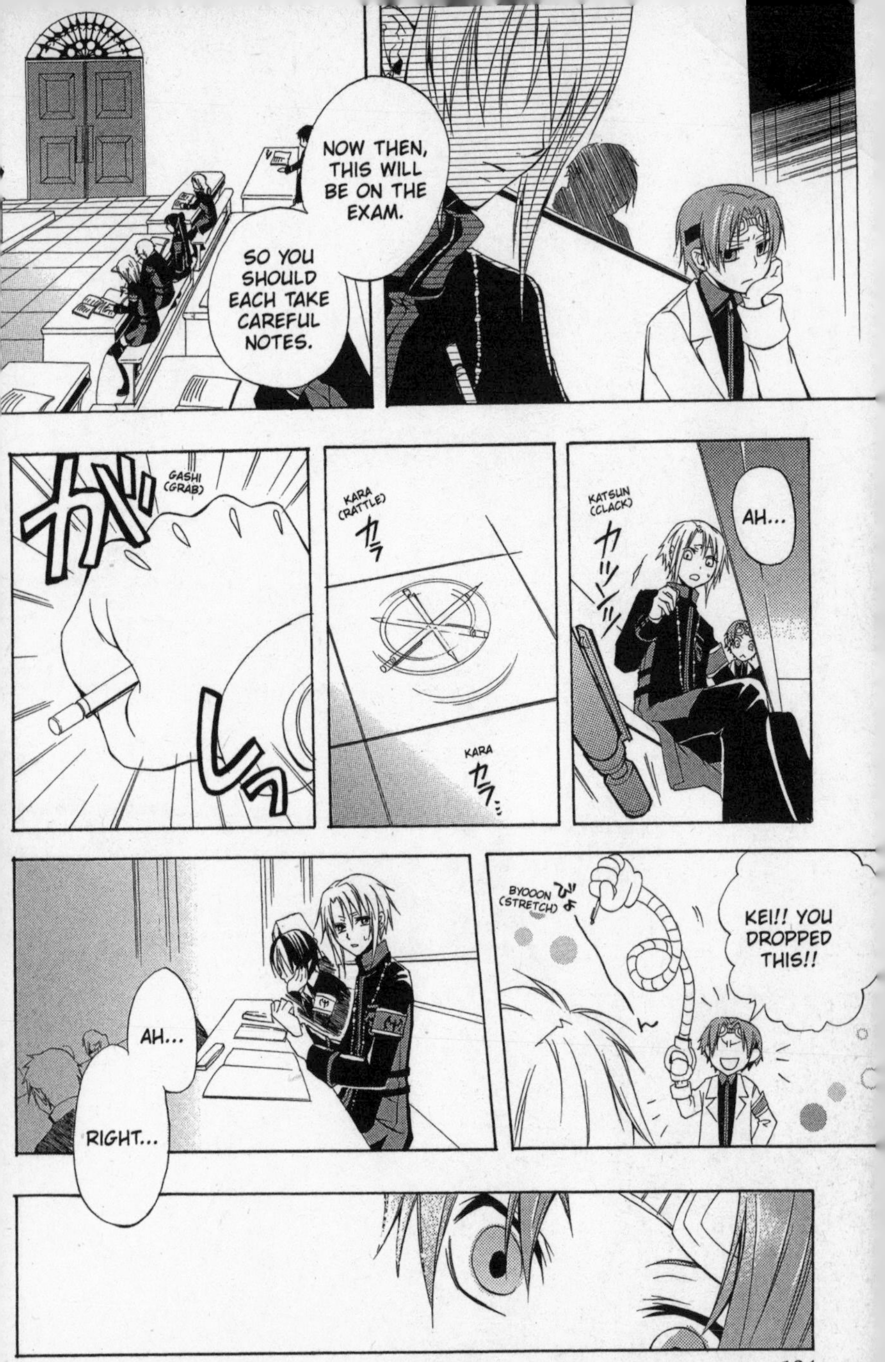
NOW THEN, THIS WILL BE ON THE EXAM.
SO YOU SHOULD EACH TAKE CAREFUL NOTES.
AH...
KATSUN (CLACK)
KARA (RATTLE)
KARA
GASHI (GRAB)
KEI!! YOU DROPPED THIS!!
BYOOON (STRETCH)
AH...
RIGHT...

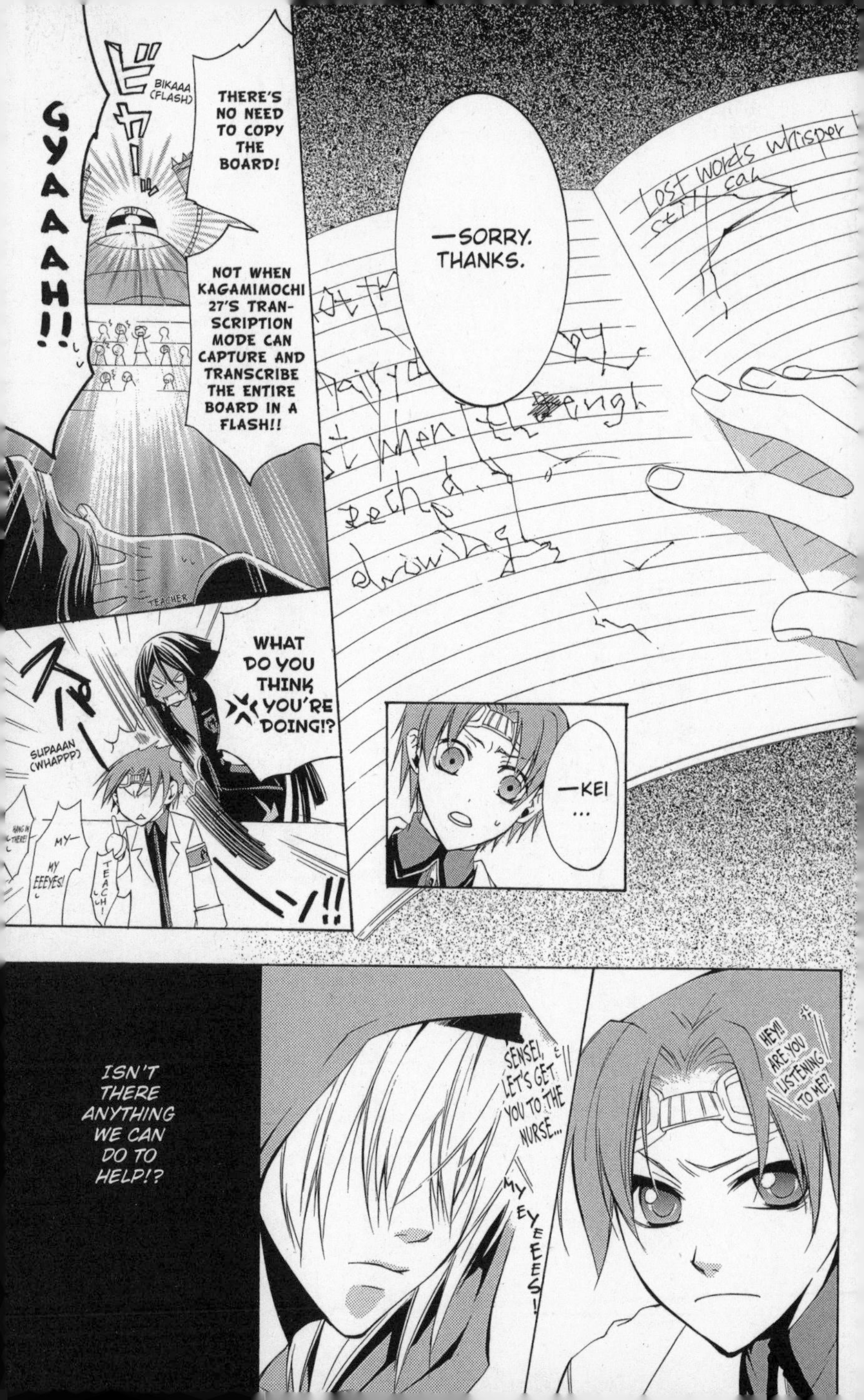

—SORRY. THANKS.
Lost words whisper
—KEI ...
BIKAAA (FLASH)
GYAAAAH!!
THERE'S NO NEED TO COPY THE BOARD!
NOT WHEN KAGAMIMOCHI 27'S TRANSCRIPTION MODE CAN CAPTURE AND TRANSCRIBE THE ENTIRE BOARD IN A FLASH!!
TEACHER
WHAT DO YOU THINK YOU'RE DOING!?
SUPAAAN (WHAPPP)
HANG IN THERE!
MY— MY EEEYES!
TEACH!
HEY! ARE YOU LISTENING TO ME!?
SENSEI, LET'S GET YOU TO THE NURSE...
MY EYEEEES!
ISN'T THERE ANYTHING WE CAN DO TO HELP!?

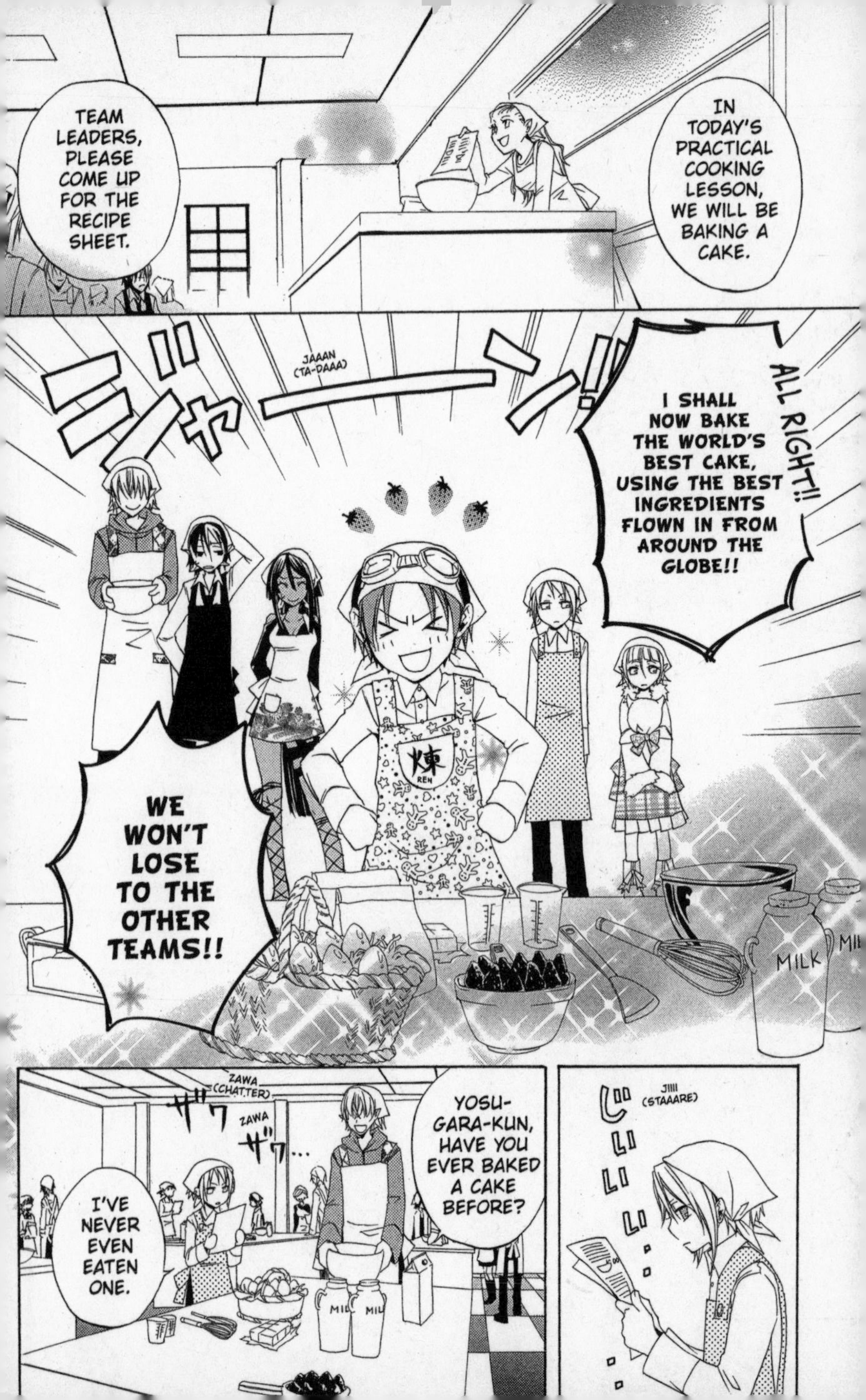
IN TODAY'S PRACTICAL COOKING LESSON, WE WILL BE BAKING A CAKE.
TEAM LEADERS, PLEASE COME UP FOR THE RECIPE SHEET.
JAAAN (TA-DAAA)
ALL RIGHT!!
I SHALL NOW BAKE THE WORLD'S BEST CAKE, USING THE BEST INGREDIENTS FLOWN IN FROM AROUND THE GLOBE!!
REN
WE WON'T LOSE TO THE OTHER TEAMS!!
MILK
JIIII (STAAARE)
ZAWA (CHATTER)
ZAWA
YOSU-GARA-KUN, HAVE YOU EVER BAKED A CAKE BEFORE?
I'VE NEVER EVEN EATEN ONE.

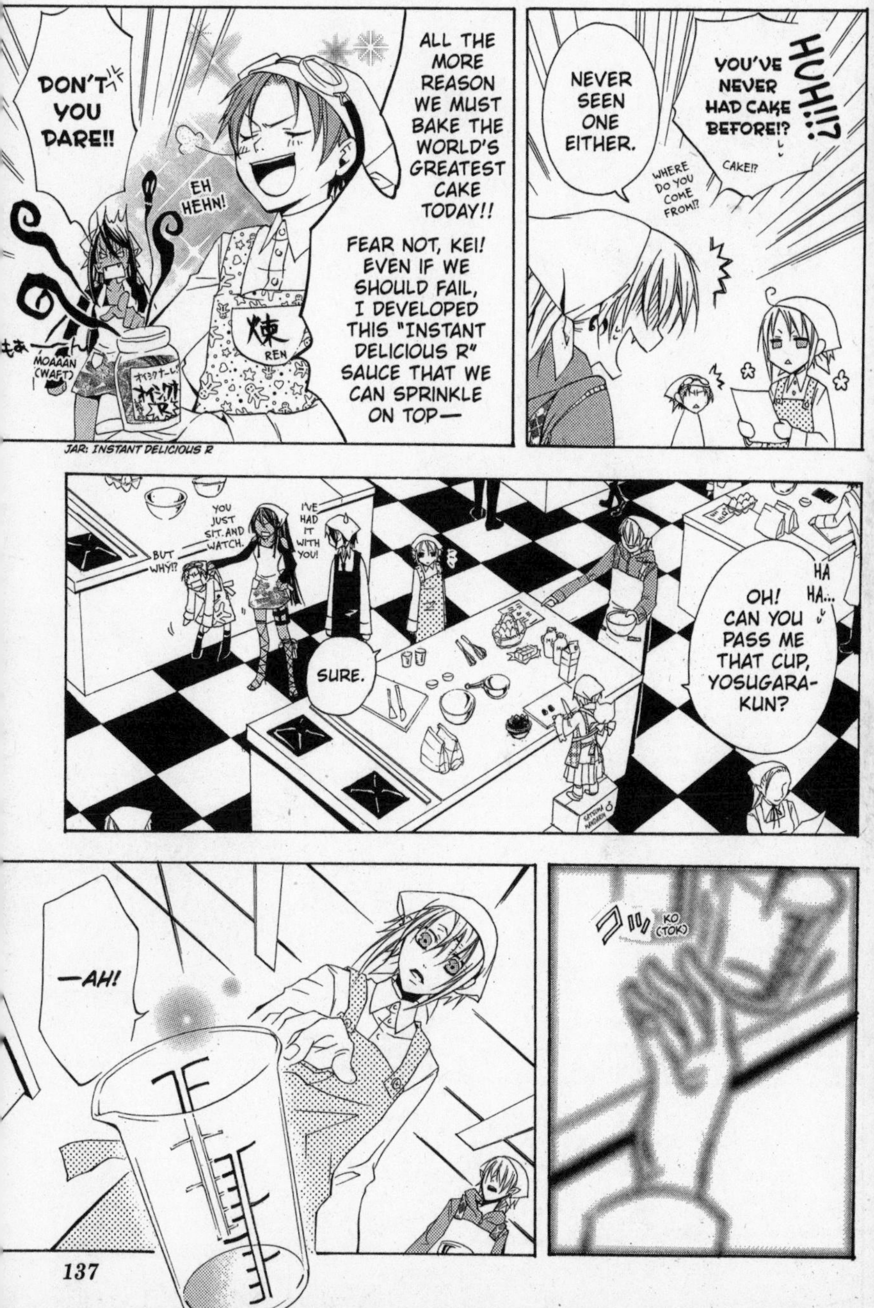
HUH!!!?
YOU'VE NEVER HAD CAKE BEFORE!?
CAKE!?
WHERE DO YOU COME FROM!?
NEVER SEEN ONE EITHER.
ALL THE MORE REASON WE MUST BAKE THE WORLD'S GREATEST CAKE TODAY!!
FEAR NOT, KEI! EVEN IF WE SHOULD FAIL, I DEVELOPED THIS "INSTANT DELICIOUS R" SAUCE THAT WE CAN SPRINKLE ON TOP—
EH HEHN!
REN
DON'T YOU DARE!!
MOAAAN (WAFT)
JAR: INSTANT DELICIOUS R
OH! CAN YOU PASS ME THAT CUP, YOSUGARA-KUN?
HA HA...
SURE.
I'VE HAD IT WITH YOU!
YOU JUST SIT AND WATCH.
BUT WHY!?
KO (TOK)
—AH!

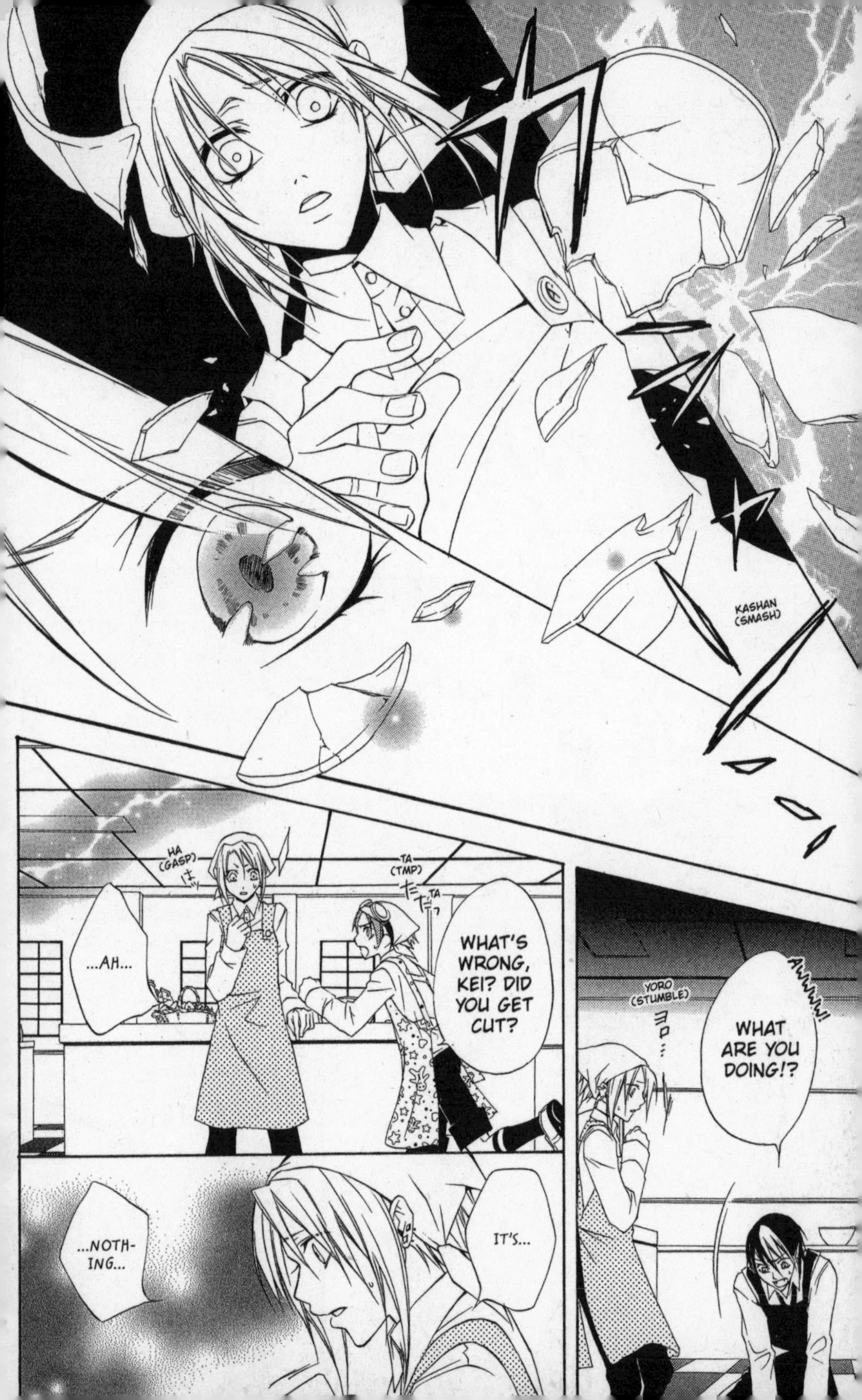
KASHAN (SMASH)
AWWWW!
WHAT ARE YOU DOING!?
YORO (STUMBLE)
TA (TMP) TA
WHAT'S WRONG, KEI? DID YOU GET CUT?
HA (GASP)
...AH...
IT'S...
...NOTHING...

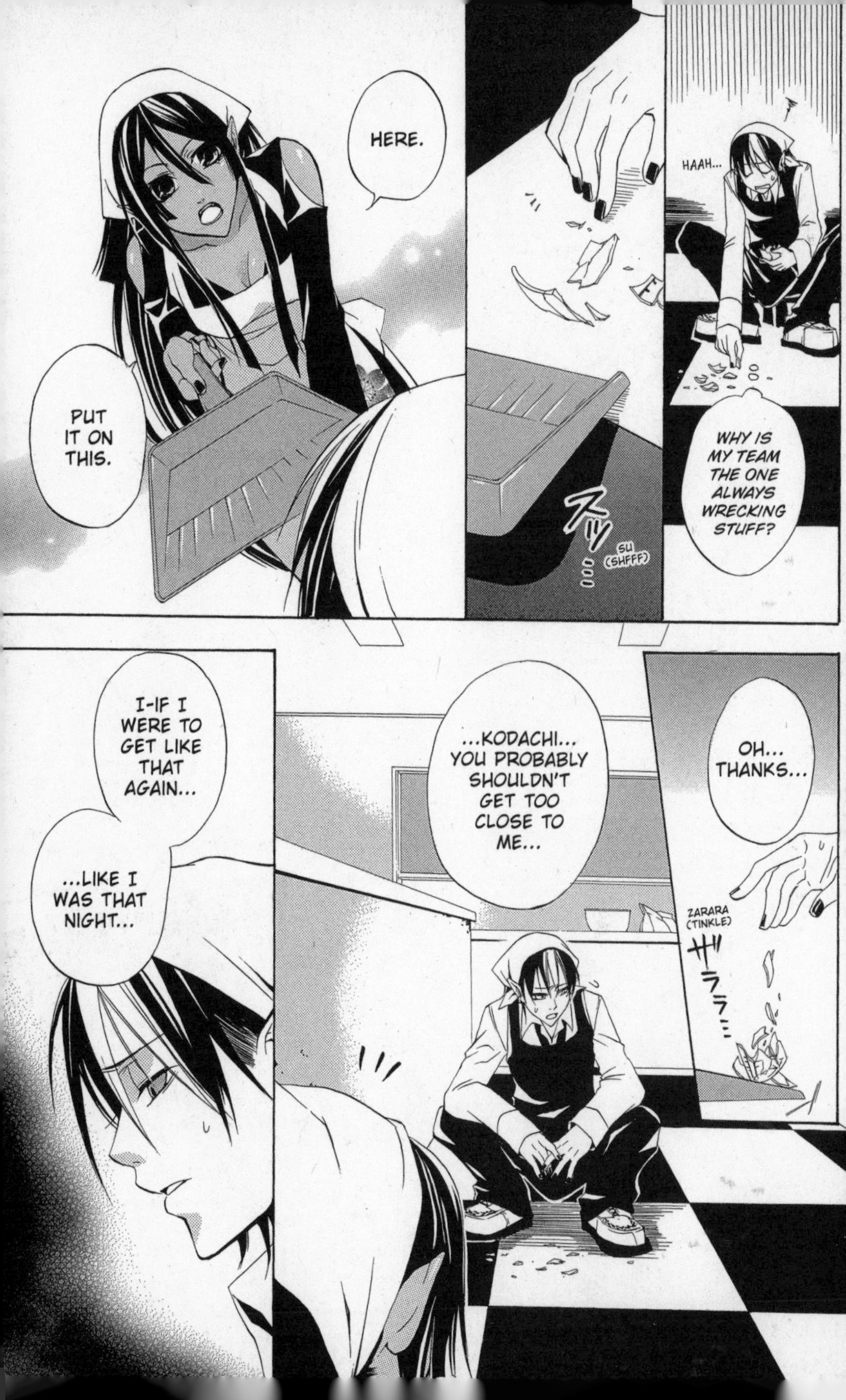
HAAH...
WHY IS MY TEAM THE ONE ALWAYS WRECKING STUFF?
SU (SHFFF)
HERE.
PUT IT ON THIS.
OH... THANKS...
ZARARA (TINKLE)
...KODACHI... YOU PROBABLY SHOULDN'T GET TOO CLOSE TO ME...
I-IF I WERE TO GET LIKE THAT AGAIN...
...LIKE I WAS THAT NIGHT...

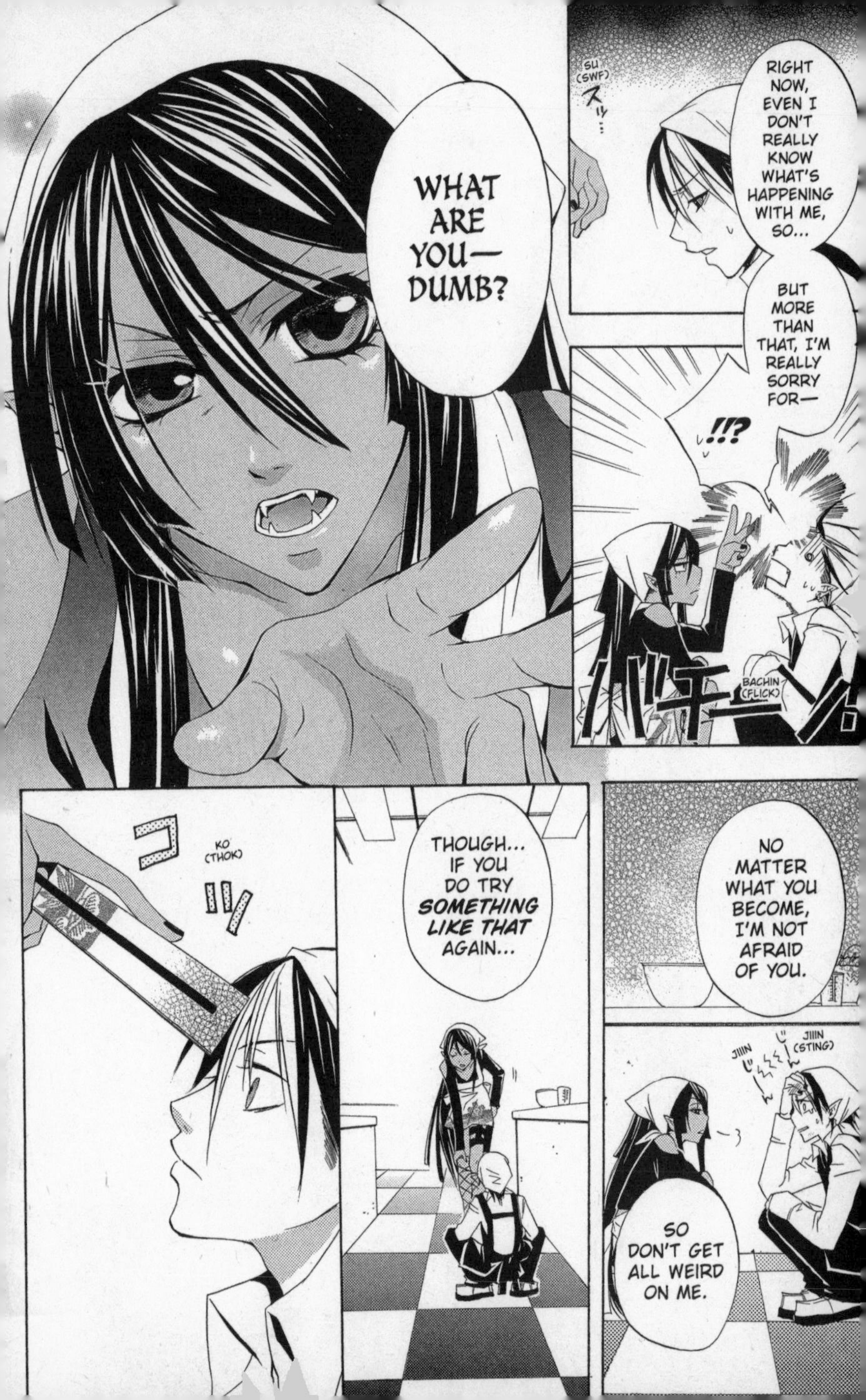
SU (SWF)
RIGHT NOW, EVEN I DON'T REALLY KNOW WHAT'S HAPPENING WITH ME, SO...
BUT MORE THAN THAT, I'M REALLY SORRY FOR—
!!?
BACHIN (FLICK)
WHAT ARE YOU— DUMB?
NO MATTER WHAT YOU BECOME, I'M NOT AFRAID OF YOU.
JIIIN JIIIN (STING)
SO DON'T GET ALL WEIRD ON ME.
THOUGH... IF YOU DO TRY *SOMETHING LIKE THAT* AGAIN...
KO (THOK)

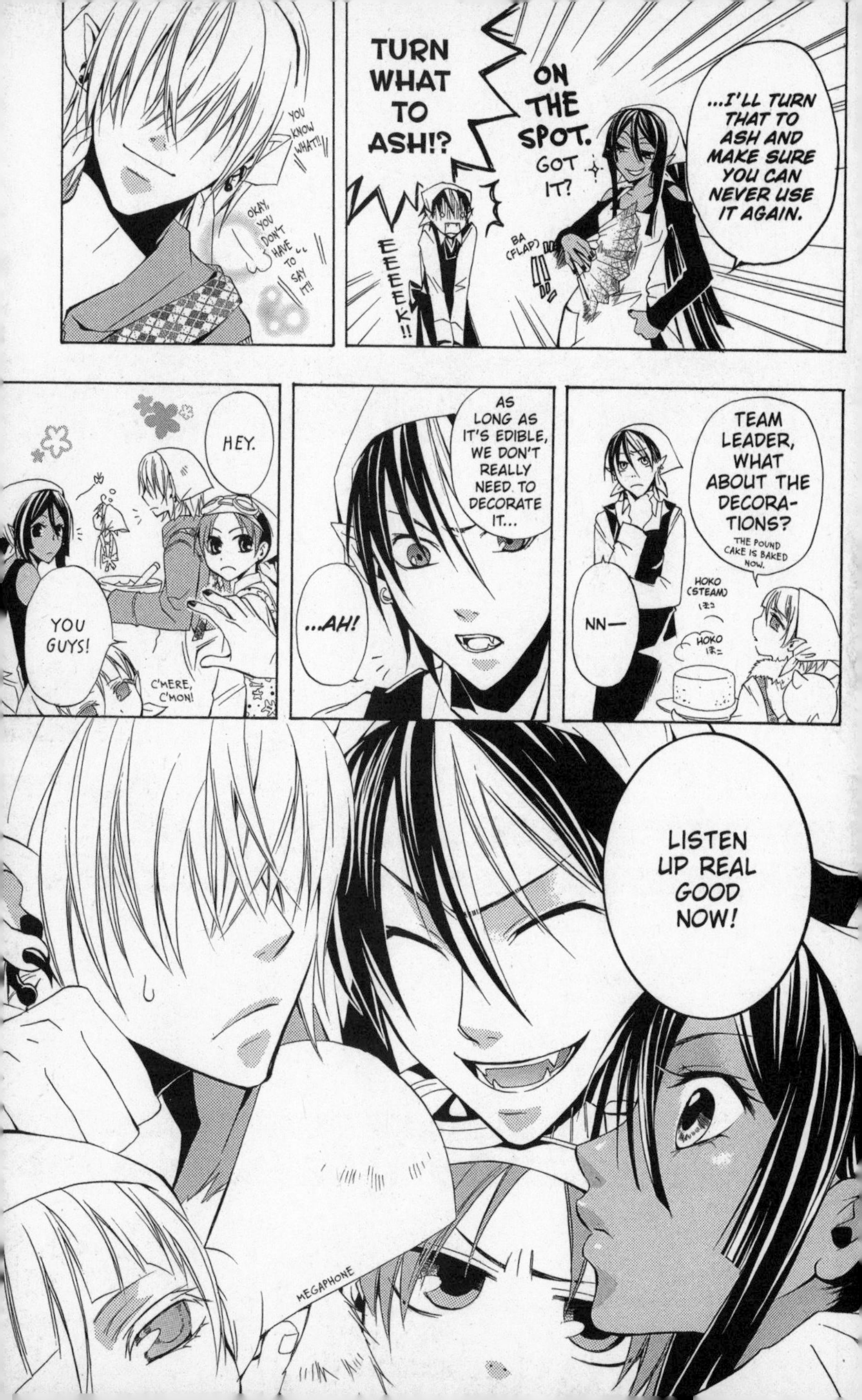
...I'LL TURN THAT TO ASH AND MAKE SURE YOU CAN NEVER USE IT AGAIN.
ON THE SPOT. GOT IT?
TURN WHAT TO ASH!?
BA (FLAP)
EEEEEK!!
YOU KNOW WHAT!!
OKAY, YOU DON'T HAVE TO SAY IT!!
TEAM LEADER, WHAT ABOUT THE DECORATIONS?
THE POUND CAKE IS BAKED NOW.
HOKO (STEAM)
HOKO
NN—
AS LONG AS IT'S EDIBLE, WE DON'T REALLY NEED TO DECORATE IT...
...AH!
HEY.
YOU GUYS!
C'MERE, C'MON!
LISTEN UP REAL GOOD NOW!
MEGAPHONE

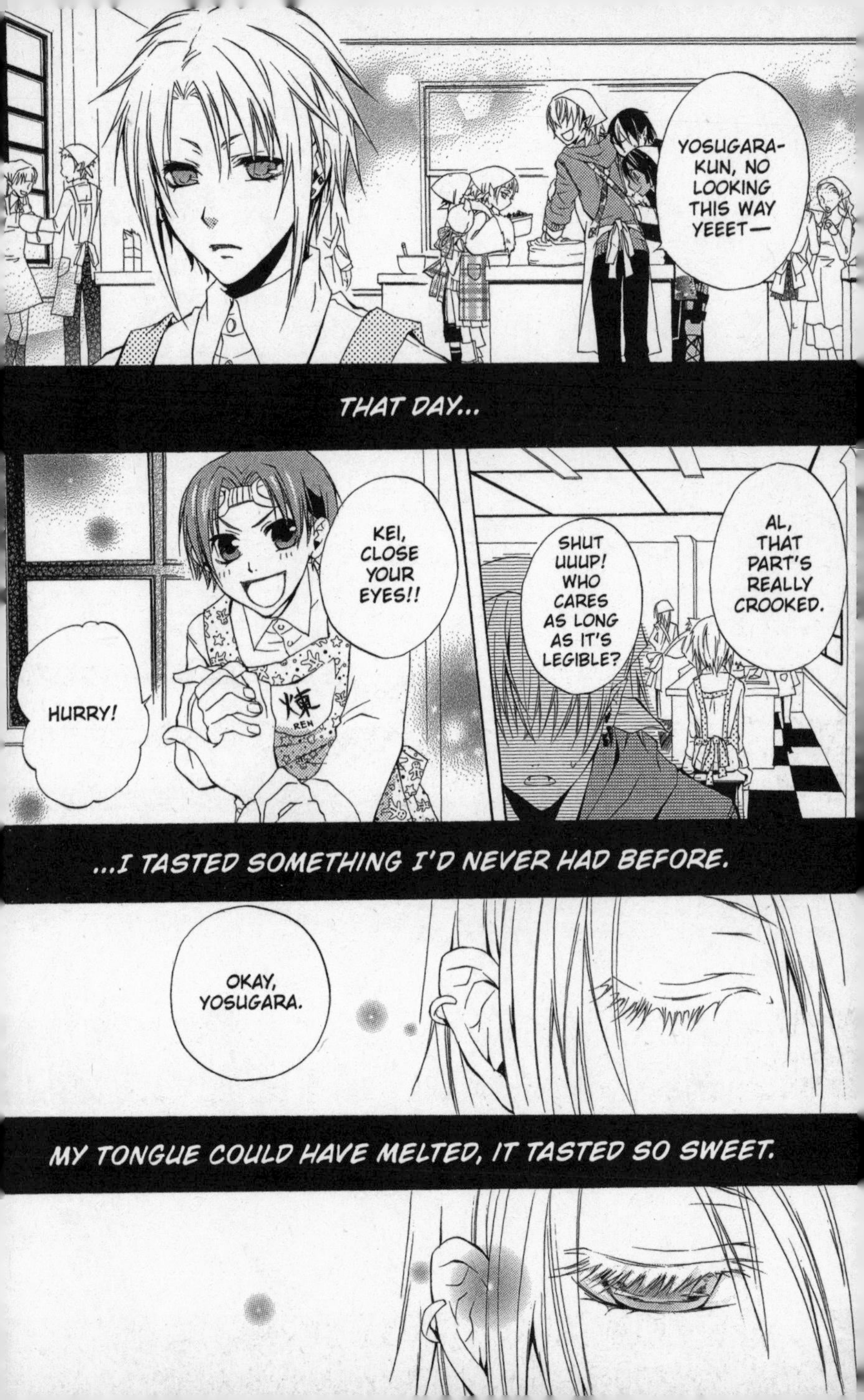
YOSUGARA-KUN, NO LOOKING THIS WAY YEEET—
THAT DAY...
AL, THAT PART'S REALLY CROOKED.
SHUT UUUP! WHO CARES AS LONG AS IT'S LEGIBLE?
KEI, CLOSE YOUR EYES!!
HURRY!
...I TASTED SOMETHING I'D NEVER HAD BEFORE.
OKAY, YOSUGARA.
MY TONGUE COULD HAVE MELTED, IT TASTED SO SWEET.

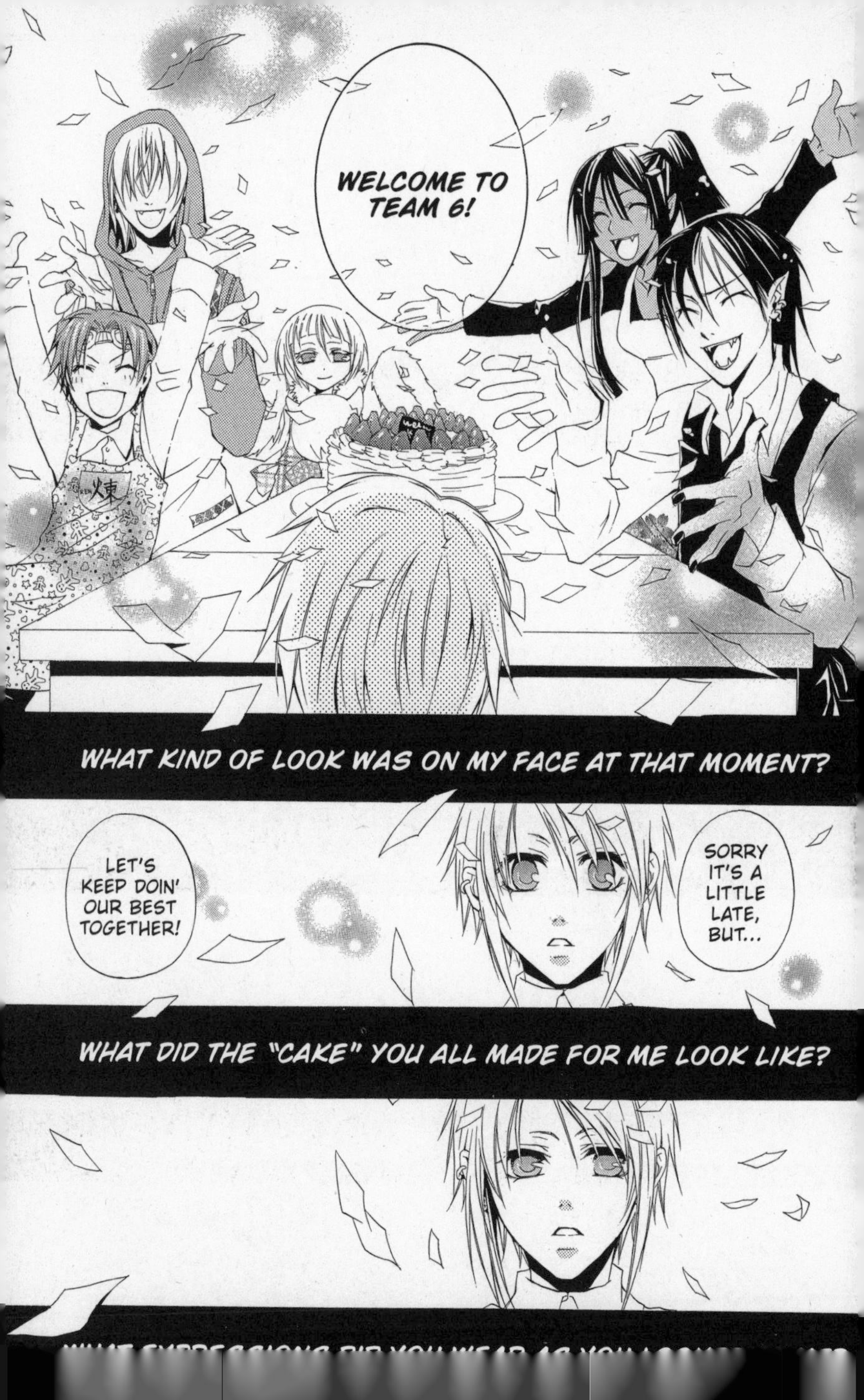
WELCOME TO TEAM 6!
WHAT KIND OF LOOK WAS ON MY FACE AT THAT MOMENT?
SORRY IT'S A LITTLE LATE, BUT...
LET'S KEEP DOIN' OUR BEST TOGETHER!
WHAT DID THE "CAKE" YOU ALL MADE FOR ME LOOK LIKE?

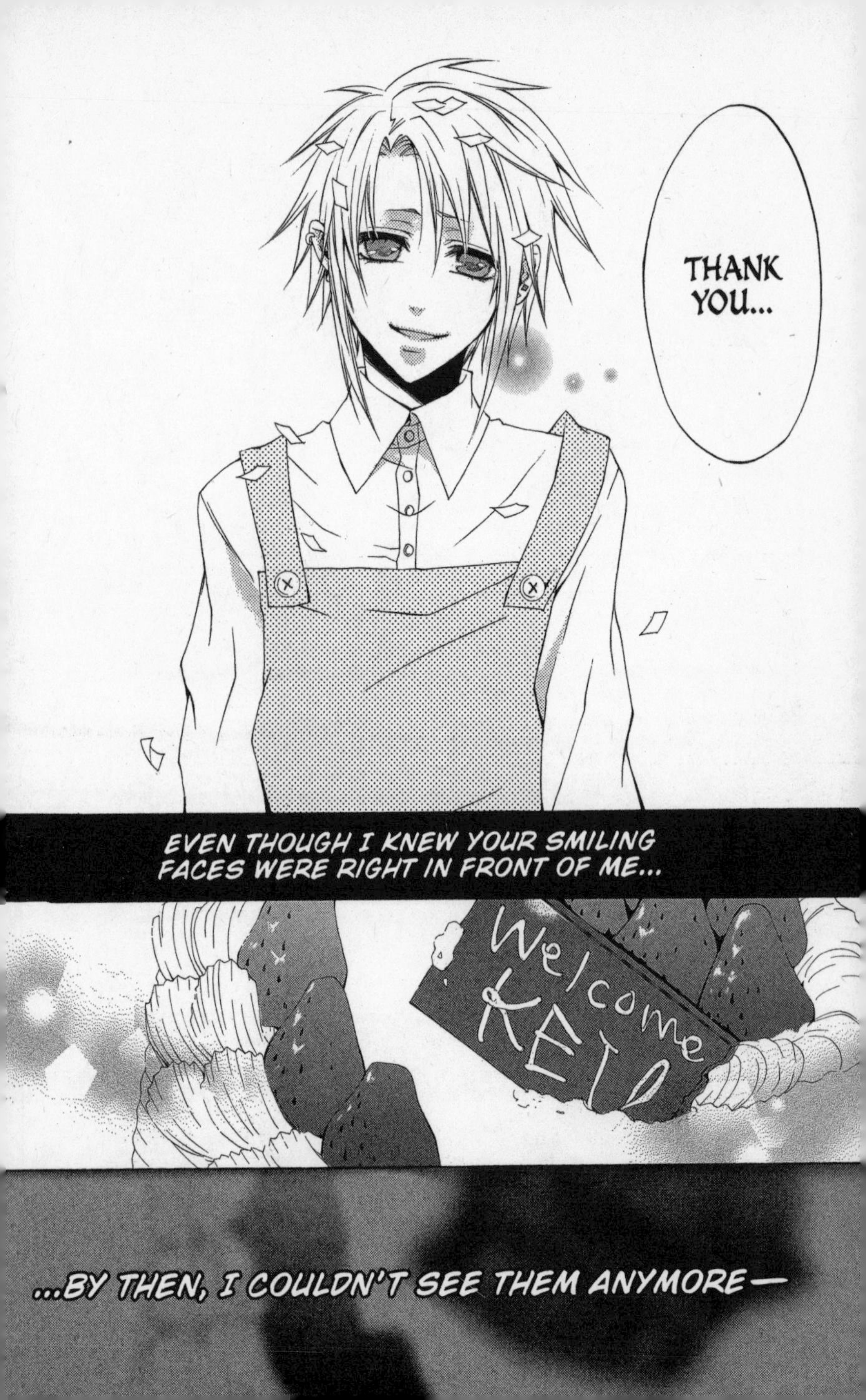
THANK YOU...
EVEN THOUGH I KNEW YOUR SMILING FACES WERE RIGHT IN FRONT OF ME...
Welcome KEI
...BY THEN, I COULDN'T SEE THEM ANYMORE—

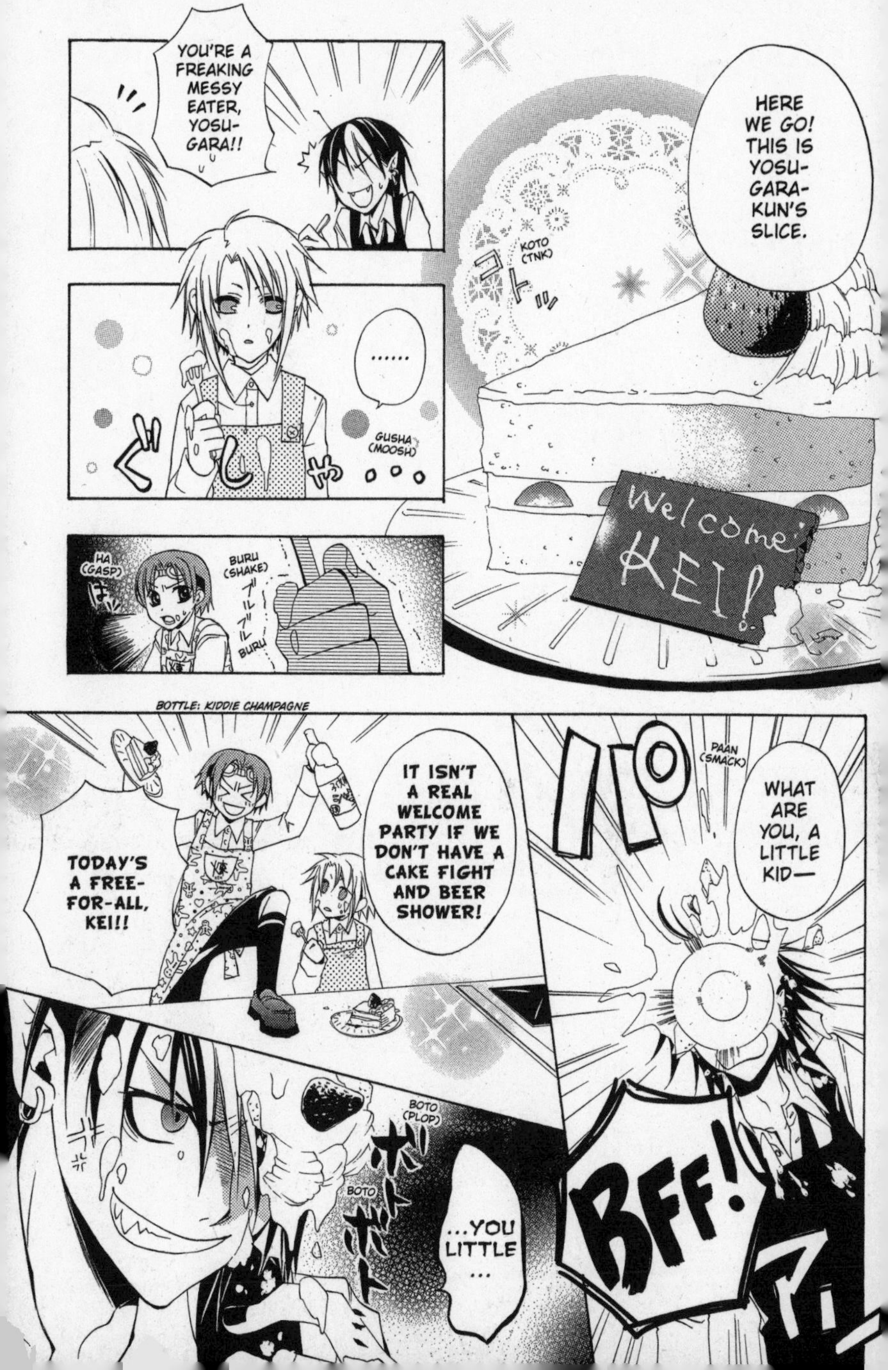
HERE WE GO! THIS IS YOSU-GARA-KUN'S SLICE.
KOTO (TNK)
YOU'RE A FREAKING MESSY EATER, YOSU-GARA!!
......
GUSHA (MOOSH)
BURU (SHAKE) BURU
HA (GASP)
BOTTLE: KIDDIE CHAMPAGNE
PAAN (SMACK)
WHAT ARE YOU, A LITTLE KID—
IT ISN'T A REAL WELCOME PARTY IF WE DON'T HAVE A CAKE FIGHT AND BEER SHOWER!
TODAY'S A FREE-FOR-ALL, KEI!!
Welcome KEI!
BFF!!
BOTO (PLOP)
BOTO
...YOU LITTLE ...

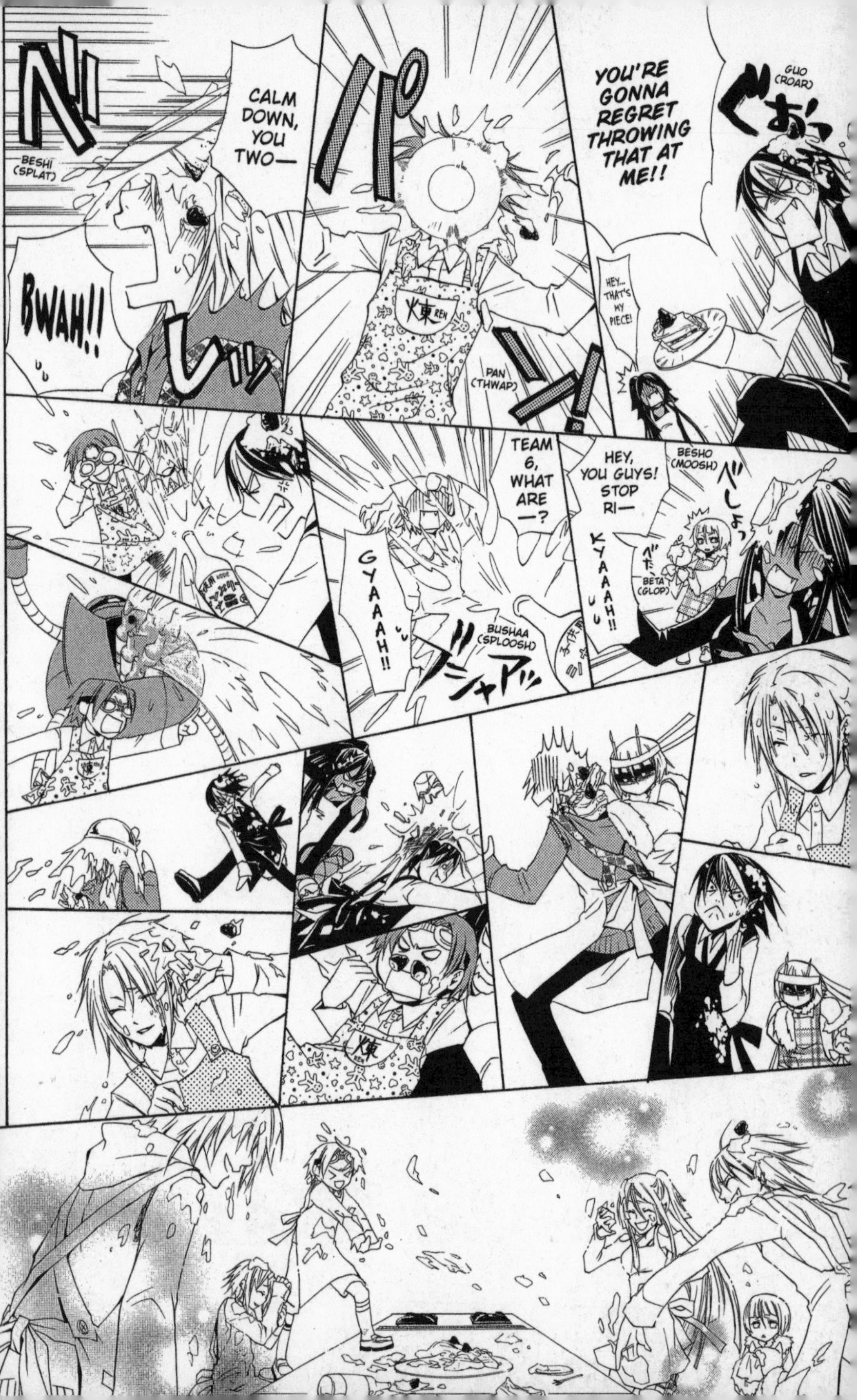
GUO (ROAR)
YOU'RE GONNA REGRET THROWING THAT AT ME!!
HEY... THAT'S MY PIECE!
PAN (THWAP)
CALM DOWN, YOU TWO—
BESHI (SPLAT)
BWAH!!
HEY, YOU GUYS! STOP RI—
BESHO (MOOSH)
BETA (GLOP)
KYAAAAH!!
TEAM 6, WHAT ARE —?
GYAAAAH!!
BUSHAA (SPLOOSH)

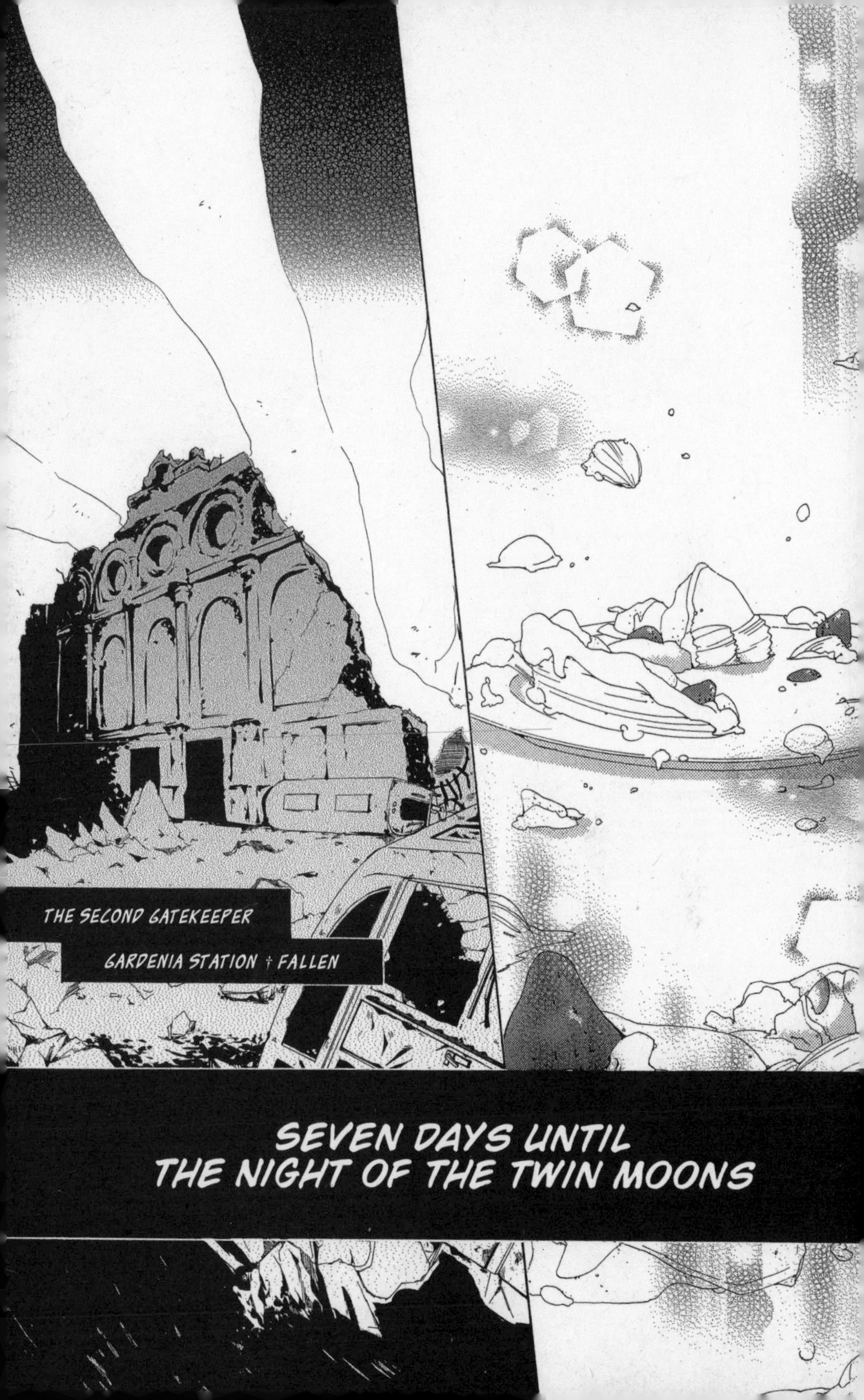
THE SECOND GATEKEEPER
GARDENIA STATION † FALLEN
SEVEN DAYS UNTIL
THE NIGHT OF THE TWIN MOONS

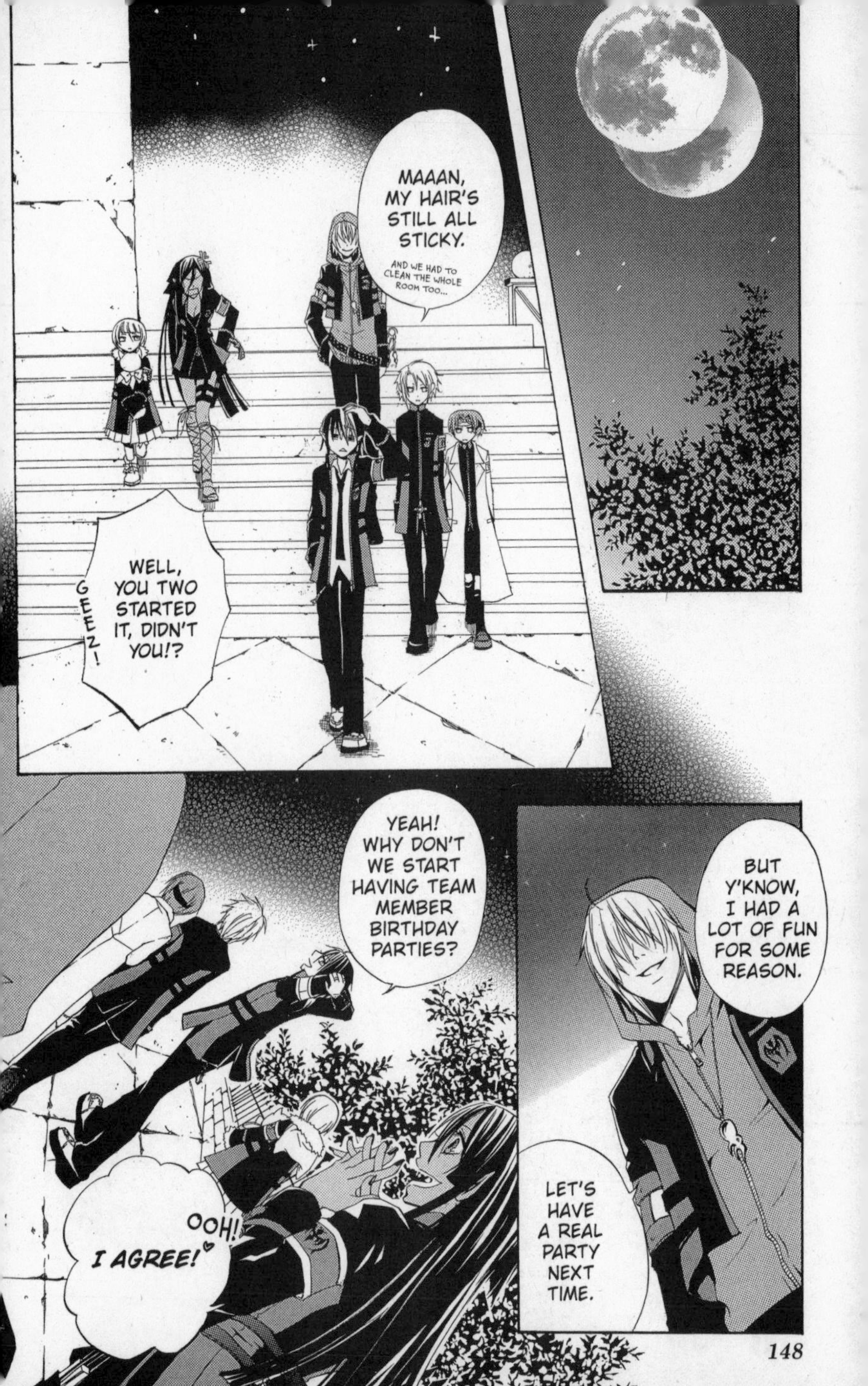
MAAAN, MY HAIR'S STILL ALL STICKY.
AND WE HAD TO CLEAN THE WHOLE ROOM TOO...
WELL, YOU TWO STARTED IT, DIDN'T YOU!?
GEEZ!
BUT Y'KNOW, I HAD A LOT OF FUN FOR SOME REASON.
LET'S HAVE A REAL PARTY NEXT TIME.
YEAH! WHY DON'T WE START HAVING TEAM MEMBER BIRTHDAY PARTIES?
OOH! I AGREE!♥

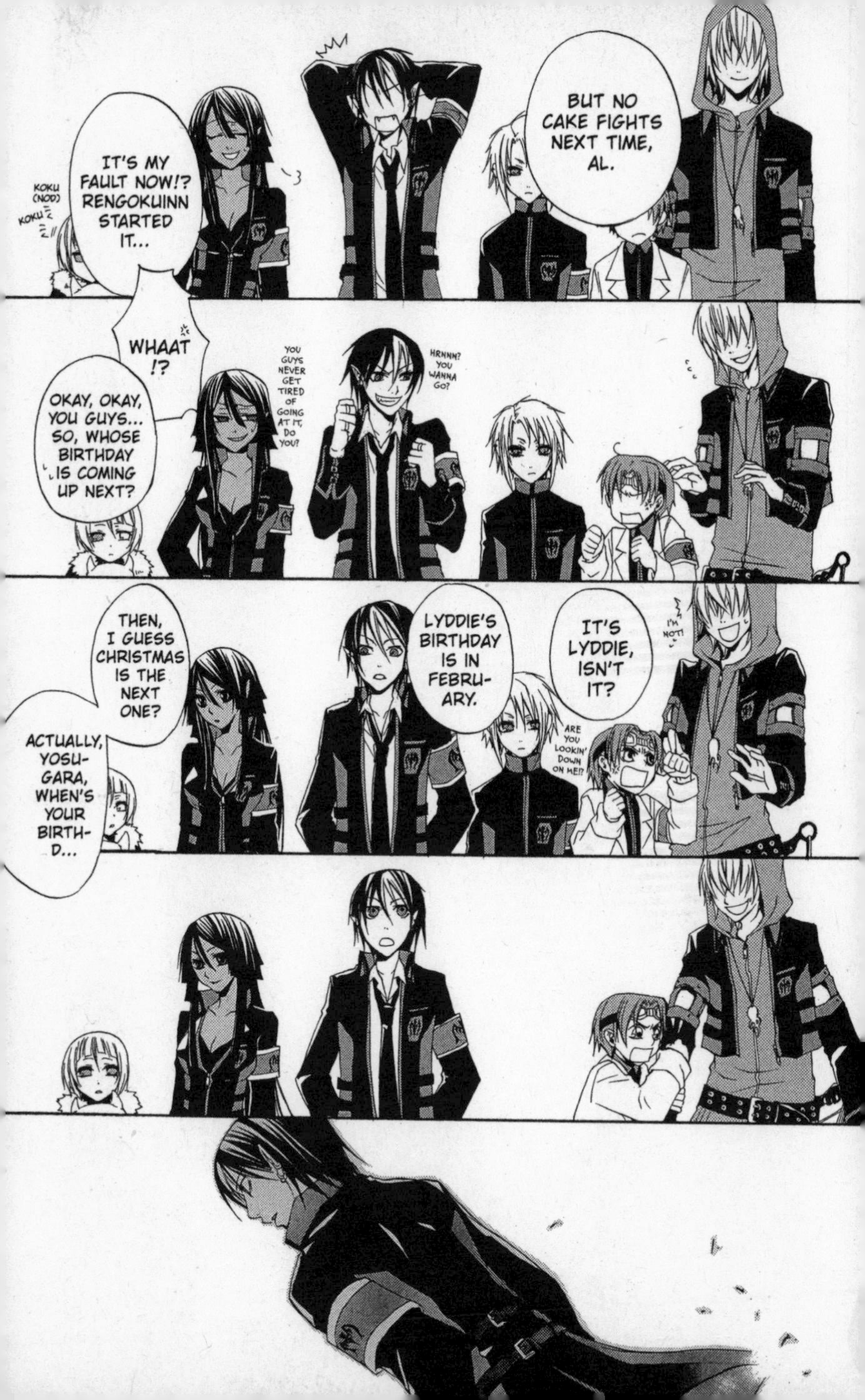
BUT NO CAKE FIGHTS NEXT TIME, AL.
IT'S MY FAULT NOW!? RENGOKUINN STARTED IT...
KOKU (NOD) KOKU
HRNNN? YOU WANNA GO?
YOU GUYS NEVER GET TIRED OF GOING AT IT, DO YOU?
WHAAT !?
OKAY, OKAY, YOU GUYS... SO, WHOSE BIRTHDAY IS COMING UP NEXT?
I'M NOT!
IT'S LYDDIE, ISN'T IT?
ARE YOU LOOKIN' DOWN ON ME!?
LYDDIE'S BIRTHDAY IS IN FEBRU-ARY.
THEN, I GUESS CHRISTMAS IS THE NEXT ONE?
ACTUALLY, YOSU-GARA, WHEN'S YOUR BIRTH-D...

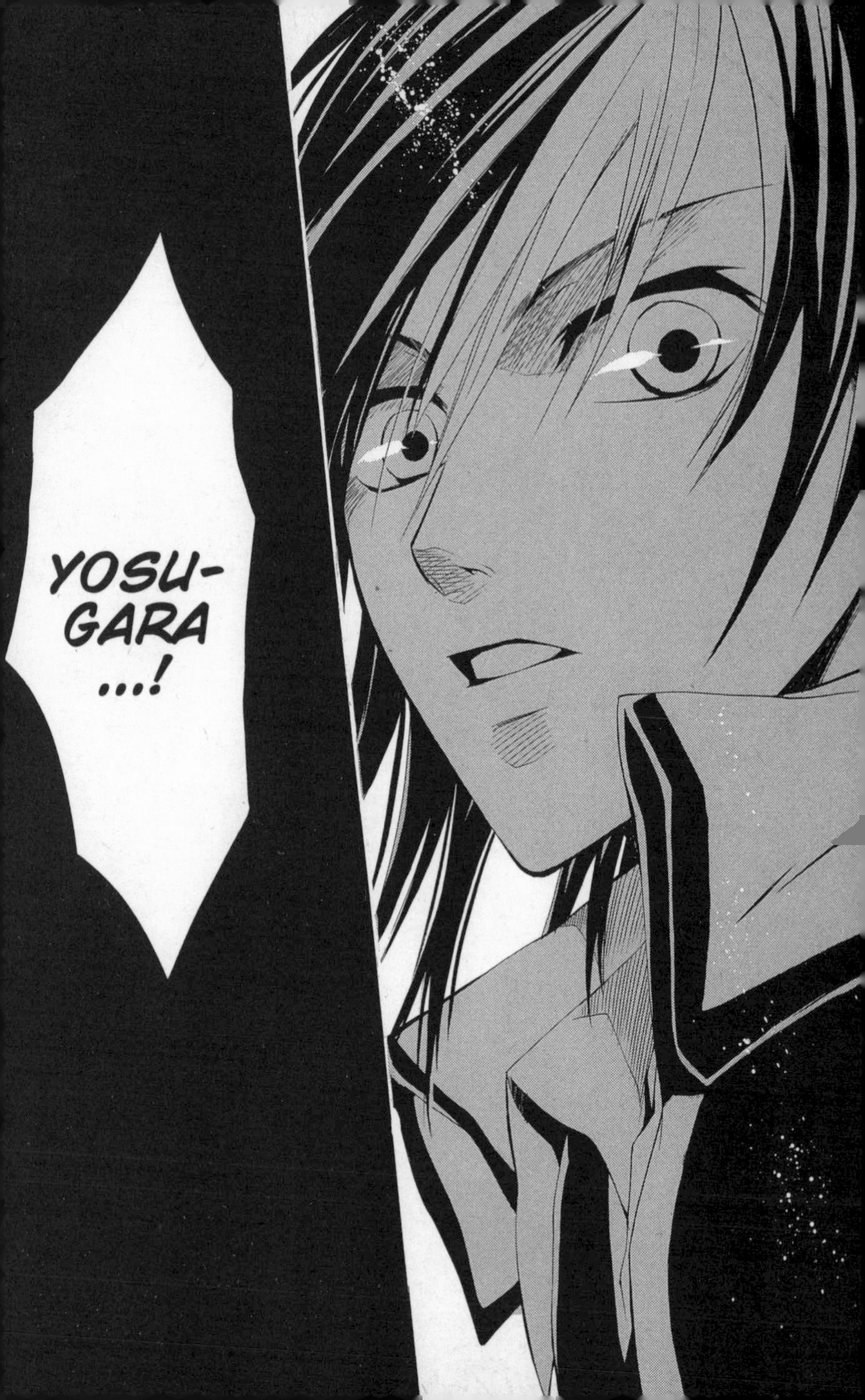
YOSU-
GARA
...!

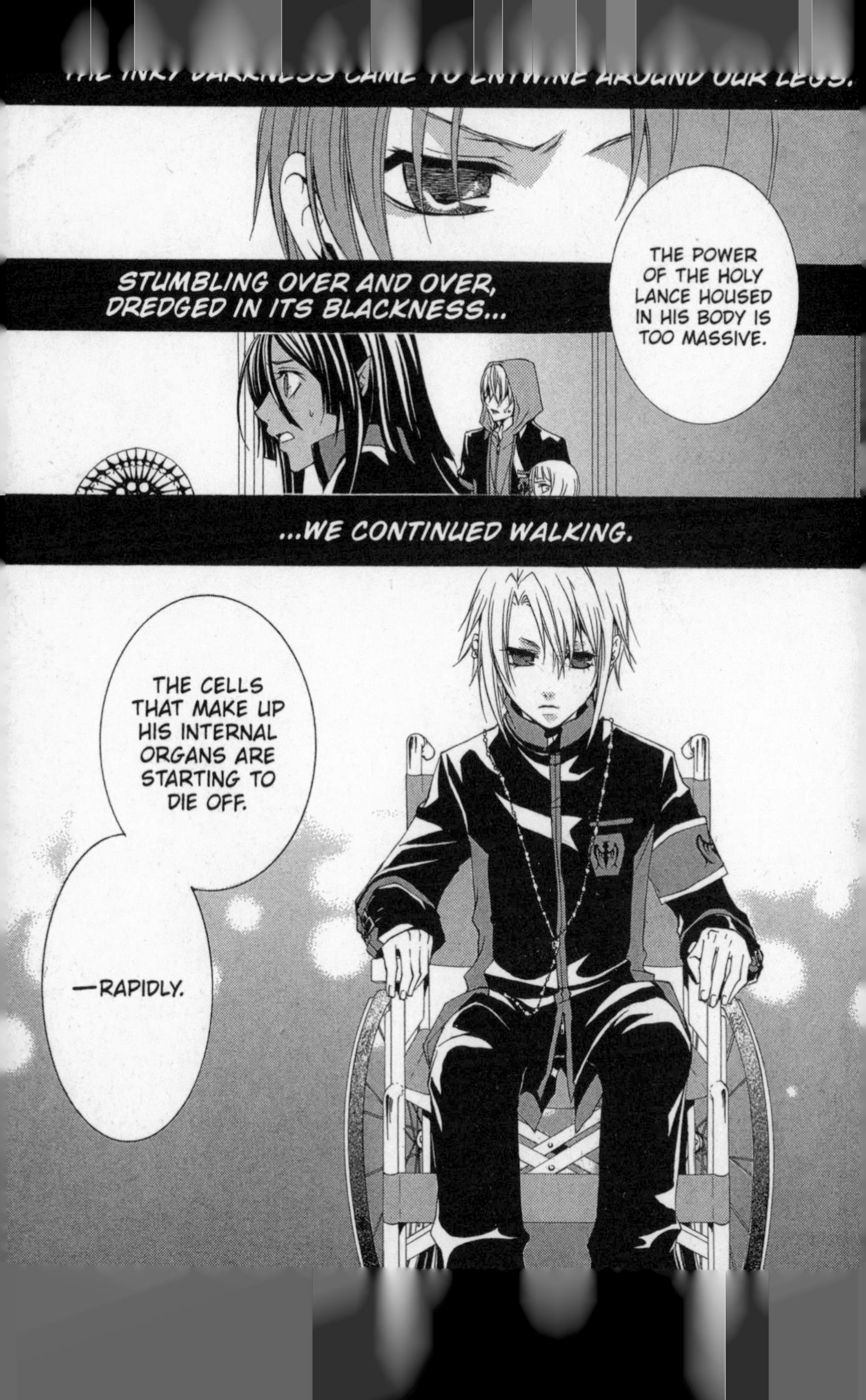
THE INKY DARKNESS CAME TO ENTWINE AROUND OUR LEGS.
THE POWER OF THE HOLY LANCE HOUSED IN HIS BODY IS TOO MASSIVE.
STUMBLING OVER AND OVER, DREDGED IN ITS BLACKNESS...
...WE CONTINUED WALKING.
THE CELLS THAT MAKE UP HIS INTERNAL ORGANS ARE STARTING TO DIE OFF.
—RAPIDLY.

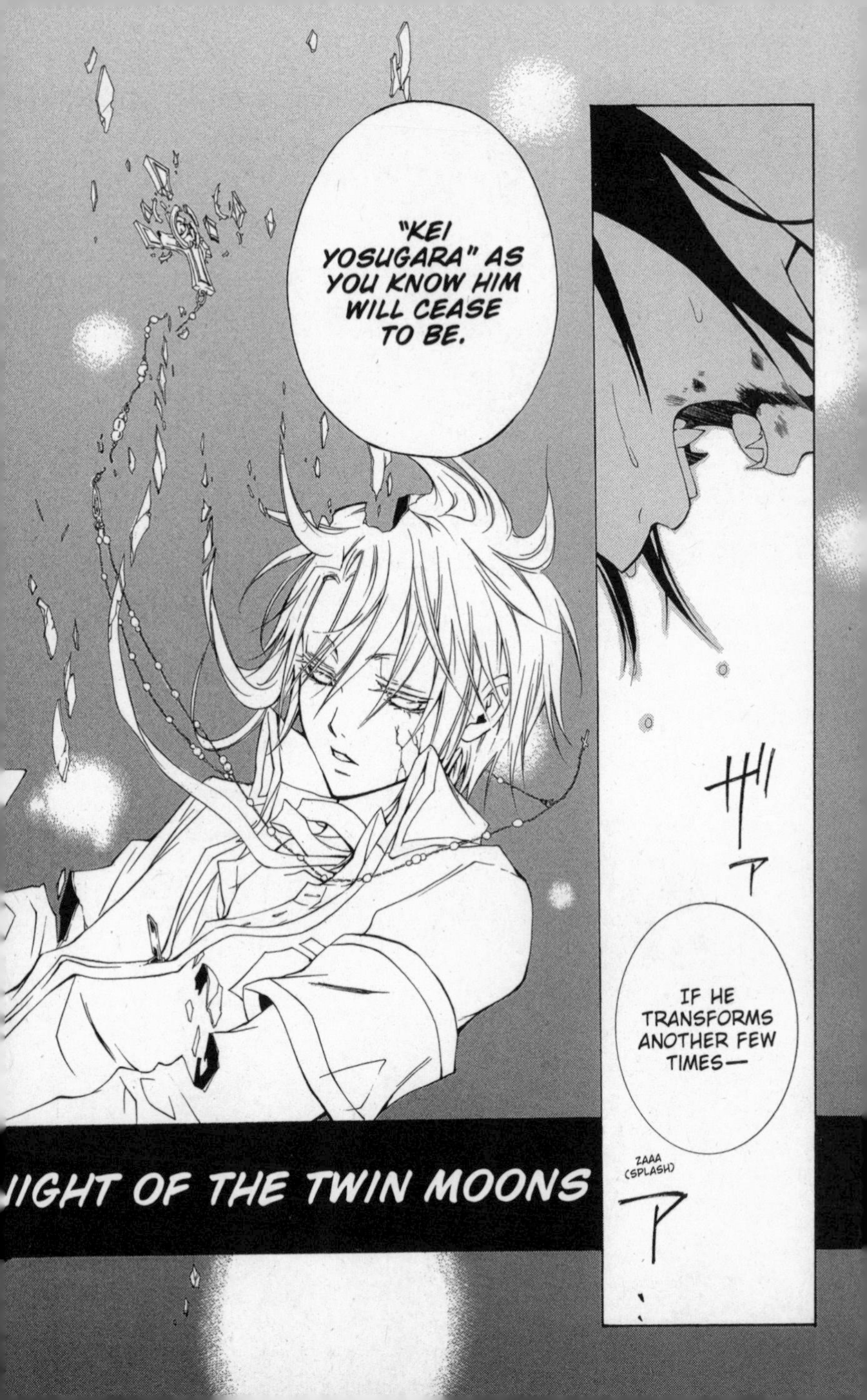
IF HE TRANSFORMS ANOTHER FEW TIMES—
ZAAA (SPLASH)
"KEI YOSUGARA" AS YOU KNOW HIM WILL CEASE TO BE.
IGHT OF THE TWIN MOONS

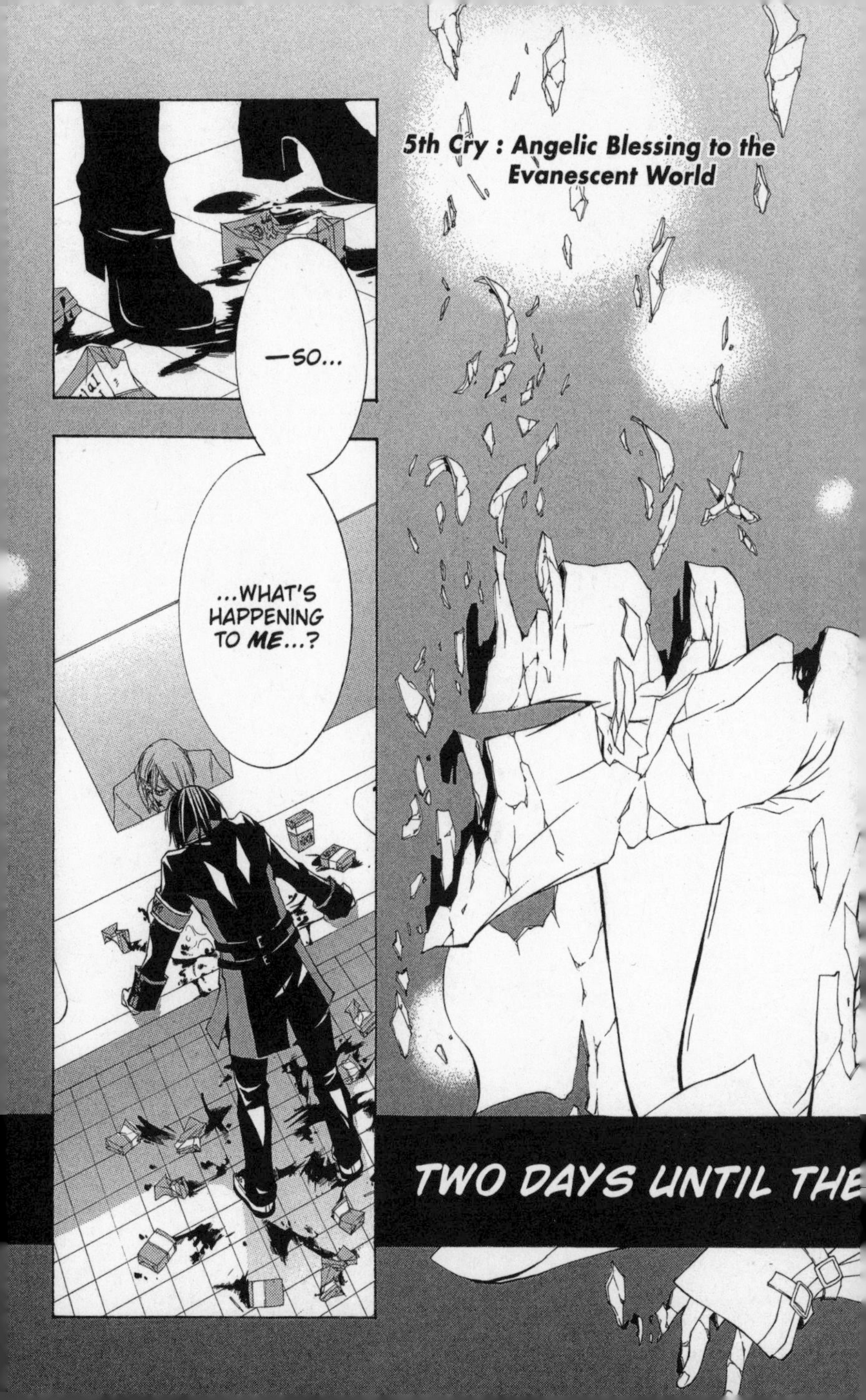
5th Cry : Angelic Blessing to the Evanescent World
TWO DAYS UNTIL THE
—SO...
...WHAT'S HAPPENING TO ME...?

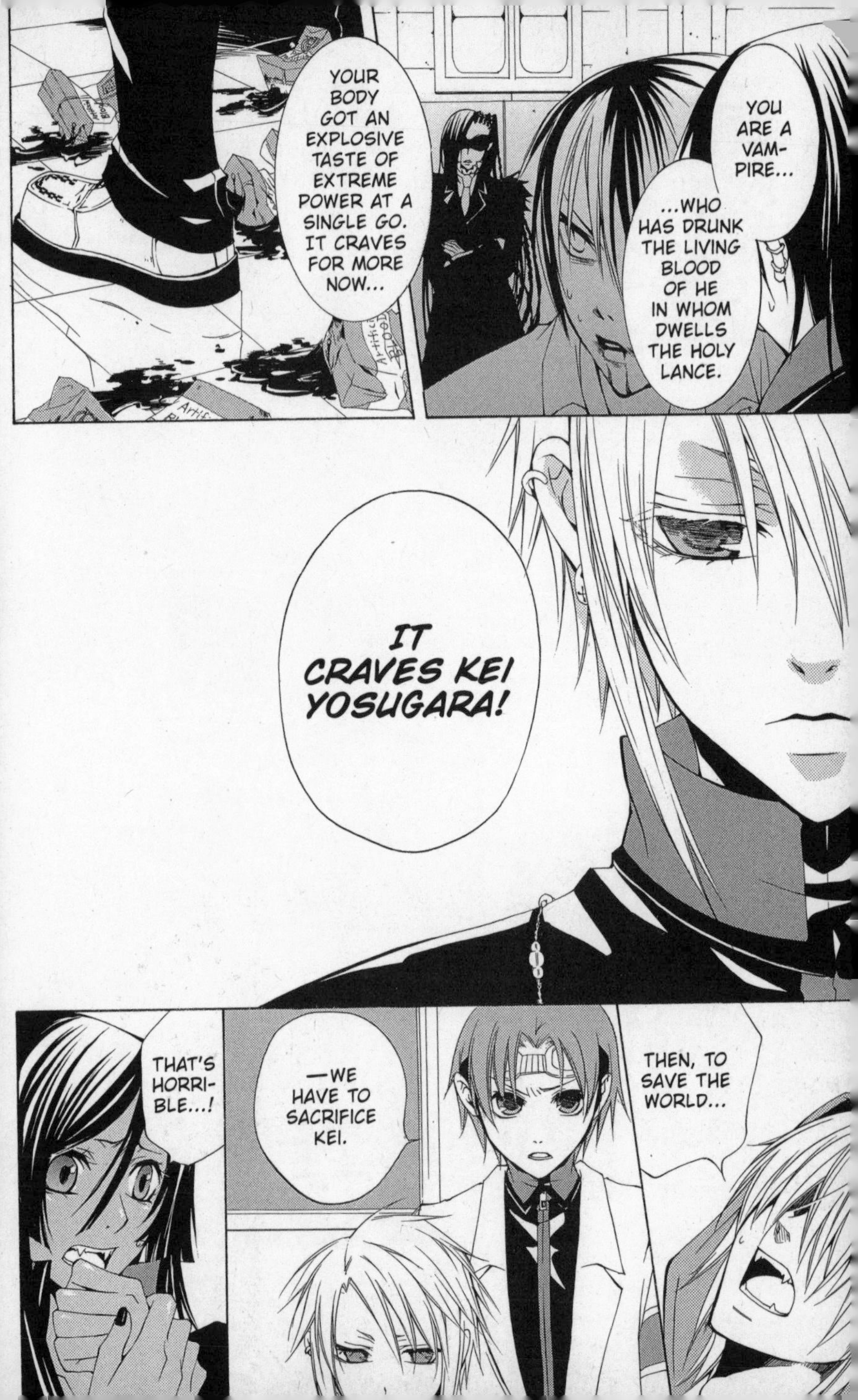
YOU ARE A VAMPIRE...
...WHO HAS DRUNK THE LIVING BLOOD OF HE IN WHOM DWELLS THE HOLY LANCE.
YOUR BODY GOT AN EXPLOSIVE TASTE OF EXTREME POWER AT A SINGLE GO. IT CRAVES FOR MORE NOW...
IT CRAVES KEI YOSUGARA!
THEN, TO SAVE THE WORLD...
—WE HAVE TO SACRIFICE KEI.
THAT'S HORRIBLE...!

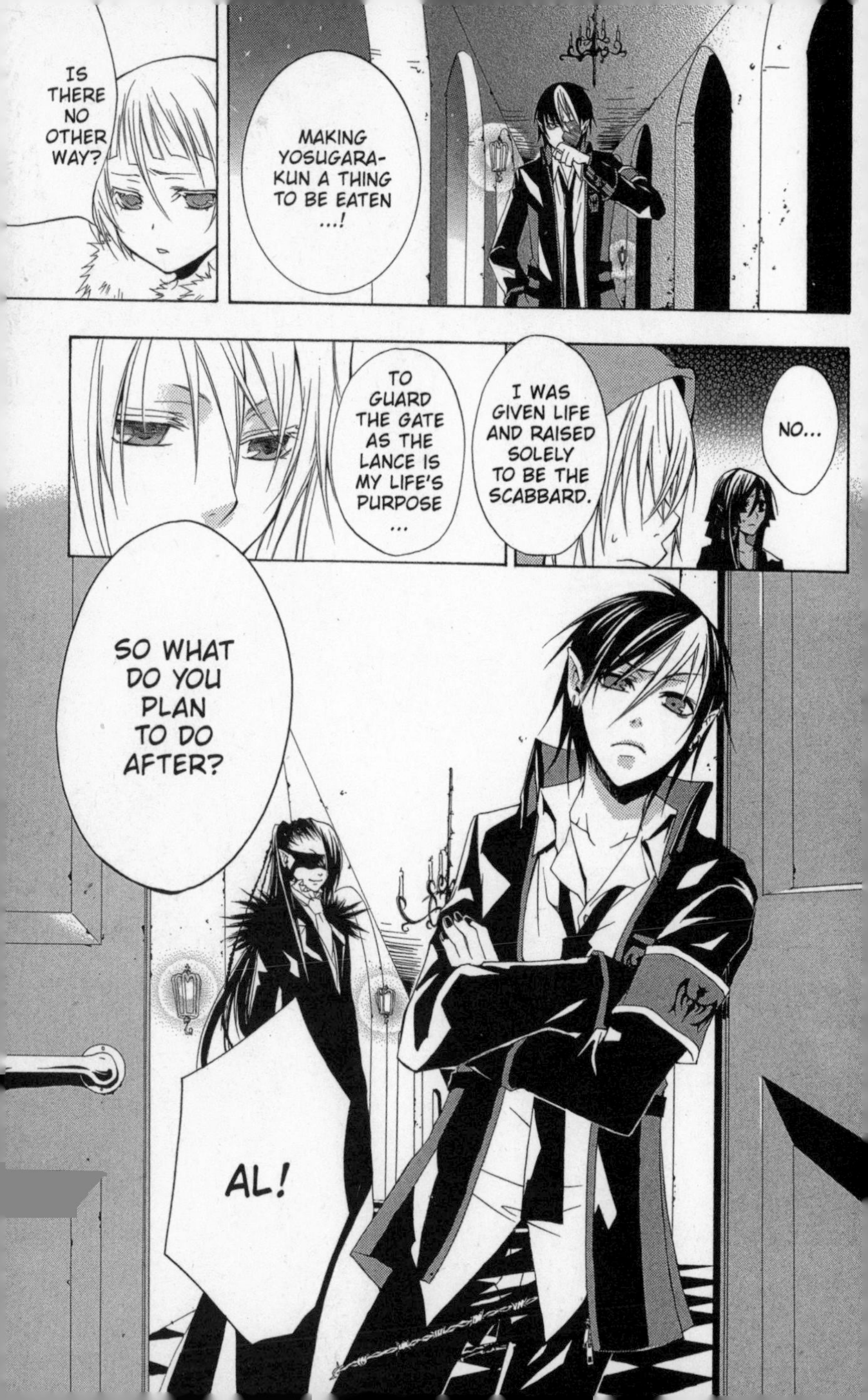
MAKING YOSUGARA-KUN A THING TO BE EATEN ...!
IS THERE NO OTHER WAY?
NO...
I WAS GIVEN LIFE AND RAISED SOLELY TO BE THE SCABBARD.
TO GUARD THE GATE AS THE LANCE IS MY LIFE'S PURPOSE ...
SO WHAT DO YOU PLAN TO DO AFTER?
AL!

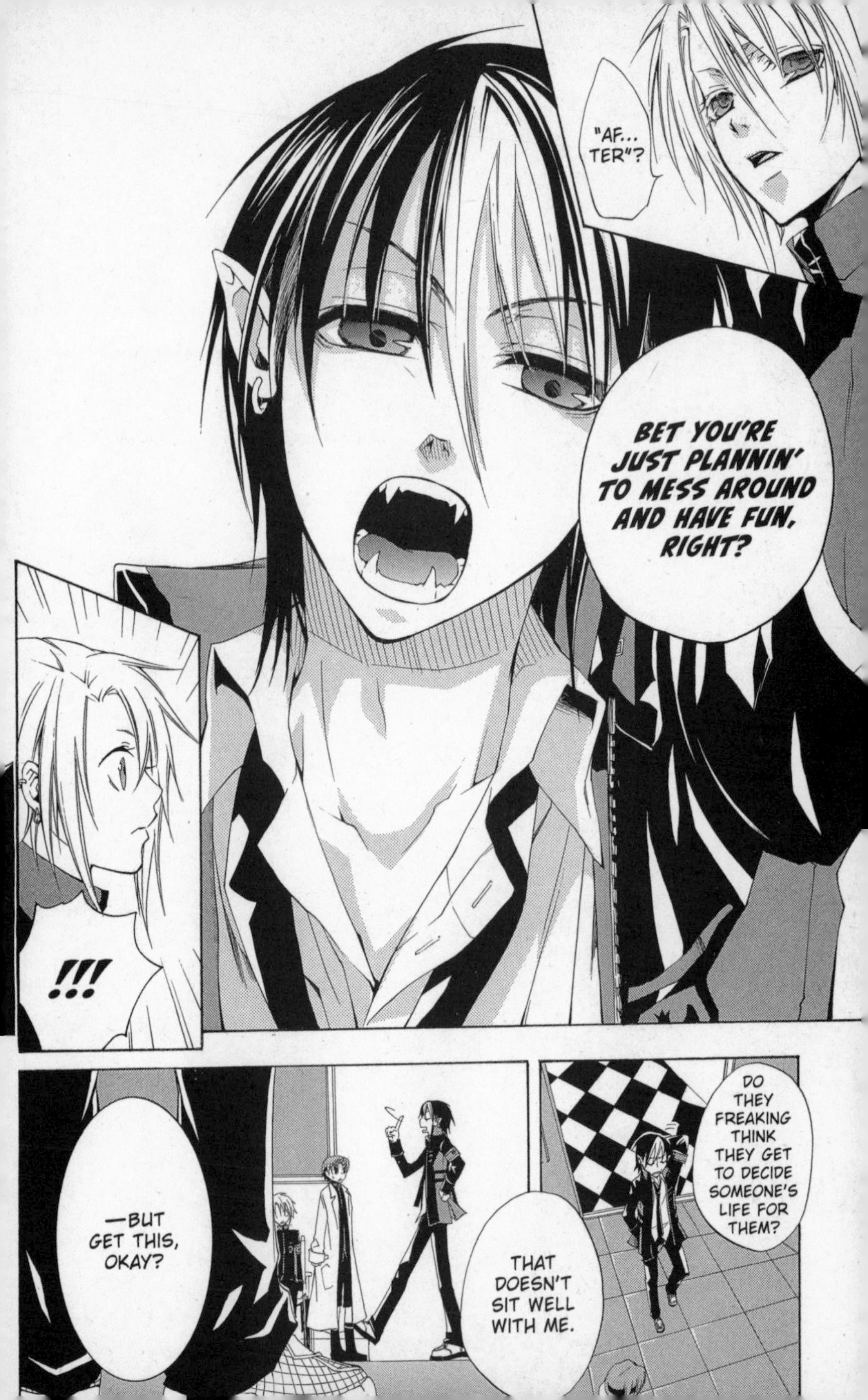
"AF... TER"?
BET YOU'RE JUST PLANNIN' TO MESS AROUND AND HAVE FUN, RIGHT?
!!!
DO THEY FREAKING THINK THEY GET TO DECIDE SOMEONE'S LIFE FOR THEM?
THAT DOESN'T SIT WELL WITH ME.
—BUT GET THIS, OKAY?

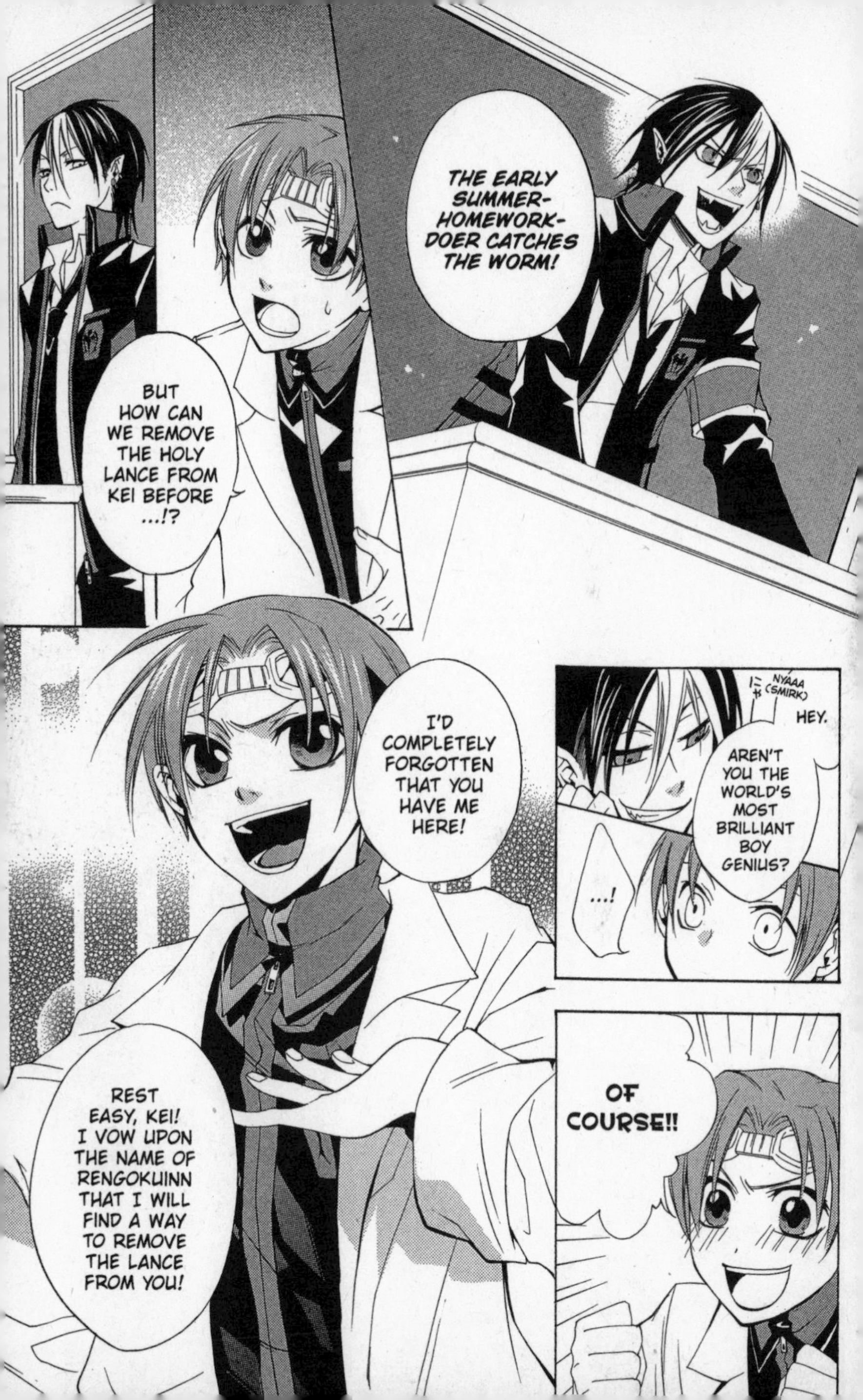
THE EARLY SUMMER-HOMEWORK-DOER CATCHES THE WORM!
BUT HOW CAN WE REMOVE THE HOLY LANCE FROM KEI BEFORE ...!?
NYAAA (SMIRK)
HEY.
AREN'T YOU THE WORLD'S MOST BRILLIANT BOY GENIUS?
...!
OF COURSE!!
I'D COMPLETELY FORGOTTEN THAT YOU HAVE ME HERE!
REST EASY, KEI! I VOW UPON THE NAME OF RENGOKUINN THAT I WILL FIND A WAY TO REMOVE THE LANCE FROM YOU!

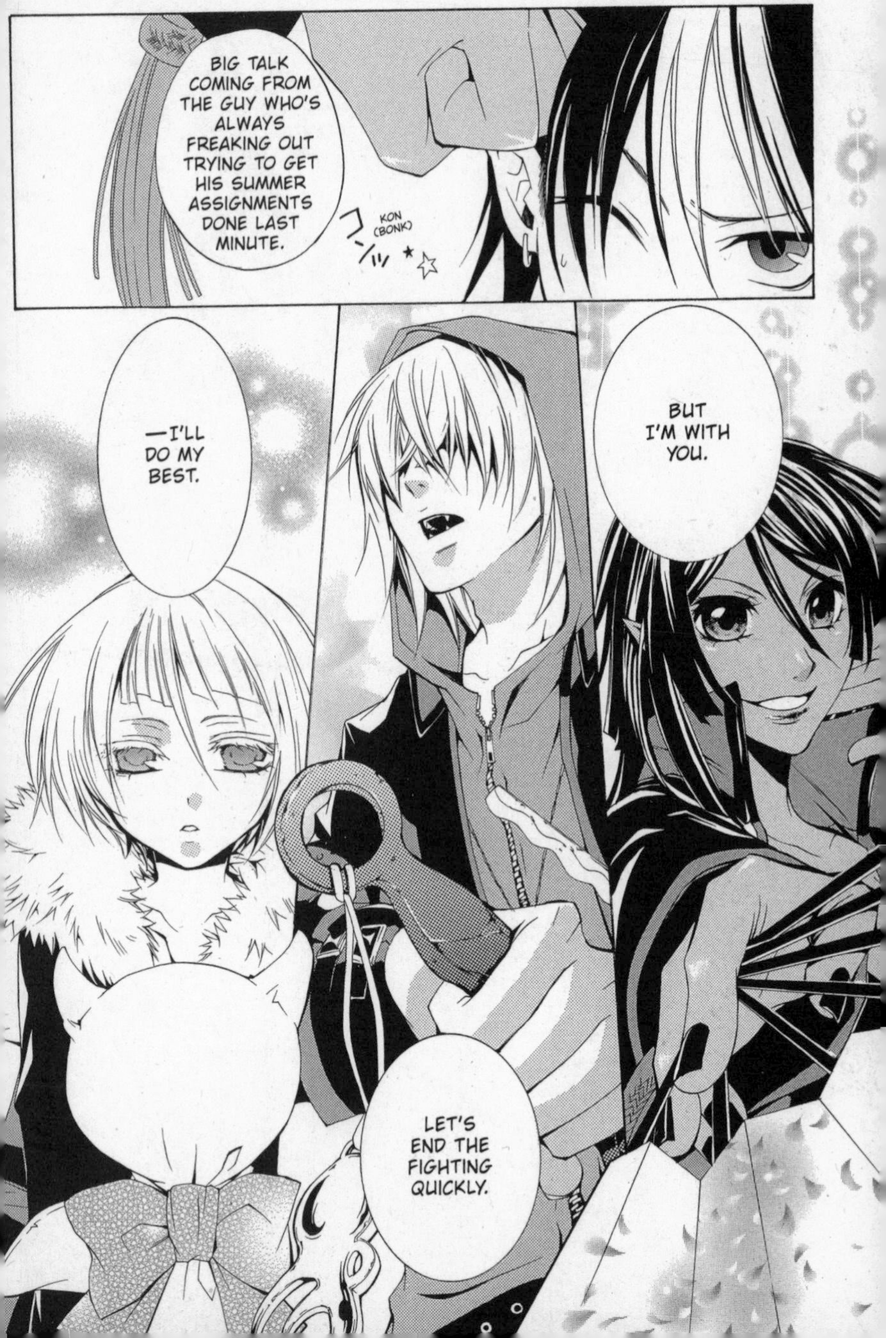
BIG TALK COMING FROM THE GUY WHO'S ALWAYS FREAKING OUT TRYING TO GET HIS SUMMER ASSIGNMENTS DONE LAST MINUTE.
KON (BONK)
BUT I'M WITH YOU.
LET'S END THE FIGHTING QUICKLY.
—I'LL DO MY BEST.

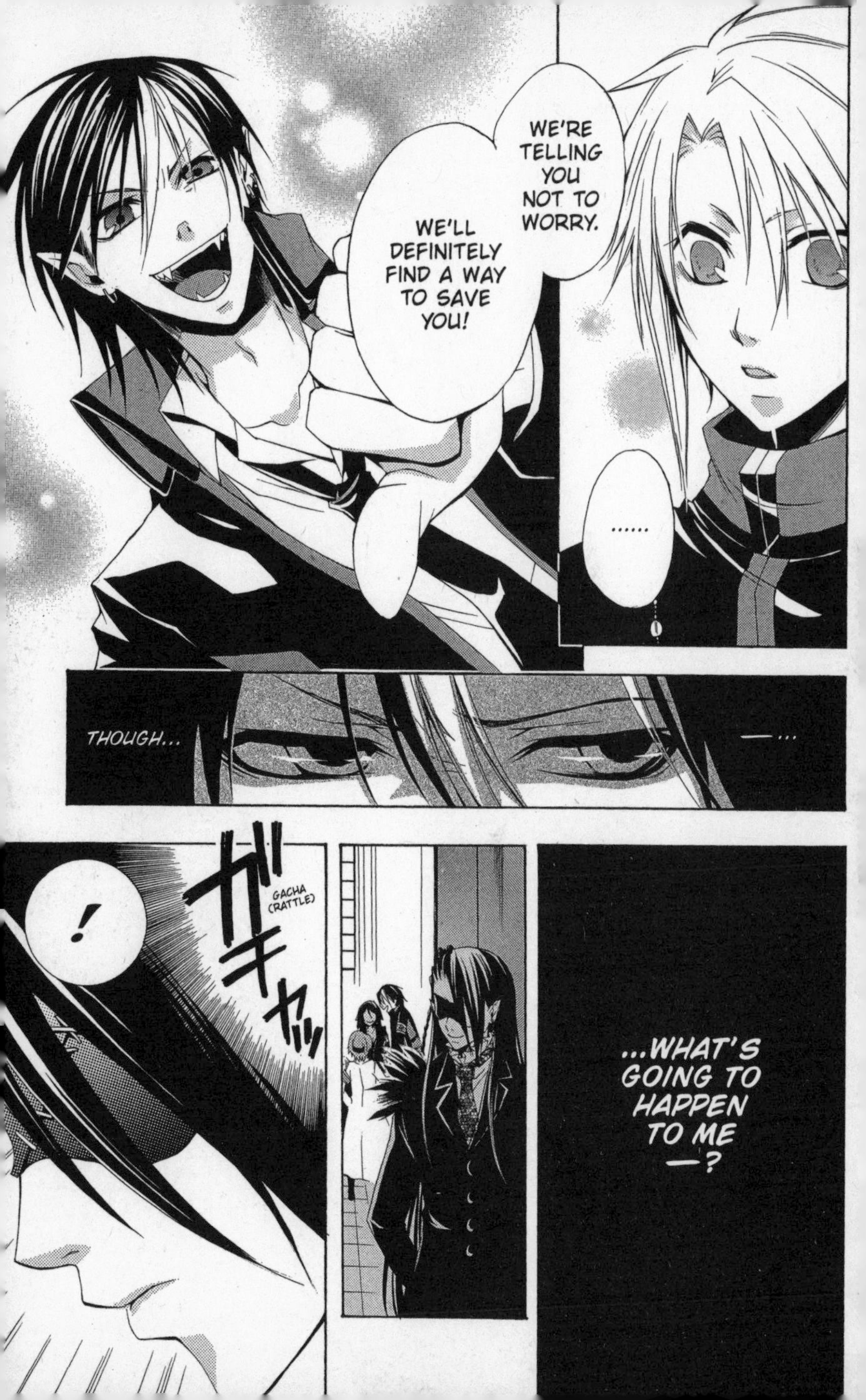
WE'RE TELLING YOU NOT TO WORRY.
WE'LL DEFINITELY FIND A WAY TO SAVE YOU!
......
—...
THOUGH...
...WHAT'S GOING TO HAPPEN TO ME —?
ガチャッ
GACHA (RATTLE)
!

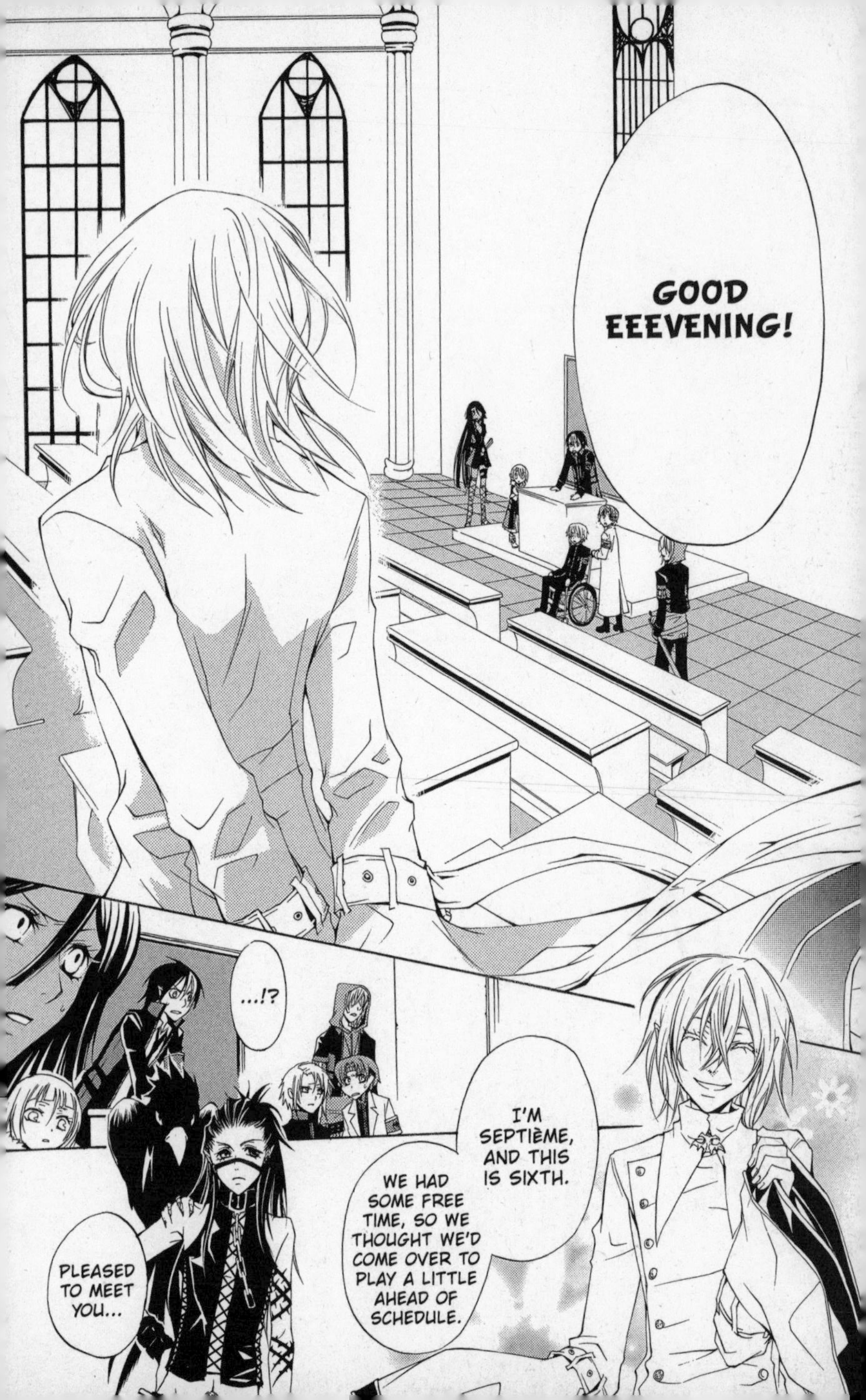
GOOD EEEVENING!
...!?
I'M SEPTIÈME, AND THIS IS SIXTH.
WE HAD SOME FREE TIME, SO WE THOUGHT WE'D COME OVER TO PLAY A LITTLE AHEAD OF SCHEDULE.
PLEASED TO MEET YOU...

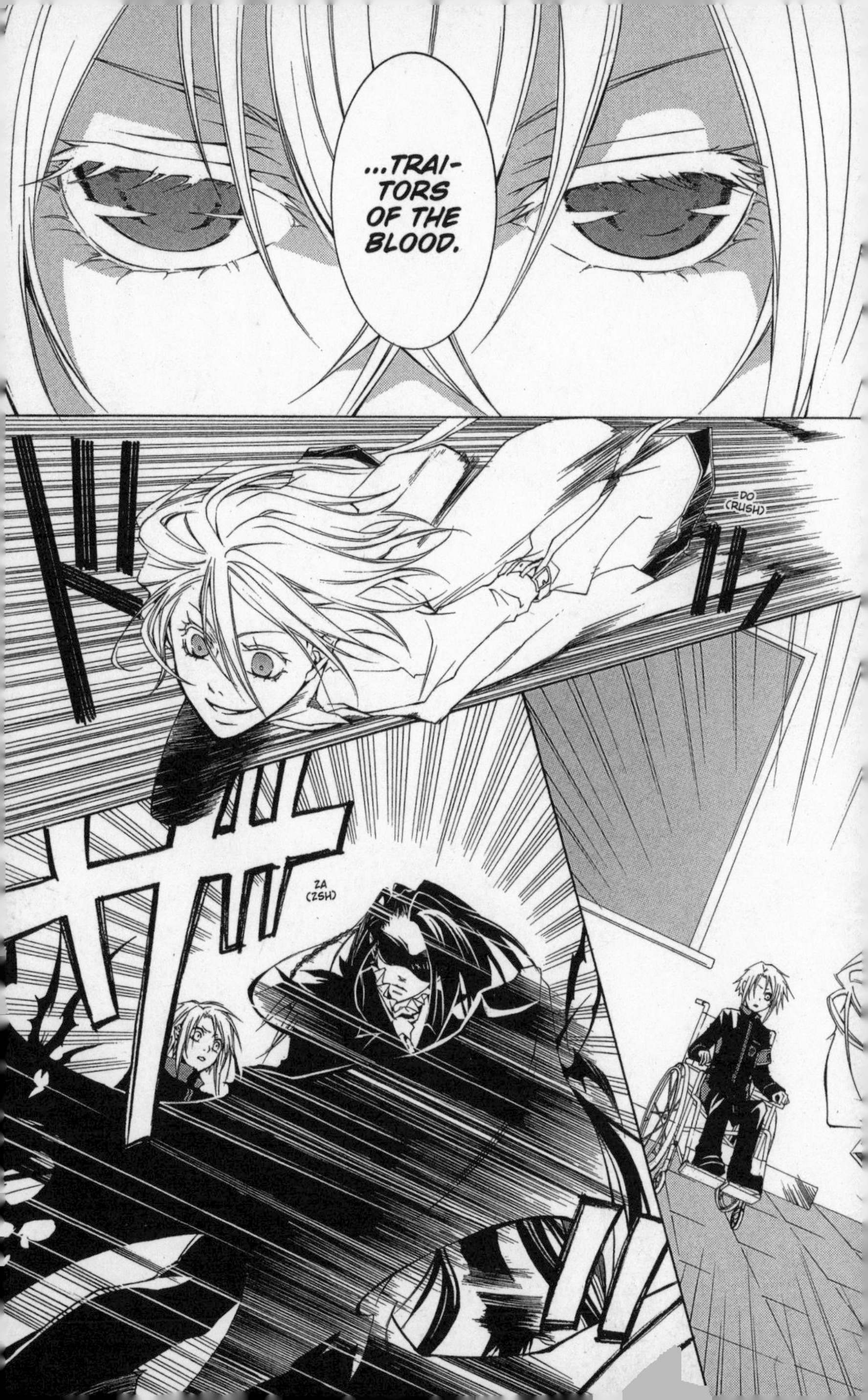
...TRAI-TORS OF THE BLOOD.
DO (RUSH)
ZA (ZSH)

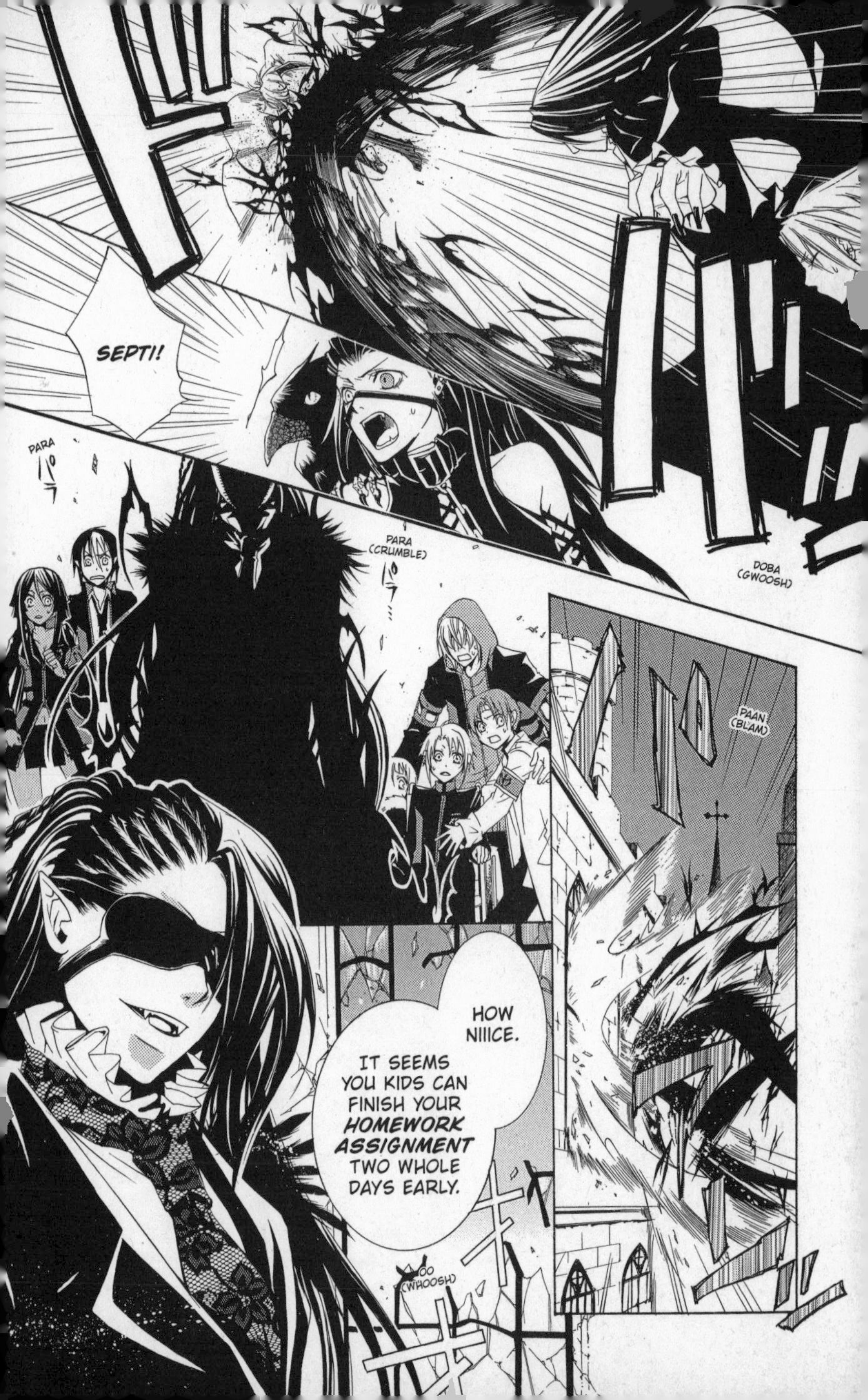
SEPTI!
DOBA (GWOOSH)
PAAN (BLAM)
PARA (CRUMBLE)
PARA
HOW NIIICE.
IT SEEMS YOU KIDS CAN FINISH YOUR **HOMEWORK ASSIGNMENT** TWO WHOLE DAYS EARLY.
OO (WHOOSH)

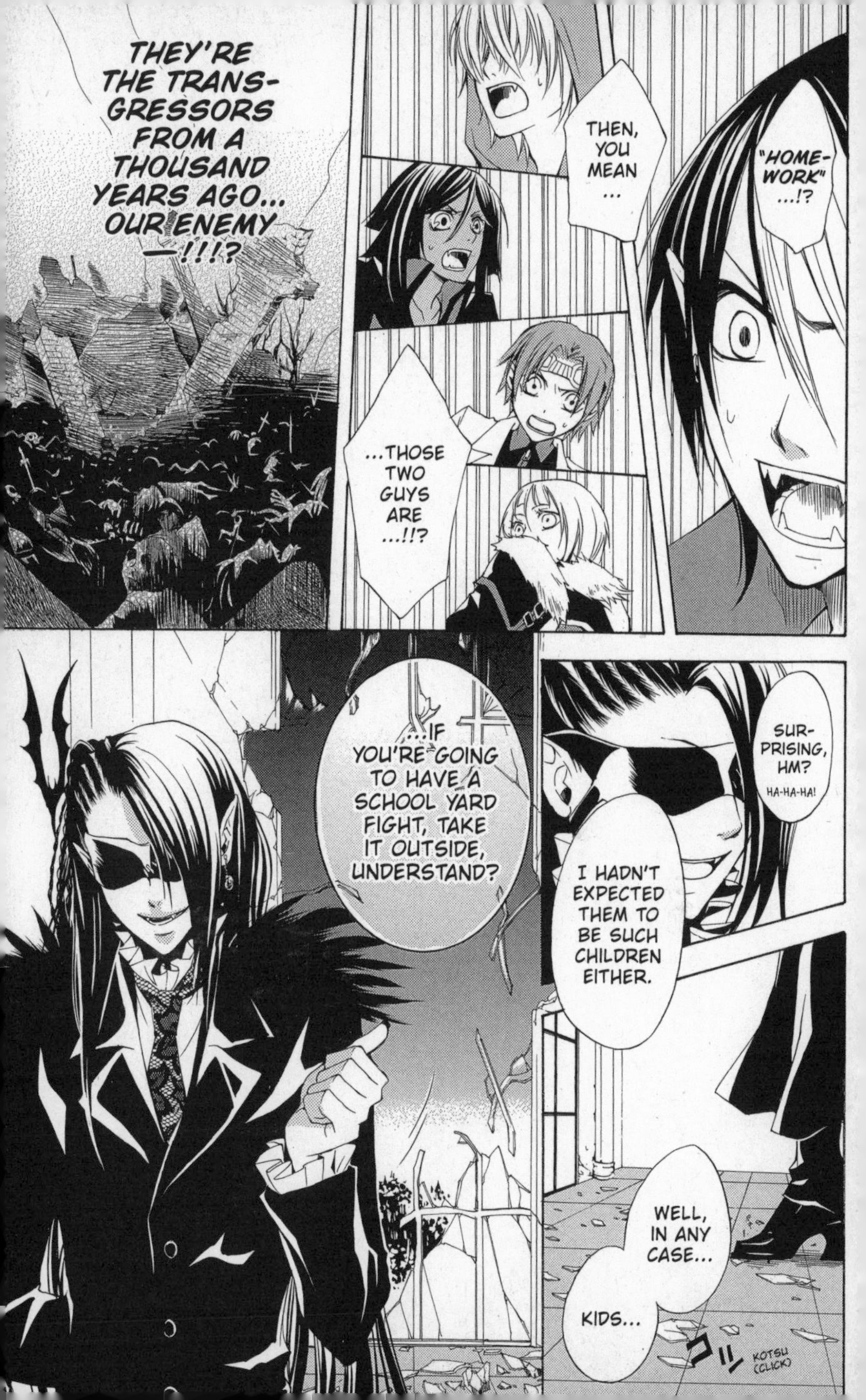
"HOME-WORK" ...!?
THEN, YOU MEAN ...
...THOSE TWO GUYS ARE ...!!?
THEY'RE THE TRANS-GRESSORS FROM A THOUSAND YEARS AGO... OUR ENEMY —!!!?
SUR-PRISING, HM?
HA-HA-HA!
I HADN'T EXPECTED THEM TO BE SUCH CHILDREN EITHER.
WELL, IN ANY CASE...
KIDS...
KOTSU (CLICK)
...IF YOU'RE GOING TO HAVE A SCHOOL YARD FIGHT, TAKE IT OUTSIDE, UNDERSTAND?

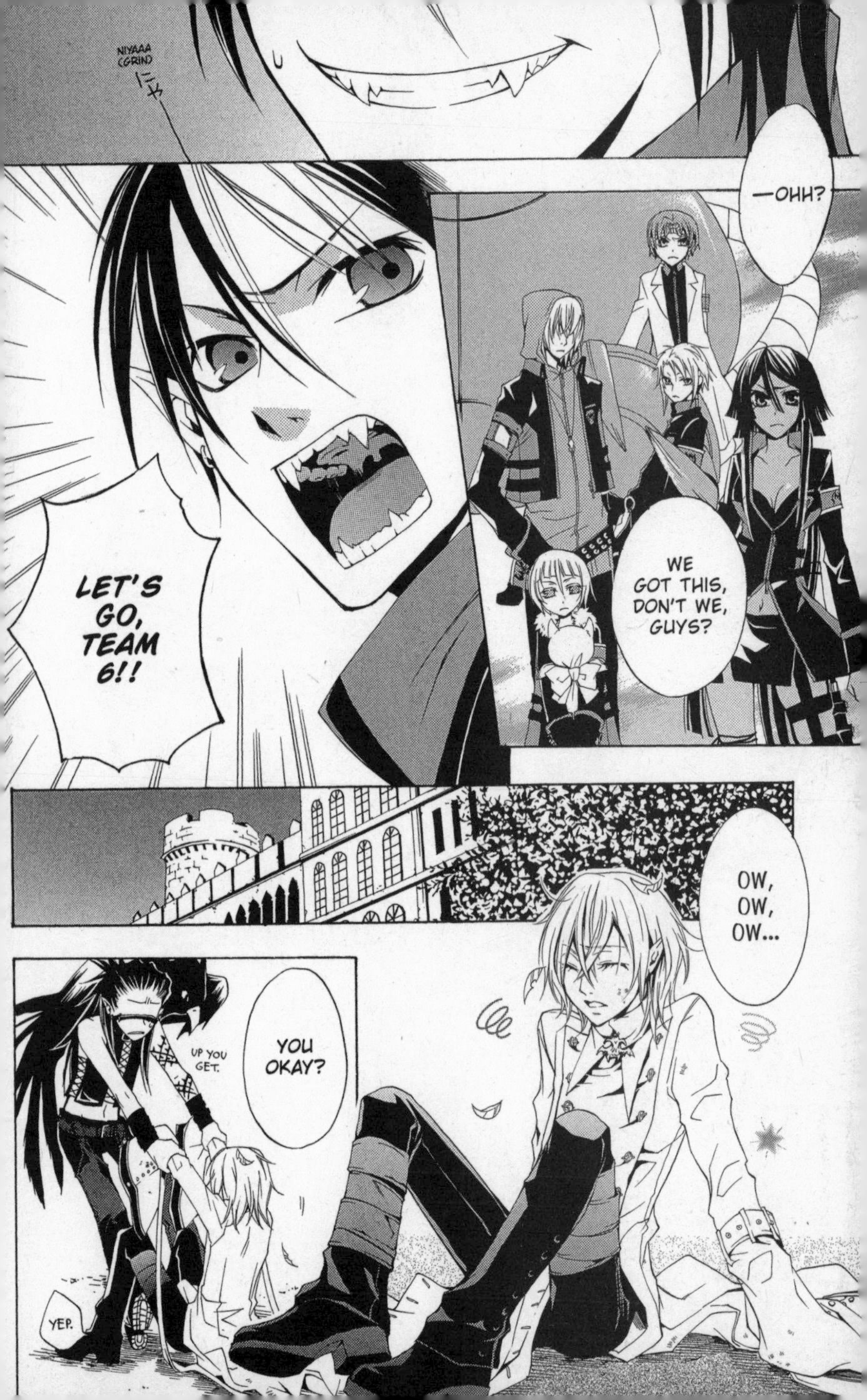
NIYAAA (GRIN)
にや
—OHH?
WE GOT THIS, DON'T WE, GUYS?
LET'S GO, TEAM 6!!
OW, OW, OW...
YOU OKAY?
UP YOU GET.
YEP.

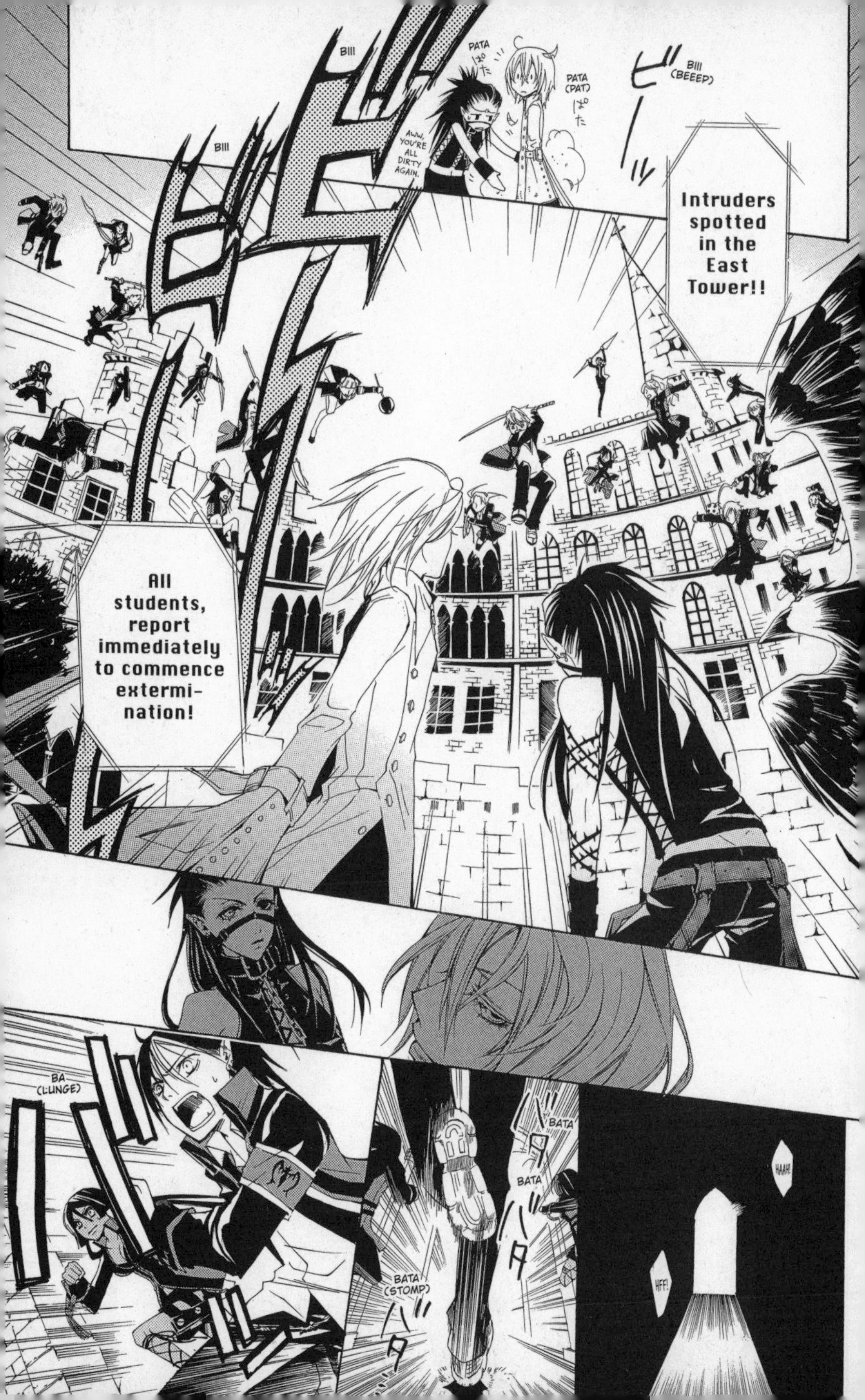

BIII (BEEEP)
PATA (PAT)
ぱた
PATA
ぱた
AWW, YOU'RE ALL DIRTY AGAIN.
BIII
BIII
Intruders spotted in the East Tower!!
All students, report immediately to commence extermi-nation!
HAAH!
HFF!
BATA
BATA
BATA (STOMP)
BA (LUNGE)

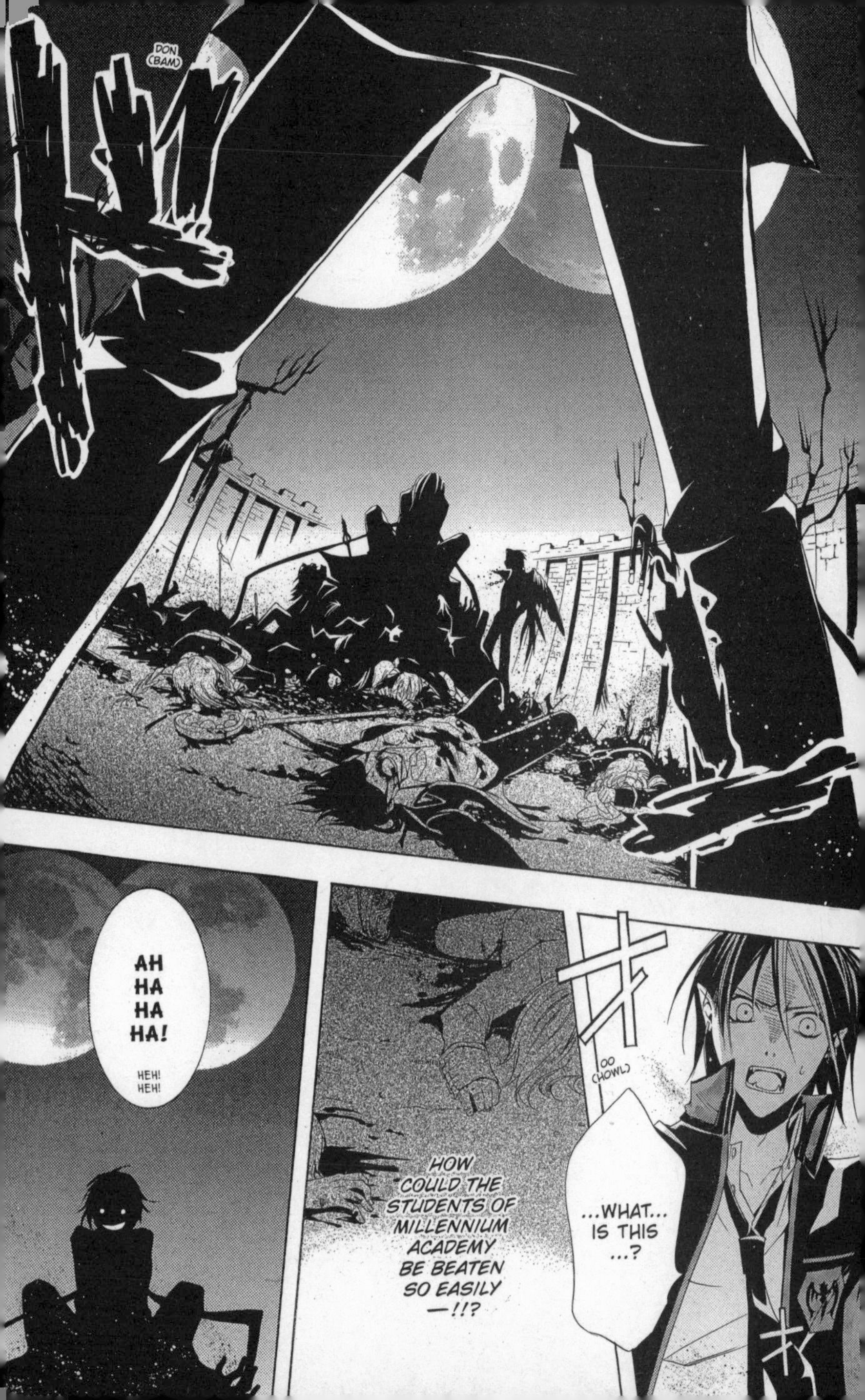
DON (BAM)
OO (HOWL)
...WHAT... IS THIS ...?
HOW COULD THE STUDENTS OF MILLENNIUM ACADEMY BE BEATEN SO EASILY —!!?
AH HA HA HA!
HEH! HEH!

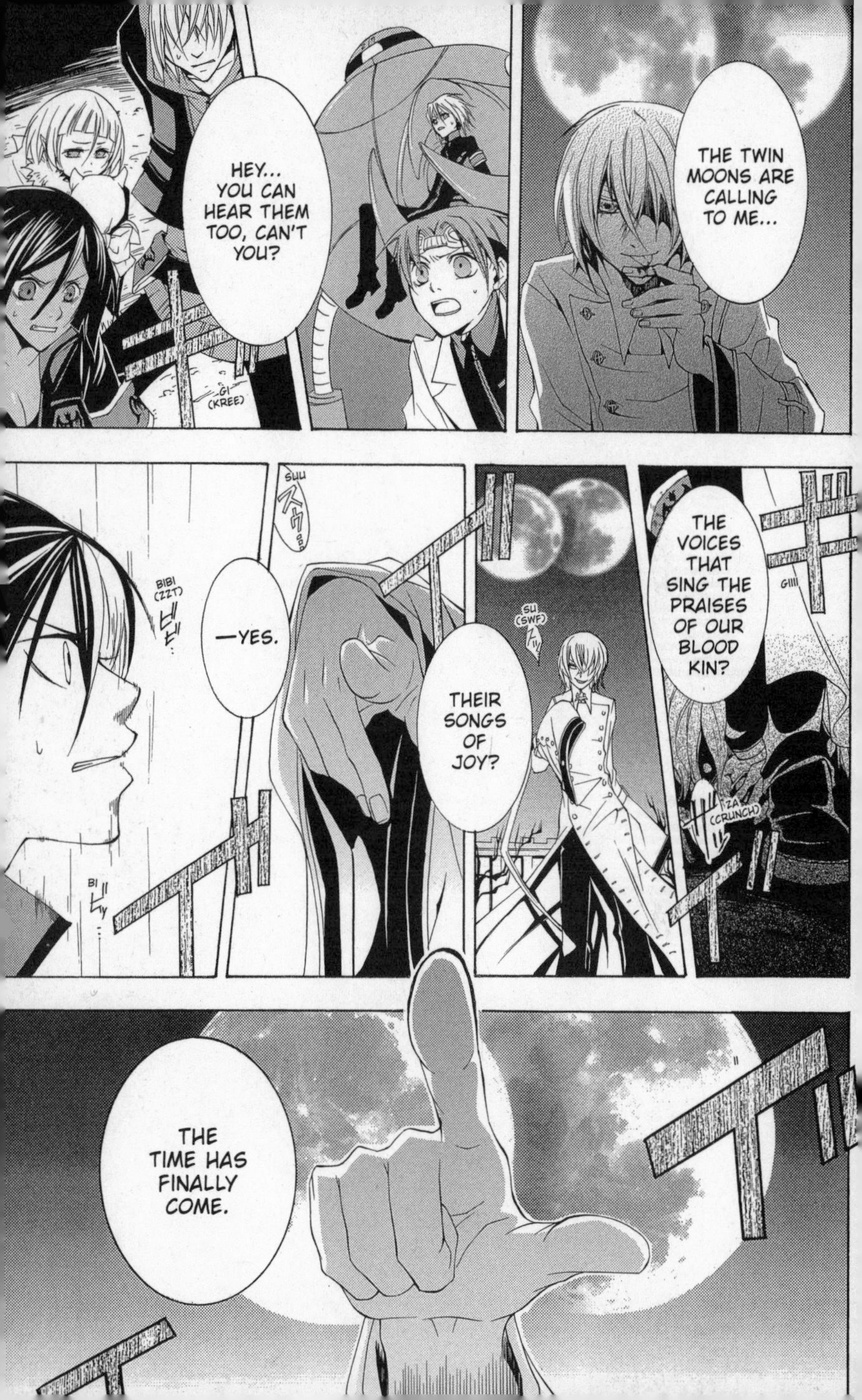
THE TWIN MOONS ARE CALLING TO ME...
HEY... YOU CAN HEAR THEM TOO, CAN'T YOU?
GI (KREE)
THE VOICES THAT SING THE PRAISES OF OUR BLOOD KIN?
GIIII
ZA (CRUNCH)
SU (SWF)
THEIR SONGS OF JOY?
SUU
—YES.
BIBI (ZZT)
BI
THE TIME HAS FINALLY COME.

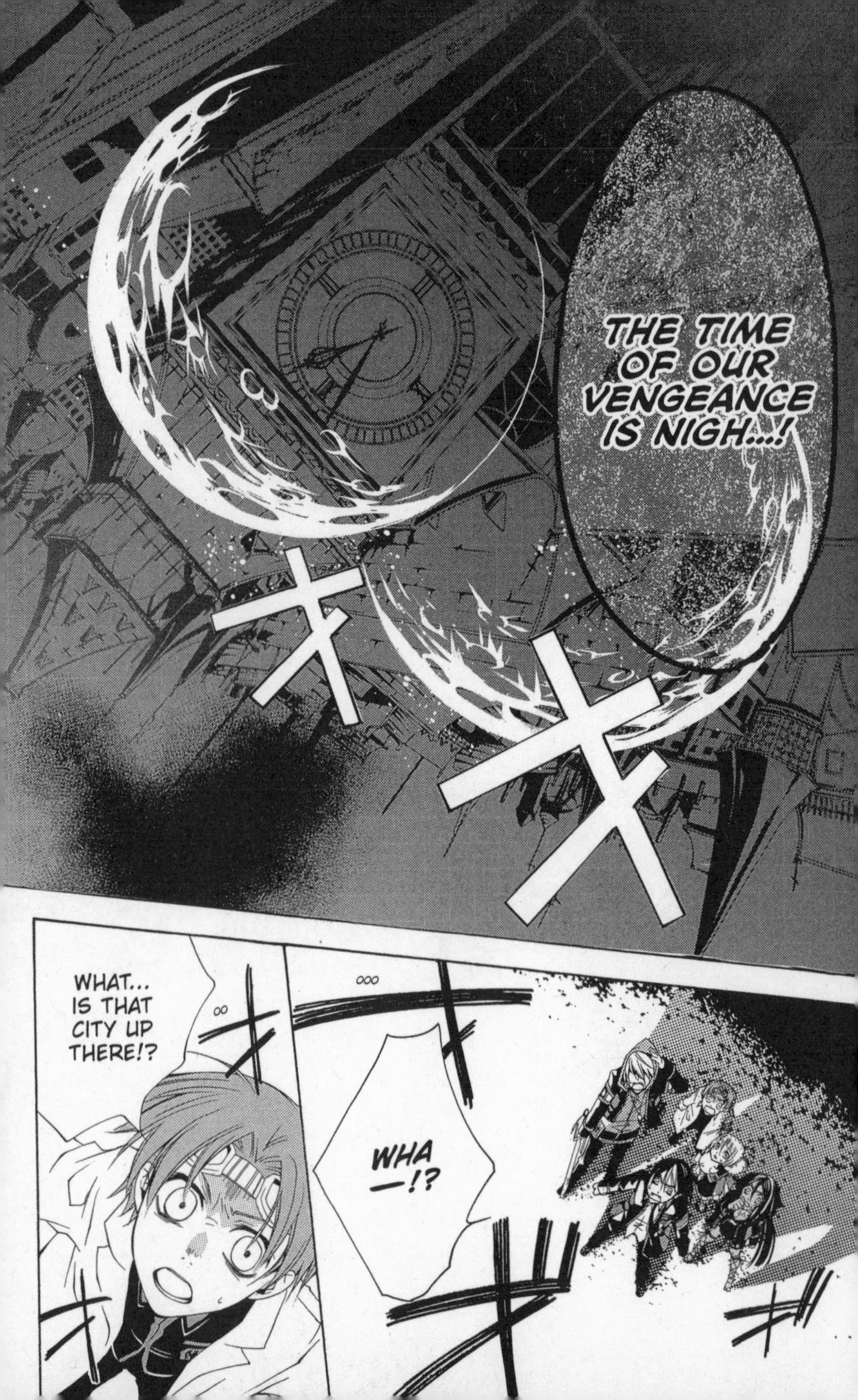
THE TIME OF OUR VENGEANCE IS NIGH...!
WHA—!?
WHAT... IS THAT CITY UP THERE!?

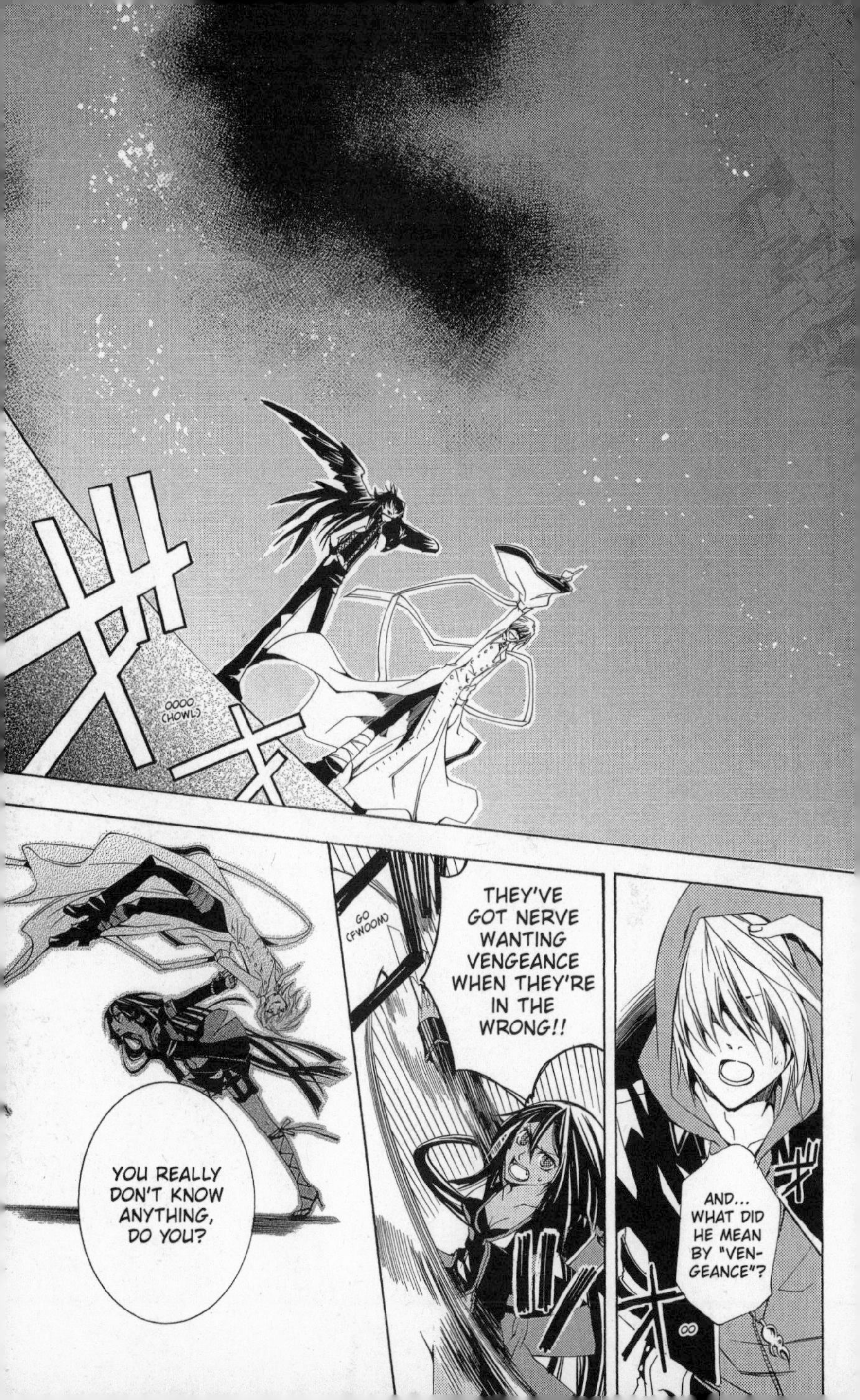
OOOO (HOWL)
AND... WHAT DID HE MEAN BY "VEN-GEANCE"?
THEY'VE GOT NERVE WANTING VENGEANCE WHEN THEY'RE IN THE WRONG!!
GO (FWOOM)
YOU REALLY DON'T KNOW ANYTHING, DO YOU?

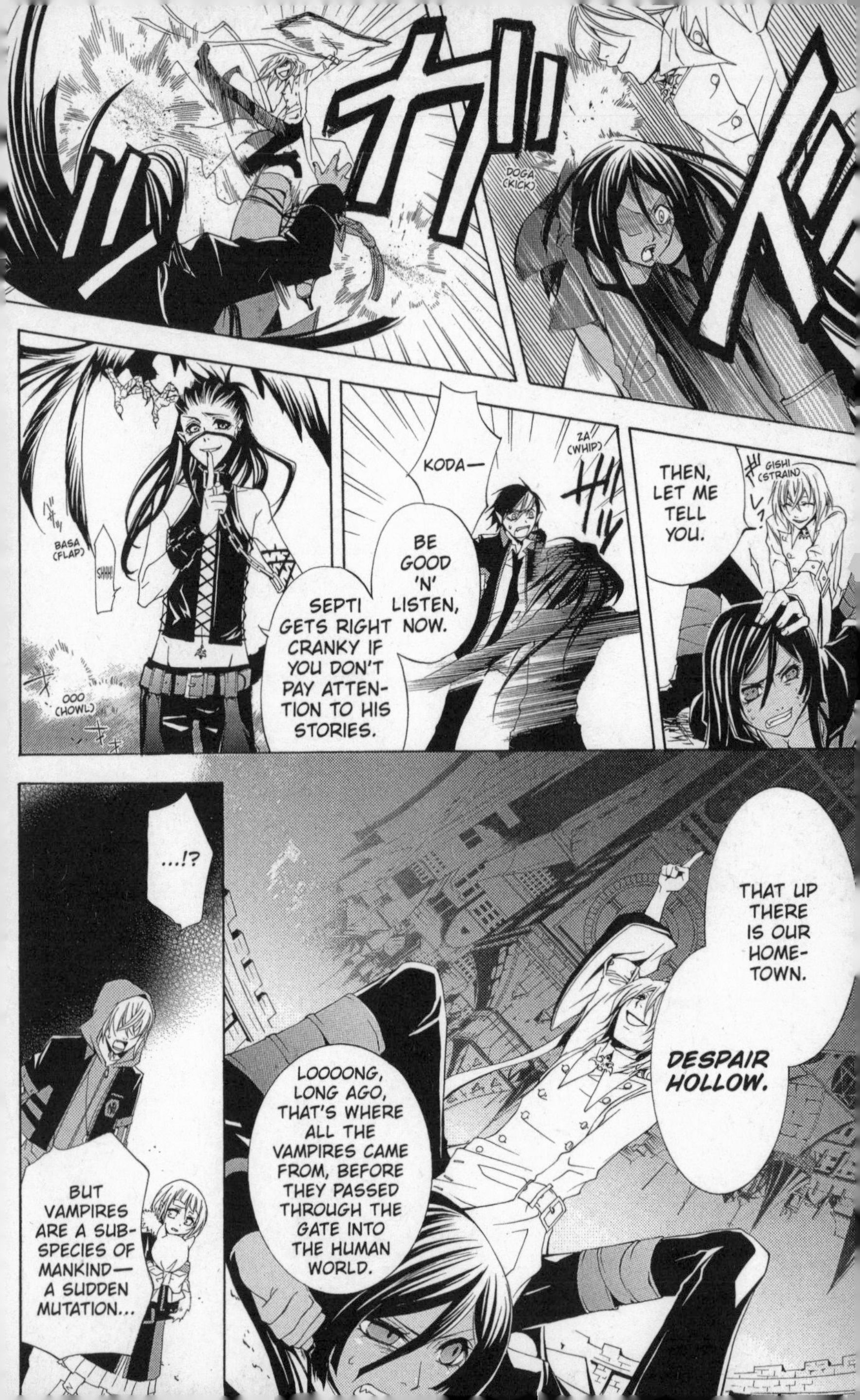
DOGA (KICK)
GISHI (STRAIN)
THEN, LET ME TELL YOU.
ZA (WHIP)
KODA—
BE GOOD 'N' LISTEN, NOW.
SEPTI GETS RIGHT CRANKY IF YOU DON'T PAY ATTEN-TION TO HIS STORIES.
BASA (FLAP)
SHHH!
OOO (HOWL)
THAT UP THERE IS OUR HOME-TOWN.
DESPAIR HOLLOW.
LOOOONG, LONG AGO, THAT'S WHERE ALL THE VAMPIRES CAME FROM, BEFORE THEY PASSED THROUGH THE GATE INTO THE HUMAN WORLD.
...!?
BUT VAMPIRES ARE A SUB-SPECIES OF MANKIND— A SUDDEN MUTATION...

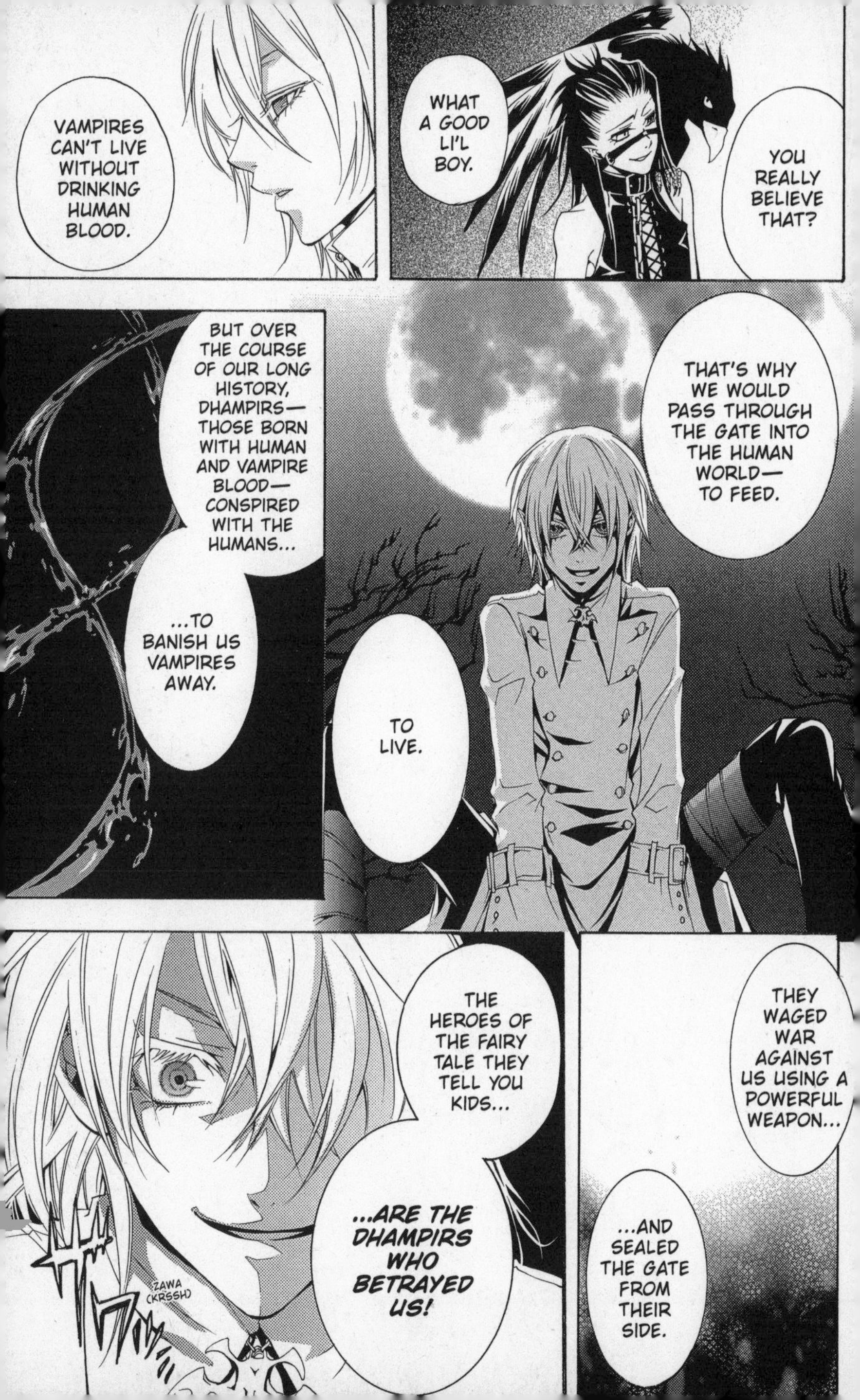
YOU REALLY BELIEVE THAT?
WHAT A GOOD LI'L BOY.
VAMPIRES CAN'T LIVE WITHOUT DRINKING HUMAN BLOOD.
THAT'S WHY WE WOULD PASS THROUGH THE GATE INTO THE HUMAN WORLD— TO FEED.
TO LIVE.
BUT OVER THE COURSE OF OUR LONG HISTORY, DHAMPIRS— THOSE BORN WITH HUMAN AND VAMPIRE BLOOD— CONSPIRED WITH THE HUMANS...
...TO BANISH US VAMPIRES AWAY.
THEY WAGED WAR AGAINST US USING A POWERFUL WEAPON...
...AND SEALED THE GATE FROM THEIR SIDE.
THE HEROES OF THE FAIRY TALE THEY TELL YOU KIDS...
...ARE THE DHAMPIRS WHO BETRAYED US!
ZAWA (KRSSH)

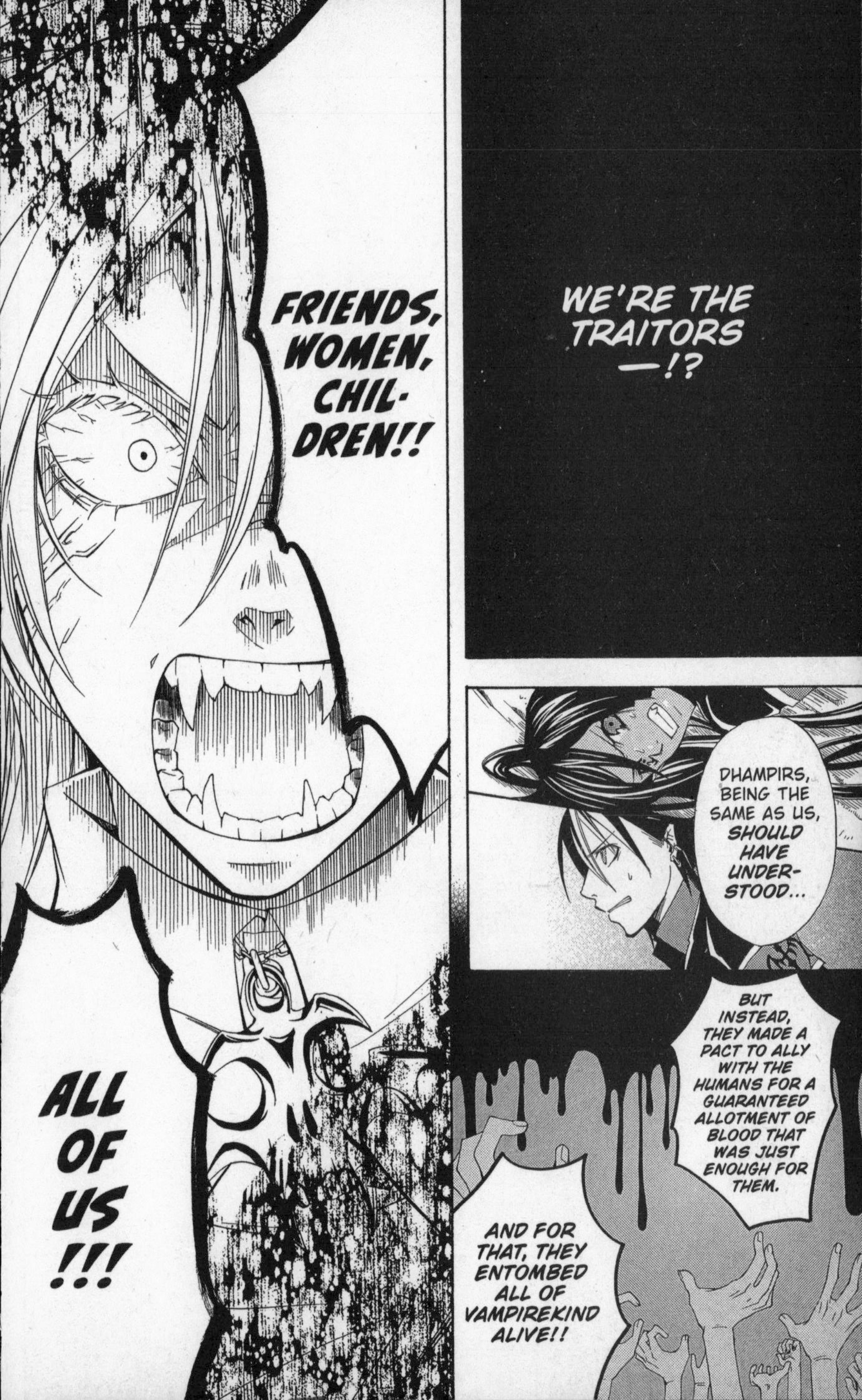
WE'RE THE TRAITORS—!?
DHAMPIRS, BEING THE SAME AS US, SHOULD HAVE UNDERSTOOD...
BUT INSTEAD, THEY MADE A PACT TO ALLY WITH THE HUMANS FOR A GUARANTEED ALLOTMENT OF BLOOD THAT WAS JUST ENOUGH FOR THEM.
AND FOR THAT, THEY ENTOMBED ALL OF VAMPIREKIND ALIVE!!
FRIENDS, WOMEN, CHILDREN!!
ALL OF US!!!

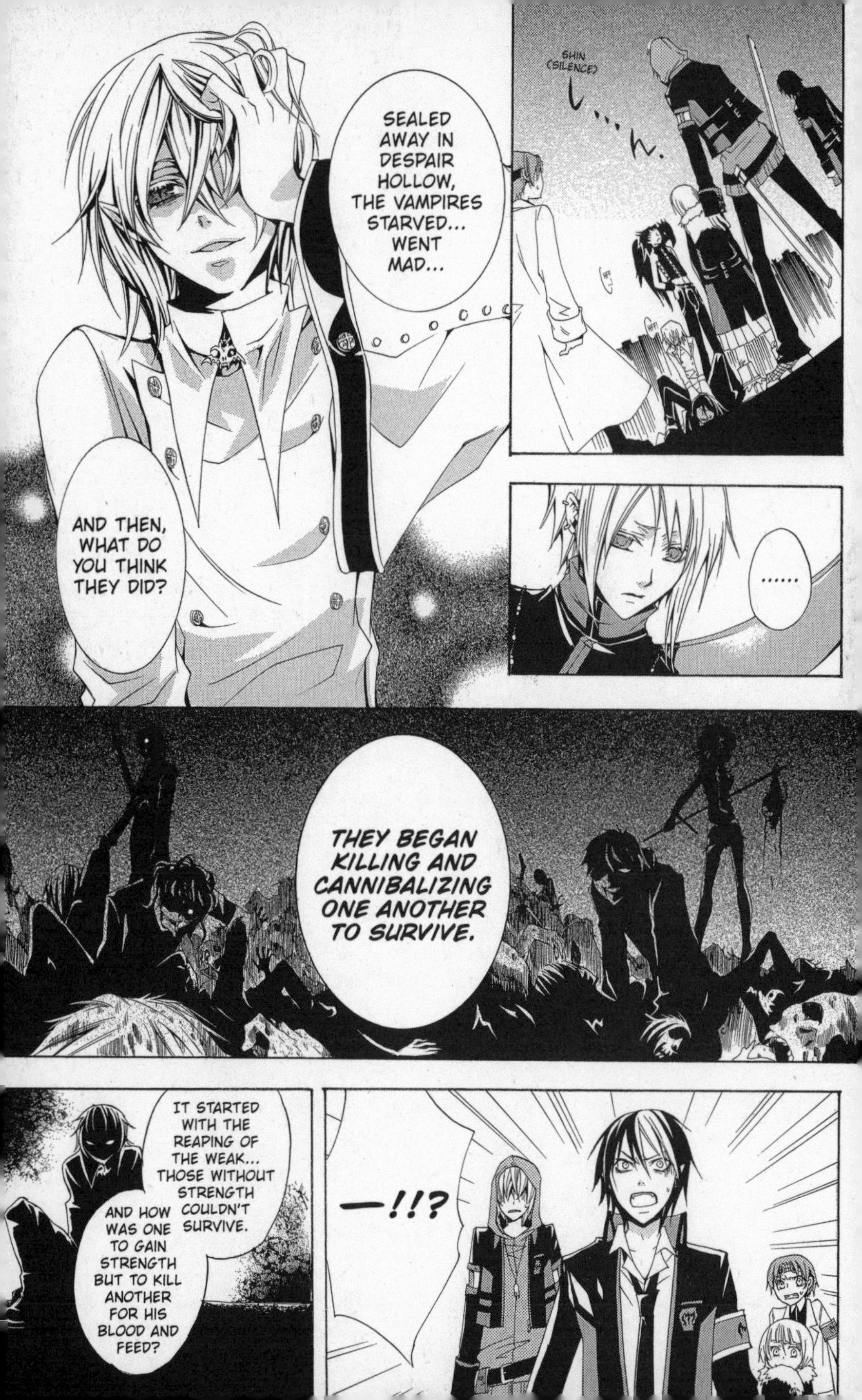
SHIN (SILENCE)
......
SEALED AWAY IN DESPAIR HOLLOW, THE VAMPIRES STARVED... WENT MAD...
AND THEN, WHAT DO YOU THINK THEY DID?
THEY BEGAN KILLING AND CANNIBALIZING ONE ANOTHER TO SURVIVE.
—!!?
IT STARTED WITH THE REAPING OF THE WEAK... THOSE WITHOUT STRENGTH COULDN'T SURVIVE.
AND HOW WAS ONE TO GAIN STRENGTH BUT TO KILL ANOTHER FOR HIS BLOOD AND FEED?

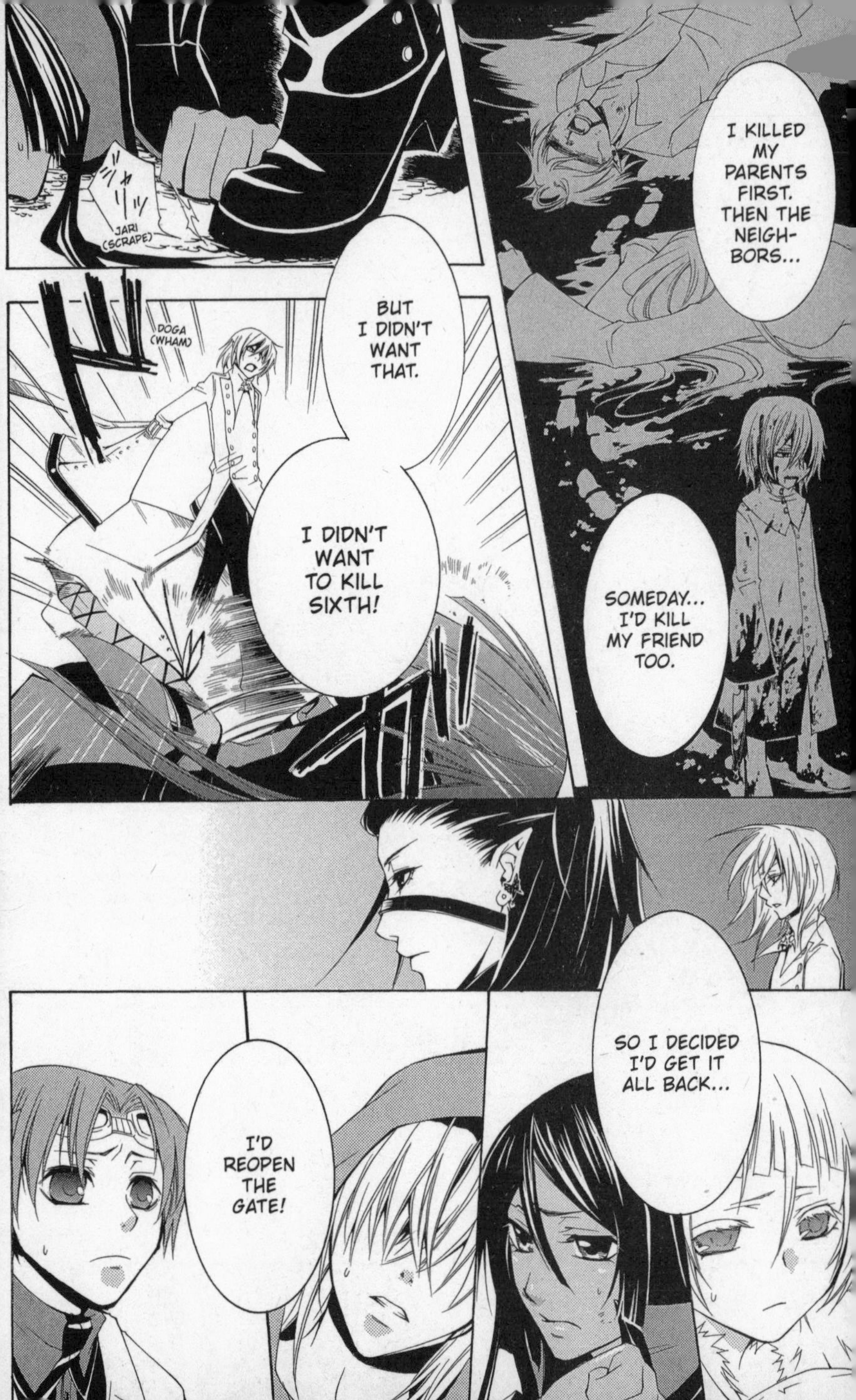
I KILLED MY PARENTS FIRST. THEN THE NEIGHBORS...
SOMEDAY... I'D KILL MY FRIEND TOO.
JARI (SCRAPE)
DOGA (WHAM)
BUT I DIDN'T WANT THAT.
I DIDN'T WANT TO KILL SIXTH!
SO I DECIDED I'D GET IT ALL BACK...
I'D REOPEN THE GATE!

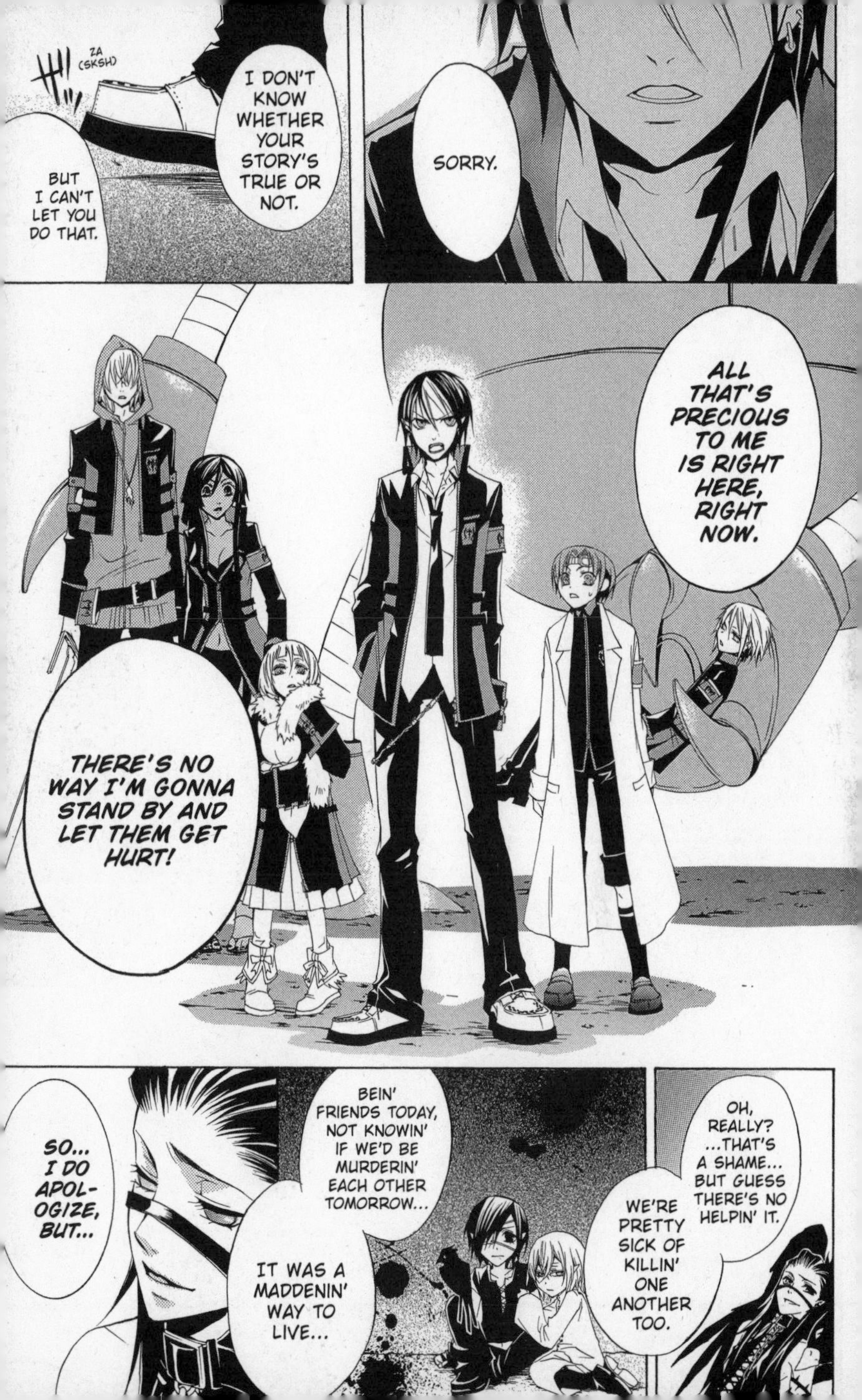
SORRY.
I DON'T KNOW WHETHER YOUR STORY'S TRUE OR NOT.
ZA (SKSH)
BUT I CAN'T LET YOU DO THAT.
ALL THAT'S PRECIOUS TO ME IS RIGHT HERE, RIGHT NOW.
THERE'S NO WAY I'M GONNA STAND BY AND LET THEM GET HURT!
OH, REALLY? ...THAT'S A SHAME... BUT GUESS THERE'S NO HELPIN' IT.
WE'RE PRETTY SICK OF KILLIN' ONE ANOTHER TOO.
BEIN' FRIENDS TODAY, NOT KNOWIN' IF WE'D BE MURDERIN' EACH OTHER TOMORROW...
IT WAS A MADDENIN' WAY TO LIVE...
SO... I DO APOLOGIZE, BUT...

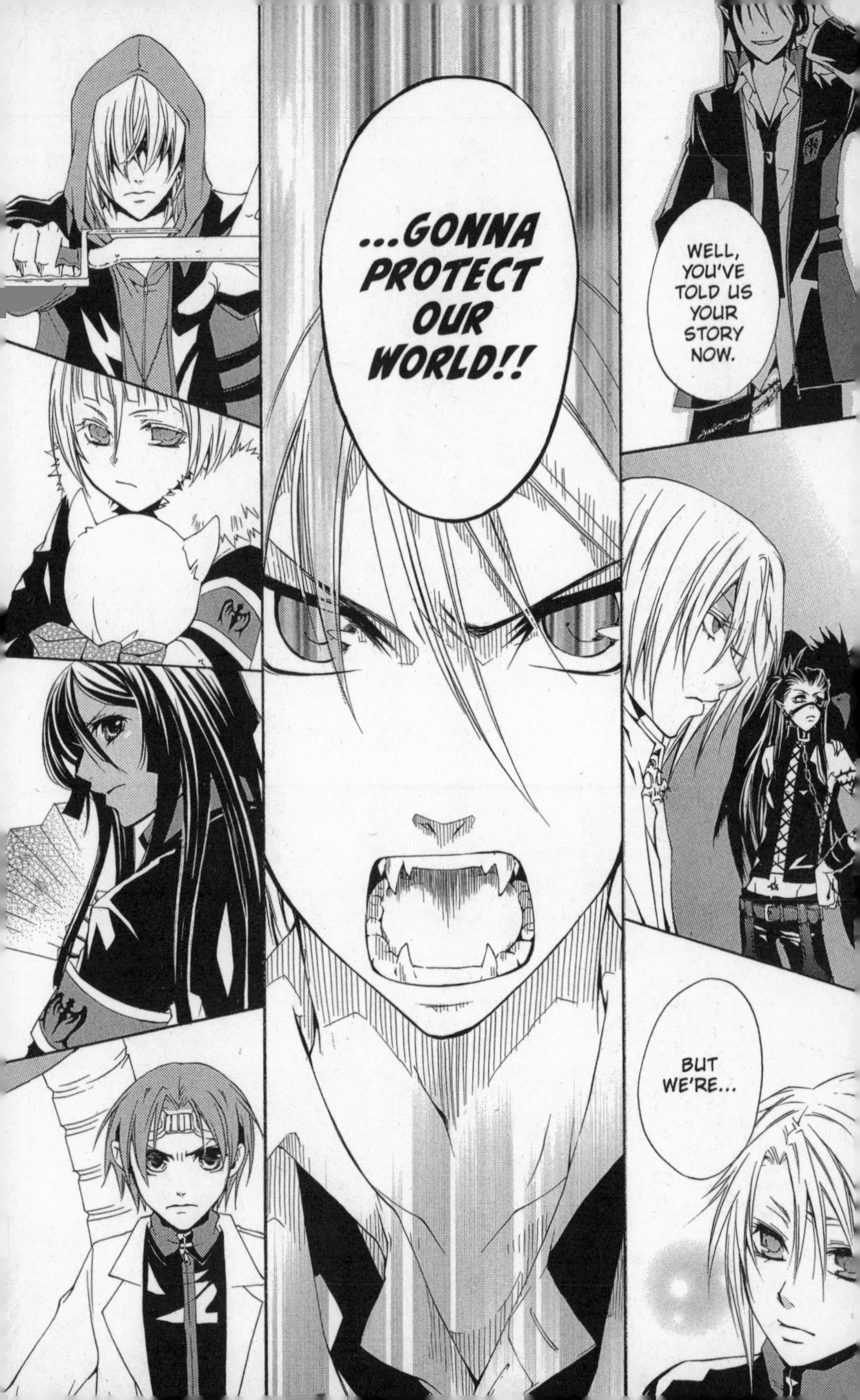
WELL, YOU'VE TOLD US YOUR STORY NOW.
BUT WE'RE...
...GONNA PROTECT OUR WORLD!!

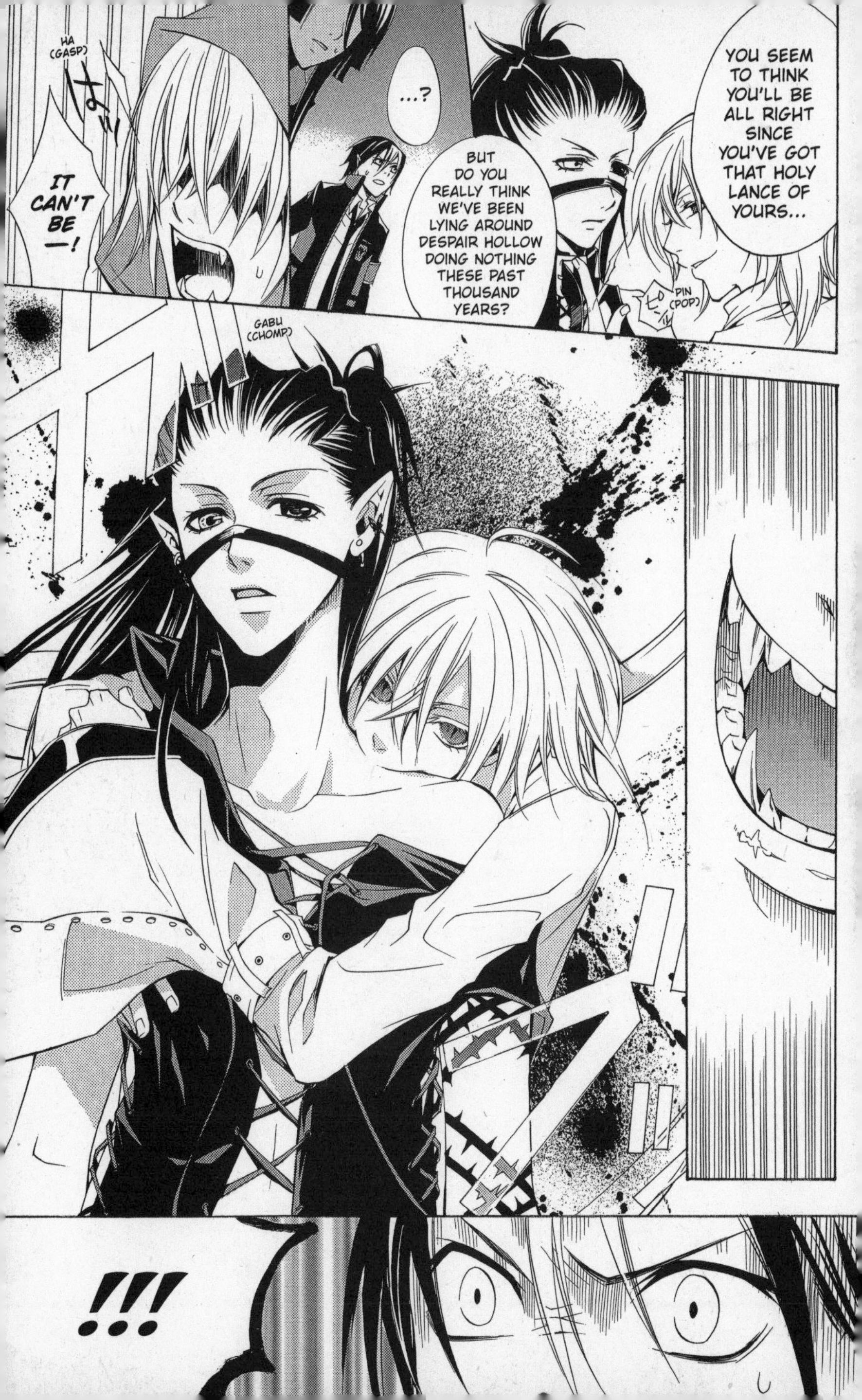
YOU SEEM TO THINK YOU'LL BE ALL RIGHT SINCE YOU'VE GOT THAT HOLY LANCE OF YOURS...
PIN (POP)
BUT DO YOU REALLY THINK WE'VE BEEN LYING AROUND DESPAIR HOLLOW DOING NOTHING THESE PAST THOUSAND YEARS?
...?
HA (GASP)
IT CAN'T BE—!
GABU (CHOMP)
!!!

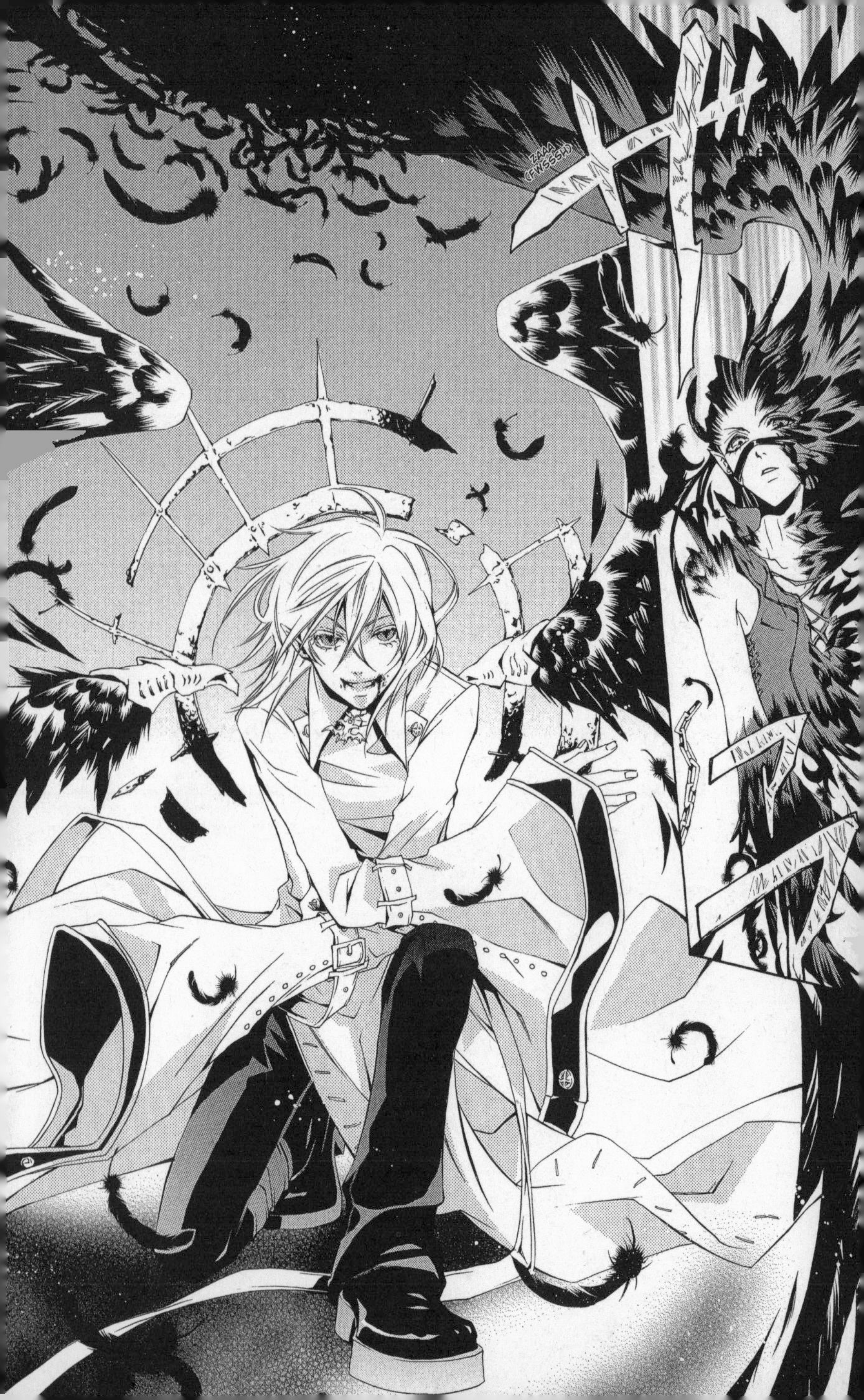
ZAAA
(FWSSSH)

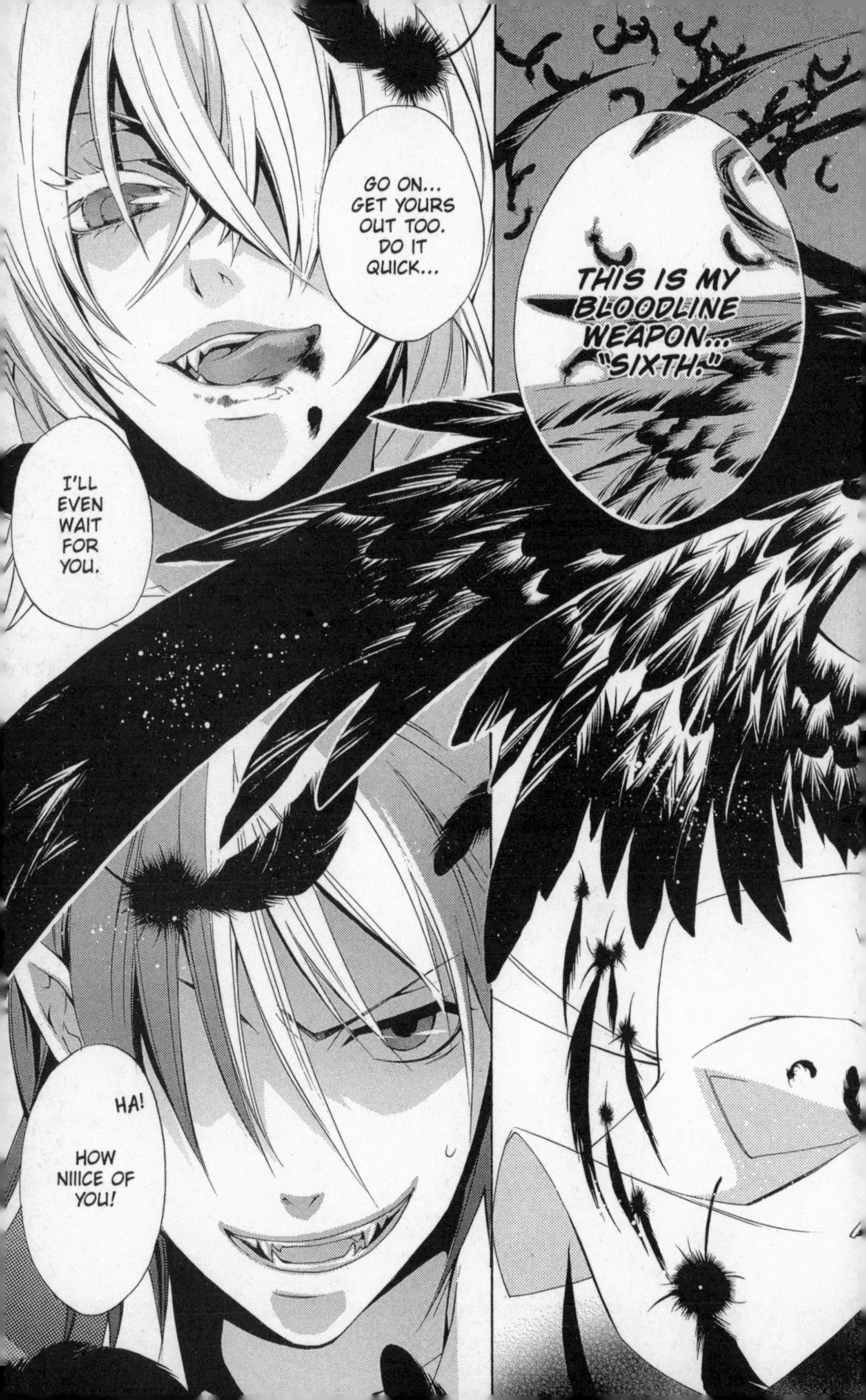
THIS IS MY BLOODLINE WEAPON... "SIXTH."
GO ON... GET YOURS OUT TOO. DO IT QUICK...
I'LL EVEN WAIT FOR YOU.
HA!
HOW NIIICE OF YOU!

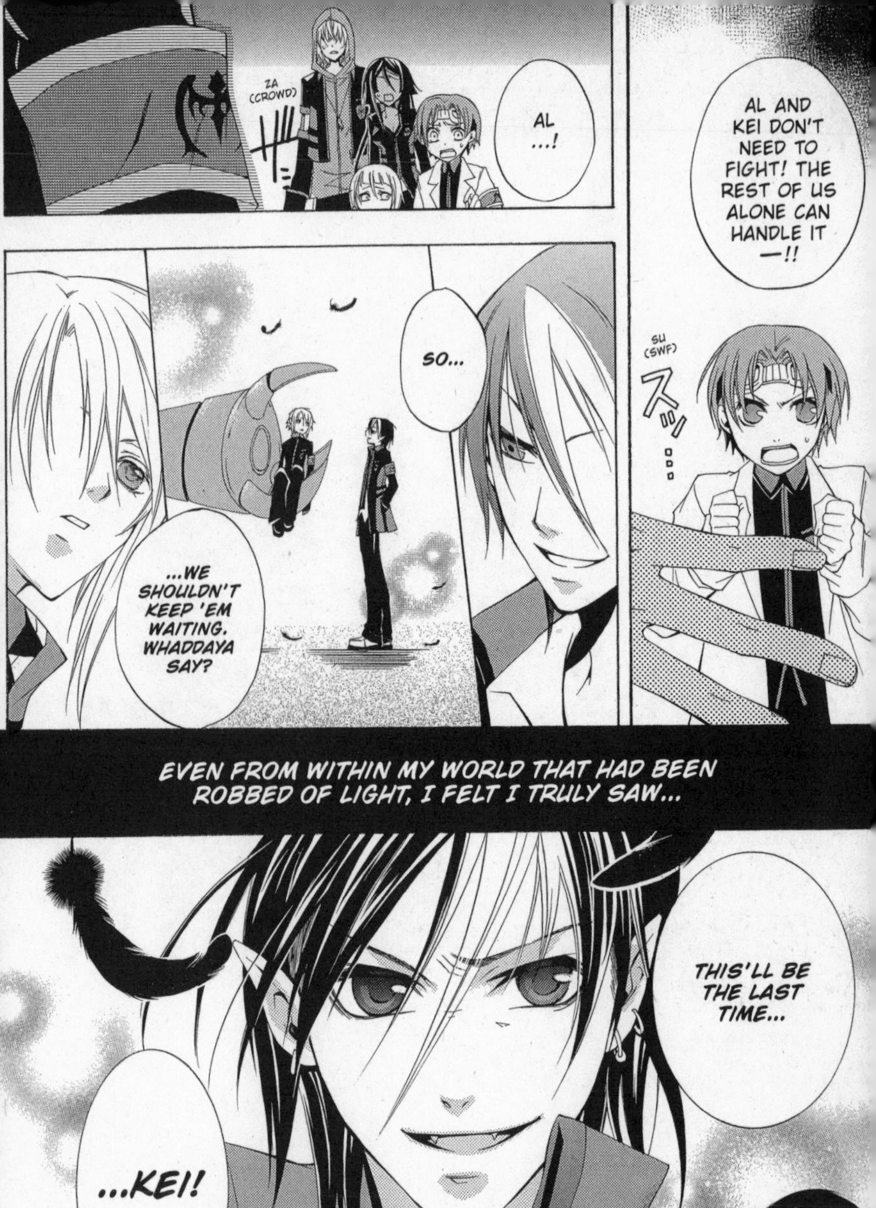
AL AND KEI DON'T NEED TO FIGHT! THE REST OF US ALONE CAN HANDLE IT—!!
SU (SWF)
AL ...!
ZA (CROWD)
SO...
...WE SHOULDN'T KEEP 'EM WAITING. WHADDAYA SAY?
EVEN FROM WITHIN MY WORLD THAT HAD BEEN ROBBED OF LIGHT, I FELT I TRULY SAW...
THIS'LL BE THE LAST TIME...
...KEI!

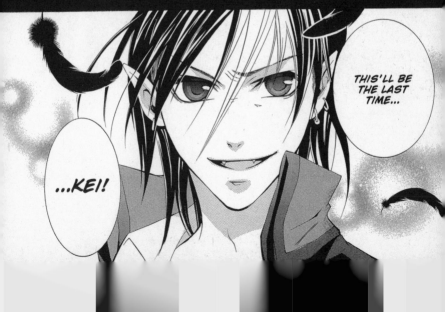

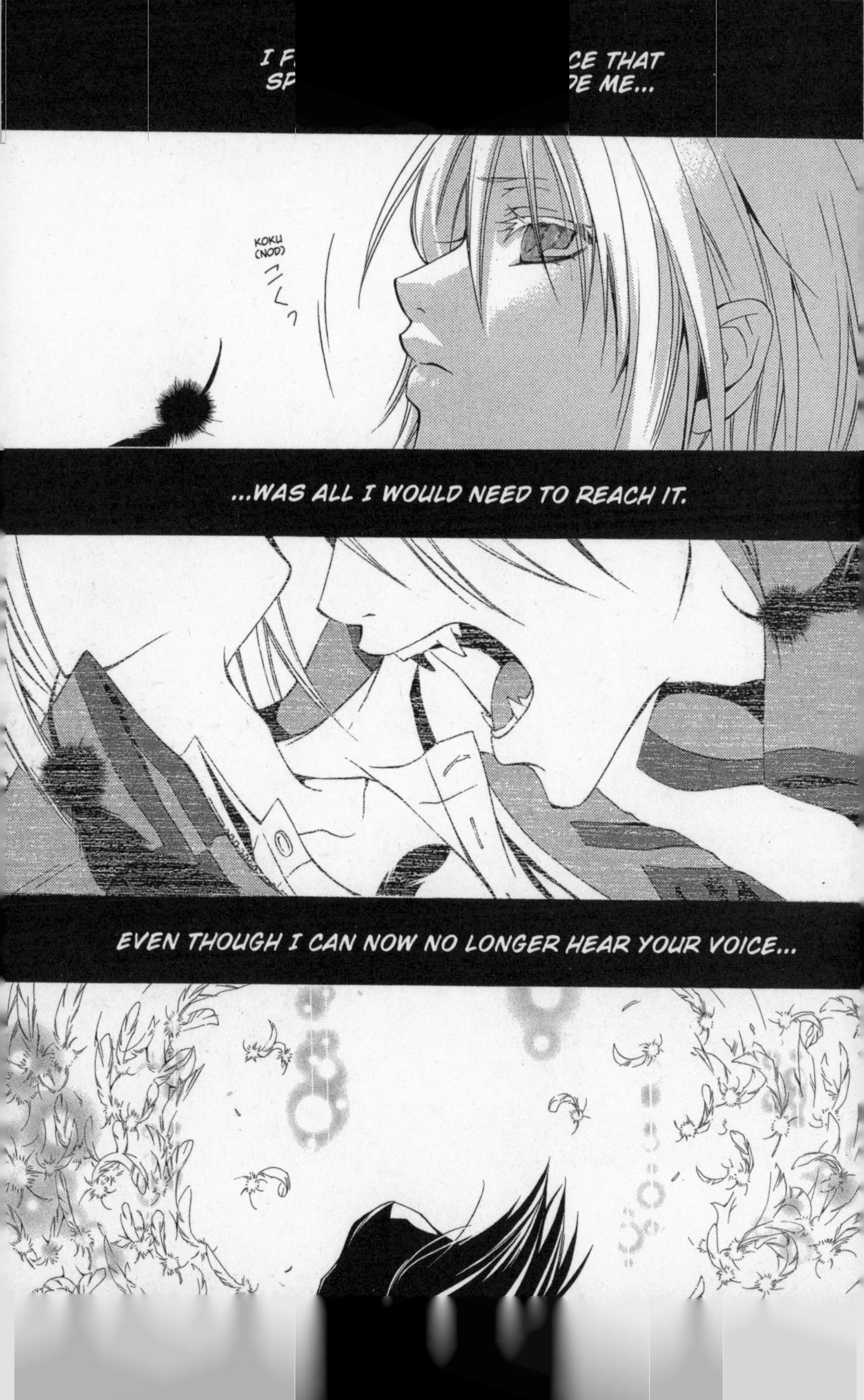
I F[redacted]CE THAT
SP[redacted]PE ME...
KOKU (NOD)
...WAS ALL I WOULD NEED TO REACH IT.
EVEN THOUGH I CAN NOW NO LONGER HEAR YOUR VOICE...

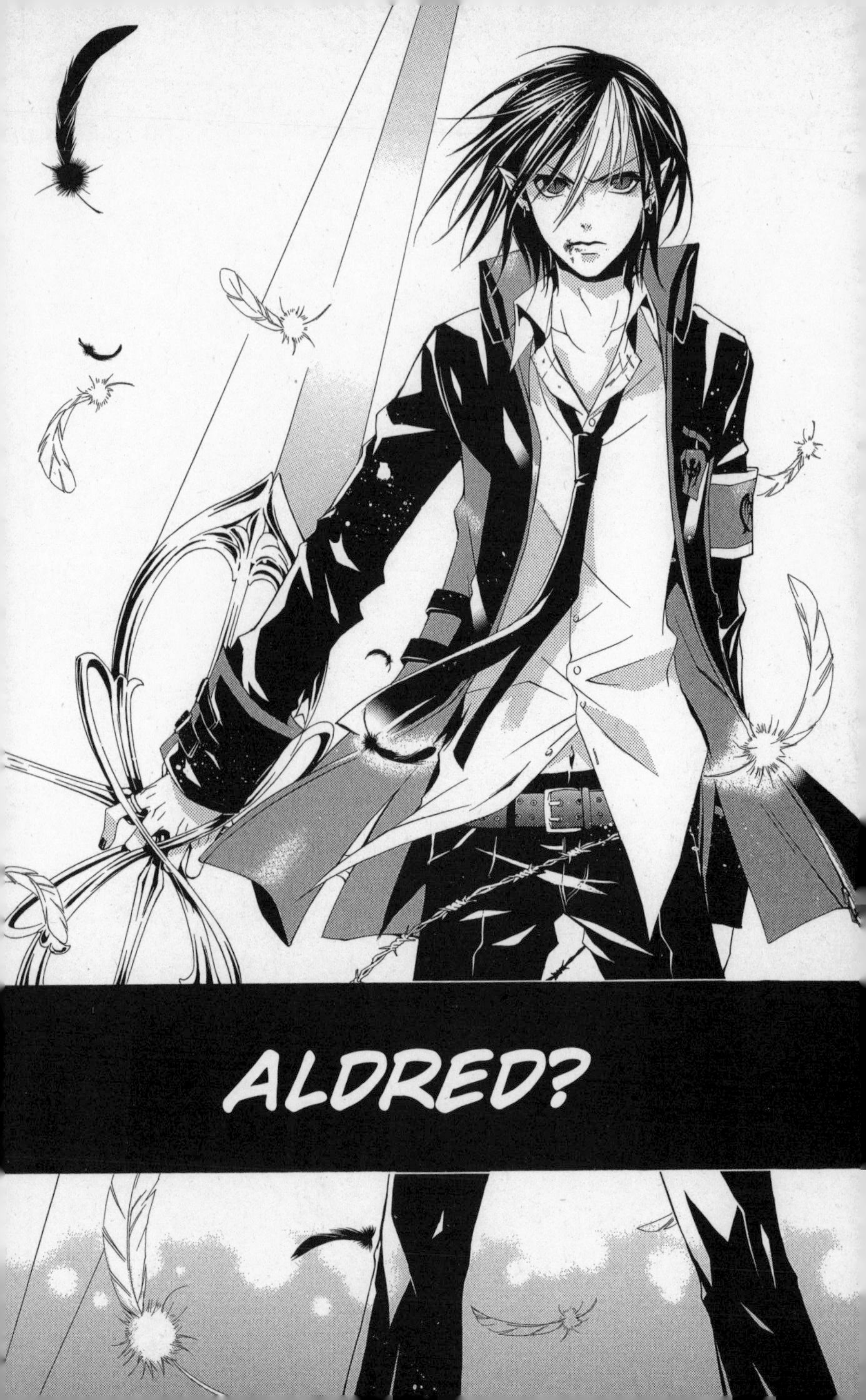
ALDRED?

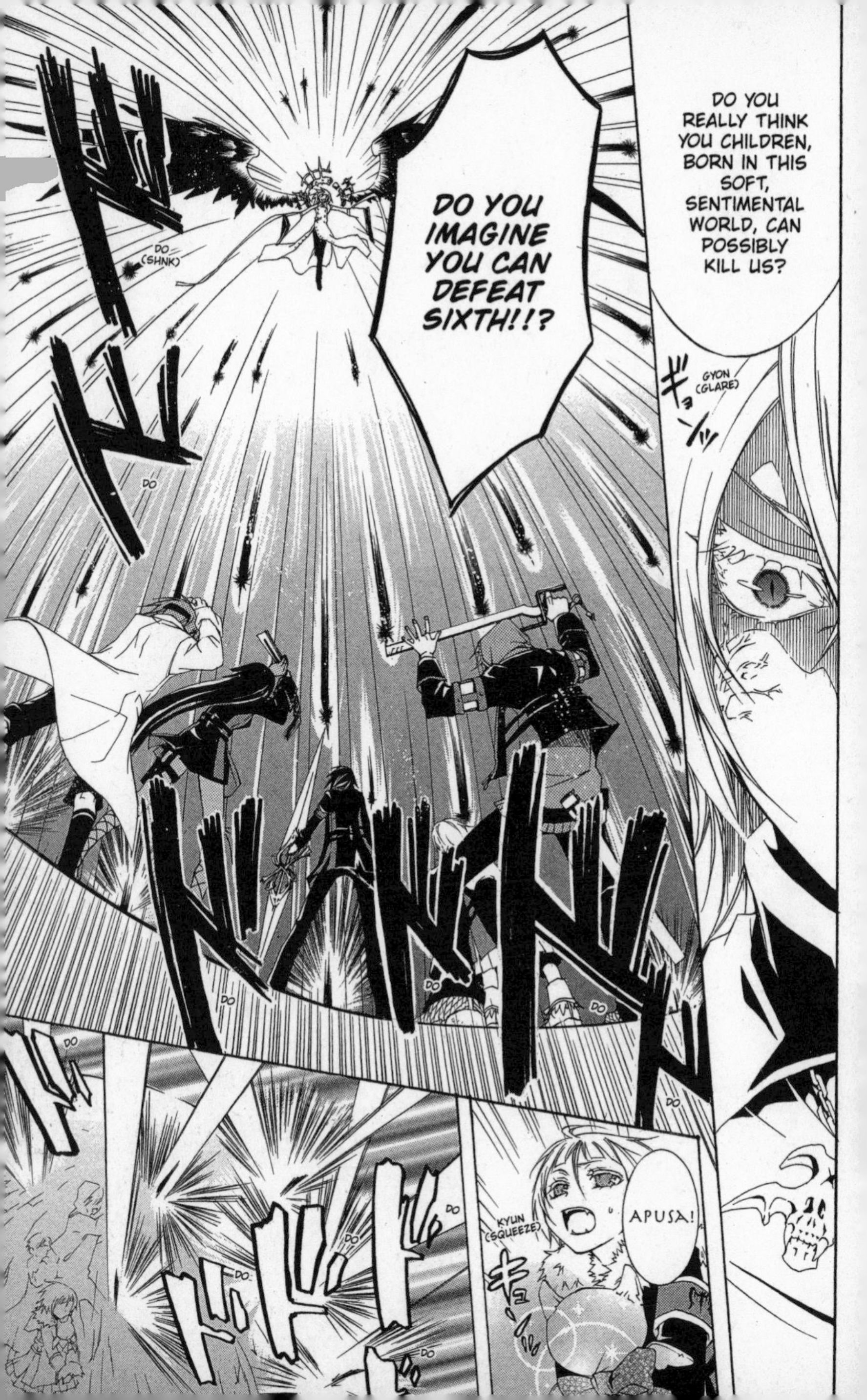
DO YOU REALLY THINK YOU CHILDREN, BORN IN THIS SOFT, SENTIMENTAL WORLD, CAN POSSIBLY KILL US?
GYON (GLARE)
DO YOU IMAGINE YOU CAN DEFEAT SIXTH!!?
DO (SHNK)
DO
DO
DO
DO
DO
DO
APUSA!
KYUN (SQUEEZE)
DO
DO
DO
DO

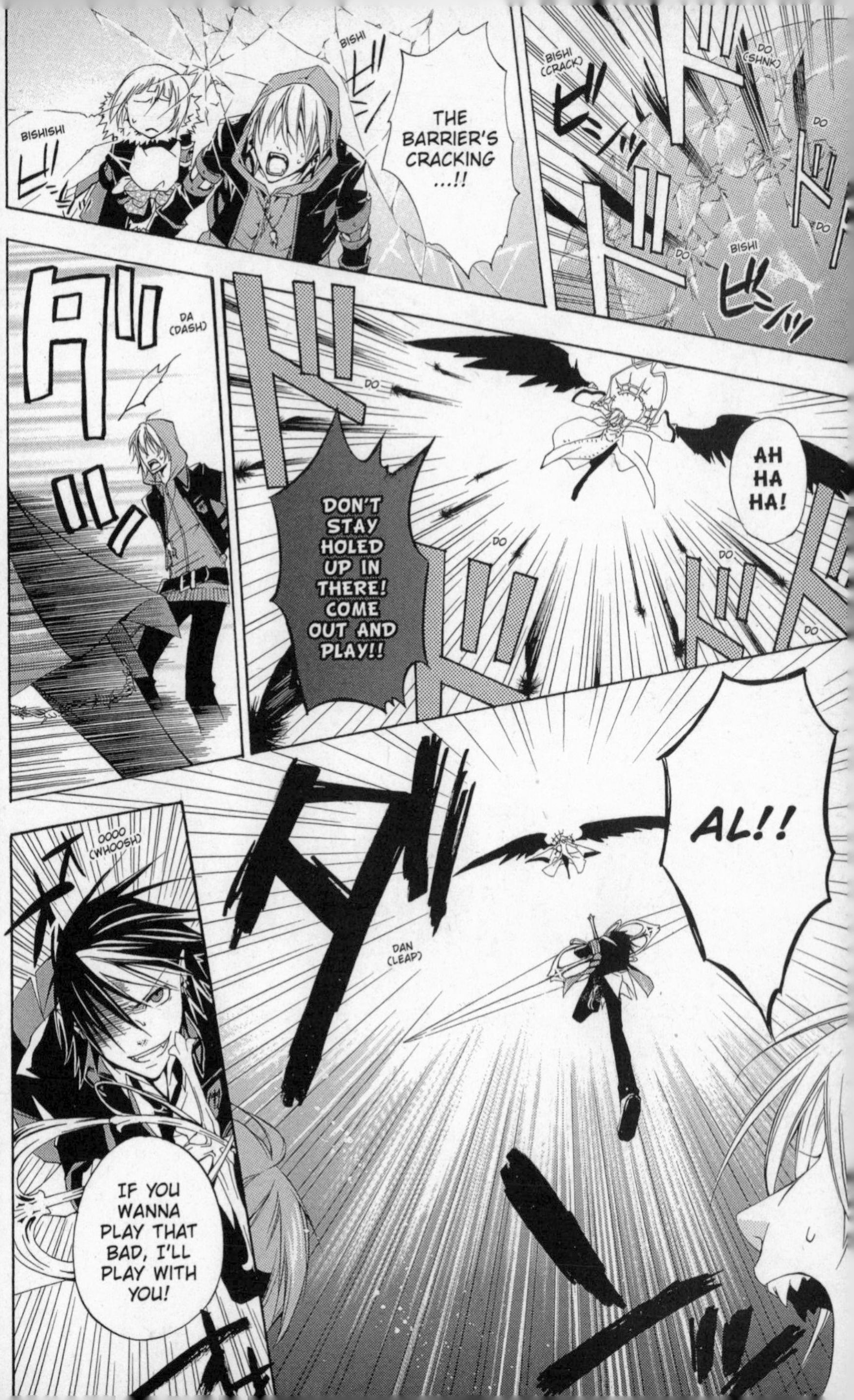

BISHI (CRACK)
DO (SHNK)
DO
DO
DO
BISHI
BISHI
THE BARRIER'S CRACKING ...!!
BISHISHI
AH HA HA!
DO
DO
DON'T STAY HOLED UP IN THERE! COME OUT AND PLAY!!
DO
DO
DA (DASH)
AL!!
DAN (LEAP)
OOOO (WHOOSH)
IF YOU WANNA PLAY THAT BAD, I'LL PLAY WITH YOU!

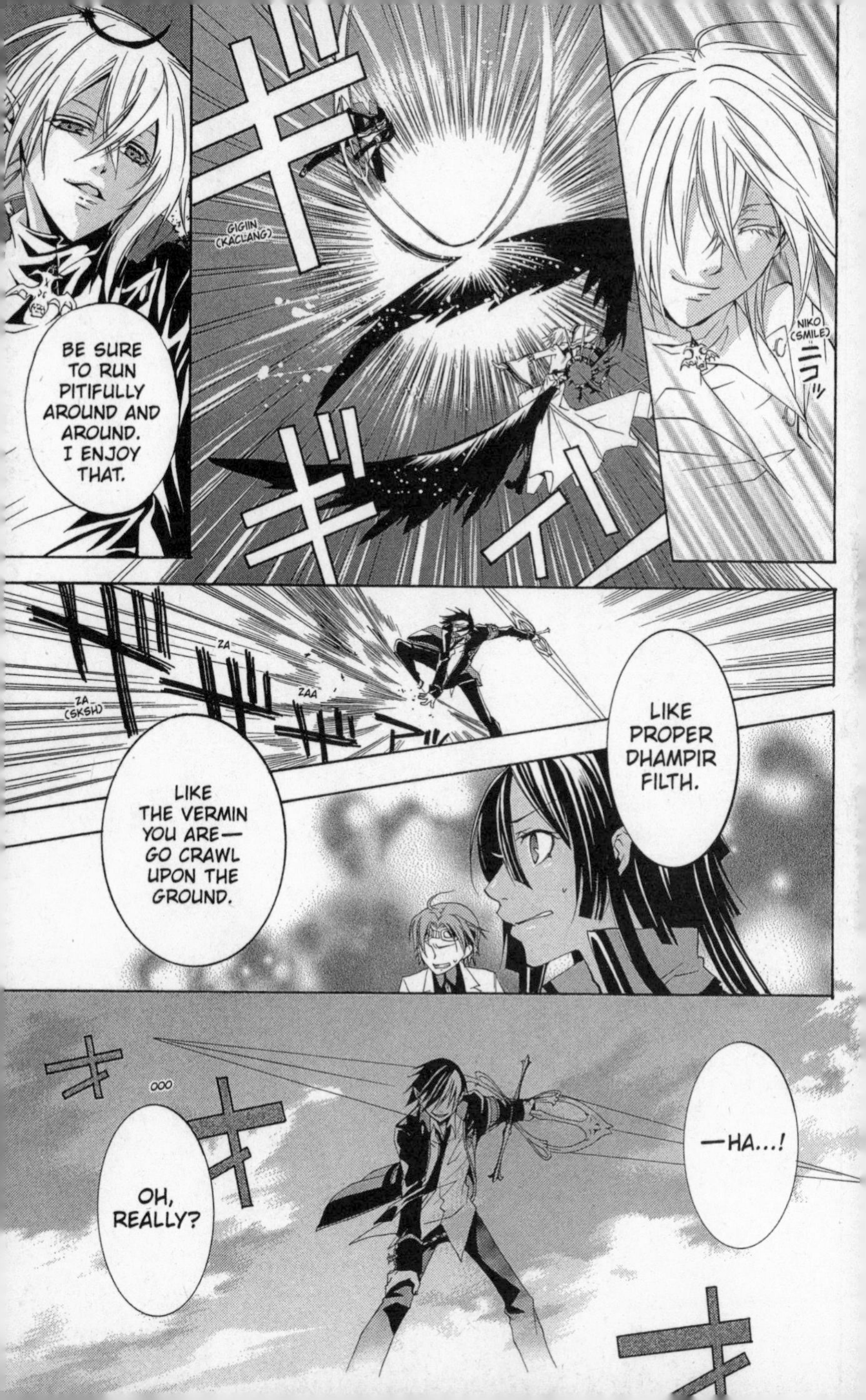
NIKO (SMILE)
GIGIIN (KACLANG)
BE SURE TO RUN PITIFULLY AROUND AND AROUND. I ENJOY THAT.
ZAA
ZA
ZA (SKSH)
LIKE PROPER DHAMPIR FILTH.
LIKE THE VERMIN YOU ARE—GO CRAWL UPON THE GROUND.
—HA...!
OOO
OH, REALLY?

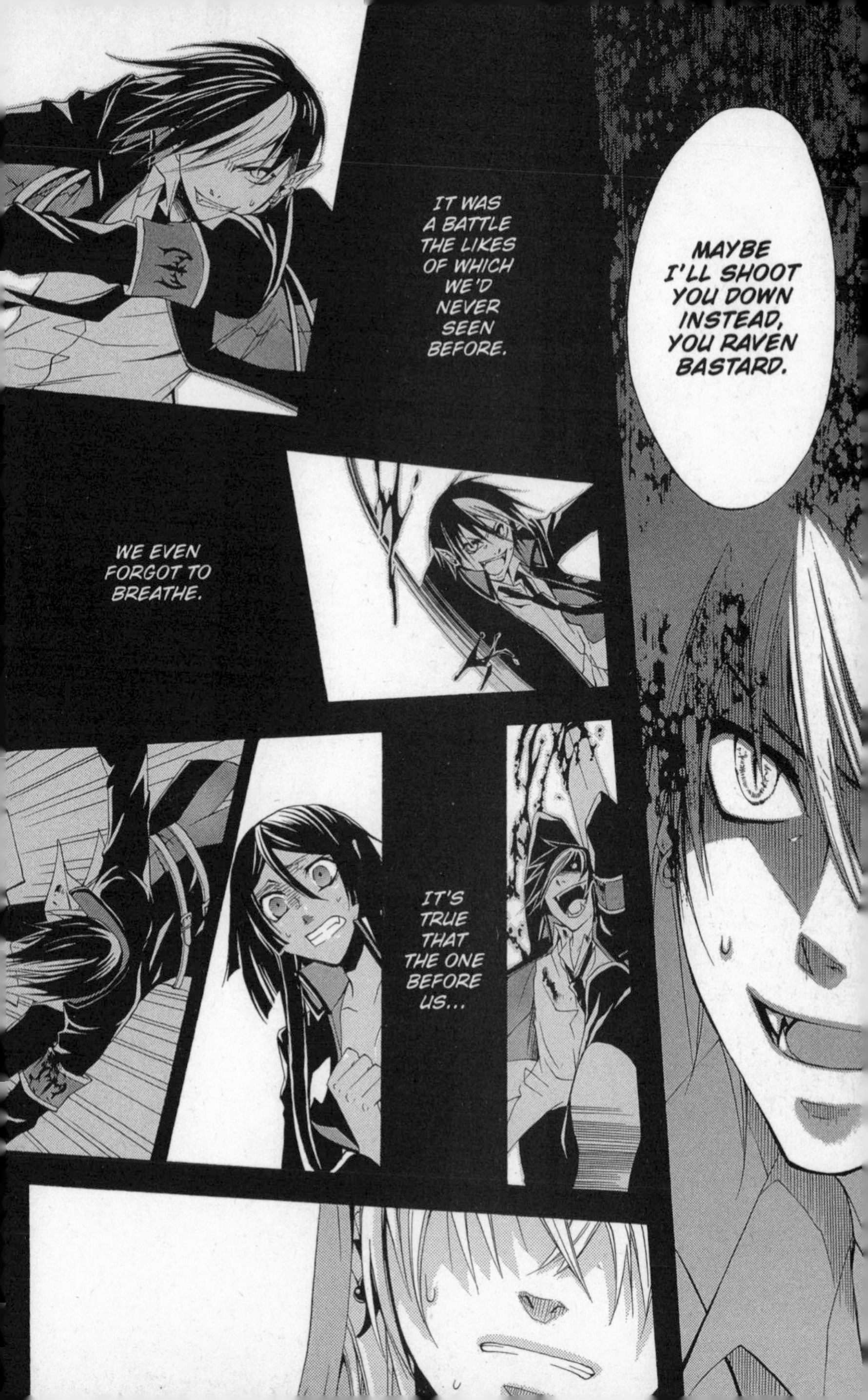
MAYBE I'LL SHOOT YOU DOWN INSTEAD, YOU RAVEN BASTARD.
IT WAS A BATTLE THE LIKES OF WHICH WE'D NEVER SEEN BEFORE.
WE EVEN FORGOT TO BREATHE.
IT'S TRUE THAT THE ONE BEFORE US...

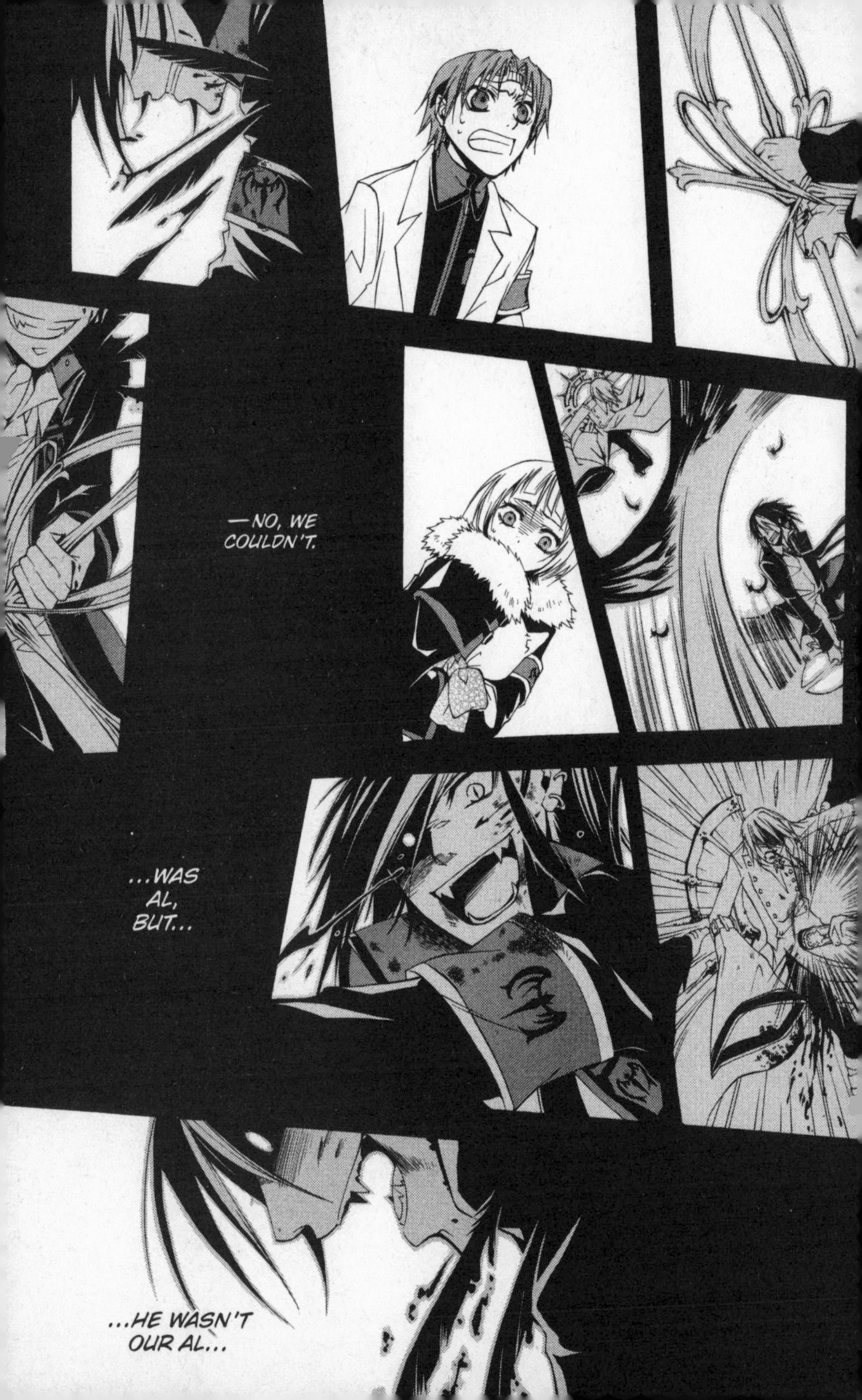
—NO, WE COULDN'T.
...WAS AL, BUT...
...HE WASN'T OUR AL...

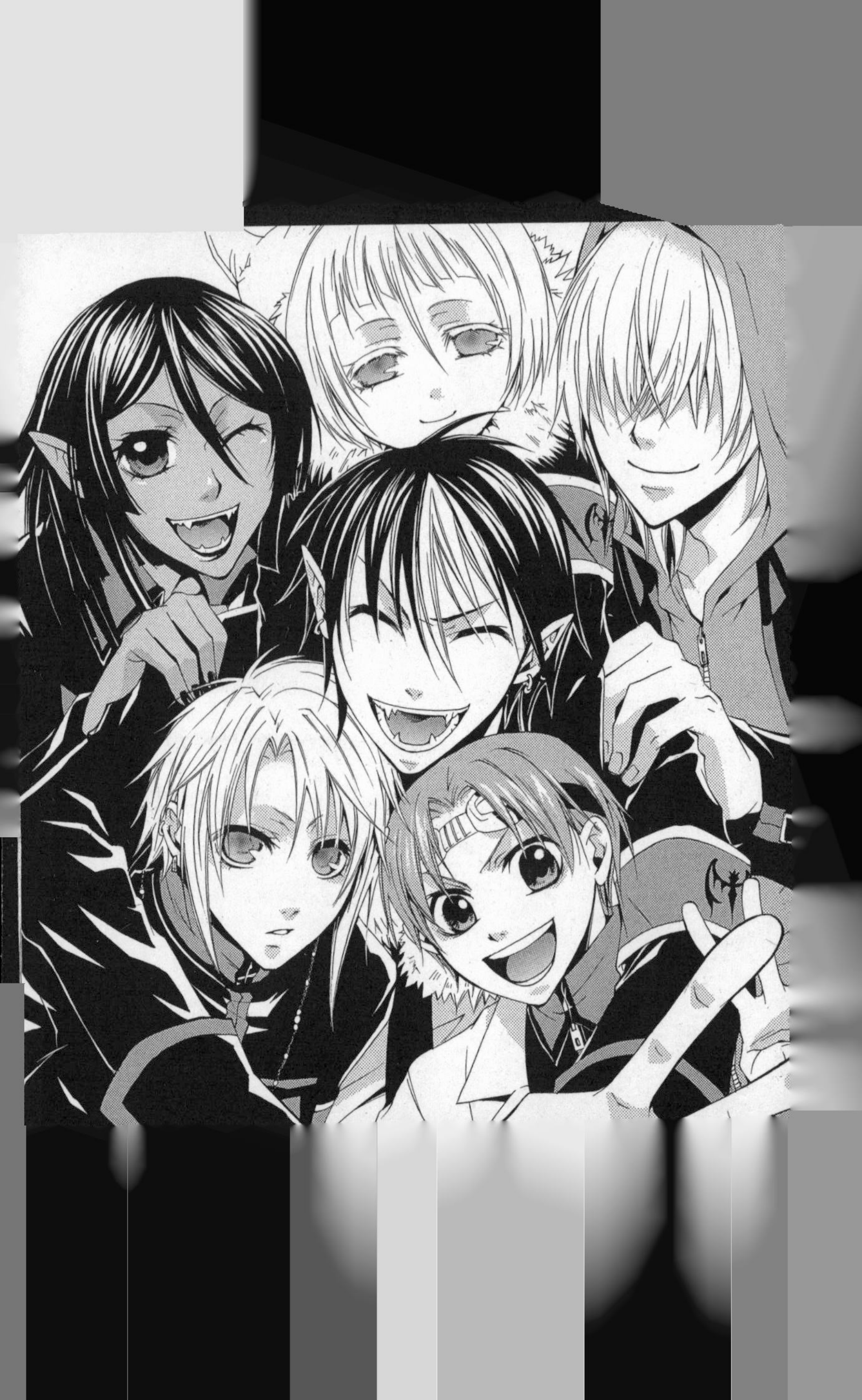

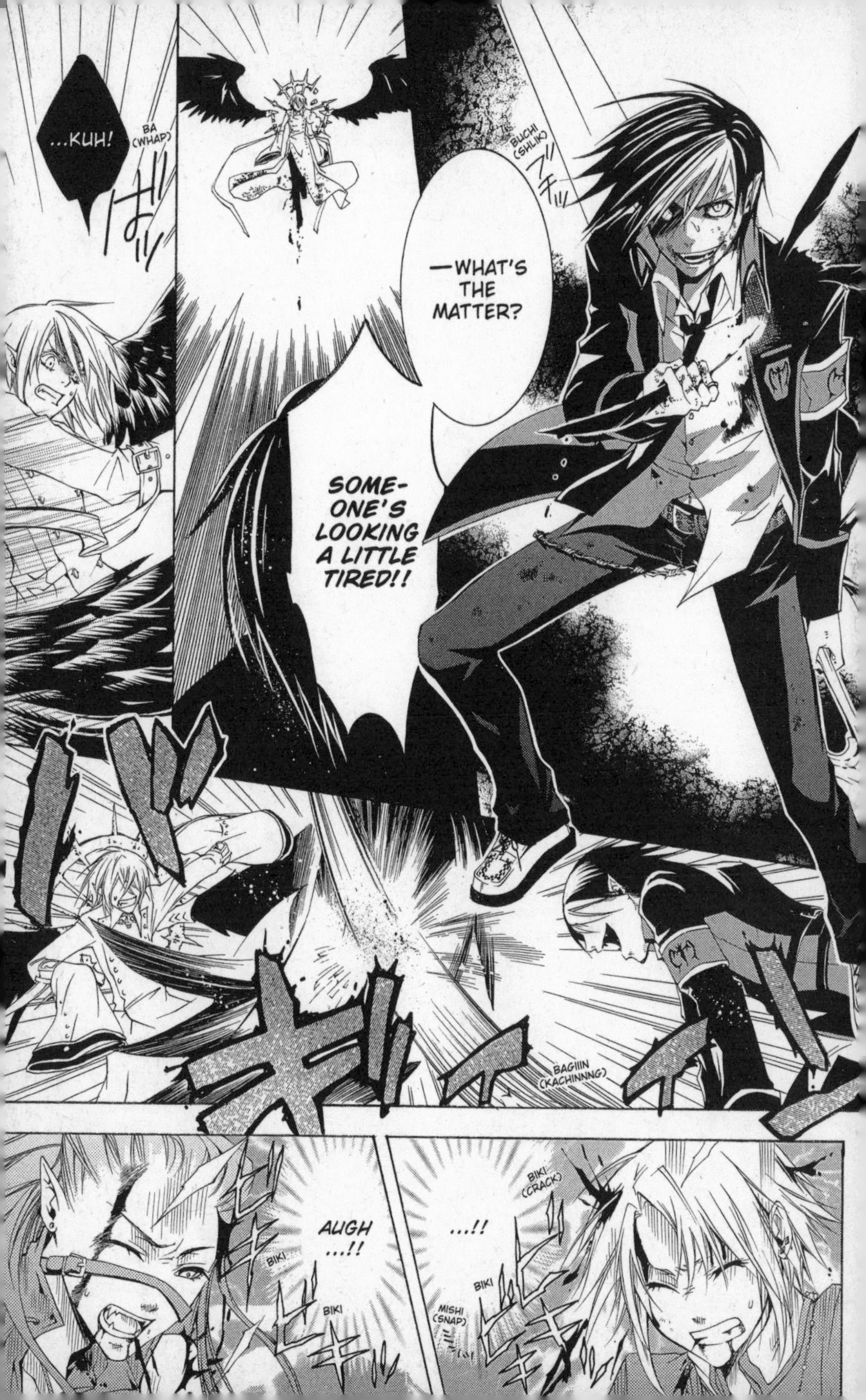
BUCHI (SHLIK)
—WHAT'S THE MATTER?
SOME-ONE'S LOOKING A LITTLE TIRED!!
BA (WHAP)
...KUH!
BAGIIN (KACHINNNG)
BIKI (CRACK)
...!!
BIKI
MISHI (SNAP)
AUGH ...!!
BIKI
BIKI

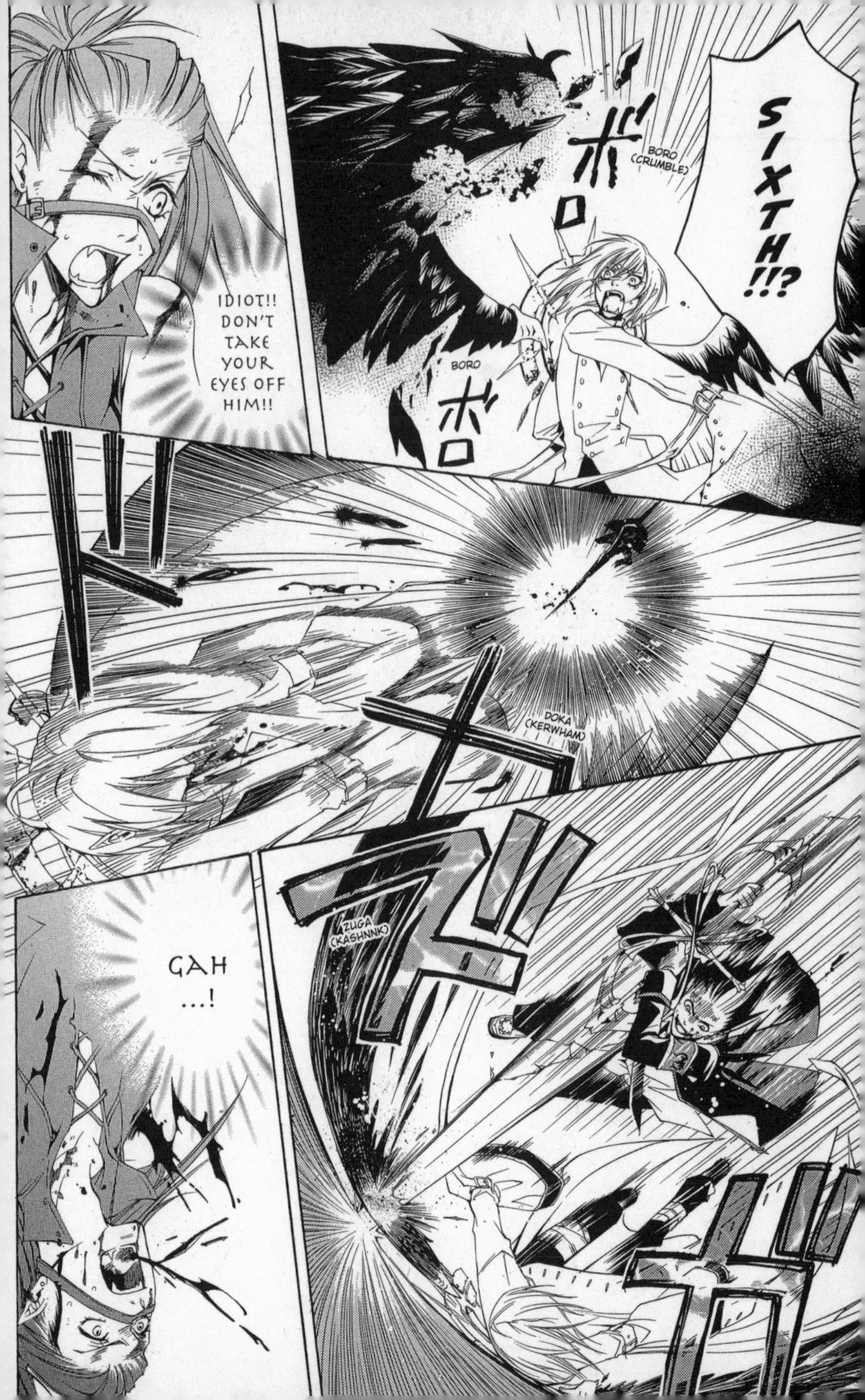
SIXTH!!?
BORO (CRUMBLE)
BORO
IDIOT!! DON'T TAKE YOUR EYES OFF HIM!!
DOKA (KERWHAM)
ZUGA (KASHNNK)
GAH ...!

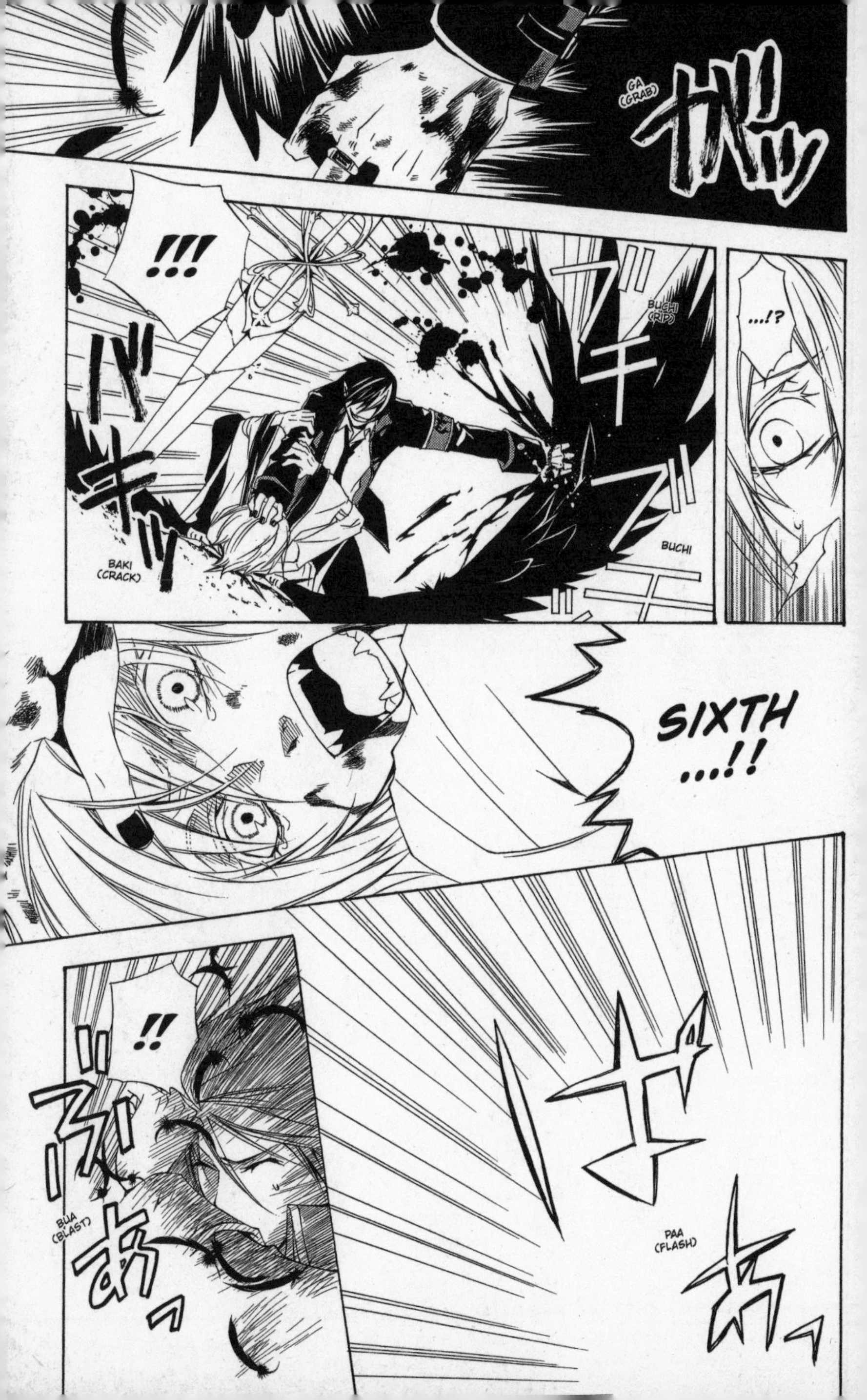
GA (GRAB)
...!?
BUCHI (RIP)
!!!
BUCHI
BAKI (CRACK)
SIXTH ...!!
PAA (FLASH)
!!
BUA (BLAST)

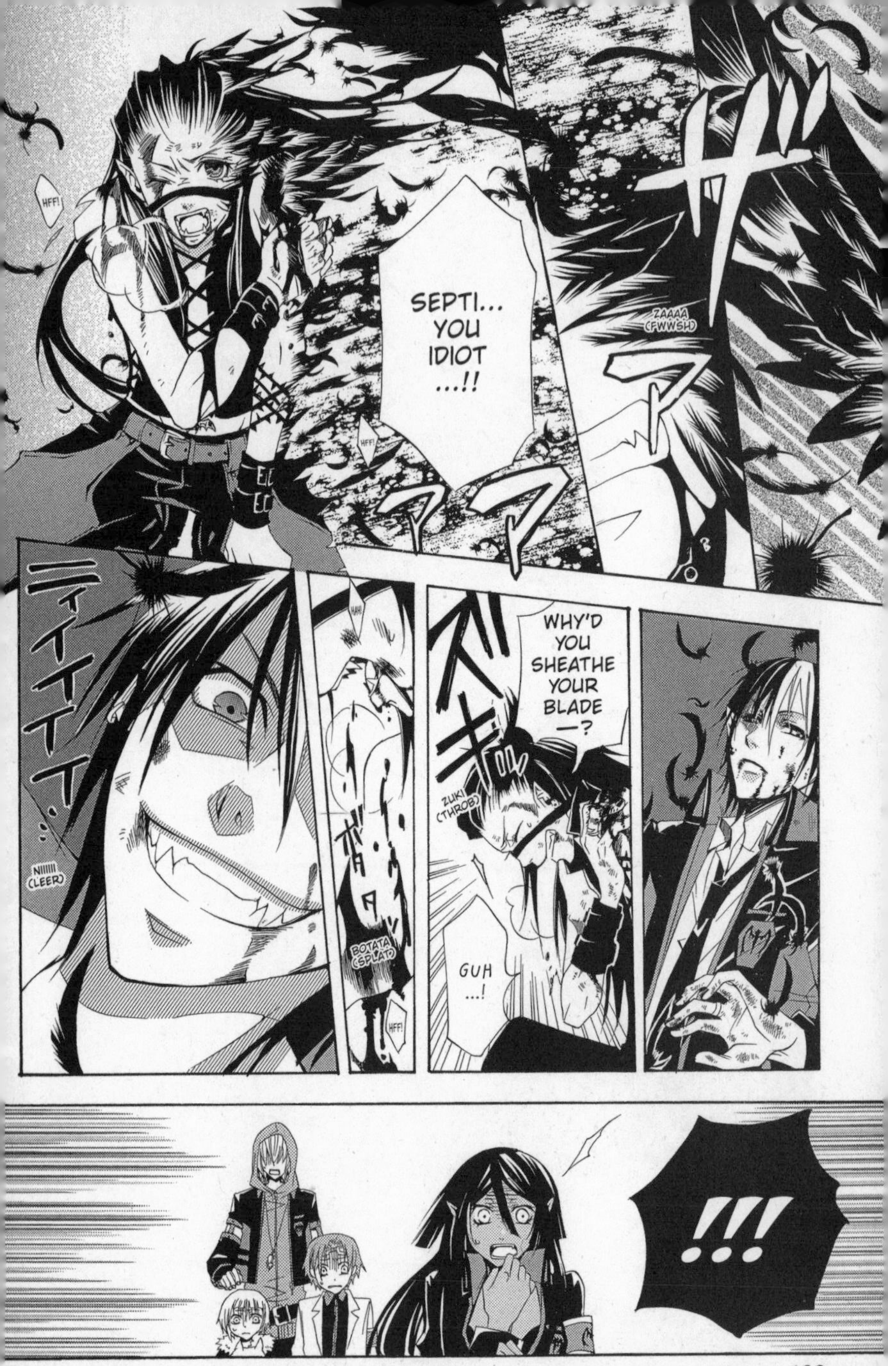
ZAAAA (FWWSH)
SEPTI... YOU IDIOT ...!!
HFF!
HFF!
WHY'D YOU SHEATHE YOUR BLADE —?
ZUKI (THROB)
GUH ...!
HAH!
BOTATA (SPLAT)
HFF!
NIIIII (LEER)
!!!

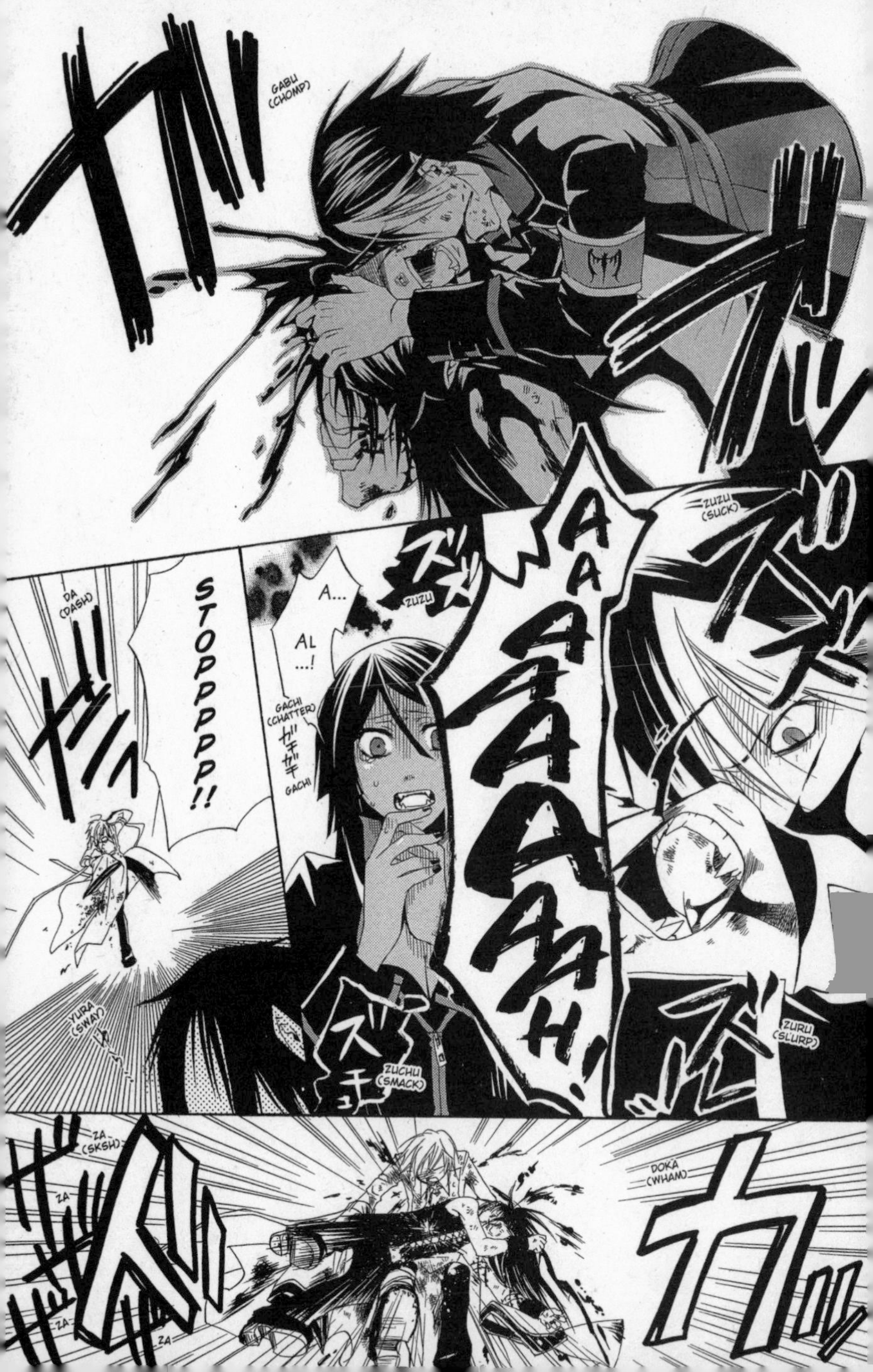
GABU (CHOMP)
ZUZU (SUCK)
AAAAAAAH!
ZURU (SLURP)
ZUZU
A...
AL ...!
GACHI (CHATTER)
GACHI
ZUCHU (SMACK)
STOPPPPPP!!
DA (DASH)
YURA (SWAY)
DOKA (WHAM)
ZA (SKSH)
ZA
ZA
ZA

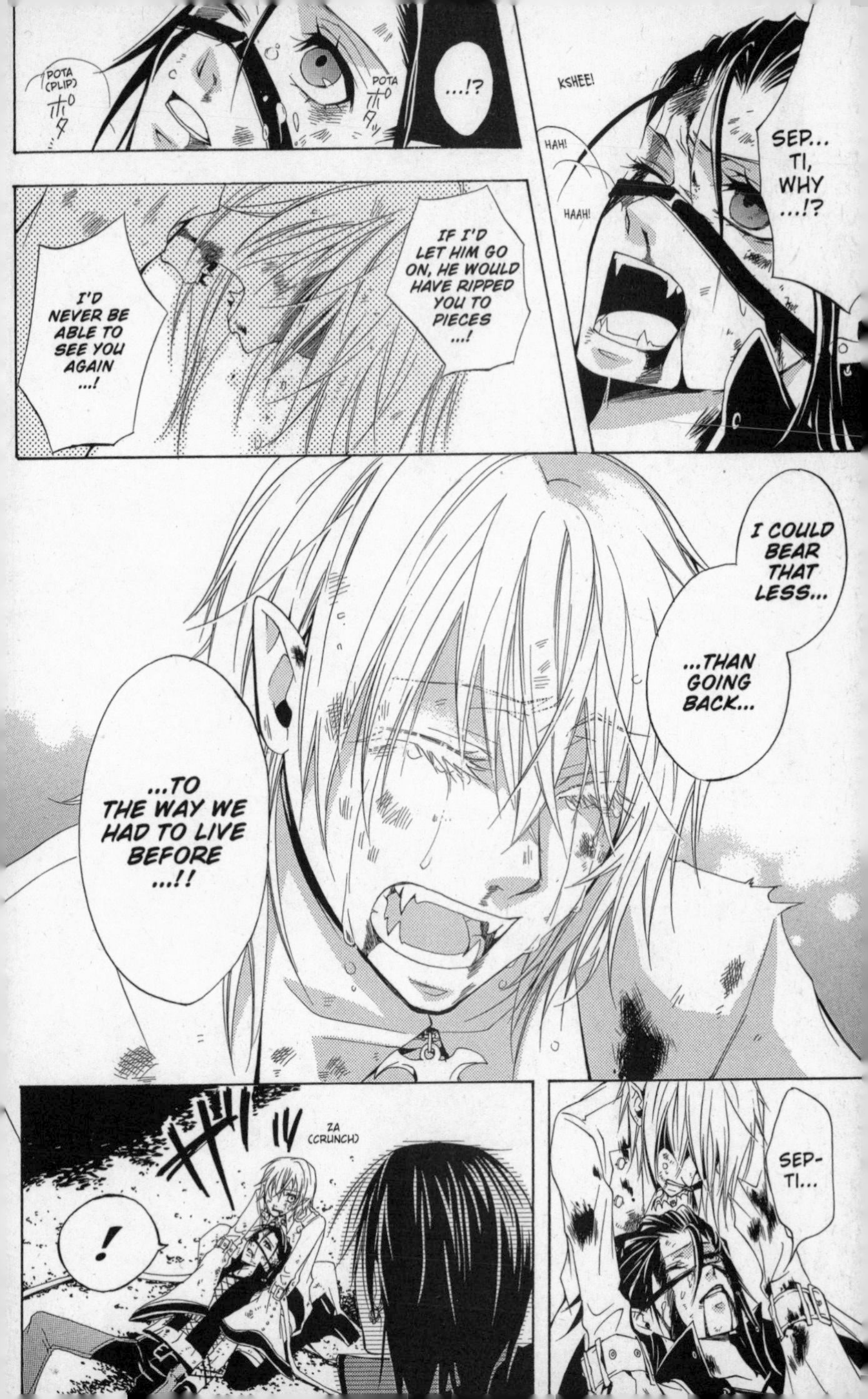
KSHEE!
HAH!
HAAH!
SEP... TI, WHY ...!?
...!?
POTA
POTA (PLIP)
IF I'D LET HIM GO ON, HE WOULD HAVE RIPPED YOU TO PIECES ...!
I'D NEVER BE ABLE TO SEE YOU AGAIN ...!
I COULD BEAR THAT LESS...
...THAN GOING BACK...
...TO THE WAY WE HAD TO LIVE BEFORE ...!!
SEP-TI...
ZA (CRUNCH)
!

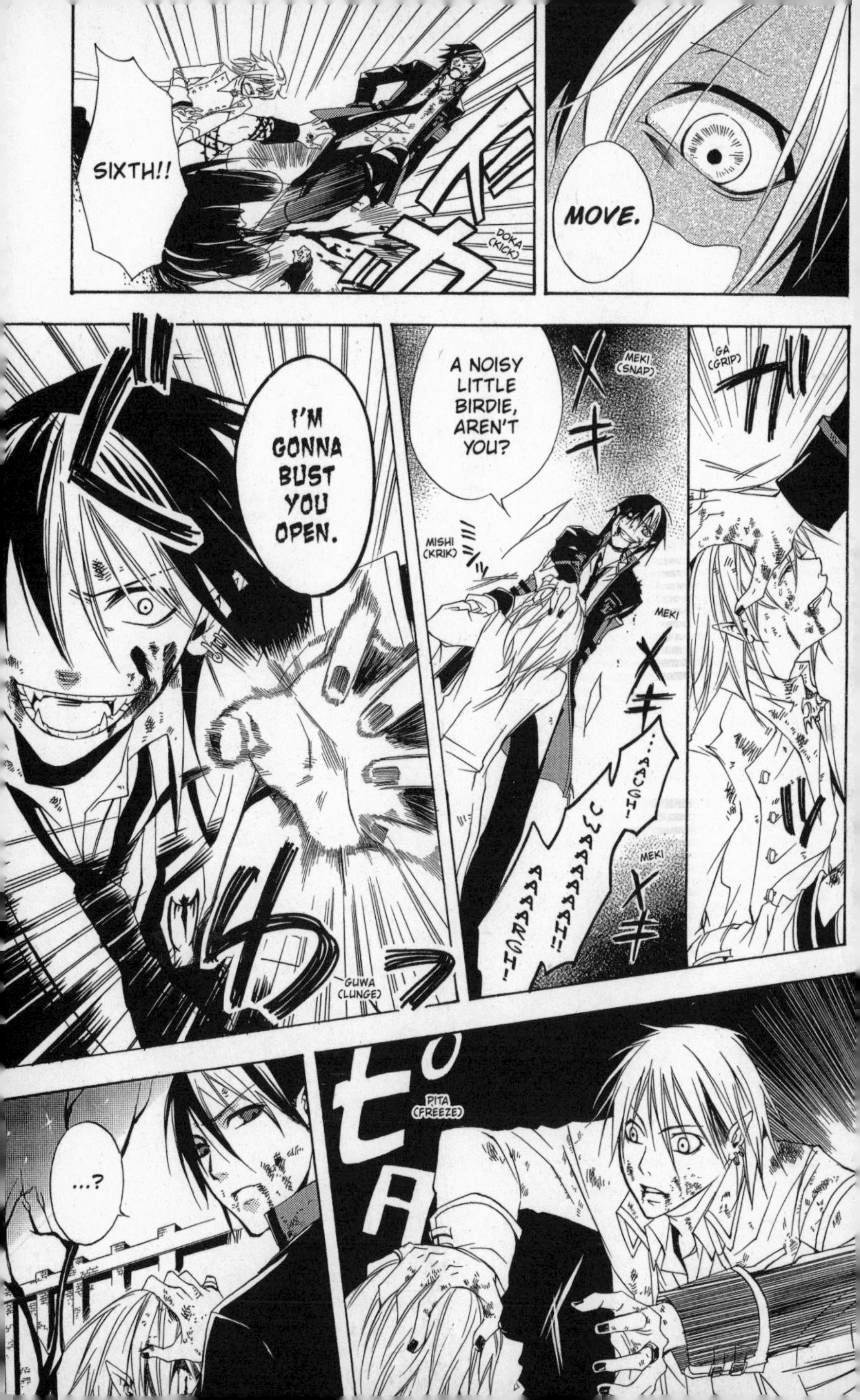
MOVE.
SIXTH!!
DOKA (KICK)
GA (GRIP)
A NOISY LITTLE BIRDIE, AREN'T YOU?
MEKI (SNAP)
MISHI (KRIK)
MEKI
...AAGH!
UWAAAAAAAH!!
AAAAARGH!
MEKI
I'M GONNA BUST YOU OPEN.
GUWA (LUNGE)
PITA (FREEZE)
...?

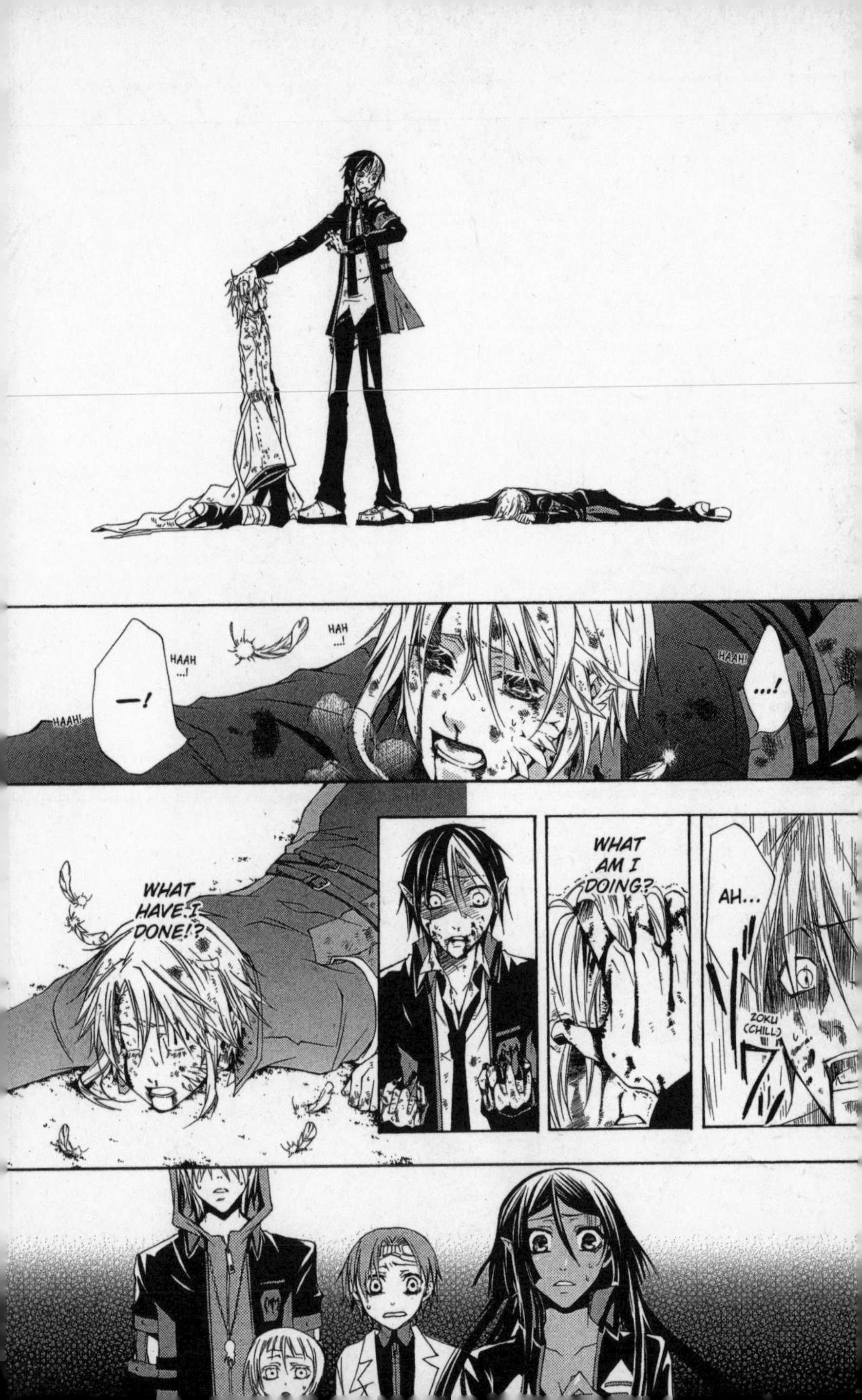
...!
HAAH!
HAH ...!
HAAH ...!
—!
HAAH!
AH...
ZOKU (CHILL)
WHAT AM I DOING?
WHAT HAVE I DONE!?

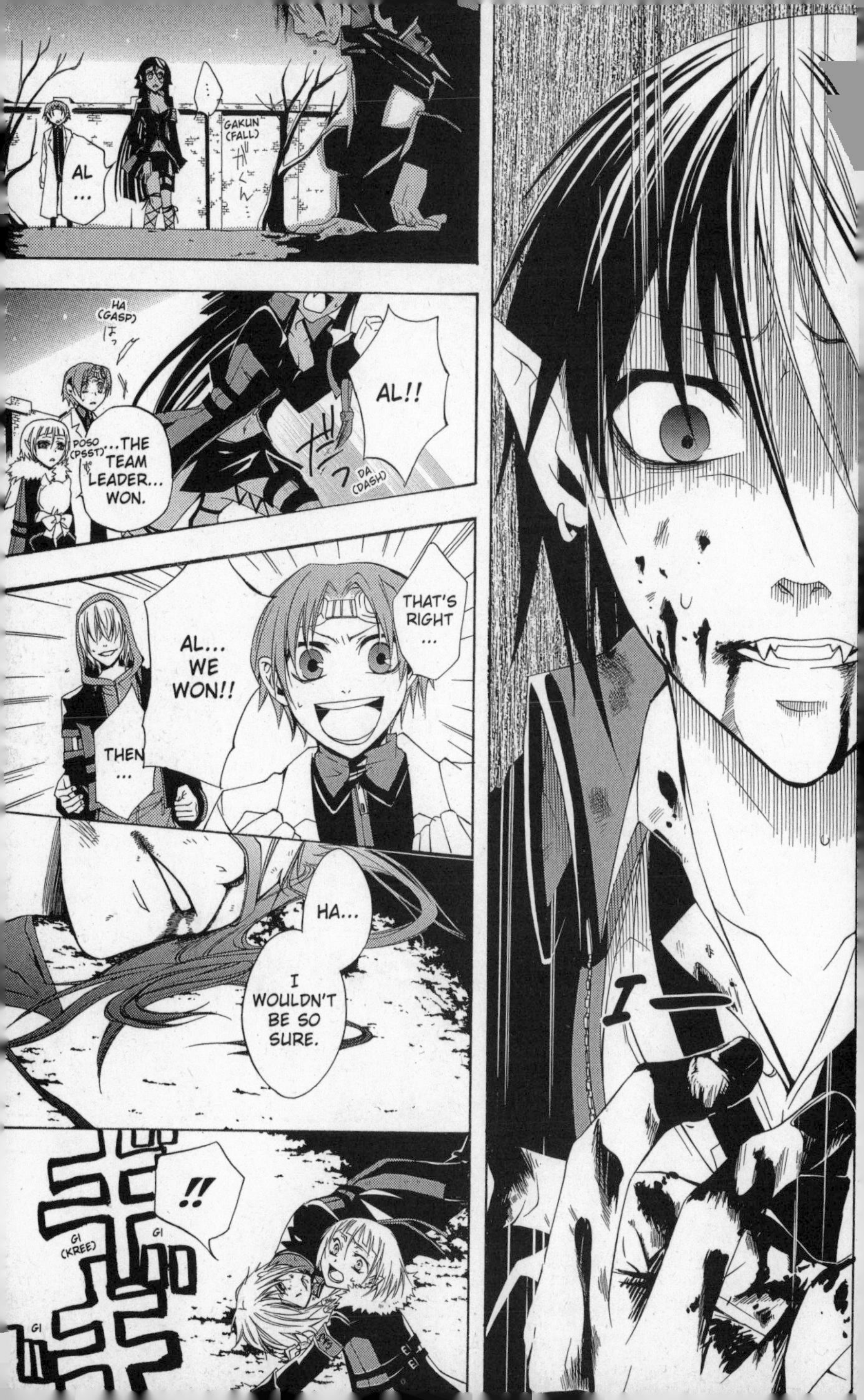
I—
...
GAKUN (FALL)
AL ...
AL!!
HA (GASP)
DA (DASH)
POSO (PSST)
...THE TEAM LEADER... WON.
THAT'S RIGHT ...
AL... WE WON!!
THEN ...
HA...
I WOULDN'T BE SO SURE.
!!
GI (KREE)
GI
GI

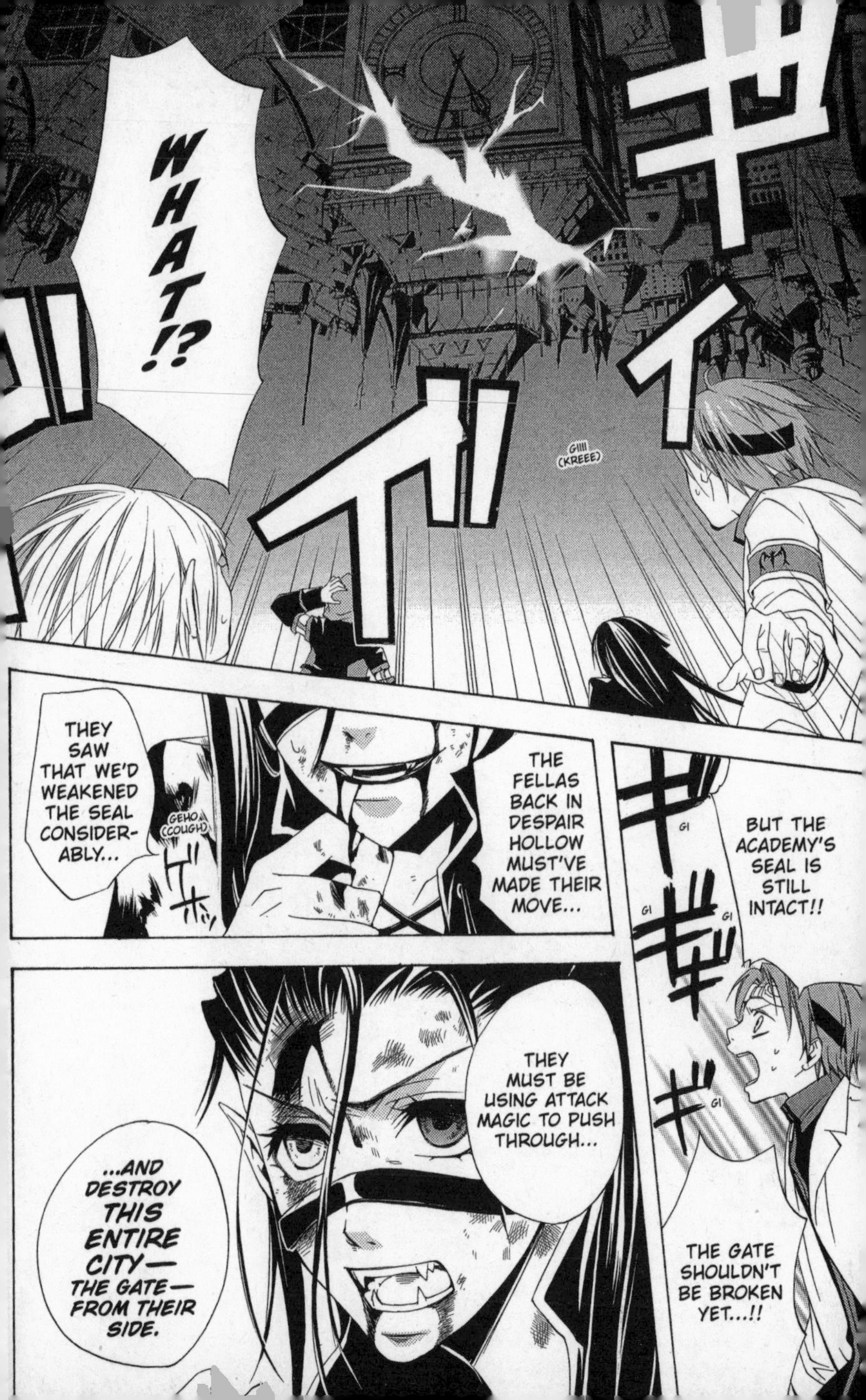
WHAT!?
GIIII (KREEE)
GI GI GI GI
BUT THE ACADEMY'S SEAL IS STILL INTACT!!
THE GATE SHOULDN'T BE BROKEN YET...!!
THE FELLAS BACK IN DESPAIR HOLLOW MUST'VE MADE THEIR MOVE...
THEY SAW THAT WE'D WEAKENED THE SEAL CONSIDERABLY...
GEHO (COUGH)
THEY MUST BE USING ATTACK MAGIC TO PUSH THROUGH...
...AND DESTROY THIS ENTIRE CITY—THE GATE—FROM THEIR SIDE.

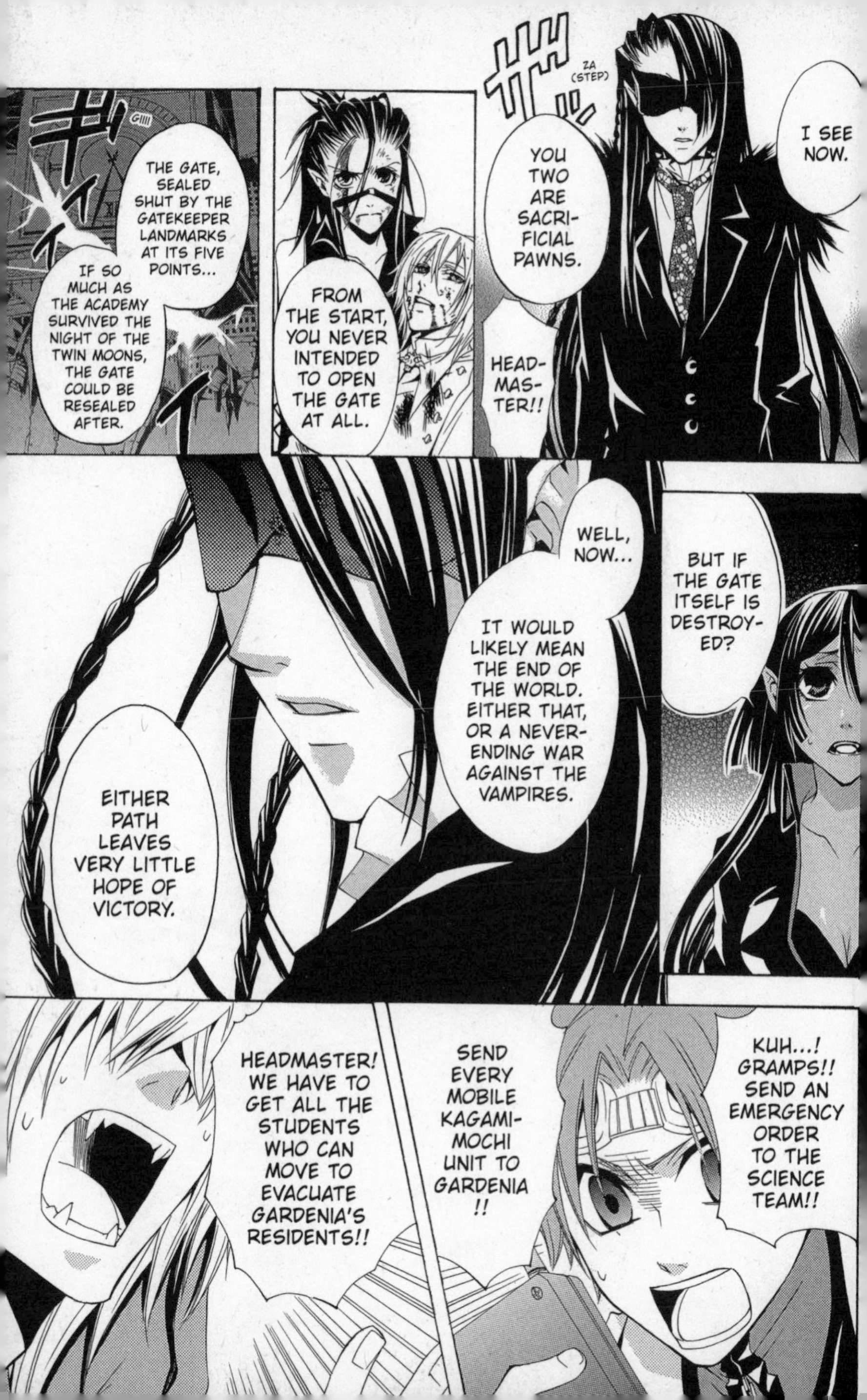
ZA (STEP)
I SEE NOW.
YOU TWO ARE SACRIFICIAL PAWNS.
HEADMASTER!!
FROM THE START, YOU NEVER INTENDED TO OPEN THE GATE AT ALL.
GIIII
THE GATE, SEALED SHUT BY THE GATEKEEPER LANDMARKS AT ITS FIVE POINTS...
IF SO MUCH AS THE ACADEMY SURVIVED THE NIGHT OF THE TWIN MOONS, THE GATE COULD BE RESEALED AFTER.
BUT IF THE GATE ITSELF IS DESTROYED?
WELL, NOW...
IT WOULD LIKELY MEAN THE END OF THE WORLD. EITHER THAT, OR A NEVER-ENDING WAR AGAINST THE VAMPIRES.
EITHER PATH LEAVES VERY LITTLE HOPE OF VICTORY.
KUH...! GRAMPS!! SEND AN EMERGENCY ORDER TO THE SCIENCE TEAM!!
SEND EVERY MOBILE KAGAMI-MOCHI UNIT TO GARDENIA!!
HEADMASTER! WE HAVE TO GET ALL THE STUDENTS WHO CAN MOVE TO EVACUATE GARDENIA'S RESIDENTS!!

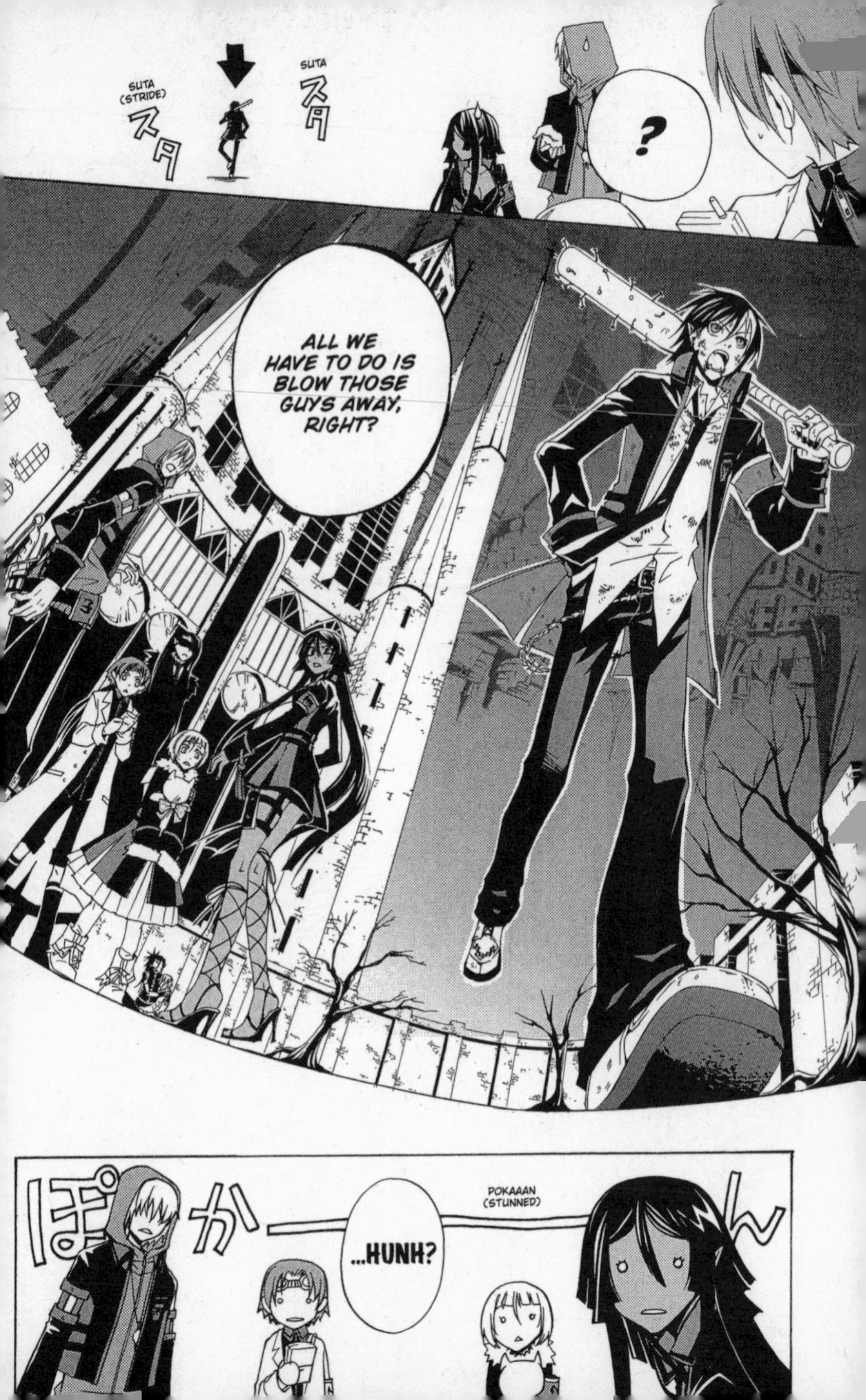
?
SUTA
スタ
SUTA (STRIDE)
スタ
ALL WE HAVE TO DO IS BLOW THOSE GUYS AWAY, RIGHT?
POKAAAN (STUNNED)
ぽか——ん
...HUNH?

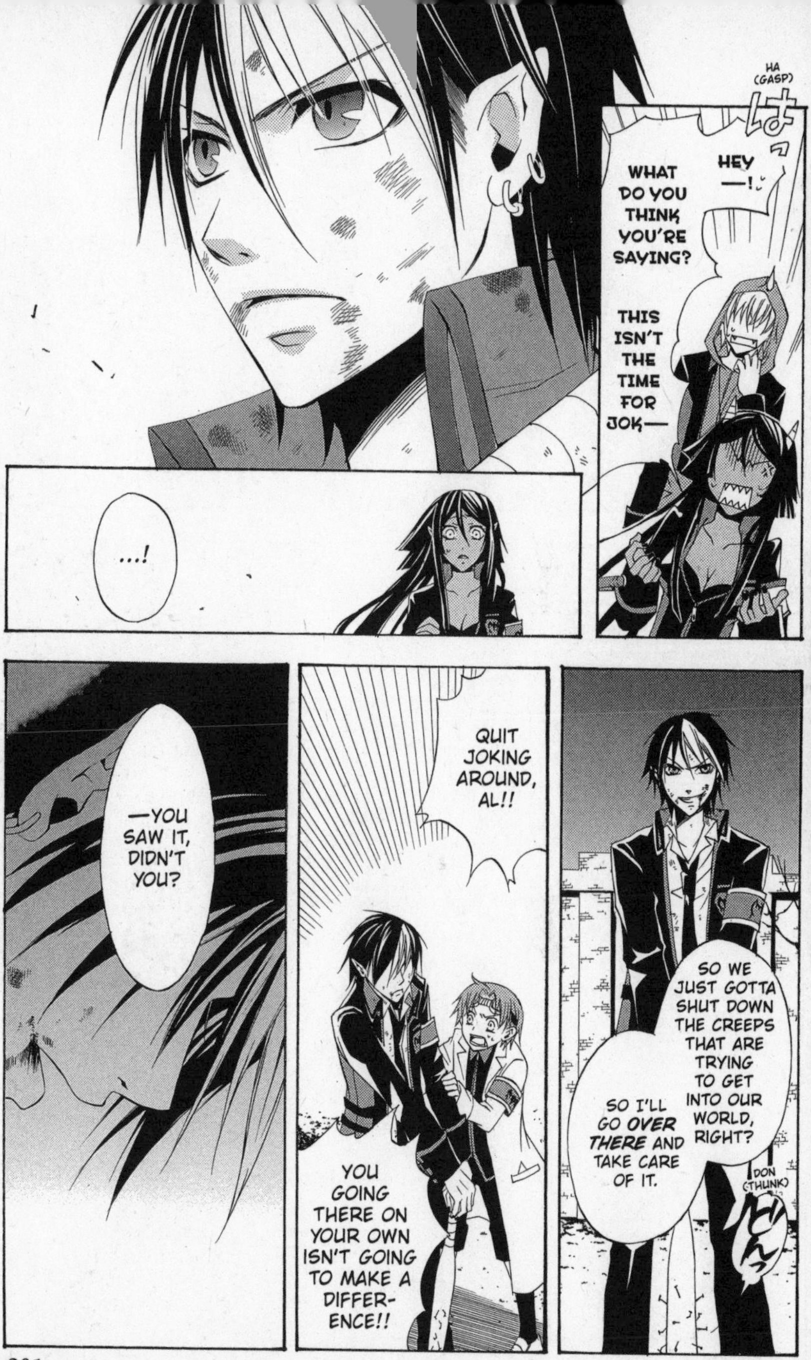

HA (GASP)
HEY—!
WHAT DO YOU THINK YOU'RE SAYING?
THIS ISN'T THE TIME FOR JOK—
...!
SO WE JUST GOTTA SHUT DOWN THE CREEPS THAT ARE TRYING TO GET INTO OUR WORLD, RIGHT?
SO I'LL GO *OVER THERE* AND TAKE CARE OF IT.
DON (THUNK)
QUIT JOKING AROUND, AL!!
YOU GOING THERE ON YOUR OWN ISN'T GOING TO MAKE A DIFFERENCE!!
—YOU SAW IT, DIDN'T YOU?

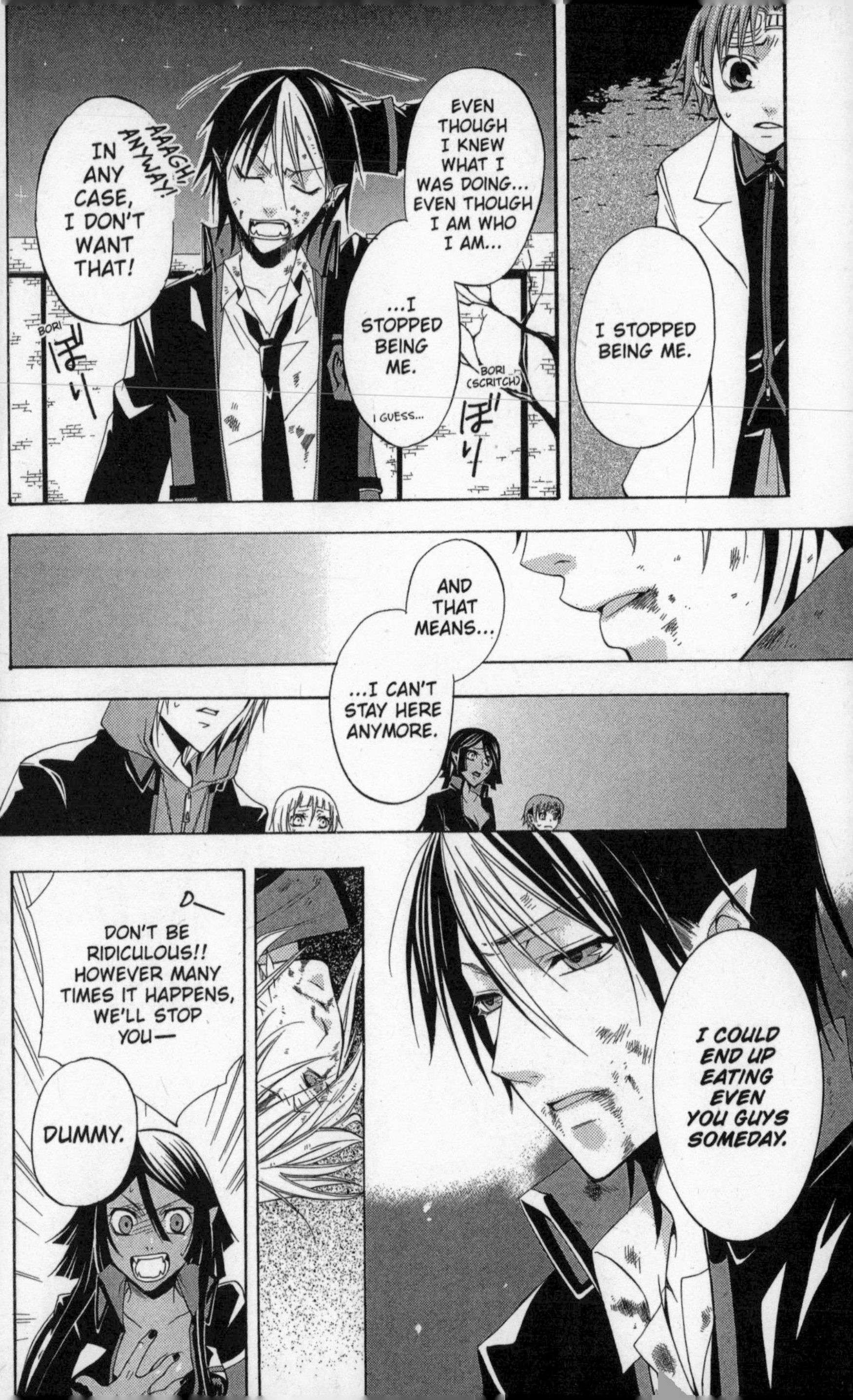
I STOPPED BEING ME.
EVEN THOUGH I KNEW WHAT I WAS DOING... EVEN THOUGH I AM WHO I AM...
...I STOPPED BEING ME.
I GUESS...
BORI (SCRITCH)
ぼり
AAAGH, ANYWAY!
IN ANY CASE, I DON'T WANT THAT!
BORI
ぼり
AND THAT MEANS...
...I CAN'T STAY HERE ANYMORE.
I COULD END UP EATING EVEN YOU GUYS SOMEDAY.
D—
DON'T BE RIDICULOUS!! HOWEVER MANY TIMES IT HAPPENS, WE'LL STOP YOU—
DUMMY.

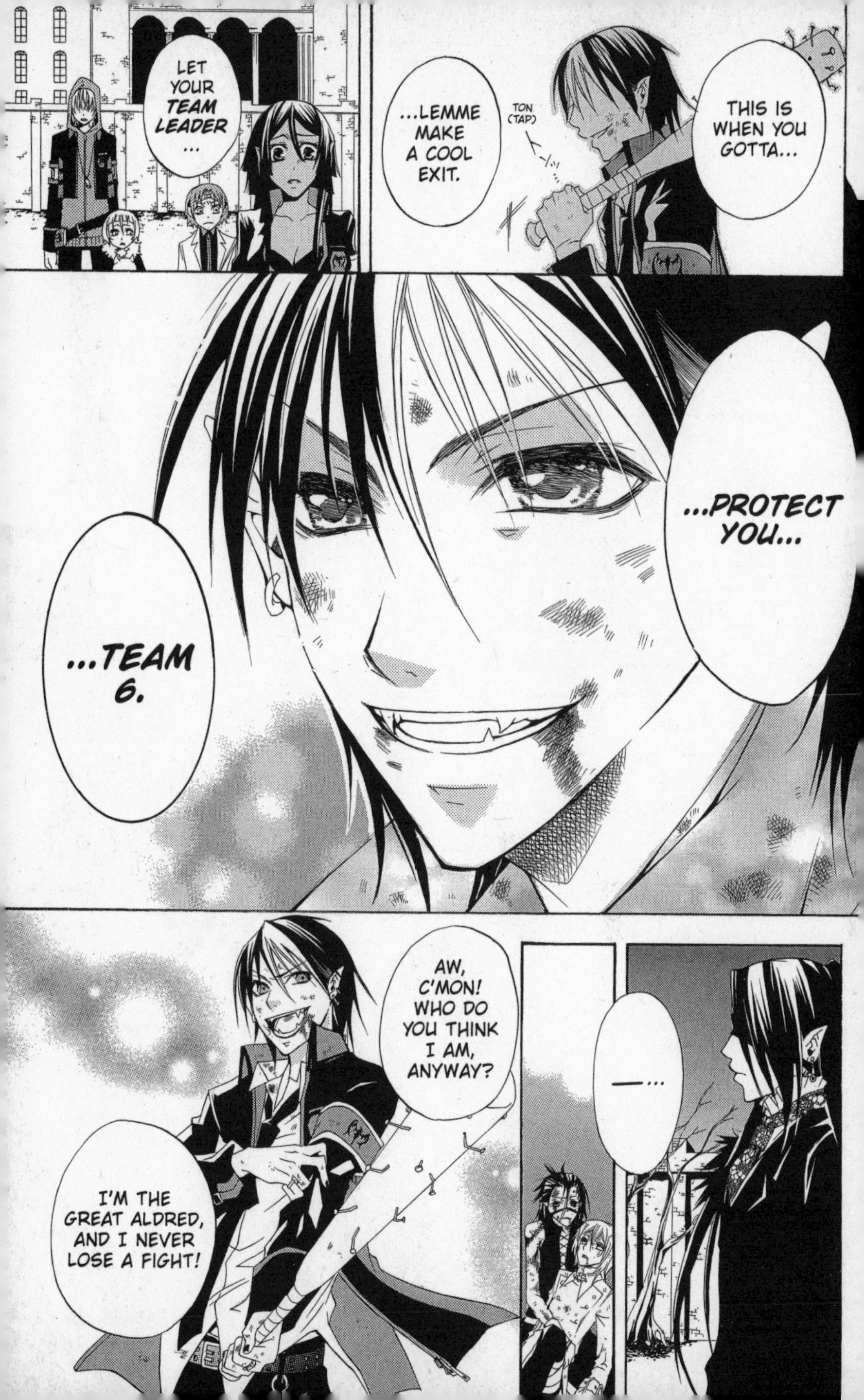
THIS IS WHEN YOU GOTTA...
TON (TAP)
...LEMME MAKE A COOL EXIT.
LET YOUR TEAM LEADER ...
...PROTECT YOU...
...TEAM 6.
—...
AW, C'MON! WHO DO YOU THINK I AM, ANYWAY?
I'M THE GREAT ALDRED, AND I NEVER LOSE A FIGHT!

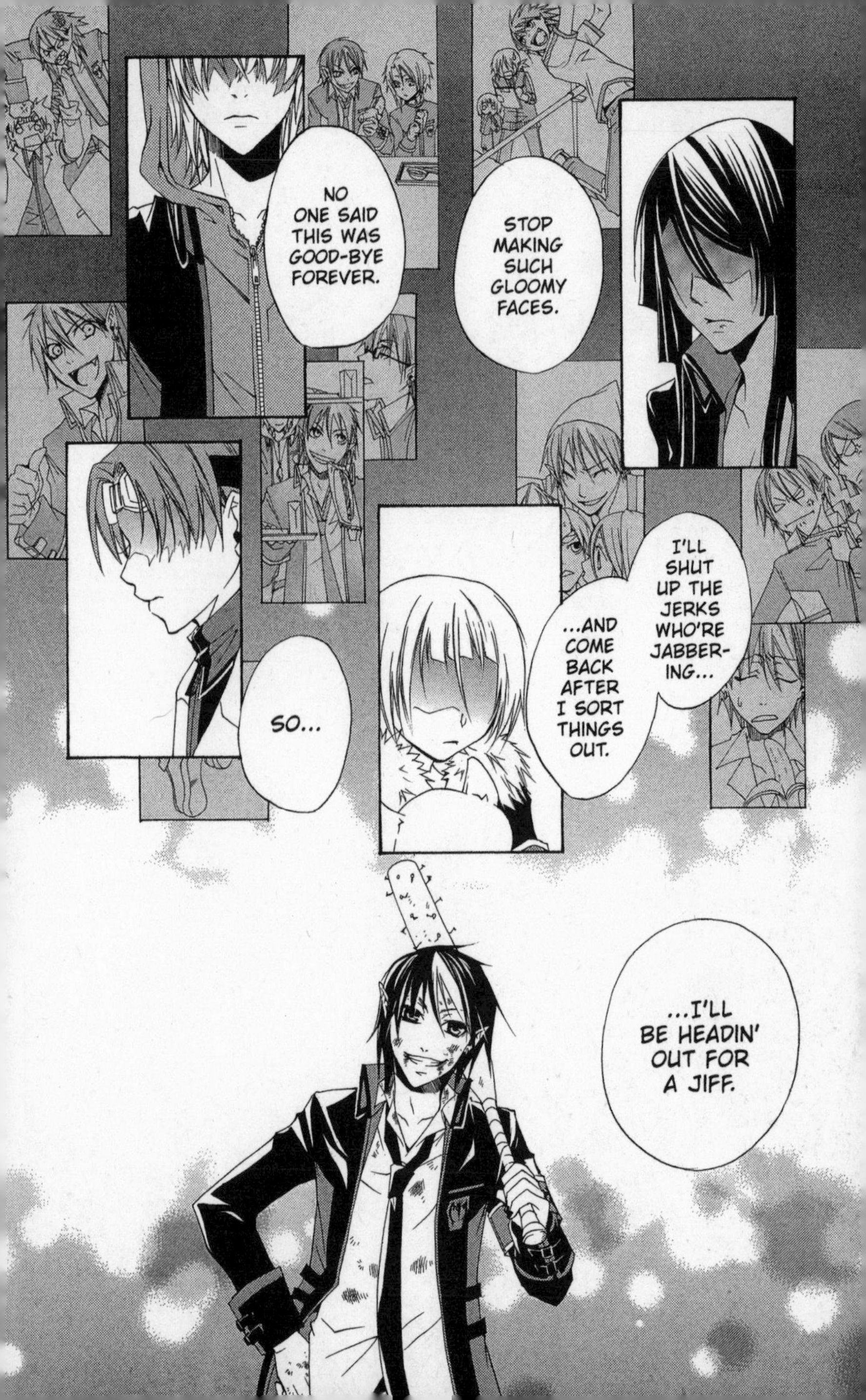
STOP MAKING SUCH GLOOMY FACES.
NO ONE SAID THIS WAS GOOD-BYE FOREVER.
I'LL SHUT UP THE JERKS WHO'RE JABBER-ING...
...AND COME BACK AFTER I SORT THINGS OUT.
SO...
...I'LL BE HEADIN' OUT FOR A JIFF.

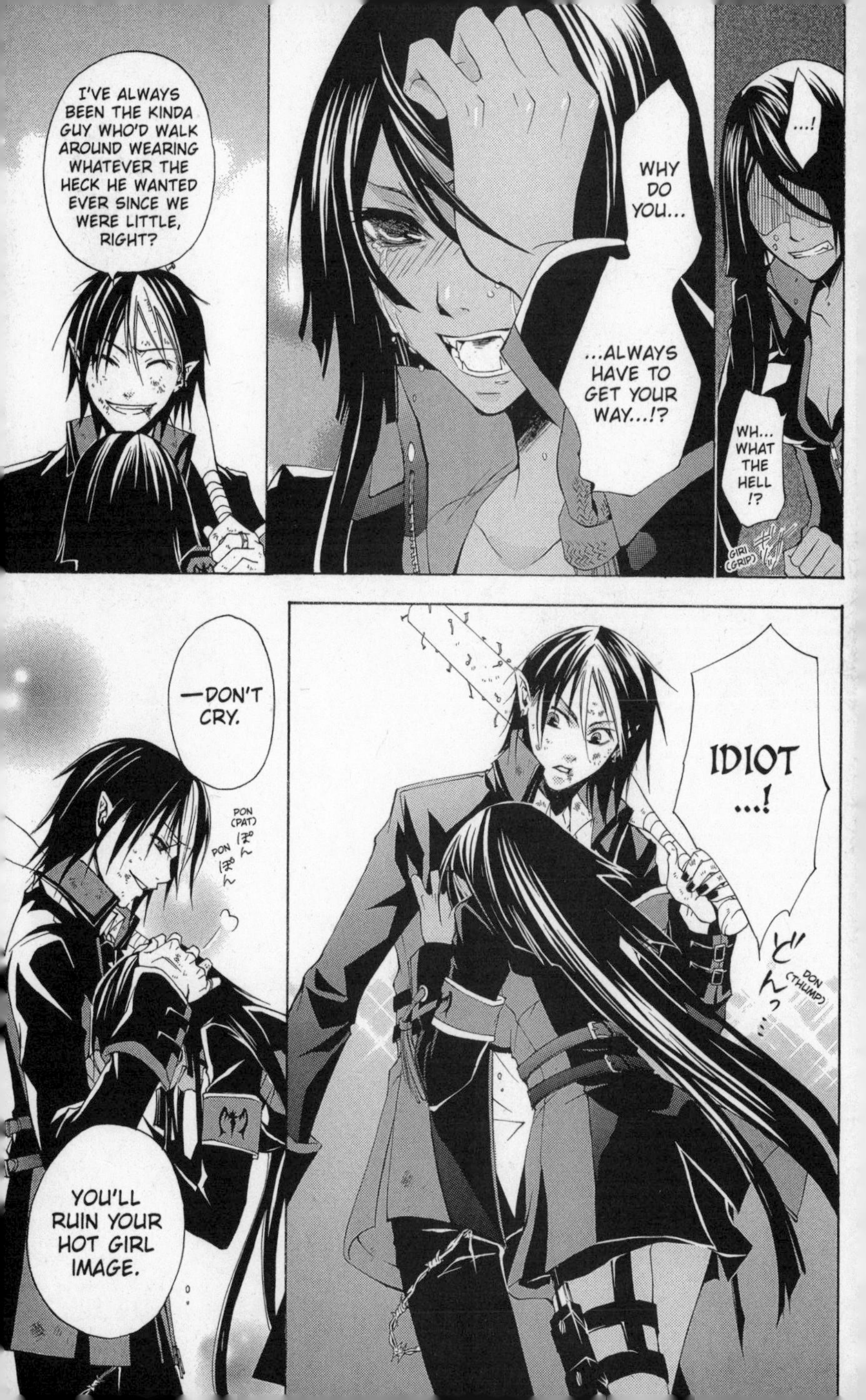
...!
WH... WHAT THE HELL !?
GIRI (GRIP)
WHY DO YOU...
...ALWAYS HAVE TO GET YOUR WAY...!?
I'VE ALWAYS BEEN THE KINDA GUY WHO'D WALK AROUND WEARING WHATEVER THE HECK HE WANTED EVER SINCE WE WERE LITTLE, RIGHT?
IDIOT ...!
どんっ
DON (THUMP)
—DON'T CRY.
PON (PAT) ぽん
PON ぽん
YOU'LL RUIN YOUR HOT GIRL IMAGE.

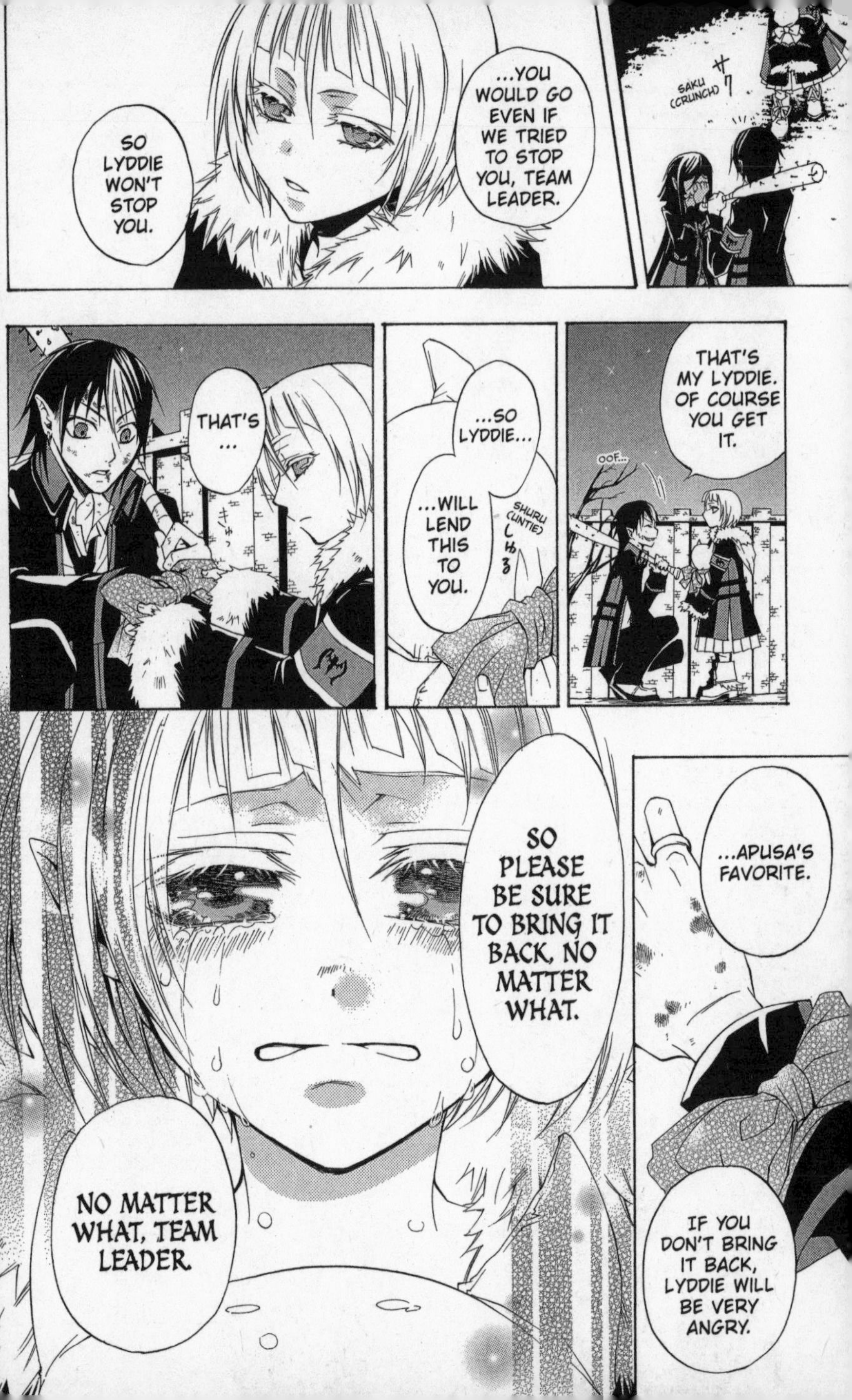
SAKU (CRUNCH)
...YOU WOULD GO EVEN IF WE TRIED TO STOP YOU, TEAM LEADER.
SO LYDDIE WON'T STOP YOU.
THAT'S MY LYDDIE. OF COURSE YOU GET IT.
OOF...
...SO LYDDIE...
SHURU (UNTIE)
...WILL LEND THIS TO YOU.
THAT'S ...
...APUSA'S FAVORITE.
IF YOU DON'T BRING IT BACK, LYDDIE WILL BE VERY ANGRY.
SO PLEASE BE SURE TO BRING IT BACK, NO MATTER WHAT.
NO MATTER WHAT, TEAM LEADER.

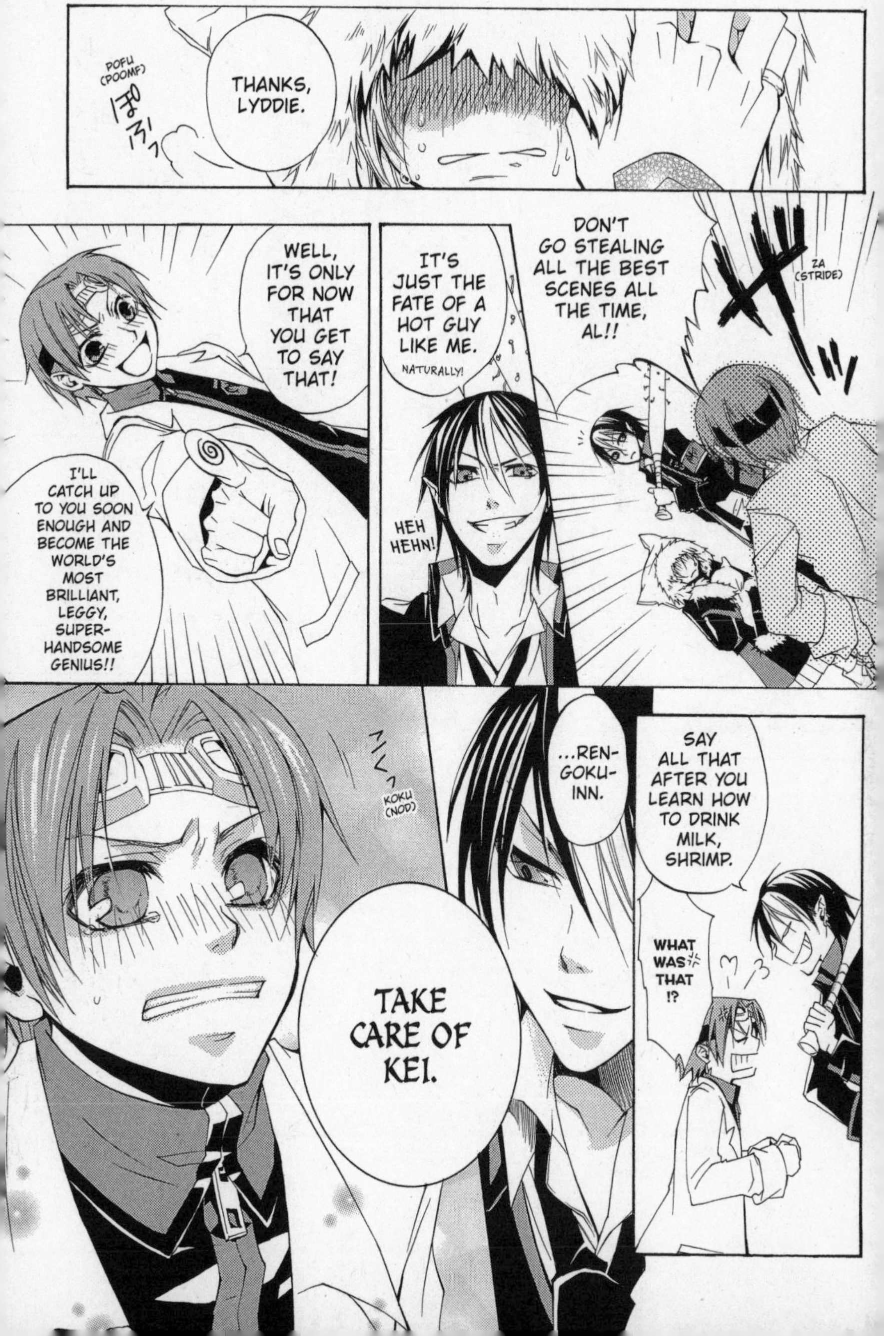
POFU (POOMP)
ぽふっ
THANKS, LYDDIE.
ZA (STRIDE)
DON'T GO STEALING ALL THE BEST SCENES ALL THE TIME, AL!!
IT'S JUST THE FATE OF A HOT GUY LIKE ME.
NATURALLY!
HEH HEHN!
WELL, IT'S ONLY FOR NOW THAT YOU GET TO SAY THAT!
I'LL CATCH UP TO YOU SOON ENOUGH AND BECOME THE WORLD'S MOST BRILLIANT, LEGGY, SUPER-HANDSOME GENIUS!!
SAY ALL THAT AFTER YOU LEARN HOW TO DRINK MILK, SHRIMP.
WHAT WAS THAT!?
...REN-GOKU-INN.
こくっ
KOKU (NOD)
TAKE CARE OF KEI.

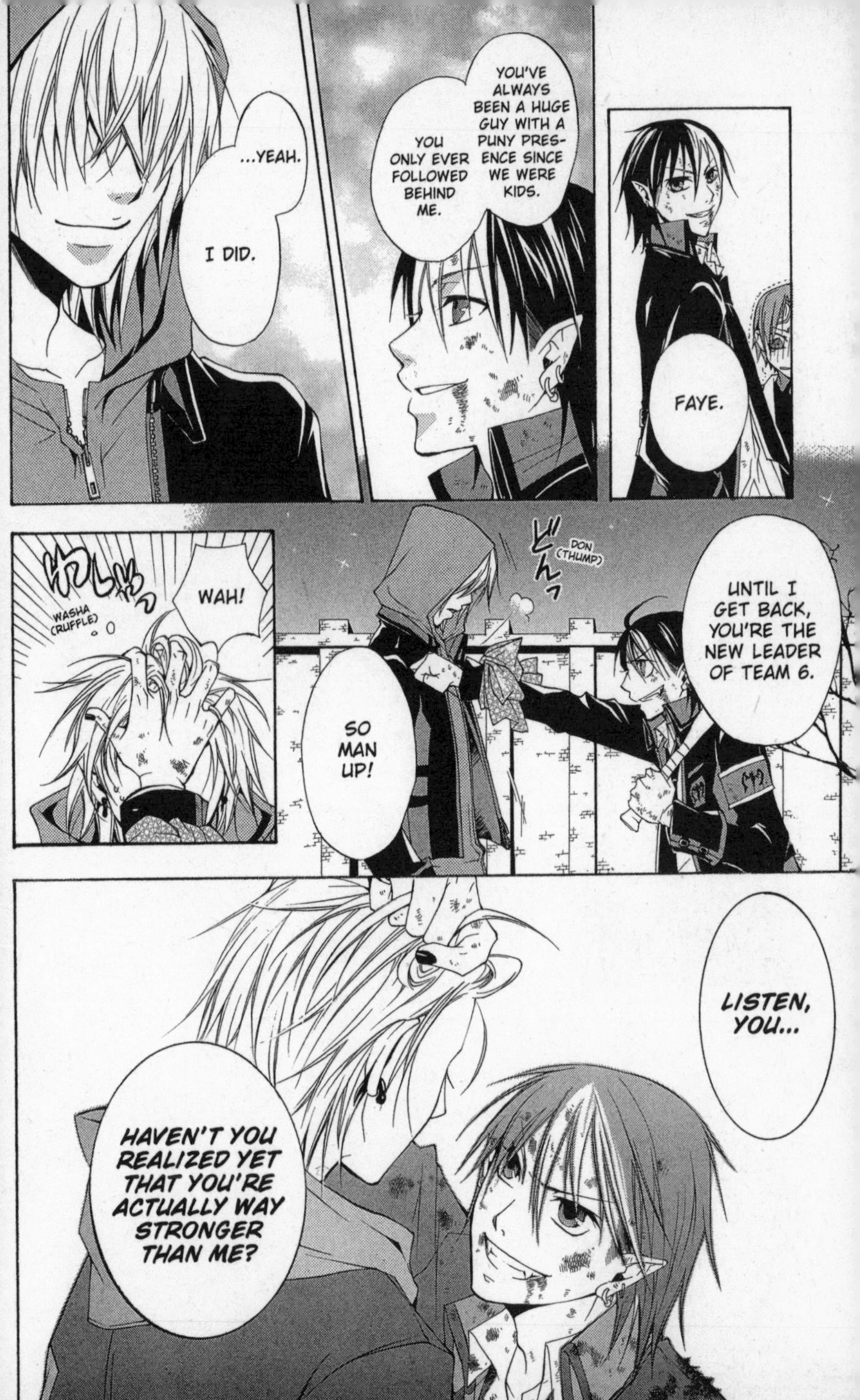
FAYE.
YOU'VE ALWAYS BEEN A HUGE GUY WITH A PUNY PRES-ENCE SINCE WE WERE KIDS.
YOU ONLY EVER FOLLOWED BEHIND ME.
...YEAH.
I DID.
どんっ
DON (THUMP)
UNTIL I GET BACK, YOU'RE THE NEW LEADER OF TEAM 6.
SO MAN UP!
わしゃっ
WASHA (RUFFLE)
WAH!
LISTEN, YOU...
HAVEN'T YOU REALIZED YET THAT YOU'RE ACTUALLY WAY STRONGER THAN ME?

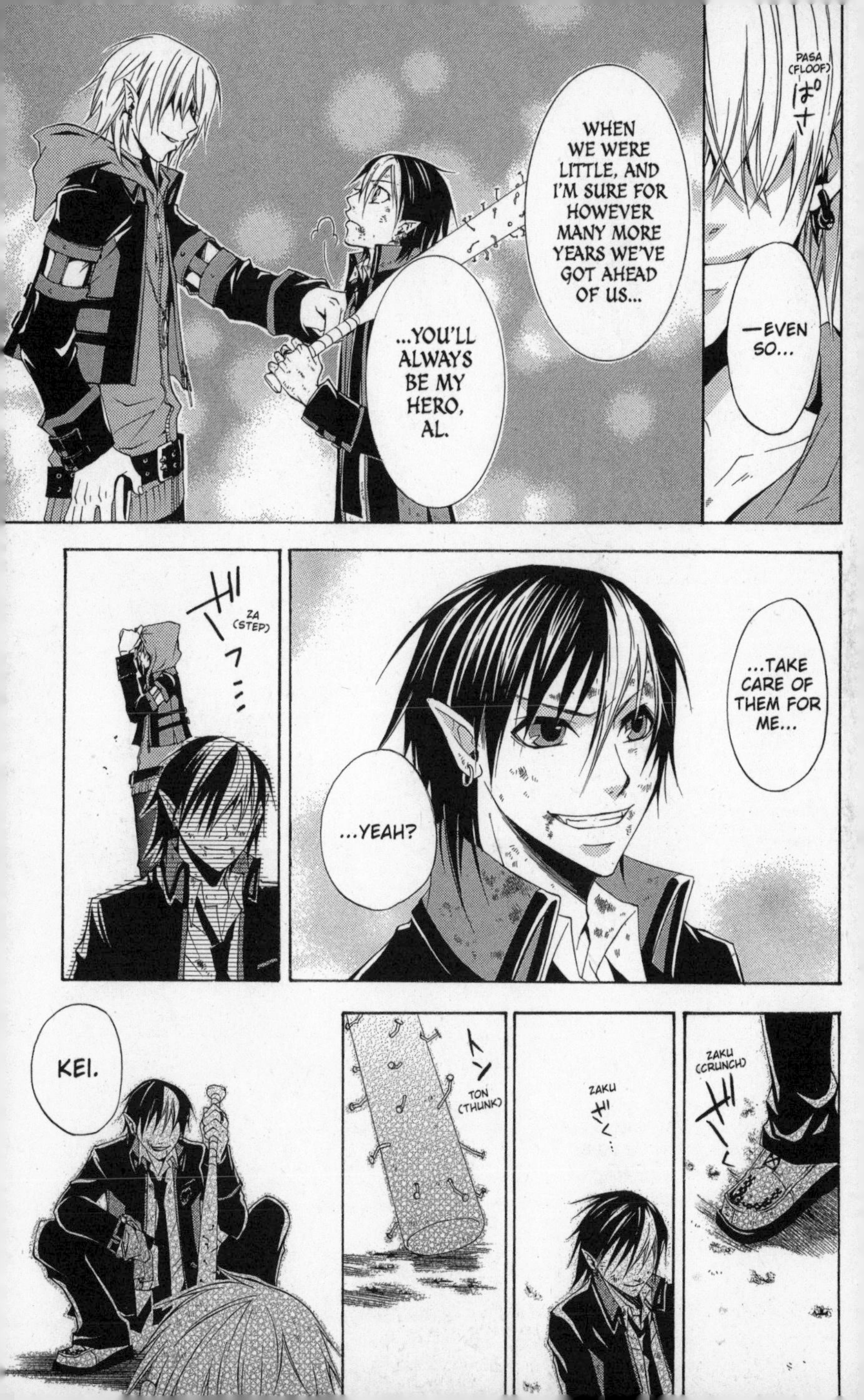
PASA (FLOOF)
—EVEN SO...
WHEN WE WERE LITTLE, AND I'M SURE FOR HOWEVER MANY MORE YEARS WE'VE GOT AHEAD OF US...
...YOU'LL ALWAYS BE MY HERO, AL.
...TAKE CARE OF THEM FOR ME...
...YEAH?
ZA (STEP)
ZAKU (CRUNCH)
ZAKU
TON (THUNK)
KEI.

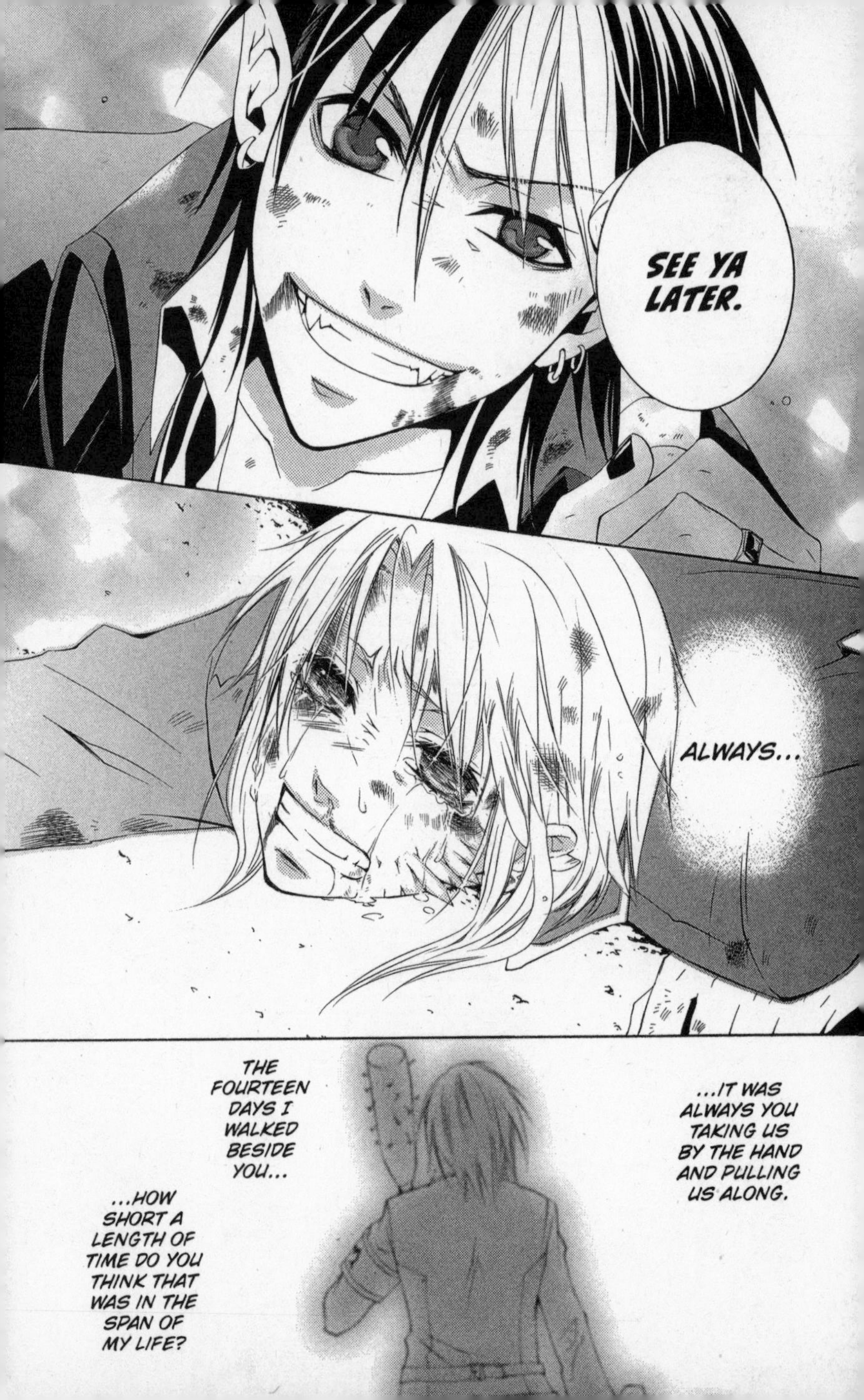
SEE YA LATER.
ALWAYS...
...IT WAS ALWAYS YOU TAKING US BY THE HAND AND PULLING US ALONG.
THE FOURTEEN DAYS I WALKED BESIDE YOU...
...HOW SHORT A LENGTH OF TIME DO YOU THINK THAT WAS IN THE SPAN OF MY LIFE?

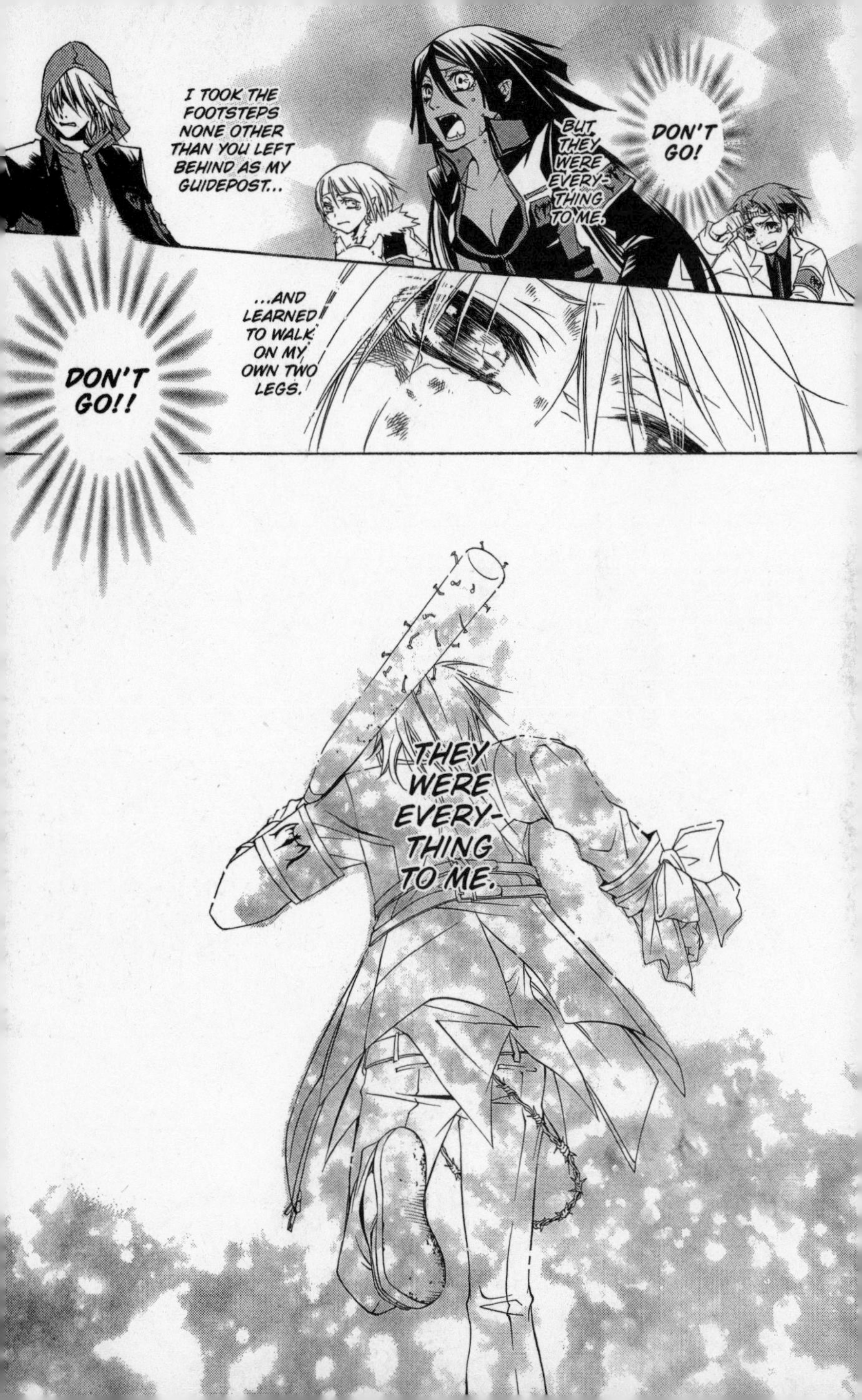
DON'T GO!
BUT THEY WERE EVERY-THING TO ME.
I TOOK THE FOOTSTEPS NONE OTHER THAN YOU LEFT BEHIND AS MY GUIDEPOST...
...AND LEARNED TO WALK ON MY OWN TWO LEGS.
DON'T GO!!
THEY WERE EVERY-THING TO ME.

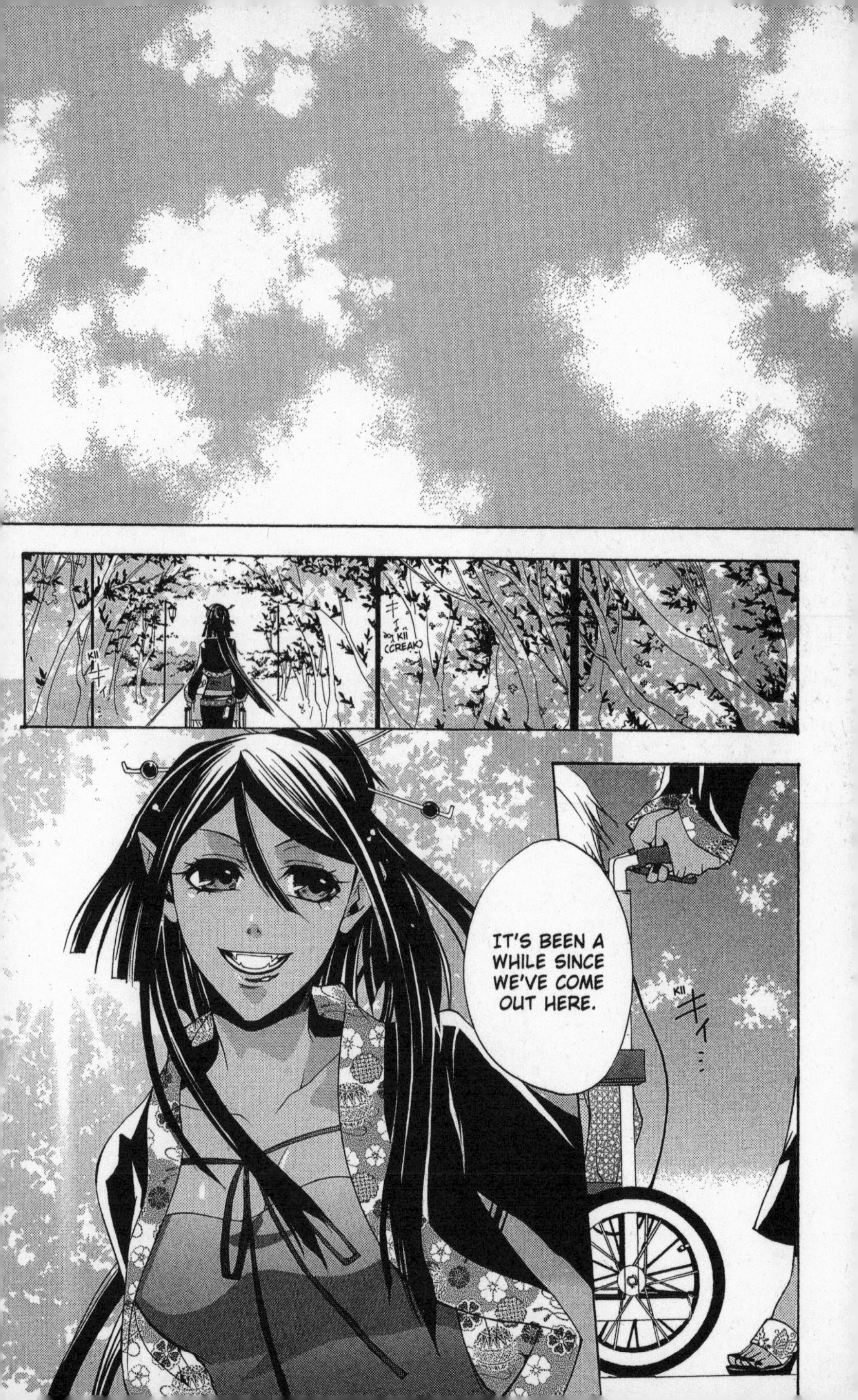
KII (CREAK)
KII
IT'S BEEN A WHILE SINCE WE'VE COME OUT HERE.
KII

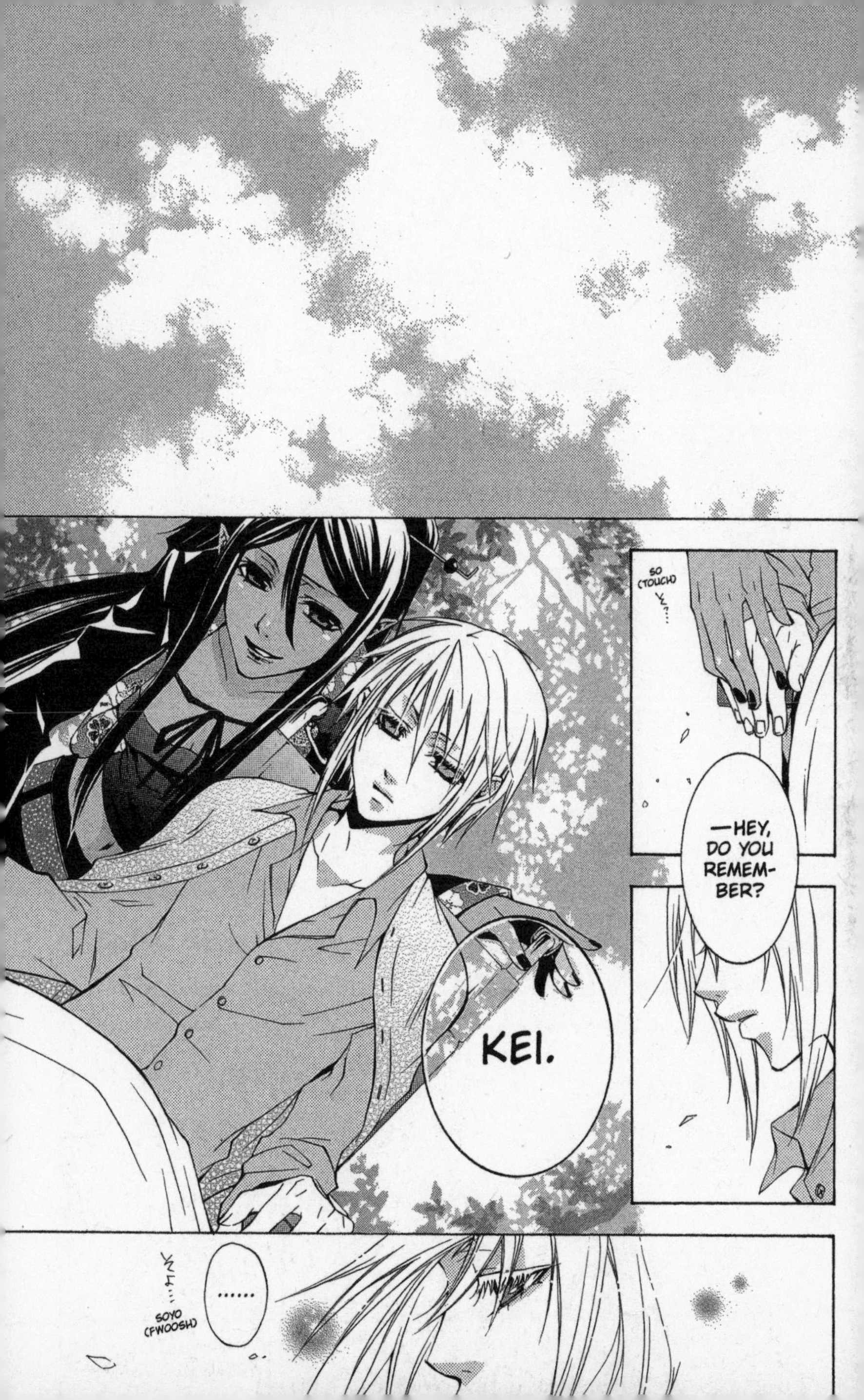
SO (TOUCH)
—HEY, DO YOU REMEMBER?
KEI.
SOYO (FWOOSH)
......

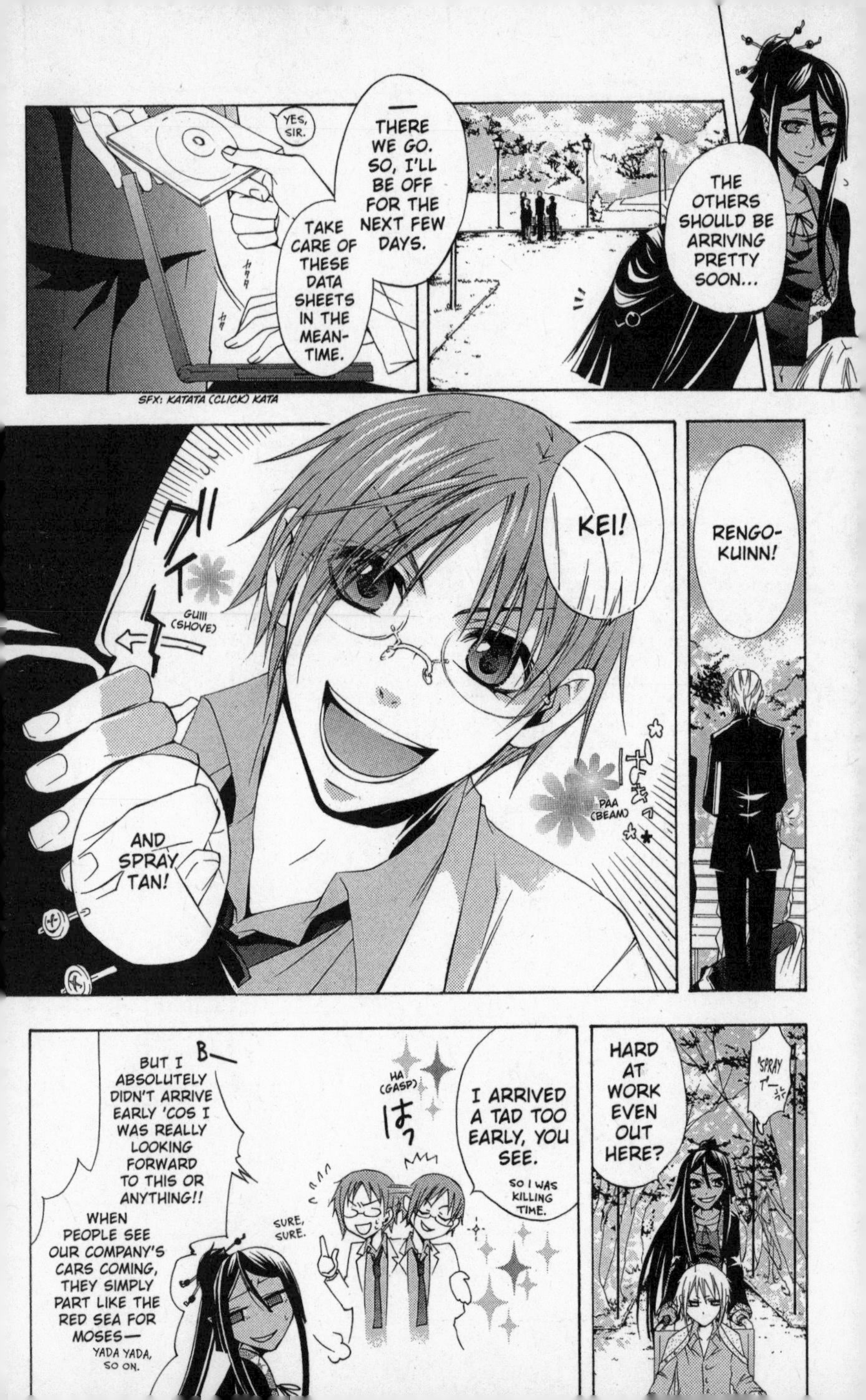
THE OTHERS SHOULD BE ARRIVING PRETTY SOON...
—THERE WE GO. SO, I'LL BE OFF FOR THE NEXT FEW DAYS.
TAKE CARE OF THESE DATA SHEETS IN THE MEAN-TIME.
YES, SIR.
SFX: KATATA (CLICK) KATA
RENGO-KUINN!
KEI!
PAA (BEAM)
GUIII (SHOVE)
AND SPRAY TAN!
SPRAY
HARD AT WORK EVEN OUT HERE?
I ARRIVED A TAD TOO EARLY, YOU SEE.
SO I WAS KILLING TIME.
HA (GASP)
B—
BUT I ABSOLUTELY DIDN'T ARRIVE EARLY 'COS I WAS REALLY LOOKING FORWARD TO THIS OR ANYTHING!!
SURE, SURE.
WHEN PEOPLE SEE OUR COMPANY'S CARS COMING, THEY SIMPLY PART LIKE THE RED SEA FOR MOSES—
YADA YADA, SO ON.

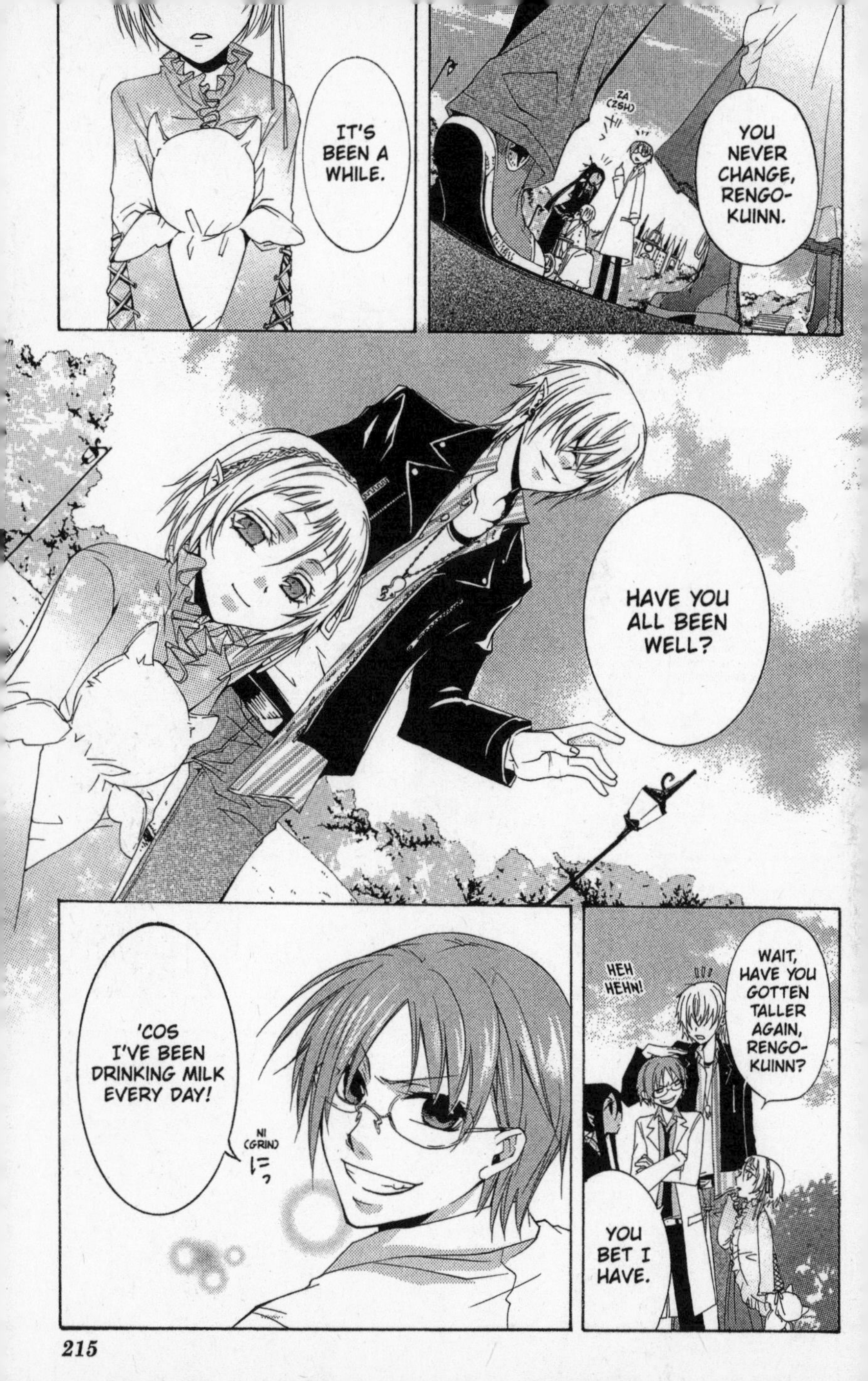
ZA (ZSH)
YOU NEVER CHANGE, RENGO-KUINN.
IT'S BEEN A WHILE.
HAVE YOU ALL BEEN WELL?
WAIT, HAVE YOU GOTTEN TALLER AGAIN, RENGO-KUINN?
HEH HEHN!
YOU BET I HAVE.
'COS I'VE BEEN DRINKING MILK EVERY DAY!
NI (GRIN)

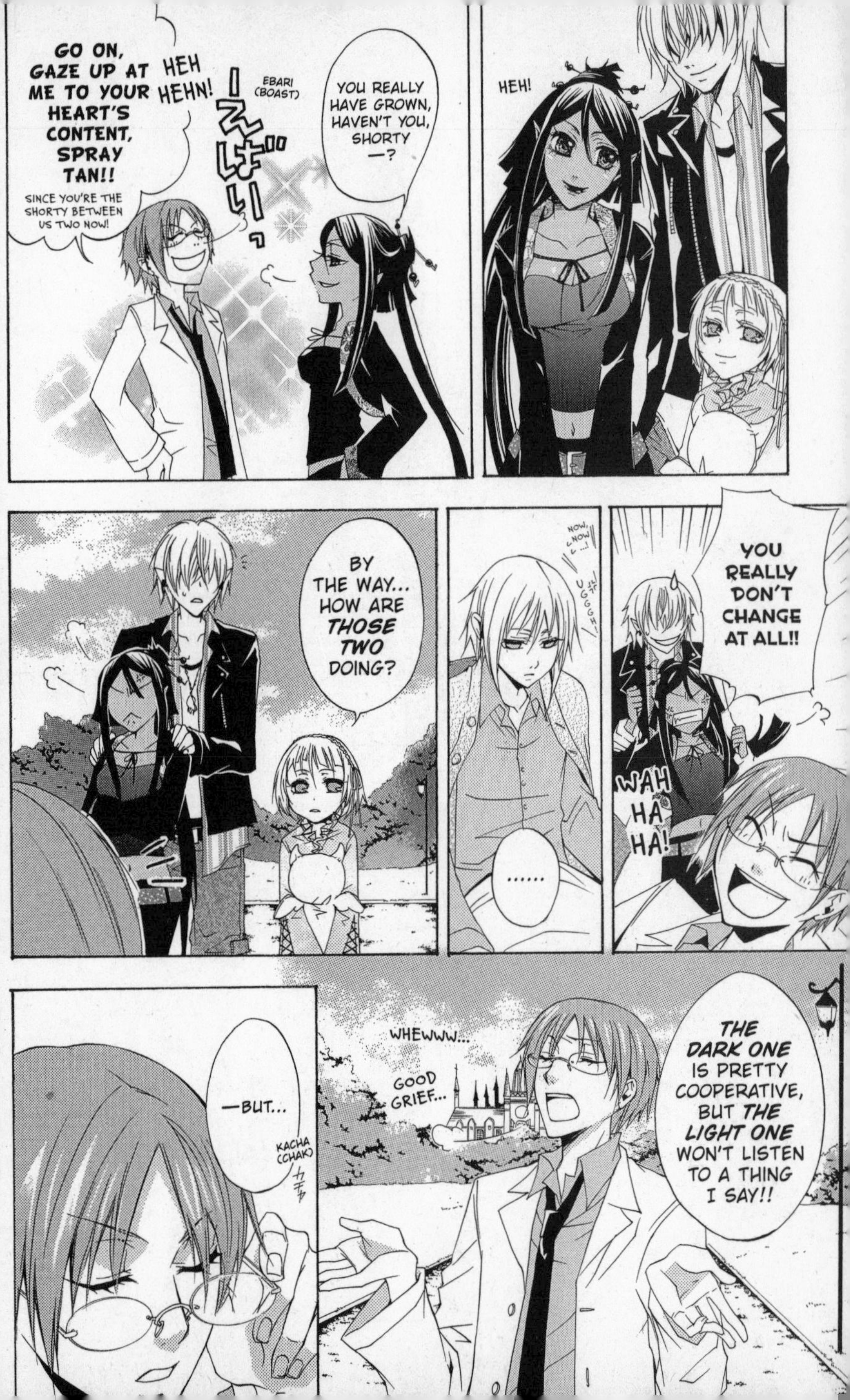
HEH!
EBARI (BOAST)
YOU REALLY HAVE GROWN, HAVEN'T YOU, SHORTY —?
HEH HEHN!
GO ON, GAZE UP AT ME TO YOUR HEART'S CONTENT, SPRAY TAN!!
SINCE YOU'RE THE SHORTY BETWEEN US TWO NOW!
YOU REALLY DON'T CHANGE AT ALL!!
WAH HA HA!
NOW, NOW...
UGGGH!
......
BY THE WAY... HOW ARE *THOSE TWO* DOING?
THE DARK ONE IS PRETTY COOPERATIVE, BUT *THE LIGHT ONE* WON'T LISTEN TO A THING I SAY!!
WHEWWW...
GOOD GRIEF...
—BUT...
KACHA (CHAK)

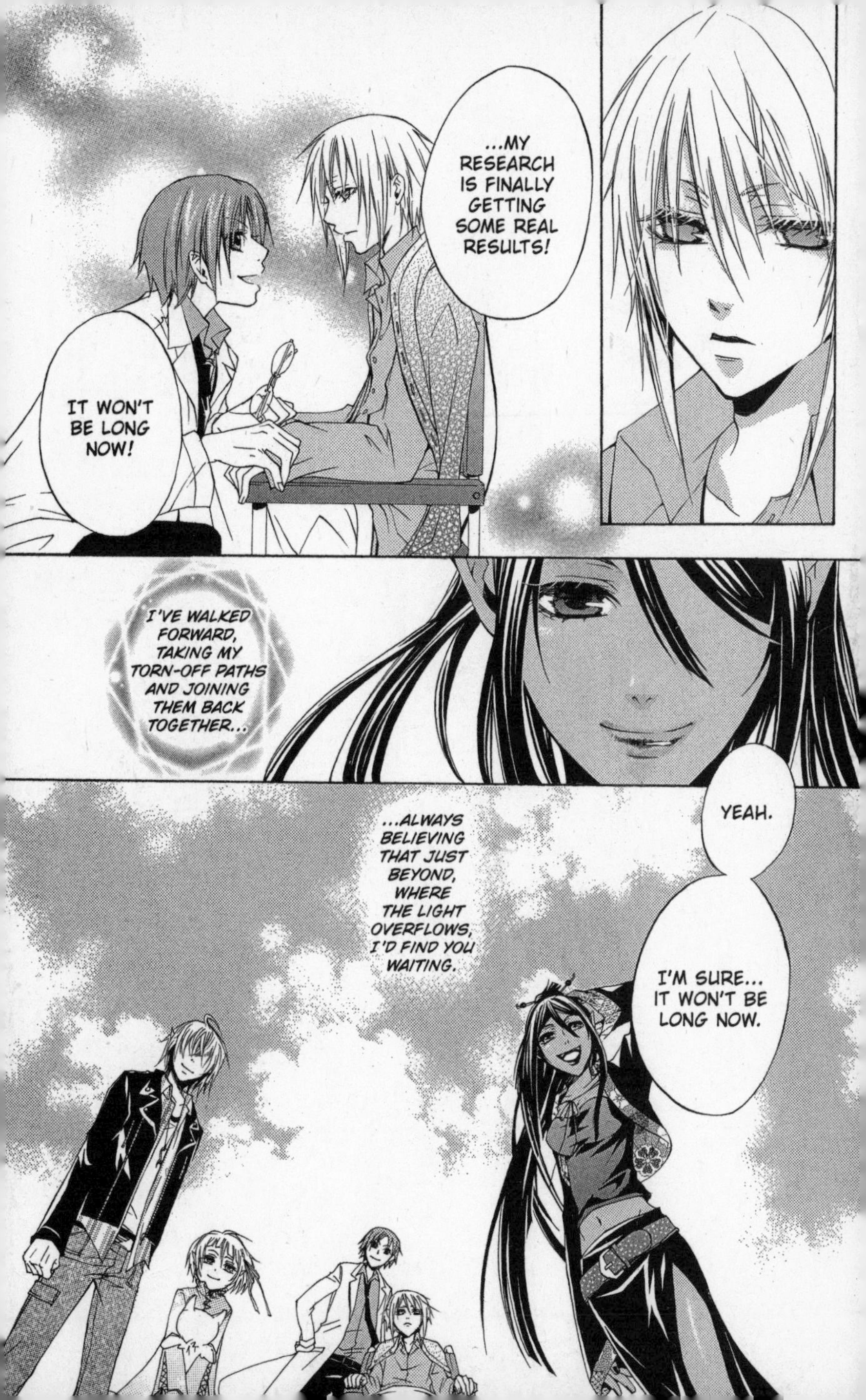
...MY RESEARCH IS FINALLY GETTING SOME REAL RESULTS!
IT WON'T BE LONG NOW!
I'VE WALKED FORWARD, TAKING MY TORN-OFF PATHS AND JOINING THEM BACK TOGETHER...
YEAH.
...ALWAYS BELIEVING THAT JUST BEYOND, WHERE THE LIGHT OVERFLOWS, I'D FIND YOU WAITING.
I'M SURE... IT WON'T BE LONG NOW.

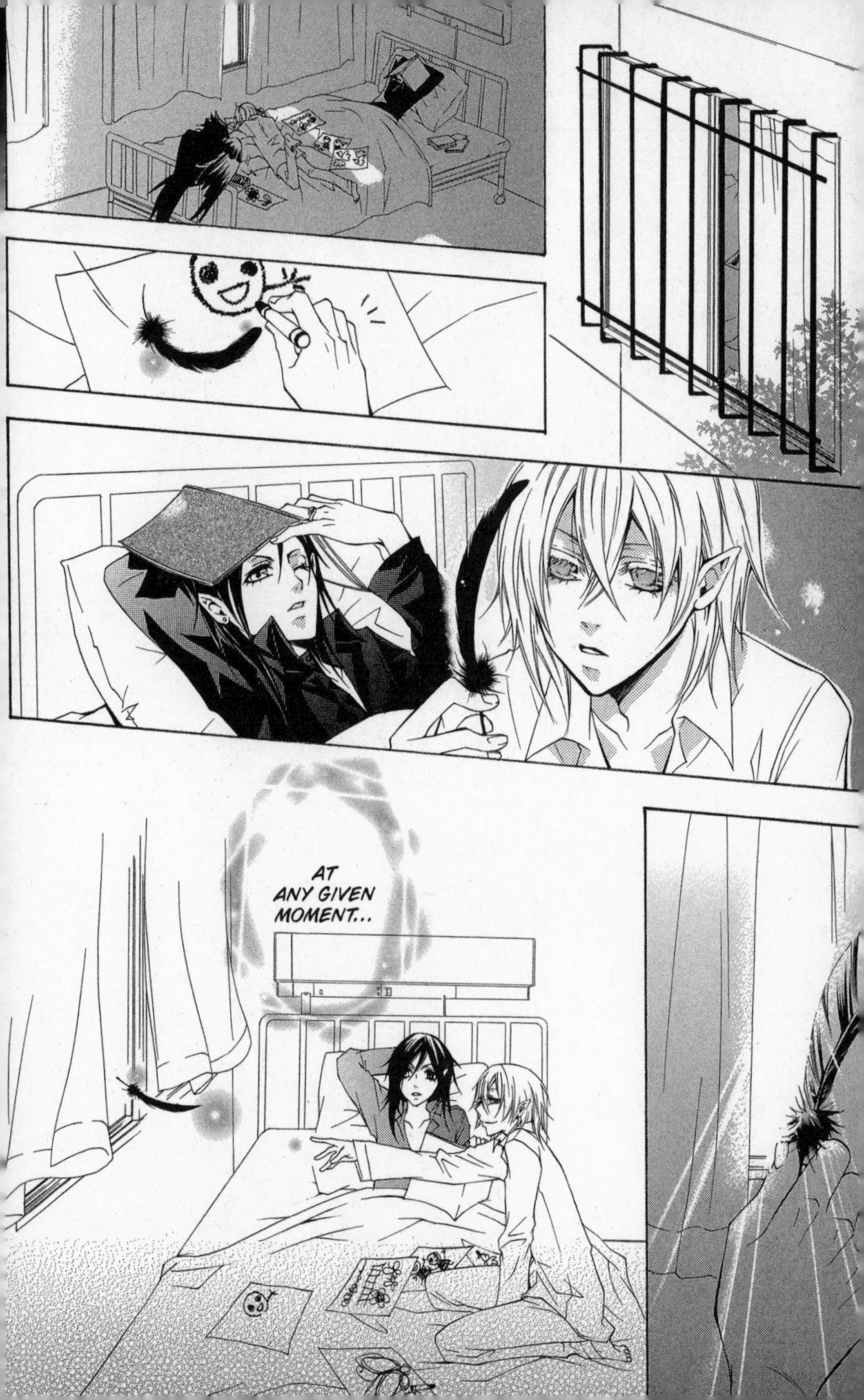
AT ANY GIVEN MOMENT...

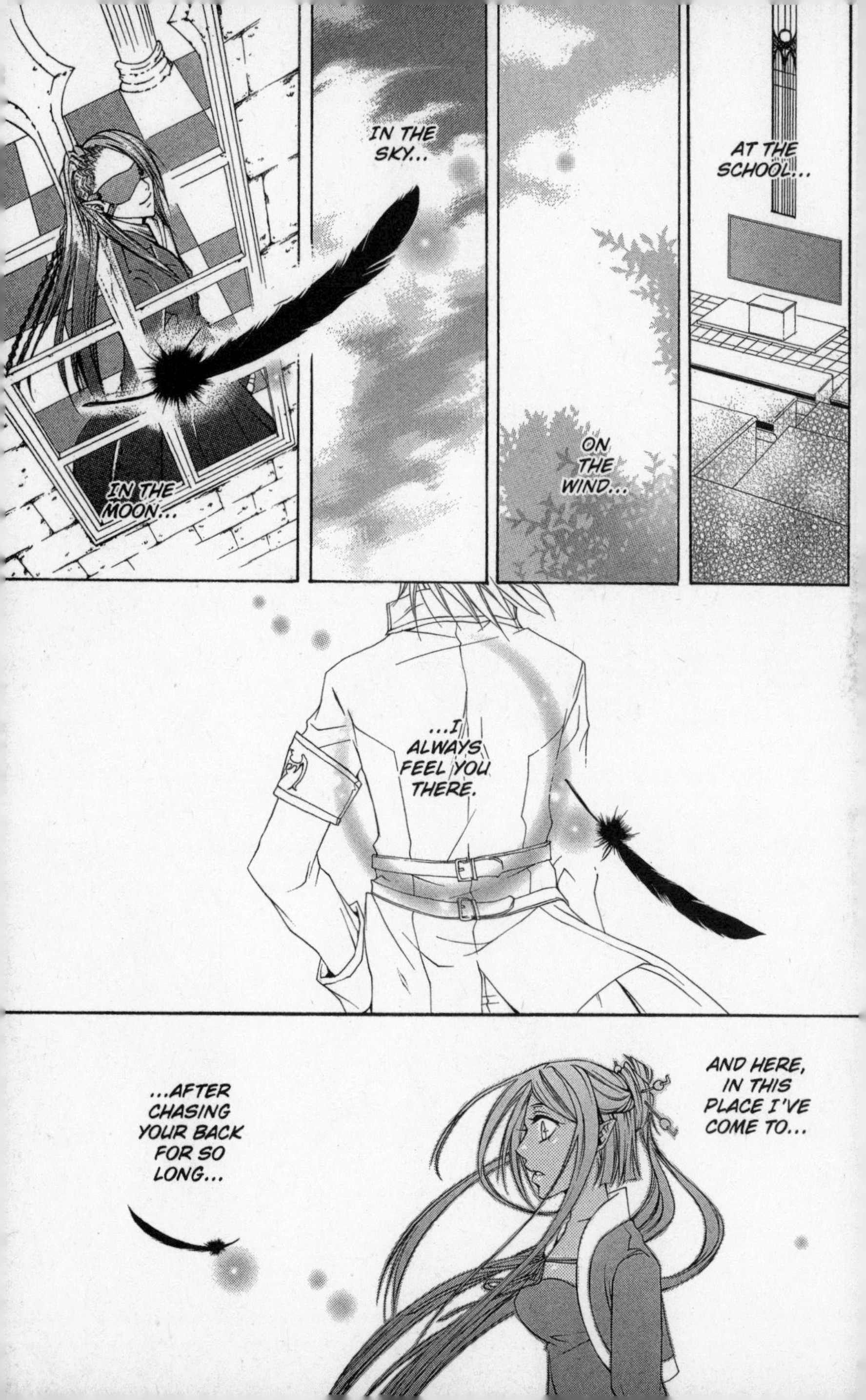
AT THE SCHOOL...
ON THE WIND...
IN THE SKY...
IN THE MOON...
...I ALWAYS FEEL YOU THERE.
AND HERE, IN THIS PLACE I'VE COME TO...
...AFTER CHASING YOUR BACK FOR SO LONG...

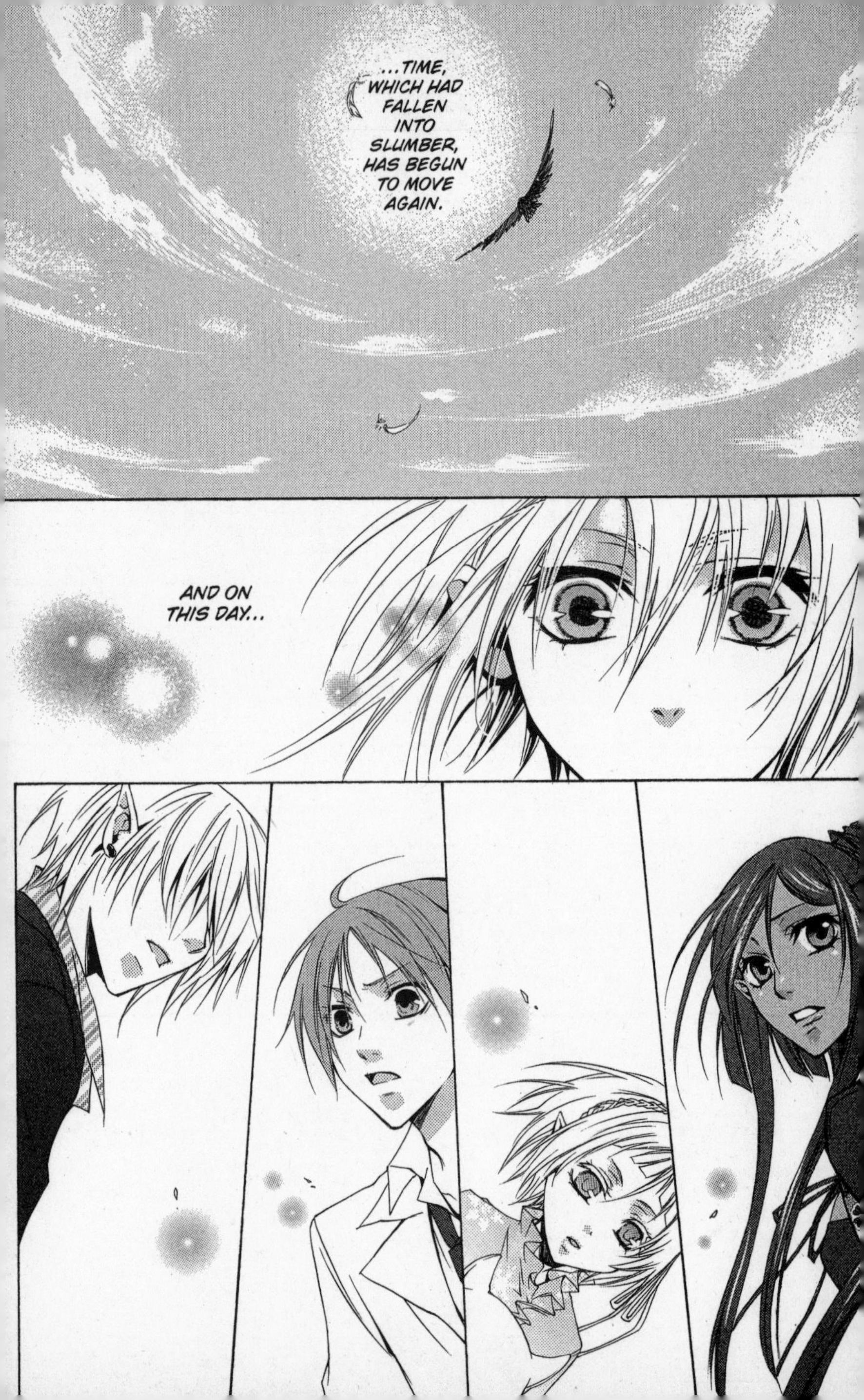
...TIME, WHICH HAD FALLEN INTO SLUMBER, HAS BEGUN TO MOVE AGAIN.
AND ON THIS DAY...

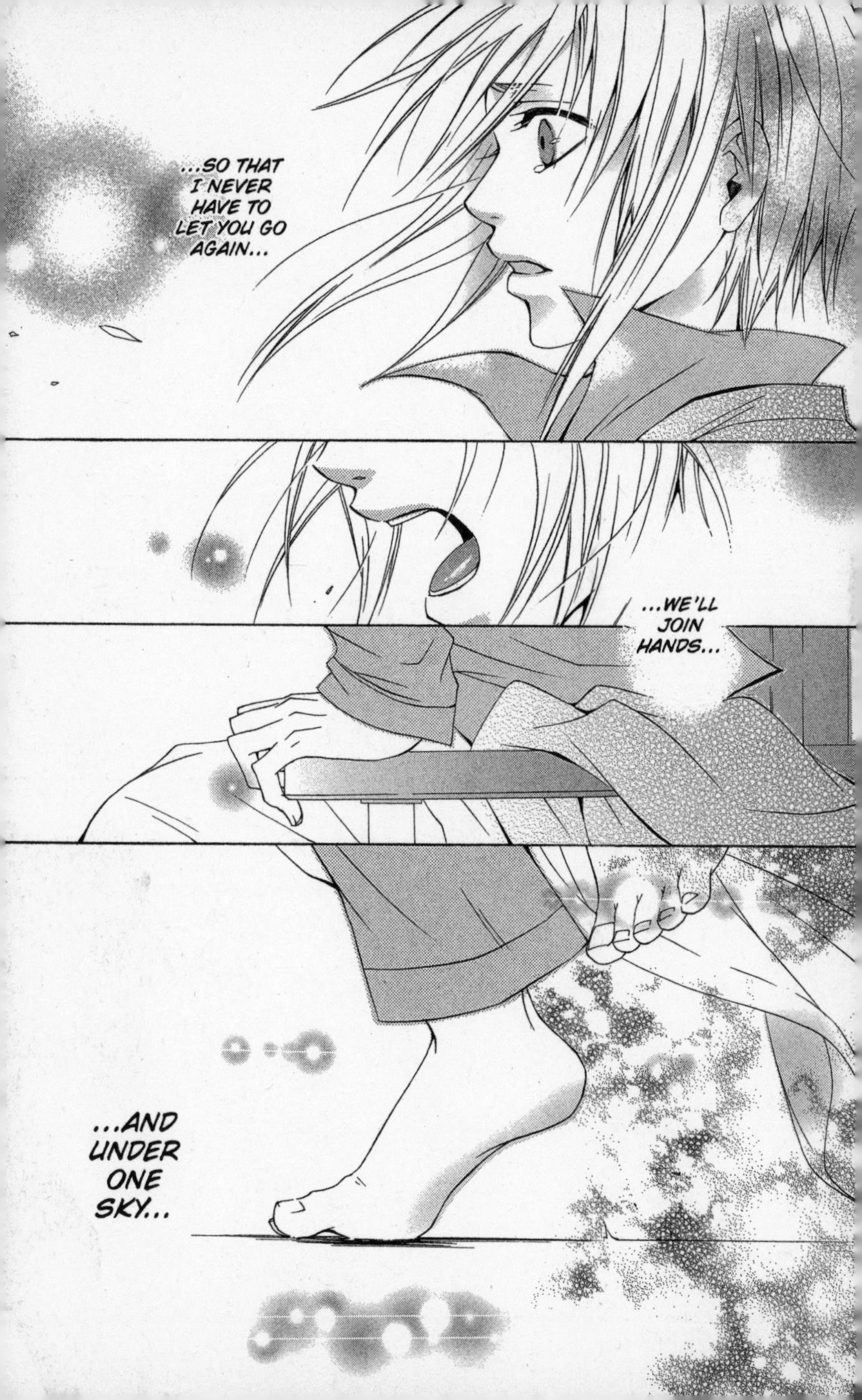
...SO THAT I NEVER HAVE TO LET YOU GO AGAIN...
...WE'LL JOIN HANDS...
...AND UNDER ONE SKY...

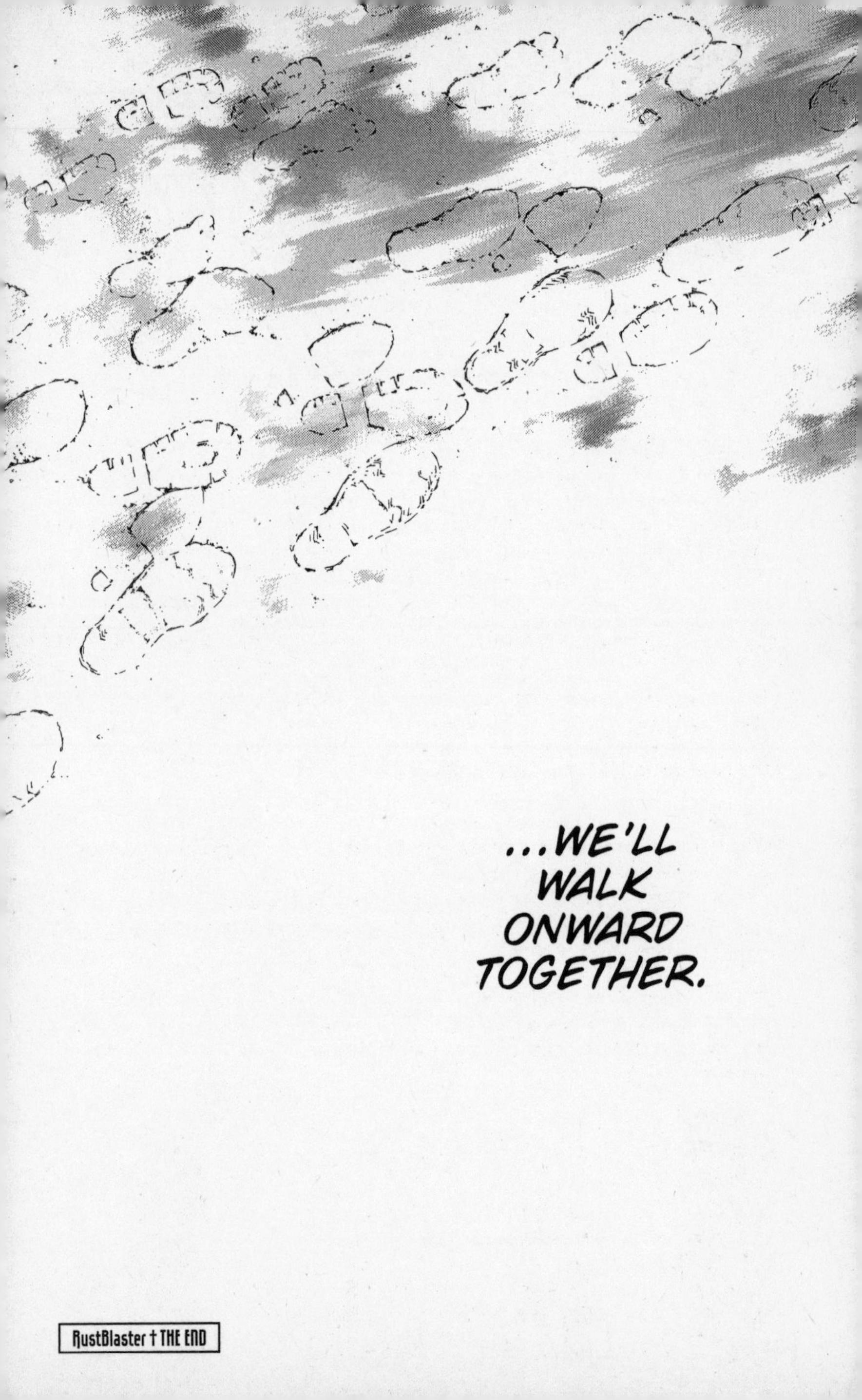
...WE'LL WALK ONWARD TOGETHER.
RustBlaster † THE END

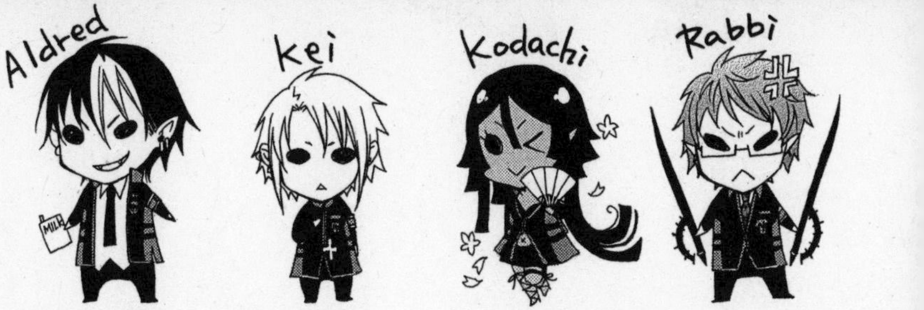
Aldred
Kei
Kodachi
Rabbi
MILK

Pleased to meet you! Hello, everyone. I am Yana Toboso. I'm a foot-dragging newcomer. And my surname is not "Hitsugi" (Japanese for "coffin"). I thank you from the bottom of my heart for purchasing **RustBlaster**, this debut manga by me, Yana Toboso!!

Now that I think about it, this was a rather difficult manga in terms of choosing a title and such. On the day my editor suggested to me, quite seriously, "Why don't we call it '**Of Moons and Milk** (for Al) **and Vampires**'?", I thought, "Is my manga really going to be serialized? ...Huh? Why am I...going into shock?" To be supported by someone with such lofty sensibilities (I mean that as a compliment) as K-san is amazing. We went through so many different titles before finally settling upon "**RustBlaster**." Though we shorten it differently!
Me = "RasuBura"
K-san = "RasuTer"—Wait, why does it sound like "spellcaster"?

In any case, I'm glad we didn't go with "Of Moons and Milk and Vampires." Really, really glad. (Yes, I said it twice.)

So with our title, I created this manga with a lot of hard work and K-san's input. I was able to include everything I wanted to draw in here (in terms of a six-chapter version of **RasuBura**, anyway!) and feel like I was able to sprint out of it along with Team 6 at the end. ...I even feel rather short of breath like I was running... ...!!! Hff! Hff...!!! I'm kind of a weakling.

No matter what world you're in, if you don't first believe in your own power, nothing can begin. Furthermore, if you don't believe in the power of the people around you, you can never progress either. The fact that a low-caliber manga artist like me could make an awesome manga like **RustBlaster** is sincerely thanks to my editor and my mother and my dear assistant-chans, who worked hard without sleep, and to you, who have kindly read my work. Thank you so very much!!

"It's okay for me to throw off my rusty old thoughts and take a flying leap into the sky!" To all of you who were nice enough to read this, I would be glad if you would think that way too. I pray to all the right arms, and moons, and so on, that we will be able to meet again soon.

2006 . Yana Toboso

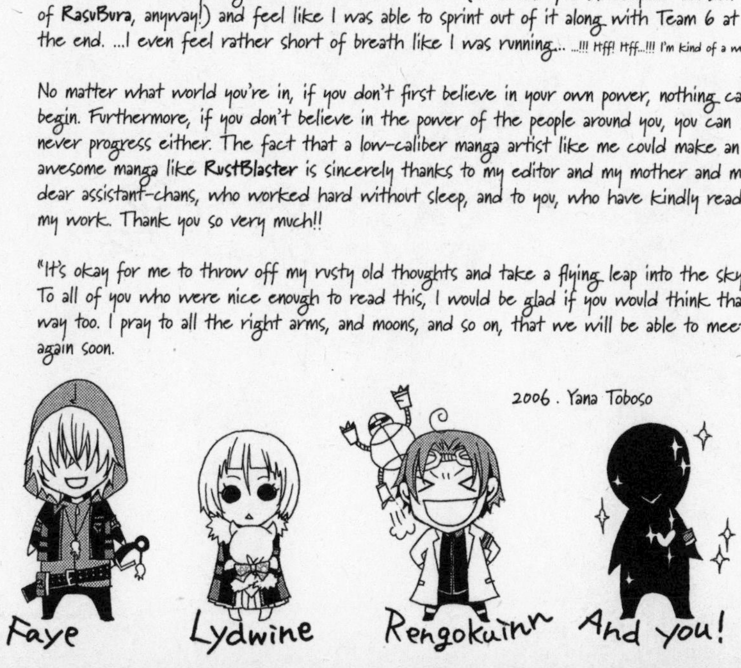
Faye
Lydwine
Rengokuinn
And you!

Staff RustBlaster are ...

comic
Yana Toboso

Editor
Takeshi Kuma

Executive Assistants
kiyo . Akiyo Satorigi
Fumi . kingyo1go!
Mai . Taku Hashiba

Special Thanx
Mine . My mother
and You.

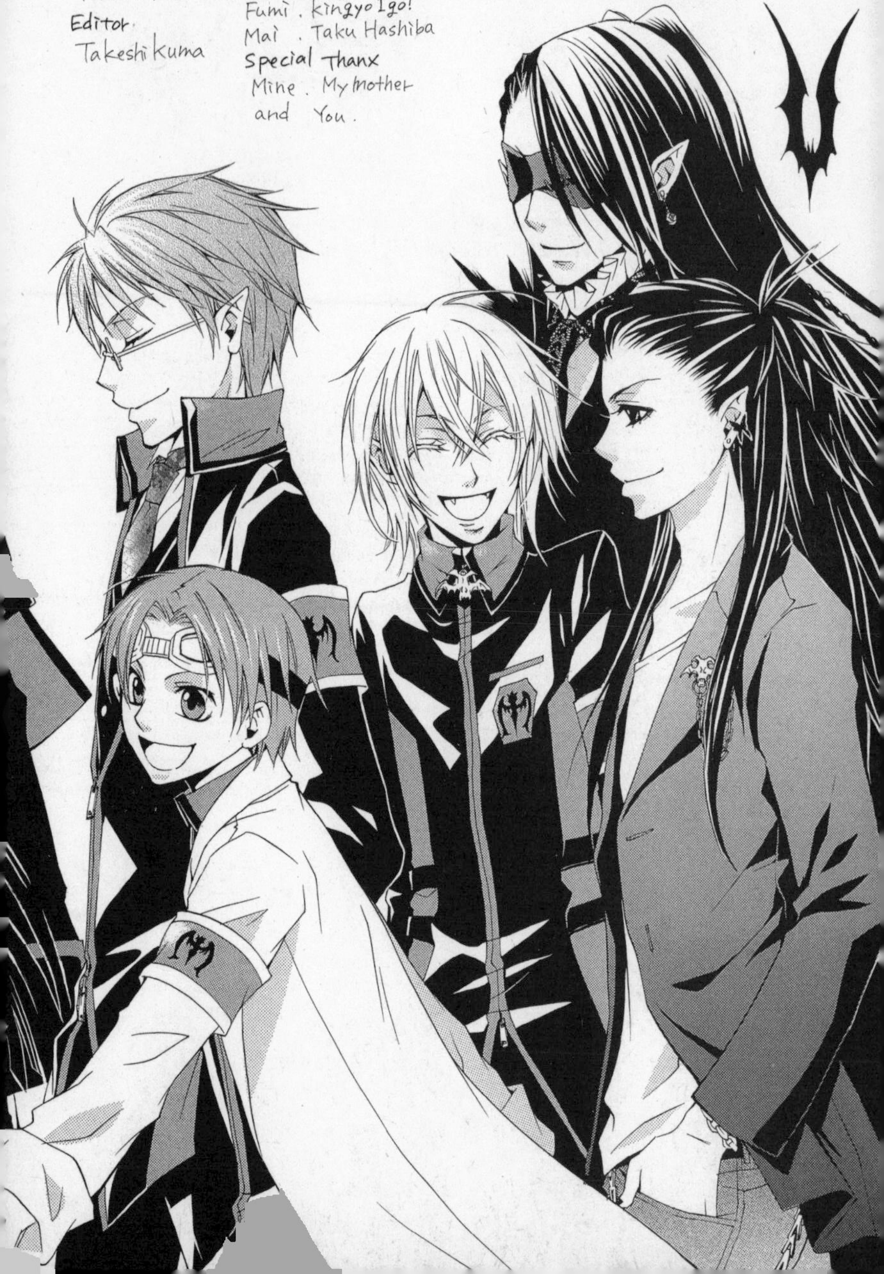

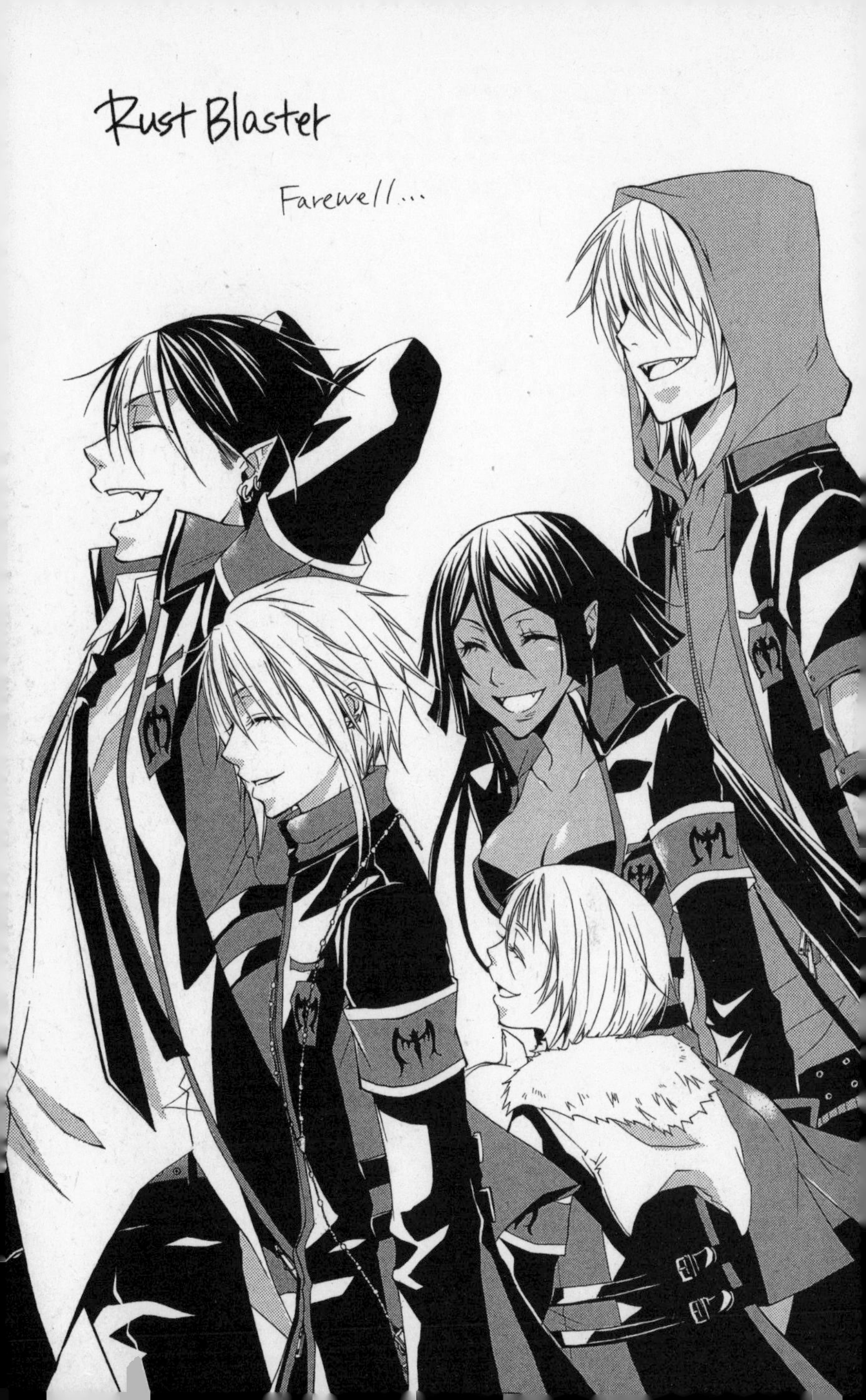
Rust Blaster
Farewell...

RustBlaster

Yana Toboso

Translation: Su Mon Han   †   Lettering: Tania Biswas

Rust Blaster © 2006 Yana Toboso / SQUARE ENIX CO., LTD. First published in Japan in 2006 by SQUARE ENIX CO., LTD. English translation rights arranged with SQUARE ENIX CO., LTD. and Hachette Book Group through Tuttle-Mori Agency, Inc.

Translation © 2015 by SQUARE ENIX CO., LTD.

Yen Press
Hachette Book Group
1290 Avenue of the Americas, New York, NY 10104

www.HachetteBookGroup.com
www.YenPress.com

Yen Press is an imprint of Hachette Book Group, Inc. The Yen Press name and logo are trademarks of Hachette Book Group, Inc.

The publisher is not responsible for websites (or their content) that are not owned by the publisher.

First Yen Press Edition: August 2015

ISBN: 978-0-316-34202-5

10 9 8 7 6 5 4 3 2 1

BVG

Printed in the United States of America